TAKING SIDES:
Clashing Views
on
Controversial Issues

To the Students of The City College of New York

 ## STAFF

Susan J. Friedman   Editor
Brenda Filley   Production Manager
Charles Vitelli   Designer
Bertha Kinne   Typesetter
Jeremy Brenner   Photographer

Howard Styles   Cover Photograph

TAKING SIDES:
Clashing Views
on
Controversial Issues

Edited, Selected, and with Introductions by

GEORGE MC KENNA

STANLEY FEINGOLD

The City College of New York

The Dushkin Publishing Group, Inc.
Guilford, Connecticut

Library of Congress Catalog Card Number: 77-
93817

Manufactured in the United States of America

First Edition, First Printing

PREFACE

Dialogue means two people talking to the same issue. Easy? Play back the next serious conversation you overhear in which a couple of true believers try to persuade one another of the truth, logic and virtue of their own views and the falsity, irrationality, and downright evil of the other's.

What's likely to go wrong? At the outset, they are unlikely to make clear the nature of the issue, defining or describing it with enough clarity and specificity to make sure that they are both talking about the same area of controversy. As they proceed, they are likely to employ vague, emotion-laden terms without spelling out the uses to which the terms are put. When the heat is on, they may resort to slinging epithets at one another, and the hoped-for meeting of minds will give way to the scoring of political points and the reinforcement of existing prejudices.

When the discussion of American involvement in Vietnam came down to the defense of it by "war criminals" in the eyes of the detractors, and the criticism of it by "traitors" in the eyes of the war's defenders, no one was really listening, and no one was learning. When the urban poor are indiscriminately categorized as "welfare loafers" and the inner city Blacks view all whites as "honkies," the possibility of effective communication and conciliation has been curtailed. On these and other divisive issues, neither detente nor resolution can be possible without verbal disarmament and abandonment of our stockpiles of mindless slogans and meaningless epithets.

People in high places are as likely as the rest of us to stoop to low phrases. President Nixon and his associates set a dubious standard for public debate with their talk about "radic-libs," "campus bums," "nattering nabobs of negativism," "effete snobs," and "querulous elitists" dispensing "ideological plugola" which was "tearing down America" and endangering "national security." The choice is not, as some super-patriots would have it, between loving America or leaving it. The choice is in reality between understanding it and not understanding it, and encouraging dialogue between opposed positions is the most certain way of enhancing our understanding.

The purpose of this book is to make a modest contribution toward the revival of political dialogue in America. What we propose to do is to examine some leading issues in American politics from the perspective of sharply opposed points of view. We have tried to select authors who argue their points vigorously but in such a way as to enhance our understanding of the issue.

For each issue we have inserted a pair of essays, one pro and one con. We hope the reader will examine each position carefully, and then take sides.

We realize, of course, that there often exist more than two sides to an issue. But this does not deter us from examining the issue in terms of pro and contra.

The reader who has thoughtfully examined two antithetical views, each of which is expressed with all the evidence and eloquence that an informed advocate can bring to bear upon the argument, will also perceive what positions can be occupied both between and beyond the sharply-differentiated essays which he or she has read.

In one sense our approach resembles a series of formal debates, of the kind conducted by debating teams and moot law courts. In another and more important sense, however, the conflicting arguments of this book represent something quite different. A debate is an intellectual game, in which opposition is explicit but artificial. By contrast, the essays included here were rarely written in direct response to one another. More important, the form in which they are expressed is that of public consideration of real issues, in which both political participants and commentators seek the widest support for their positions. In every instance we have chosen what we believe to be an appropriate and well-reasoned statement by a committed advocate. If this often adds passion to reason, it is an element which the student of American politics cannot afford to ignore. But passion with substance is much different from empty rhetoric and name-calling.

Although we have attempted (in the Introduction) to indicate the major alignments in American politics, a reflective reader of these essays is bound to realize that the mere ascription of a label will not dispose of the position. Every analysis presented here has merit—insofar as it reflects some sense of political reality and represents a viewpoint shared by some Americans—and each analysis therefore demands to be dealt with on its merit.

We hope that the reader who confronts lively and thoughtful statements on vital issues will be stimulated to ask some of the critical questions about American politics. What are the highest-priority issues with which government must deal today? What positions should be taken on these issues? What should be the attitude of Americans toward their government? To what extent, if any, does it need to be changed? How should it be organized in order to achieve the goals we set for it? What are these goals? Our conviction is that a healthy, stable democracy requires a citizenry which considers these questions and participates, however indirectly, in the answering of them. The alternative is apathy, passivity, and, sooner or later, the rule of tyrants.

We wish to acknowledge the encouragement and support given to this project by Rick Connelly of the Dushkin Publishing Group. We are grateful as well to Susan Friedman for her very able editorial supervision. We must also thank Mirella Baroni Harris, who directed our attention to one of the selections on poverty in America. Finally, we thank our wives, Sylvia McKenna and Fumiko Feingold, for the support and understanding they showed during the period in which we prepared this book.

George McKenna
Stanley Feingold

CONTENTS

Part II: Does American Government Govern Properly?

INTRODUCTION

George McKenna
Stanley Feingold

LABELS AND ALIGNMENTS IN AMERICAN POLITICS

Like commercial products on store shelves, political positions usually have labels affixed to them. Political labels are sometimes misleading and invariably say less than is necessary for making a rational choice. In American politics the most common labels are "liberal" and "conservative." There are also brands which are either less well-known or less well-regarded, such as "radical," "reactionary," "elitist," and "pluralist," names which attract smaller shares of the political market.

Not everyone thinks that using these labels is a good idea. President John F. Kennedy scorned these "traditional labels and worn-out slogans." Former Vice President Nelson Rockefeller also deplored the idea of approaching problems with either a liberal or a conservative perspective. "It is," he said, "a little like the man who said, 'Don't confuse me with the facts; my mind is made up.' " One obvious reason why successful politicians may resist either characterization is their fear of alienating voters who identify with the other. Jimmy Carter's ability to seem conservative to conservatives and liberal to liberals surely contributed significantly to his success in getting elected President.

But if this demonstrates the risks a politician runs in getting labeled, it proves at the same time the potency of labels for the electorate. Most people are prepared to characterize particular stands on public issues as conservative or liberal, or at least as leaning in one direction or the other. The proverbial man in the street uses the labels intuitively, without exploring either their origins or logical implications, but with a sense at least of their recent history and usage.

Our own view is that all of the terms we have cited have fairly stable and coherent meanings, but that the meanings should be examined periodically if they are to retain their usefulness in political dialogue. Since this book is dedicated to dialogue, and since many of the essays in it either use some of the terms or can be described by them, we believe that it is incumbent upon us to attempt some clarification.

Let us begin with this question: What are the underlying differences between liberals and conservatives? The answer, put simply, is that they differ in their views of human nature. Liberalism tends toward optimism, conservatism toward pessimism (the conservative would say realism). Liberals have in some historical periods gone so far as to believe in the perfectibility of humankind, and have thus placed great store in universal education, the closed ballot, and the direct primary as means of bringing about fuller participation in government. If the hopes held for these reforms have proven excessive, liberals are undaunted in their championing of the rights and welfare of the poor and oppressed. The underlying belief is that there are virtually no limits to what a person can become if he or she is given a fair chance and a decent environment. Liberals are often secularists who see themselves on the side of the angels.

Conservatives scorn what they consider to be liberal illusions. They believe that the mass of people has a limited capacity for self-improvement, and if political practicality and democratic doctrine require that everyone shall have a voice in the government of society, we should not be gulled into believing that the mass of prejudices and half-truths that pass for the political opinions of most people constitute the collective voice of wisdom. Conservatism of the American variety does not imply a yearning for feudalism, slavery, or absolute monarchy, but it does inveigh against "the tyranny of the majority," and against those restraints which the majority might impose upon the most able and intelligent members of society.

Classical liberalism. Liberalism has undergone a number of changes since it was first introduced as a political doctrine in the early nineteenth century. At that time, what is now called "classical liberalism" attacked the power of the state, including excessive taxation, licensing, the state church, armies of soldiers and armies of public officials, and laws inhibiting free speech and press. The French called it *laissez-faire,* literally "leave to be," that is: leave people alone. The objective was to foster the flowering of all that is best in the human personality, an objective which has remained constant over the years.

New Deal liberalism. Today, however, those who call themselves liberals generally have abandoned their faith in laissez-faire as an instrument for liberating human potential. In an industrial society individuals acting by themselves lack the resources to eliminate poverty, hunger, ignorance, prejudice, and other varieties of human misery—especially when they have to fight opponents who are often well-organized and well-heeled. Despite earlier social reform movements, the need for state intervention to deal with the problems did not become manifest in the United States until the Great Depression of 1929. Its disastrous effects—poverty, mass unemployment, widespread misery—opened the way to a new administration. "I pledge you, I pledge myself," Franklin Roosevelt said in accepting the Democratic nomination in 1932, "to a new deal for the American people." Roosevelt's "new deal" was an attempt to effect relief and recovery from the Depression; it employed a variety of means, including welfare programs, public works projects, and regulation of business, most of which involved government intervention in the economy. The New Deal's claim to the title of liberalism was based upon its reliance on democratic government to liberate people from poverty, oppression, and economic exploitation. At the same time, the New Dealers claimed to be at least as zealous as the classical liberals in defending political and civil liberties.

The reconciliation of laissez-faire liberalism and welfare state liberalism can only be found in the conviction that both are dedicated to the fulfillment of the human personality, and different circumstances dictated the employment of different means to achieve that goal. It was this very flexibility about means which the New Dealers considered essential for fighting modern social problems. The striking characteristic of the New Deal administrations was their pragmatic and experimental approach to policy. Programs were tried, and if found wanting, abandoned. All means were possible, including even alliances with the very bankers and businessmen whom the New Dealers excoriated in their speeches.

New Politics liberalism. Some post-New Deal liberals and most conservatives have noted that the New Deal did not end the Depression (World War II did that), it did not substantially alter the distribution of wealth (after all the legal assaults on monopoly and all the verbal assaults on "economic royalists," economic power in America remains about as concentrated as it was a half-century ago), and it did not level the barriers to racial equality (it virtually ignored the race issue). Some of the later liberals, advocates of what they called "New Politics," deplored the New Deal's alliances with big-city political machines, the growth of "the imperial presidency," and the increasing bureaucratization and remoteness of government. Other "New Politics" liberals faulted liberal administrations for not doing enough, quickly enough. The note of urgency was a recurrent theme among civil rights workers, Vietnam protesters, and anti-poverty demonstrators during the 1960s, and was carried over into the 1970s to include ecologists and feminists. "Freedom Now," a slogan of the civil rights movement, expressed a mood which was broadly shared by all advocates of the New Politics.

Conservatism. The same kind of pushing and pulling would be evident if we attempted a capsule history of conservatism in recent America. A casual observer might understandably conclude that a liberal or conservative stance is mere rationalization. During most of the New Deal, and in reaction to welfare measures since that period, conservatives have argued that more government means more interference in our lives, more regulation of our private conduct, more bureaucratic control of economic enterprise, more advantages for the less energetic at the expense of the more energetic, and, of course, more taxes. This sounds like the position of classical liberals, and many who adopt these views about the welfare state eschew the label "conservative," preferring to be called "libertarians." But there are many more critics of the welfare state who are not at all reluctant to call themselves conservatives, and, we think, with good reason. First, unlike classical liberals, these critics of the welfare state are not optimistic about human nature. They worry about "welfare loafers," "do-gooders," and others who either take advantage of well-intentioned programs or else go around generating the good intentions. When it comes to temperament and expectation, these critics of the welfare state really have little in common with Jefferson or the other early liberals. Second, they do not share the classical liberal's aversion to all government intrusion into the private sphere. When it comes to the maintenance of order and stability they are quite prepared to sanction government programs, and even massive government spending, to combat crime, subversion, and foreign enemies.

The point is that few conservatives and perhaps fewer liberals are doctrinaire with respect to the power of the state. Both are quite prepared to use the state for *their* purposes. It is true that some recent "activist" Presidents, such as Franklin D. Roosevelt and John F. Kennedy, were liberals. But Richard Nixon was also an "activist," and, while he may be difficult to classify, he was closer to being a conservative than to being a liberal. Going much further back in our history, we ought to recall that it was a liberal Jefferson who counseled against "energetic government" and conservative Alexander Hamilton who helped design bold powers for the new central government.

Given the seeming contradictions, Americans may wonder if there is any continuity in either liberalism or conservatism over a considerable period of time. Despairing of qualitative differences, some Americans resort to a quantitative measure, a left-right ruler on which "left" represents those who want more government spending to achieve more social ends and "right" represents those who want less of both. This runs the risk of equating extreme liberalism with totalitarianism, a doctrine which proclaims the right of the state to control all of our lives, and extreme conservatism with anarchy, or no government at all. As a matter of fact, some conservatives do see liberalism as a half-way house to communist totalitarianism, and some liberals view conservatism as a kind of abdication of responsibility. But these are caricatures of the real divisions in American political thought, and they obscure real differences which may be less dramatic but are more relevant to deciding among the practicable alternatives on divisive issues.

The real differences may be illustrated in relation to real issues. The liberal is committed to the widest access to higher education, in order to fulfill human potential, to compensate for inequities in elementary education and social background, and to compensate for the intellectual and cultural advantages that money can buy. The conservative is skeptical as to whether everyone can profit from more years of schooling, and would rather advocate education, which is graded according to the varying ability of each class. (The American conservative will concede that class barriers can be transcended, and even rearranged, but never abolished, since inequality is inevitable.)

The liberal is at least in spirit sworn to outlaw poverty, to tear down slums and erect an environment in which less fortunate members of society will enjoy greater opportunity to fulfill their intellectual, esthetic, and moral natures.

Moreover, insofar as is possible, the liberal would have the poor shape these programs and guide their own destinies. Conservatives recoil from the prospect of "community action" which, they are convinced, is bound to lead to corruption and violence instead of the liberal's dream of participatory democracy. The lower classes, the conservative would say, generally lack the forethought, thrift, industry, and ability to defer pleasure which alone can elevate them; to put it bluntly, although it might be unpolitic for the conservative to put it so publicly, the poor are poor because they lack the merit to be otherwise.

From the preceding illustrations, we might conclude that the liberal is likely to argue for change, while the conservative exalts the *status quo*. This is generally true, though it needs qualification. The liberal is much taken with the notion of "progress," and anxious to free people from "obsolete" institutions and practices. Conservatives are likely to stress the virtues of "stability" and "order." Nevertheless, conservatives have been known to innovate for the sake of preservation, while liberals never hesitate to go back to ancient sources when it serves their ends. The whole loyalty-security apparatus of the 1950s, including new laws against "subversives," was introduced by conservatives and resisted by liberals in the name of a two-hundred year tradition of civil liberties.

Having examined liberalism and conservatism—the most commonly used labels in America's marketplace of ideas—let us go on to consider some of those which are used less frequently.

Radicals and reactionaries. The label "reactionary" is almost always an epithet, and the label "radical" is worn with pride only by a few zealots on the banks of the political mainstream. A reactionary is not a conserver but a backward-mover, dedicated to turning the clock back to better times. Most of the rest of us harbor the suspicion that the reactionary would restore us to a time that never was except in political myth, and the repeal of industrialism or universal education or the twentieth century does not commend itself as a practical, let alone a desirable, political program.

Radicalism (literally meaning "from the roots" or "going to the foundation") implies fundamental reconstruction of the social order. Taken in that sense, it is possible to speak of right-wing radicalism as well as left-wing radicalism, radicalism which restores or newly inaugurates an elitist society, which acknowledges inequality and rewards persons unequally, as well as a radicalism which eliminates privilege and advantage and initiates an equality of chances for all persons. The term is sometimes used in both of these senses, but most often radicalism is reserved to characterize more liberal change. Where the liberal would effect change through conventional democratic processes, the radical is likely to be skeptical as to the ability of the established machinery to bring about the needed change and might be prepared to sacrifice a "little" liberty to bring about a great deal more equality.

Both major parties in the United States know that it is suicidal to be identified by the public as either reactionary or radical. Sides are not to be sharply drawn. One reason is that many Americans are reluctant to choose. Reform? Yes, of course, but conserve too. Moderation is well-regarded in this country. Our self-image has both a progressive face and another of a preserved heritage. So we sometimes seek to make haste slowly, or as the Supreme Court once memorably put it, "with all deliberate speed." Why not have the best of both worlds, that which we possess and cherish, and also that which our ingenuity and idealism can bring into being? It is easier said than done. Those who insist we must choose sides unequivocally argue that the middle of the road is an unsafe lane of travel. On the other hand, some thoughtful Americans have chosen a political principle which seems to combine liberal and conservative elements. The principle is called pluralism, and it is important because it is embodied in the constitutional system of the United States.

Pluralism. Pluralism espouses diversity, in a society containing many interest groups and in a government containing competing units of power. Because this implies the widest expression of competing ideas, pluralism expresses sympathy with an important element of liberalism. But pluralism, as Madison and Hamilton analyzed its sources in *The Federalist* commentaries on the Constitution, springs from a profoundly pessimistic view of human nature, and in this respect it corresponds more closely with conservatism. James Madison, who was possibly the single most influential member of the convention that wrote the Constitution, hoped that in a large and varied nation, no single interest group could control the government. Even if there were a majority interest, it would be unlikely to capture all of the national agencies of government—the House of Representatives, the Senate, the President, and the federal judiciary—each of which was chosen in a different way by a different constituency for a different term of office. Moreover, to make certain that no one branch exercised excessive power, each was equipped with "checks and balances" which enabled any agency of national government to curb the powers of the others. The clearest statement of Madison's, and the Constitution's, theory is to be found in the Fifty-first paper of *The Federalist:*

> It may be a reflection on human nature that such devices should be necessary to control the abuses of government. But what is government itself, but the greatest of all reflections on human nature? If men were angels, no government would be necessary.

This pluralist position may be analyzed in conflicting ways. It is conservative insofar as it rejects simple majority rule. It is liberal insofar as it similarly rejects rule by any single elite. It is conservative in its pessimistic appraisal of human nature. At the same time, pluralism's pessimism is a kind of egalitarianism, holding as it does that no one can be trusted with power, and that majority interests no less than minority interests will use power for selfish ends. It is at least defensible to suggest that in America pluralism represents an alternative to both liberalism and conservatism, in that where liberalism is majoritarian and conservatism is elitist, pluralism is anti-majoritarian and anti-elitist, and combines some elements of both!

Because a pluralist constitutional system makes change difficult to accomplish, it "tilts" toward conservatism. The *status quo* is not immovable, but it is never easily routed, at least not in the United States. The U.S. Constitution has been amended only fifteen times in the nearly two hundred years since the adoption of the Bill of Rights, and most of these amendments are technical in character. Nevertheless, liberals have derived advantages from the "flexibility" of our Constitution, or more precisely, of the manner in which the Constitution has been interpreted by our courts. Although "strict constructionists" have held that the Constitution must be taken literally, so-called "loose constructionists" have prevailed in the sense that constitutional clauses have been given expanded meaning, leading to a growth in national power that the Framers could not have anticipated. At every point where the meaning of constitutional phrases has been stretched or enlarged, "strict constructionists" have cried that the Constitution was being undermined. In reality, positions on whether to interpret the Constitution strictly or loosely have depended more on conservative or liberal outlook than on some abstract theory of the nature of constitutions. Conservatism is identified with strict constructionism in the traditional defense of states' rights, and the preservation of that balance between national and state power which existed at the time of the Constitution's adoption. The states' rights position was that of the *status quo*, tradition, inherited practice, and local elites resisting the nationalization of majority rule. At the same time, we must acknowledge that liberalism has been not less strict in its interpretation of the First Amendment defense of free speech. When "Congress shall make no law . . . abridging the freedom of speech" is held to mean *no* law against subversive, violent, peace-disrupting, or obscene speech, liberalism becomes literalism in constitutional interpretation.

The really formidable obstacle to change in the American constitutional system is the separation of powers among the three branches of national government; the legislative branch is itself composed of two houses, which are often deadlocked. A mere majority is thus unlikely to gain control of the government and to shape public policy. At the same time, the constitutional system is not traditionally conservative in thwarting the will of elite groups which are unlikely to gain sufficient influence to control governmental action. Perhaps pluralism comes closer to describing the governmental process, although it is not always of the kind that Madison envisaged. Determined minority interests, intent on influencing decision-making only in a confined area, seem to possess enhanced access to the places of power, thanks to the absence of party government and the presence of a fragmentation of power in Congress and the federal bureaucracy. A special interest will be content merely to reach and influence the ranking members of the appropriate congressional committees and the commissioners or other federal officials who deal with their interest on a regular basis.

Some applications. Despite our efforts to define the principal alignments in American politics, the edges will remain blurred. Some positions will seem simply more or less liberal, more or less conservative, without neatly filling a model type. The reader of this book will reach his or her own conclusions, but we may suggest some alignments to be found here both in order to demonstrate the variety of viewpoints and to stimulate the reader's thought. In the essays on political parties (Issue 2), H. R. Shapiro sees political parties as boss-driven associations which have destroyed the amateur spirit of participatory democracy. Against Shapiro's New Politics liberalism which condemns clubhouse politics and commends "citizen action," David Broder argues for political reform through strong political parties, much as was the case during the New Deal. In the essays on the presidency (Issue 6), Theodore Sorensen echoes New Deal liberalism in stressing the positive features of the modern presidency, while Michael Novak would cut the presidency down to more controllable size, as conservatives—and some New Politics liberals—would. In Issue 10, a New Politics liberal, Herbert Hill, expresses urgency about the need to end racism, and insists that only affirmative action programs will give discriminated minorities equal opportunity now, while a New Deal liberal, Nathan Glazer, warns that such programs substitute new inequities for old.

Conservatism finds expression in Martin Diamond's defense of the electoral college method of electing the President (Issue 4), Ernest van den Haag's advocacy of retention of the death penalty (Issue 9), and Edward Banfield's critical analysis of lower-class culture in relation to the eradication of poverty (Issue 11). Pluralism is championed by David Riesman in his identification of power with a plurality of groups (Issue 1), by John Fischer in his claim that government by interest groups makes the American system both representative and moderate (Issue 3), and by Jerome Barron in his advocacy of the inclusion of more factional viewpoints in the mass media (Issue 13).

These characterizations hardly suggest the complexity and subtlety of these essays, but they indicate that there are philosophical reverberations beyond the immediate issues considered in the essays.

The thoughtful reader will independently assess the viewpoints in these essays in order to determine which are conservative or liberal or pluralist or otherwise, and which are right and which are wrong. The empirical evidence to support judgments of right and wrong is often scant. Does capital punishment deter criminals from committing murder? Does obscenity contribute to a breakdown of morals and the commission of sex crimes? Even more often, right and wrong are matters of value judgment, so that at bottom one's position expresses a moral preference. Instead of deterrence, we might consider retribution: Is society entitled to exact an eye for an eye? Instead of social consequences, we might consider the rights of society: May society enforce a particular code of moral behavior and expression?

Obviously, one's position on these issues will be affected by circumstances. After Vietnam and Watergate, for example, many who had once championed the strong presidency have adopted the opposite view. But we would like to think that the essays in this book are durable enough to last through several seasons of events and controversies. We can be certain that the issues will survive, and the search for coherence and consistency in our use of political labels underlines the options open to us and reveals their consequences. The result must be more mature judgments about what is best for America. That, of course, is the ultimate aim of public debate and decision-making, and it transcends all labels and categories.

PART I

HOW DEMOCRATIC IS THE AMERICAN POLITICAL PROCESS?

ISSUE 1

WHO RULES AMERICA?

Since the framing of the United States Constitution behind closed doors in 1787 there have been periodic charges that America is controlled, or in imminent danger of being controlled, by a power elite. All representative government is necessarily government by elites (i.e., small, selective ruling groups), but those who raise the specter of a power elite are charging that America is run by an *unrepresentative* elite, one which is unaccountable to the majority of voters. Almost invariably, it is added that this elite is not just political but economic as well. Although all industrial societies have gradations of wealth, democracy is supposed to counter the weight of money with the weight of numbers. The basic contention of the elite-theorists, then, is not simply that there are rich and poor in America but that the very rich—or a small elite working in league with them—are making all the crucial decisions.

Fear of elitism has a long history in America. Richard Henry Lee, a signer of the Declaration of Independence, spoke for many "anti-federalists" who opposed ratification of the Constitution, when he warned that the proposed charter shifted power away from the people and into the hands of the "aristocrats" and "moneyites," those who "avariciously grasp at all power and property." Long after these fears were more or less quieted there still remained a residue of suspicion that the wealthy were manipulating the machinery of government for their own purposes. Andrew Jackson's battle against the federally chartered Bank of the United States involved a number of issues, but one of the most prominent was the fear of elitism. "It is to be regretted," Jackson wrote in his veto message, "that the rich and powerful too often bend the acts of government to their selfish purposes." The growing controversy over slavery shifted the leading issues away from these typical Jacksonian concerns, but within a generation after the Civil War they had returned, and with greater force than ever. For the populist movement of the 1880s and 1890s, the American Revolution was not just a break with England but a grand rebellion against all forms of kingship or aristocracy. Sadly, the populists lamented, elitism had crept back, in the form of economic royalism; behind the facade of democracy were the "robber barons," rich capitalists who manipulated the politicians and ran the government at the expense of "the plain people."

Despite populism's decline as an active political movement, what has not died out is the assertion that America is controlled by an unrepresentative elite. That assertion is sometimes ridiculed without being examined on its own terms. "The paranoid style" one writer called it, and others have referred disparagingly to "cabalism" and "conspiracy theories." It is true, of course, that the theory of elite-domination has many crackpot variants: Jewish conspiracies, Papist plots, Communists poisoning our reservoirs, and so on. But this does not permit us to treat all theories of elitism as if they were evidence of mental disorder. Just as there is thoughtful patriotism on the one hand and mindless flag-waving on the other, so there are sophisticated theories, as opposed to wild talk, about elitism in America.

The best-known modern formulation of the position that a powerful self-perpetuating elite governs America is that of the late C. Wright Mills, in *The Power Elite*. Others have elaborated upon his thesis, and still others have defined the ruling class in other ways. Nevertheless, Mills' analysis remains vivid and challenging.

By contrast, David Riesman in *The Lonely Crowd* portrayed a shift away from a ruling group to a society where many groups are capable of exercising a veto upon political decisions which are adverse to their interests. It contains echoes of James Madison's analysis of constitutional decision-making in *The Federalist* essays and John C. Calhoun's *Disquisition on Government*. Although Mills and Riesman were writing in the 1950s, they were formulating answers to a perennial American question: who rules us?

David Riesman

A PLURALITY OF GROUPS

There has been in the last fifty years a change in the configuration of power in America, in which a single hierarchy with a ruling class at its head has been replaced by a number of "veto groups" among which power is dispersed. This change has many complex roots and complex consequences, including the change in political mood from moralizing to tolerance. A clear-cut power structure helped to create the clarity of goals of the inner-directed; an amorphous power structure helps to create the consumer orientation of the other-directed. . . .*

The Leaders and the Led

There have been two periods in American history in which a sharply defined ruling class emerged. In the late eighteenth and early nineteenth centuries the Federalist leadership—landed-gentry and mercantilist-money leadership—certainly thought of itself as, and was, a ruling group. Long before its leadership was actually dislodged, its power was disputed and, in decisive instances, overruled in the northern and middle states by yeoman farmers and artisans. These latter, having little time or gift for politics, ordinarily left it to their "betters," but they retained a veto on what was done and occasionally, as with Jackson, moved into a more positive command. After the Civil War, however, farmers and artisans lost their capacity to check what was done, and the captains of industry emerged as a ruling class. During their hegemony the images and the actualities of power in America coincided more closely than I think they do today. . . .

Ruling-class theories, applied to contemporary America, seem to be spectral survivals of this earlier time. The captain of industry no longer runs business, no longer runs politics, and no longer provides legitimate "spiritual comfort." . . .

In the focus of public attention the old captains of industry have been replaced by an entirely new type: the Captains of Nonindustry, of Consumption and Leisure . . . .

Proportionately, actors, artists, entertainers, get more space than they used

Continued on p. 6

---

*Riesman distinguishes between "inner-directed" people, who aim their lives toward the achievement of clear-cut goals, and "other-directed" types, who feel much more uncertainty about goals and who therefore are constantly watching others for cues. "Inner-directedness" flourished in the nineteenth century, while the "other-directed" style predominates today. [Editors.]

From David Riesman, *The Lonely Crowd* (New Haven, Conn.: Yale University Press, 1961).

C. Wright Mills

A POWER ELITE

The Higher Circles

The powers of ordinary men are circumscribed by the everyday worlds in which they live, yet even in these rounds of job, family, and neighborhood they often seem driven by forces they can neither understand nor govern. "Great changes" are beyond their control, but affect their conduct and outlook none the less. The very framework of modern society confines them to projects not their own, but from every side, such changes now press upon the men and women of the mass society, who accordingly feel that they are without purpose in an epoch in which they are without power.

But not all men are in this sense ordinary. As the means of information and of power are centralized, some men come to occupy positions in American society from which they can look down upon, so to speak, and by their decisions mightily affect, the everyday worlds of ordinary men and women. They are not made by their jobs; they set up and break down jobs for thousands of others; they are not confined by simple family responsibilities; they can escape. They may live in many hotels and houses, but they are bound by no one community. They need not merely "meet the demands of the day and hour"; in some part, they create these demands, and cause others to meet them. Whether or not they profess their power, their technical and political experience of it far transcends that of the underlying population. What Jacob Burckhardt said of "great men," most Americans might well say of their elite: "They are all that we are not."

The power elite is composed of men whose positions enable them to transcend the ordinary environments of ordinary men and women; they are in positions to make decisions having major consequences. Whether they do or do not make such decisions is less important than the fact that they do occupy such pivotal positions; their failure to act, their failure to make decisions, is itself an act that is often of greater consequence than the decisions they do make. For they are in command of the major hierarchies and organizations of modern society. They rule the big corporations. They run the machinery of the state and claim its prerogatives. They direct the military establishment. They occupy the strategic command posts of the social structure, in which are now centered the effective means of the power and the wealth and the celebrity which they enjoy.

Continued on p. 10

1. WHO RULES AMERICA?

(Riesman, cont. from p. 4)

to, and the heroes of the office, hustings, and factory get less. . . .

But, of course, these captains of consumption are not leaders. They are still only personalities, employed to adorn movements, not to lead them. Yet the actual leaders have much in common with them.

For an illustration we can turn to a recent American leader—undoubtedly a leader—who shared many characteristics of the artist and entertainer: Franklin D. Roosevelt. We are accustomed to thinking of him as a man of great power. Yet his role in leading the country into war was very different from that of McKinley or even of Wilson. Think of McKinley pacing the floor of his study, deciding whether or not to ask for a declaration of war on Spain—when he already knew that Spain would capitulate. McKinley felt it was up to him; so did Wilson. Roosevelt felt he could only maneuver within very narrow limits, limits which came close to leaving the decision to the enemy. . . .

The old-time captain of industry was also a captain of consumption: what standards were set, were set by him. He was also a captain of politics. The new captain of consumption who has usurped his place in the public eye is limited severely to the sphere of consumption—which itself has of course greatly expanded. Today, the personalities from the leisure world, no matter how much loved, lack the strength and the situation for leadership. If a movie star of today tries to put across a political message, in or out of films, he finds himself vulnerable to all sorts of pressures. The movie producer is no more powerful. The Catholics, the Methodists, the organized morticians, the state department, the southerners, the Jews, the doctors, all put their pressure on the vehicle that is being prepared for mass distribution. Piety or decency protects some minority groups that have no lobbies. The movie maker acts as a broker among these veto groups in a situation much too intricate to encourage his taking a firm, moralizing stance. At best, he or someone in his organization may sneak a moral and political message into the film as Roosevelt or someone in his organization sneaked over an appointment or a new coordinating agency. The message, the appointment, the agency—none of them could get very far in the Alice in Wonderland croquet game of the veto groups.

Who Has the Power?

The shifting nature of the lobby provides us with an important clue as to the difference between the present American political scene and that of the age of McKinley. The ruling class of businessmen could relatively easily (though perhaps mistakenly) decide where their interests lay and what editors, lawyers, and legislators might be paid to advance them. The lobby ministered to the clear leadership, privilege, and imperative of the business ruling class.

Today we have substituted for that leadership a series of groups, each of which has struggled for and finally attained a power to stop things conceivably inimical to its interests and, within far narrower limits, to start things. The various business groups, large and small, the movie-censoring groups, the farm groups and the labor and professional groups, the major ethnic groups and major regional groups, have in many instances succeeded in maneuvering themselves into a position in which they are able to neutralize those who might attack them. The very increase in the number of these groups, and in the kinds of interests "practical" and "fictional" they are protecting, marks, therefore, a decisive change from the lobbies of an earlier day. There is a change in method, too, in the way the groups are organized, the way they handle each other, and the way they handle the public, that is, the unorganized.

These veto groups are neither leader-groups nor led-groups. The only leaders of national scope left in the United States today are those who can placate the veto groups. The only followers left in the United States today are those unorganized and sometimes disorganized unfortunates who have not yet invented their group.

Within the veto groups, there is, of course, the same struggle for top places that goes on in other bureaucratic setups. Among the veto groups competition is monopolistic; rules of fairness and fellowship dictate how far one can go. Despite the rules there are, of course, occasional "price wars," like the jurisdictional disputes of labor unions or Jewish defense groups; these are ended by negotiation, the division of territory, and the formation of a roof organization for the previously split constituency. These big monopolies, taken as a single group, are in devastating competition with the not yet grouped, much as the fair-trade economy competes against the free-trade economy. These latter scattered followers find what protection they can in the interstices around the group-minded.

Each of the veto groups in this pattern is capable of an aggressive move, but the move is sharply limited in its range by the way in which the various groups have already cut up the sphere of politics and arrayed certain massive expectations behind each cut. Both within the groups and in the situation created by their presence, the political mood tends to become one of other-directed tolerance. The vetoes so bind action that it is hard for the moralizers to conceive of a program that might in any large way alter the relations between political and personal life or between political and economic life. In the amorphous power structure created by the veto groups it is hard to distinguish rulers from the ruled, those to be aided from those to be opposed, those on your side from those on the other side. This very pattern encourages the inside-dopester who can unravel the personal linkages, and discourages the enthusiast or indignant who wants to install the good or fend off the bad. Probably, most of all it

1. WHO RULES AMERICA?

encourages the new-style indifferent who feels and is often told that his and everyone else's affairs are in the hands of the experts and that laymen, though they should "participate," should not really be too inquisitive or aroused.

By their very nature the veto groups exist as defense groups, not as leadership groups. If it is true that they do "have the power," they have it by virtue of a necessary mutual tolerance. More and more they mirror each other in their style of political action, including their interest in public relations and their emphasis on internal harmony of feelings. There is a tendency for organizations as differently oriented as, say, the Young Socialists and the 4-H Club, to adopt similar psychological methods of salesmanship to obtain and solidify their recruits.

This does not mean, however, that the veto groups are formed along the lines of character structure. As in a business corporation there is room for extreme inner-directed and other-directed types, and all mixtures between, so in a veto group there can exist complex symbiotic relationships among people of different political styles. Thus a team of lobbyists may include both moralizers and inside-dopesters, sometimes working in harness, sometimes in conflict; and the constituency of the team may be composed mainly of new-style political indifferents who have enough literacy and organizational experience to throw weight around when called upon. Despite these complications I think it fair to say

that the veto groups, even when they are set up to protect a clear-cut moralizing interest, are generally forced to adopt the political manners of the other-directed.

In saying this I am talking about the national scene. The smaller the constituency, of course, the smaller the number of veto groups involved and the greater the chance that some one of them will be dominant. Thus, in local politics there is more indignation and less tolerance, just as even the *Chicago Tribune* is a tolerant paper in comparison with the community throwaways in many Chicago neighborhoods.

The same problem may be considered from another perspective. Various groups have discovered that they can go quite far in the amorphous power situation in America without being stopped. Our society is behaviorally open enough to permit a considerable community of gangsters a comfortable living under a variety of partisan political regimes. In their lack of concern for public relations these men are belated businessmen. So are some labor leaders who have discovered their power to hold up the economy, though in most situations what is surprising is the moderation of labor demands—a moderation based more on psychological restraints than on any power that could effectively be interposed. Likewise, it is sometimes possible for an aggressive group, while not belonging to the entrenched veto-power teams, to push a bill through a legislature. Thus, the original Social Security Act went through Congress, so far as

I can discover, because it was pushed by a devoted but tiny cohort; the large veto groups including organized labor were neither very much for it nor very much against it.

For similar reasons those veto groups are in many political situations strongest whose own memberships are composed of veto groups, especially veto groups of one. The best example of this is the individual farmer who, after one of the farm lobbies has made a deal for him, can still hold out for more. The farm lobby's concern for the reaction of other veto groups, such as labor unions, cuts little ice with the individual farmer. This fact may strengthen the lobby in a negotiation: it can use its internal public relations problems as a counter in bargaining, very much as does a diplomat who tells a foreign minister that he must consider how Senator so-and-so will react. For, no matter what the other-directedness of the lobby's leaders, they cannot bind their membership to carry out a public relations approach. Many labor unions have a similar power because they cannot control their memberships who, if not satisfied with a deal made by the union, can walk off or otherwise sabotage a job.

In contrast, those veto groups are often weaker whose other-directed orientation can dominate their memberships. Large corporations are vulnerable to a call from the White House because, save for a residual indignant like Sewell Avery, their officials are themselves other-directed and because, once the word from the chief goes out, the factory superintendents, no matter how boiling mad, have to fall into line with the new policy by the very nature of the centralized organization for which they work: they can sabotage top management on minor matters but not, say, on wage rates or tax accounting. As against this, the American Catholic Church possesses immense veto-group power because it combines a certain amount of centralized command—and a public picture of a still greater amount—with a highly decentralized priesthood (each priest is in a sense his own trade association secretary) and a membership organization of wide-ranging ethnic, social, and political loyalties; this structure permits great flexibility in bargaining.

These qualifications, however, do not change the fact that the veto groups, taken together, constitute a new buffer region between the old, altered, and thinning extremes of those who were once leaders and led. It is both the attenuation of leaders and led, and the other-oriented doings of these buffers, that help to give many moralizers a sense of vacuum in American political life.

The veto groups, by the conditions their presence creates and by the requirements they set for leadership in politics, foster the tolerant mood of other-direction and hasten the retreat of the inner-directed indignants.

Is There a Ruling Class Left?

Nevertheless, people go on acting

9

1. WHO RULES AMERICA?

as if there still were a decisive ruling class in contemporary America. In the postwar years, businessmen thought labor leaders and politicians ran the country, while labor and the left thought that "Wall Street" ran it, or the "sixty families." Wall Street, confused perhaps by its dethronement as a telling barometer of capital-formation weather, may have thought that the midwestern industrial barons, cushioned on plant expansion money in the form of heavy depreciation reserves and undivided profits, ran the country. They might have had some evidence for this in the fact that the New Deal was much tougher with finance capital—e.g., the SEC and the Holding Company Act—than with industrial capital and that when, in the undistributed profits tax, it tried to subject the latter to a stockholder and money-market control, the tax was quickly repealed.

(Cont. from p. 5, Mills, "Power Elite")

The power elite are not solitary rulers. Advisers and consultants, spokesmen and opinion-makers are often the captains of their higher thought and decision. Immediately below the elite are the professional politicians of the middle levels of power, in the Congress and in the pressure groups, as well as among the new and old upper classes of town and city and region. Mingling with them, in curious ways which we shall explore, are those professional celebrities who live by being continually displayed but are never, so long as they remain celebrities, displayed enough. If such celebrities are not at the head of any dominating hierarchy, they do often have the power to distract the attention of the public or afford sensations to the masses, or, more directly, to gain the ear of those who do occupy positions of direct power. More or less unattached, as critics of morality and technicians of power, as spokesmen of God and creators of mass sensibility, such celebrities and consultants are part of the immediate scene in which the drama of the elite is enacted. But that drama itself is centered in the command posts of the major institutional hierarchies.

The truth about the nature and the power of the elite is not some secret which men of affairs know but will not tell. Such men hold quite various theories about their own roles in the sequence of event and decision. Often they are uncertain about their roles, and even more often they allow their fears and their hopes to affect their assessment of their own power. No matter how great their actual power, they tend to be less acutely aware of it than of the resistances of others to its use. Moreover, most American men of affairs have learned well the rhetoric of public relations, in some cases even to the point of using it when they are alone, and thus coming to believe it. The personal awareness of the actors is only one of the several sources one must examine in order to understand the higher circles. Yet many who believe that there is no elite, or at any rate none of any consequence, rest their argument upon what men of affairs believe about themselves, or at least assert in public.

There is, however, another view: those who feel, even if vaguely, that a compact and powerful elite of great importance does now prevail in America often base that feeling upon the historical trend of our time. They have felt, for example, the domination of the military event, and from this they infer that generals and admirals, as well as other men of decision influenced by them, must be enormously powerful. They hear that the Congress has again abdicated to a handful of men decisions clearly related to the issue of war or peace. They know that the bomb was dropped over Japan in the name of the United States of America, although they were at no time consulted about the matter. They feel that they live in a time of big decisions; they know that they are not making any. Accordingly, as they consider the present as history, they infer that at its center, making decisions or failing to make them, there must be an elite of power.

On the one hand, those who share this feeling about big historical events assume that there is an elite and that its power is great. On the other hand, those who listen carefully to the reports of men apparently involved in the great decisions often do not believe that there is an elite whose powers are of decisive consequence.

Both views must be taken into account, but neither is adequate. The way to understand the power of the American elite lies neither solely in recognizing the historic scale of events nor in accepting the personal awareness reported by men of apparent decision. Behind such men and behind the events of history, linking the two, are the major institutions of modern society. These hierarchies of state and corporation and army constitute the means of power; as such they are now of a consequence not before equaled in human history—and at their summits, there are now those command posts of modern society which offer us the sociological key to an understanding of the role of the higher circles in America.

Within American society, major national power now resides in the economic, the political, and the military domains. Other institutions seem off to the side of modern history, and, on occasion, duly subordinated to these. No family is as directly powerful in national affairs as any major corporation; no church is as directly powerful in the external biographies of young men in America today as the military establishment; no college is as powerful in the shaping of momentous events as the National Security Council. Religious, educational, and family institutions are not autonomous centers of national power; on the contrary, these decentralized areas are increasingly shaped by the big three, in which developments of decisive and immediate consequence now occur. Families and churches and schools adapt to modern life; governments and armies and corporations shape it; and, as they do so, they turn these lesser institutions into means for their ends. Religious institutions provide chaplains to the armed forces where they are used as a means of increasing the effectiveness of its morale to kill. Schools select and train men for their jobs in corporations and their specialized tasks in the armed forces. The extended family has, of course, long been broken up by the industrial revolution, and now the son and the father are removed from the family, by compulsion if need be, whenever the army of the state sends out the call. And the symbols of all these lesser institutions are used to legitimate the power and the decisions of the big three.

The life-fate of the modern individual depends not only upon the family into which he was born or which he enters by marriage, but increasingly upon the corporation in which he spends the most alert hours of his best years; not only upon the school where he is educated as a child and adolescent, but also upon the state which touches him throughout his life; not only upon the church in which on occasion he hears the word of God, but also upon the army in which he is disciplined.

If the centralized state could not rely upon the inculcation of nationalist loyalties in public and private schools, its leaders would promptly seek to modify the decentralized educational system. If the bankruptcy rate among the top five hundred corporations were as high as the general divorce rate among the thirty-seven million married couples, there would be economic catastrophe on an international scale. If members of armies gave to them no more of their lives than do believers to the churches to which they belong, there would be a military crisis.

Within each of the big three, the typical institutional unit has become enlarged, has become administrative, and, in the power of its decisions, has become centralized. Behind these developments there is a fabulous technology, for as institutions, they have incorporated this technology and guide it, even as it shapes and paces their developments.

The economy—once a great scatter of small productive units in autonomous balance—has become dominated by two or three hundred giant corporations, administratively and politically interrelated, which together hold the keys to economic decisions.

The political order, once a decentralized set of several dozen states with a weak spinal cord, has become a centralized, executive establishment which has taken up into itself many powers previously scattered, and now enters into each and every cranny of the social structure.

The military order, once a slim establishment in a context of distrust fed by state militia, has become the largest and most expensive feature of government, and, although well versed in smiling public relations, now has all the grim and clumsy efficiency of a sprawling bureaucratic domain.

In each of these institutional areas, the means of power at the disposal of decision makers have increased enormously; their central executive powers have been enhanced; within each of them modern administrative routines have been elaborated and tightened up.

As each of these domains becomes enlarged and centralized, the consequences of its activities become greater, and its traffic with the others increases. The decisions of a handful of corporations bear upon military and political as well as upon economic developments around the world. The decisions of the military establishment rest upon and grievously affect political life as well as the very level of economic activity. The decisions made within the political domain determine economic activities and military programs. There is no longer, on the one hand, an economy, and, on the other hand, a political order containing a military establishment unimportant to politics and to money-making. There is a political economy linked, in a thousand ways, with military institutions and decisions. On each side of the world-split running through central Europe and around the Asiatic rimlands, there is an ever-increasing interlocking of economic, military, and political structures. If there is government intervention in the corporate economy, so is there corporate intervention in the govern-

mental process. In the structural sense, this triangle of power is the source of the interlocking directorate that is most important for the historical structure of the present.

The fact of the interlocking is clearly revealed at each of the points of crisis of modern capitalist society—slump, war, and boom. In each, men of decision are led to an awareness of the interdependence of the major institutional orders. In the nineteenth century, when the scale of all institutions was smaller, their liberal integration was achieved in the automatic economy, by an autonomous play of market forces, and in the automatic political domain, by the bargain and the vote. It was then assumed that out of the imbalance and friction that followed the limited decisions then possible a new equilibrium would in due course emerge. That can no longer be assumed, and it is not assumed by the men at the top of each of the three dominant hierarchies.

For given the scope of their consequences, decisions—and indecisions—in any one of these ramify into the others, and hence top decisions tend either to become coordinated or to lead to a commanding indecision. It has not always been like this. When numerous small entrepreneurs made up the economy, for example, many of them could fail and the consequences still remain local; political and military authorities did not intervene. But now, given political expectations and military commitments, can they afford to allow key units of the private corporate economy to break down in slump? Increasingly, they do intervene in economic affairs, and as they do so, the controlling decisions in each order are inspected by agents of the other two, and economic, military, and political structures are interlocked.

At the pinnacle of each of the three enlarged and centralized domains, there have arisen those higher circles which make up the economic, the political, and the military elites. At the top of the economy, among the corporate rich, there are the chief executives; at the top of the political order, the members of the political directorate; at the top of the military establishment, the elite of soldier-statesmen clustered in and around the Joint Chiefs of Staff and the upper echelon. As each of these domains has coincided with the others, as decisions tend to become total in their consequence, the leading men in each of the three domains of power—the warlords, the corporation chieftains, the political directorate—tend to come together, to form the power elite of America.

The Theory of Balance

Not wishing to be disturbed over moral issues of the political economy, Americans cling to the idea that the government is a sort of automatic machine, regulated by the balancing of competing interests. This image of politics is simply a carry-over from the official image of the economy: in both, an equilibrium is achieved by the pulling and hauling of many interests, each restrained only by legalistic and amoral interpretations of what the traffic will bear.

The ideal of the automatic balance reached its most compelling elaboration in eighteenth-century economic terms: the market is sovereign and in the magic economy of the small entrepreneur there is no authoritarian center. And in the political sphere as well: the division, the equilibrium, of powers prevails, and hence there is no chance of despotism. "The nation which will not adopt an equilibrium of power," John Adams wrote, "must adopt a despotism. There is no other alternative." As developed by the men of the eighteenth century, equilibrium, or checks and balances, thus becomes the chief mechanism by which both economic and political freedom were guaranteed and the absence of tyranny insured among the sovereign nations of the world.

Nowadays, the notion of an automatic political economy is best known to us as simply the practical conservatism of the anti-New Dealers of the 'thirties. It has been given new—although quite false—appeal by the frightening spectacle of the totalitarian states of Germany yesterday and Russia today. And although it is quite irrelevant to the political economy of modern America, it is the only rhetoric that prevails widely among the managerial elite of corporation and state.

It is very difficult to give up the old model of power as an automatic balance, with its assumptions of a plurality of independent, relatively equal, and conflicting groups of the balancing society. All these assumptions are explicit to the point of unconscious caricature in recent statements of "who rules America." According to Mr. David Riesman, for example, during the past half century there has been a shift from "the power hierarchy of a ruling class to the power dispersal" of "veto groups." Now no one runs anything: all is undirected drift. "In a sense," Mr. Riesman believes, "this is only another way of saying that America is a middle-class country ... in which, perhaps people will soon wake up to the fact that there is no longer a 'we' who run things and a 'they' who don't or a 'we' who don't run things and a 'they' who do, but rather that all 'we's' are 'they's' and all 'they's' are 'we's.' "

"The chiefs have lost the power, but the followers have not gained it," and in the meantime, Mr. Riesman takes his psychological interpretation of power and of the powerful to quite an extreme, for example: "if businessmen *feel* weak and dependent, they *are* weak and dependent, no matter what material resources may be ascribed to them."

" . . . The future," accordingly, "seems to be in the hands of the small business and professional men who control Congress: the local realtors, lawyers, car salesmen, undertakers, and so on; of the military men who control defense and, in part, foreign policy; of the big business managers and their

lawyers, finance-committee men and other counselors who decide on plant investment and influence the rate of technological change; of the labor leaders who control worker productivity and worker votes; of the black belt whites who have the greatest stake in southern politics; of the Poles, Italians, Jews, and Irishmen who have stakes in foreign policy, city jobs, and ethnic religious and cultural organizations; of the editorializers and storytellers who help socialize the young, tease and train the adult, and amuse and annoy the aged; of the farmers— themselves warring congeries of cattlemen, corn men, dairymen, cotton men, and so on—who control key departments and committees and who, as the living representatives of our inner-directed past, control many of our memories; of the Russians and, to a lesser degree, other foreign powers who control much of our agenda of attention; and so on. The reader can complete the list."

Here indeed is something that measures up "to the modern standards of being fully automatic and completely impersonal. Yet there is some reality in such romantic pluralism, even in such a *pasticcio* of power as Mr. Riesman invents: it is a recognizable, although a confused, statement of the middle levels of power, especially as revealed in Congressional districts and in the Congress itself. But it confuses, indeeed it does not even distinguish between the top, the middle, and the bottom levels of power. In fact, the strategy of all such romantic pluralism, with its image of a semi-

1. WHO RULES AMERICA?

organized stalemate, is rather clear:

You elaborate the number of groups involved, in a kind of bewildering, Whitmanesque enthusiasm for variety. Indeed, what group fails to qualify as a "veto group"? You do not try to clarify the hodge-podge by classifying these groups, occupations, strata, organizations according to their political relevance or even according to whether they are organized politically at all. You do not try to see how they may be connected with one another into a structure of power, for by virtue of his perspective, the romantic conservative focuses upon a scatter of milieux rather than upon their connections within a structure of power. And you do not consider the possibility of any community of interests among the top groups. You do not connect all these milieux and miscellaneous groups with the big decisions: you do not ask and answer with historical detail: exactly *what*, directly or indirectly, did "small retailers" or "brick masons" have to do with the sequence of decision and event that led to World War II? What did "insurance agents," or for that matter, the Congress, have to do with the decision to make or not to make, to drop or not to drop, the early model of the new weapon? Moreover, you take seriously the public-relations-minded statements of the leaders of all groups, strata, and blocs, and thus confuse psychological uneasiness with the facts of power and policy. So long as power is not nakedly displayed, it must not be power. And of course you do not consider the difficulties posed for you as an observer by the fact of secrecy, official and otherwise.

In short, you allow your own confused perspective to confuse what you see and, as an observer as well as an interpreter, you are careful to remain on the most concrete levels of description you can manage, defining the real in , terms of the existing detail.

The balance of power theory, as Irving Howe has noted, is a narrow-focus view of American politics. With it one can explain temporary alliances within one party or the other. It is also narrow-focus in the choice of time-span: the shorter the period of time in which you are interested, the more usable the balance of power theory appears. For when one is up-close and dealing journalistically with short periods, a given election, for example, one is frequently overwhelmed by a multiplicity of forces and causes. One continual weakness of American "social science," since it became ever so empirical, has been its assumption that a mere enumeration of a plurality of causes is the wise and scientific way of going about understanding modern society. Of course it is nothing of the sort: it is a paste-pot eclecticism which avoids the real task of social analysis: that task is to go beyond a mere enumeration of all the facts that might conceivably be involved and weigh each of them in such a way as to understand how they fit together, how they form a model of what it is you are trying to understand.

Undue attention to the middle levels of power obscures the structure of power as a whole, especially the top and the bottom. American politics, as discussed and voted and campaigned for, have largely to do with these middle levels, and often only with them. Most "political" news is news and gossip about middle-level issues and conflicts. And, in America, the political theorist too is often merely a more systematic student of elections, of who voted for whom. As a professor or as a free-lance intellectual, the political analyst is generally on the middle levels of power himself. He knows the top only by gossip; the bottom, if at all, only by "research." But he is at home with the leaders of the middle level, and, as a talker himself, with their "bargaining."

Commentators and analysts, in and out of the universities, thus focus upon the middle levels and their balances because they are closer to them, being mainly middle-class themselves; because these levels provide the noisy content of "politics" as an explicit and reported-upon fact; because such views are in accord with the folklore of the formal model of how democracy works; and because, accepting that model as good, especially in their current patrioteering, many intellectuals are thus able most readily to satisfy such political urges as they may feel.

When it is said that a "balance of power" exists, it may be meant that no one interest can impose its will or its terms upon others; or that any

one interest can create a stalemate; or that in the course of time, first one and then another interest gets itself realized, in a kind of symmetrical taking of turns; or that all policies are the results of compromises, that no one wins all they want to win, but each gets something. All these possible meanings are, in fact, attempts to describe what can happen when, permanently or temporarily, there is said to be "equality of bargaining power." But, as Murray Edelman has pointed out, the goals for which interests struggle are not merely given; they reflect the current state of expectation and acceptance. Accordingly, to say that various interests are "balanced" is generally to evaluate the *status quo* as satisfactory or even good; the hopeful ideal of balance often masquerades as a description of fact.

"Balance of power" implies equality of power, and equality of power seems wholly fair and even honorable, but in fact what is one man's honorable balance is often another's unfair imbalance. Ascendant groups of course tend readily to proclaim a just balance of power and a true harmony of interest, for they prefer their domination to be uninterrupted and peaceful. So large businessmen condemn small labor leaders as "disturbers of the peace" and upsetters of the universal interests inherent in business-labor cooperation. So privileged nations condemn weaker ones in the name of internationalism, defending with moral notions what has been won by force against

17

those have-nots whom, making their bid for ascendancy or equality later, can hope to change the *status quo* only by force.

The Power Elite

The idea of the power elite rests upon and enables us to make sense of (1) the decisive institutional trends that characterize the structure of our epoch, in particular, the military ascendancy in a privately incorporated economy, and more broadly, the several coincidences of objective interests between economic, military, and political institutions; (2) the social similarities and the psychological affinities of the men who occupy the command posts of these structures, in particular the increased interchangeability of the top positions in each of them and the increased traffic between these orders in the careers of men of power; (3) the ramifications, to the point of virtual totality, of the kind of decisions that are made at the top, and the rise to power of a set of men who, by training and bent, are professional organizers of considerable force and who are unrestrained by democratic party training.

Negatively, the formation of the power elite rests upon (1) the relegation of the professional party politician to the middle levels of power, (2) the semi-organized stalemate of the interests of sovereign localities into which the legislative function has fallen, (3) the virtually complete absence of a civil service that constitutes a politically neutral, but politically relevant, depository of brainpower and executive skill, and (4) the increased official secrecy behind which great decisions are made without benefit of public or even Congressional debate.

As a result, the political directorate, the corporate rich, and the ascendant military have come together as the power elite, and the expanded and centralized hierarchies which they head have encroached upon the old balances and have now relegated them to the middle levels of power. Now the balancing society is a conception that pertains accurately to the middle levels, and on that level the balance has become more often an affair of intrenched provincial and nationally irresponsible forces and demands than a center of power and national decision.

POSTSCRIPT

WHO RULES AMERICA?

Few rebuttals to the charge that America is ruled by a "power elite" contend that the majority always rules in America. To say that would not only fly in the face of the facts, it would also run contrary to some deeply held American values. Whether these values go by the name of "minority rights," "individualism," or "constitutionalism," the point is that Americans are usually reluctant to put all their eggs in one basket of majority head-counts.

David Riesman, then, does not try to say that America is always and everywhere run by the majority. His point is that minorities play an important role in the governing process, but their role is primarily negative: minority groups can *prevent* the passage of measures which threaten their vital interest. And even this limited power is not the monopoly of any one minority; every organized group possesses this weapon of self-defense. Mills, on the other hand, sees the power of the minority as being more than simply negative. In his view, the power elite occupies the "command posts" of our nation. As for how broadly the power is shared, Mills confines it to three interlocking groups: military chiefs, industrial leaders, and the top officials of the executive branch.

The literature of political science and sociology contains many expressions of these conflicting views of power in America. Robert Dahl's *Who Governs?* (Yale, 1961) studied New Haven, Connecticut in the late 1950s and concluded that it was run by a broad coalition of interest groups and politicians but not by any single minority. Dahl suggested that the New Haven model also fits the United States as a whole. Very different from Dahl's view is that of G. William Domhoff. In *Who Rules America* (Prentice-Hall, 1967) and *The Higher Circles* (Random House, 1970) Domhoff argued that America is controlled by representatives of the upper class. Arnold Rose, on the other hand (*The Power Structure,* Oxford, 1967), presented a picture of America which resembles Riesman's. He concluded that the "power structure of the United States is highly complex and diversified," and that "the political system is more or less democratic."

It is certainly not easy to decide which school of analysis is more accurate. Much, obviously, depends upon the data produced by each, but a great deal also depends upon how we weigh the data and judge its importance. For example, Mills agrees with Riesman that there is a clash of interest groups in the "middle" levels of power, e.g., in Congress, but contends that this is not where the "big" decisions are made. In choosing sides, then, we must make our own judgments as to whether Congress is really a "middle"-level decision-maker, and whether the "big" decisions are made elsewhere. For this we need information, but we also need to use our instincts and our common sense.

ISSUE 2

WHAT GOOD
ARE POLITICAL PARTIES?

"If I could not go to heaven but with a party, I would not go there at all." Thus did Thomas Jefferson express his feelings about political parties in America. Jefferson regarded them as dangerous institutions which tended to subvert the spirit of republican government. George Washington, in a speech probably written by Alexander Hamilton, took much the same view. In his Farewell Address he warned against "all combinations and associations" which aim to "direct, control, counteract or awe the regular deliberation of the constituted authorities." Another Founding Father, James Madison, seemed to be talking about parties when he ruminated about the mischiefs of "faction" in Federalist 10. At any rate, not a single one of the Founders ever said a good word about parties.

Yet nearly all of them belonged to one. In fact, Washington and Hamilton were the leaders of our first organized party as an independent nation, the Federalists. Madison and Jefferson later led in the formation of an opposition party, the Republicans (no kin to the present party by that name) which decisively beat the Federalists in the election of 1800. From that point the history of our parties becomes rather involved, with new parties appearing and old ones dying, until the present two-party alignment took shape shortly before the Civil War. From the time of Andrew Jackson until the death of Franklin Roosevelt parties enjoyed great popular support in America. People tended to identify themselves—and their families, their regions, their ethnic groups— with one of the two major parties.

For better or for worse, those days seem to be over. A Gallup poll taken in 1974 showed that only 23 percent of Americans identify themselves as Republicans. The Democrats fare better—but not that much better, since Americans today commonly split their tickets or desert "their" party without any qualms. It should not be surprising, then, that the fastest-growing group of voters are the so-called "independents," those who refuse to identify with any party. They number 33 percent of American voters, 10 percent more than Republicans. Among young people the "independent" route seems to be especially popular, and on many Northern university campuses about half the students so designate themselves.

2. WHAT GOOD ARE POLITICAL PARTIES?

Why the rejection of parties? In part it may have to do with the disgrace of Vietnam and Watergate, associated respectively with a Democratic and a Republican administration. The decline of parties also seems to correlate with the rise of television, a medium which tends to make party politics look either suspicious or ridiculous. To understand the erosion of party loyalty in the broadest sense, however, we must take into account the increasing mobility and sophistication of Americans. As our people move from farm to city, from city to suburb, and from high school to college, they break the bands which once tied their families to one or another of the parties.

One can always ask, of course, whether American parties ever deserved the loyalty of any particular class of Americans. Compared to those of Europe, American parties have not shown very clear-cut differences in approaching the issues. Both support capitalism ("free enterprise") while recognizing a legitimate role of government in the economy; both profess concern about poverty and racial discrimination in America (while differing about strategies for dealing with these problems); both call for an America which is at once peaceful and strong militarily; both are highly critical of Communism but, in the wake of Vietnam, extremely reluctant to engage in any more foreign wars. Despite these similarities, some students of American politics have concluded that the two parties moved into sharper opposition, at least on domestic issues, during the 1960s—the Republicans becoming more conservative, the Democrats more liberal. All of this awaits conclusive demonstration.

What does seem clear is that American parties, whether loosely or tightly defined, are losing favor with the voters. More and more Americans seem to be returning to the Founding Fathers' attitude toward parties as "factions," institutions to be avoided if possible, but at least to be kept under control by an alert citizenry. What can be said in opposition to this trend? There are serious political thinkers, not simply party propagandists, who view the erosion of partisan ties with great concern. Political parties, they argue, have served a variety of purposes essential to American democracy, and the absence of parties would leave a dangerous political vacuum. In the selections that follow, *Washington Post* columnist David Broder argues this point, while H.R. Shapiro reaffirms the position of the Founders.

David S. Broder

PARTIES
PROMOTE DEMOCRACY

In its 1950 report, "Toward a More Responsible Two-Party System," the committee on political parties of the American Political Science Association said there were four dangers to our democracy which "warrant special emphasis," dangers which they prophesied would become more acute unless the forces weakening our party system were combated.

"The first danger," the report said, "is that the inadequacy of the party system in sustaining well-considered programs and providing broad public support for them may lead to grave consequences in an explosive era."

The weakness of our party system has made it very difficult to build and maintain support for the long-term enterprises we need to pursue at home and abroad. The task of supporting international economic development, of constructing a stable world peace, of building a strong domestic economy and equitably distributing its products and wealth, of reforming our governmental structures and finding adequate resources for our urgent national needs cannot be accomplished by a single Congress or a single President. We have paid a high price for the instability and weakness of our governing coalitions. Ambitious programs have been launched, but funds to finance them withheld. Commitments made by a President have been undercut by Congress. Funds voted by Congress have been vetoed or impounded by a President. No party has been able to move ahead on its own agenda for very long, and the result has been sixteen years of government by fits and starts, with a mounting backlog of unkept promises and unmet needs.

"The second danger," the APSA committee said, "is that the American people may go too far for the safety of constitutional government in compensating for this inadequacy by shifting excessive responsibility to the President."

We have seen that happen, too. The weakness and frustration of responsible party government at the state and local levels—which is, if anything, even more serious than at the national level—has sent most of our major issues to Washington for resolution. And in Washington power has increasingly been stripped from Congress and the departments and been centralized in the

Continued on p. 24

H. R. Shapiro

PARTIES HAVE UNDERMINED DEMOCRACY

Several decades have passed since political parties were the subject of high public debate and comprehensive legislation. Several decades have passed since men in elected office made serious efforts to curb the power of political parties over the governments of this Republic. Since that time, such efforts have come to seem naive or even retrograde. What is more common, they have come to seem almost incomprehensible. Political debates about political parties? Why parties, we are told, are what you mean by "politics." Curb the power of parties over government? Why parties, we are told, are the very instruments of government and the competition between them the sole practical means by which popular government becomes possible at all.

An elaborate political ideology has grown up around America's "two-party system," surrounding it, justifying it and buttressing it. It pervades the speeches of politicians; it provides the stuff of daily newspaper reporting and the assumptions of learned essays in "political science." Constantly we are asked to look upon political reality through the lens of the party system. When we do, however, the one thing we can never see or understand is political reality. That is the purpose of the ideology.

In outline, the official conception of party government is simplicity itself. A party is an organization of party workers "regulars" or "stalwarts," party leaders and office seekers united around a single exclusive goal: to win elections for public office. This exclusive desire for victory is a party's reason for being and it is held to have two beneficial consequences. It makes each party a sensitive instrument for gauging the "popular mood"—for how else can the party succeed in putting up winning candidates? Secondly it provides a ceaseless competition for office between the two "major" parties. This competition guarantees representative government, for if the men of one party fail to represent the citizenry, the other party provides the voters with an opportunity to elect more representative leaders. This competition is held to be enhanced when the organization leaders of the party are strong enough to control the party nominations, for then they can hold their candidates to the party's principles and programs and the voters know who they are voting for when they vote the party label.

Continued on p. 30

From H. R. Shapiro, *The Bureaucratic State* (Brooklyn, N.Y.: Samizdat Press, 1975).

2. WHAT GOOD ARE POLITICAL PARTIES?

(Broder, cont. from p.22)

White House. Bereft of the sustained support a responsible party system could provide for passage and implementation of a long-term program, each of the last four Presidents has been forced to improvise his governmental policies and tactics on a day-to-day basis, hoping some temporary alliance would permit him to overcome the inherent immobility of the vast governmental system. As the APSA committee predicted, this situation has produced the type of "President who exploits skillfully the arts of demagoguery, who uses the whole country as his political backyard, and who does not mind turning into the embodiment of personal government." But even the highly personalized presidency of our era has not managed to cope successfully with the problems challenging America.

"The third danger," the APSA committee said in 1950, "is that with growing public cynicism and continuing proof of the ineffectiveness of the party system, the nation may eventually witness the disintegration of the two major parties." That has not yet happened, but we are appreciably closer to that danger than we were twenty years ago. Popular dissatisfaction with the two-party system is manifested in many ways: by the decline in voting; by the rise in the number of voters who refuse to identify themselves with either party; by the increase in ticket splitting, a device for denying either party responsibility for government;

and by the increased use of third parties or ad hoc political coalitions to pressure for change.

"The fourth danger," the APSA committee said, "is that the incapacity of the two parties for consistent action based on meaningful programs may rally support for extremist parties, poles apart, each fanatically bent on imposing on the country its particular panacea."

Regrettably, we have seen altogether too much of this kind of political polarization in the past twenty years. This has been an era of confrontation politics: whites vs. blacks; hard hats vs. students; demonstrators vs. police. The extremist parties are yet small, but the extremist movements are growing, and as our domestic political process becomes increasingly polarized, polemicized and violent, there is real danger the end result may be a totalitarian party of the left or right.

What must concern us is the rising level of public frustration with government-and-politics-as-usual. It is not just a few radical students who say and believe the political system is not working; millions of ordinary, hard-working Americans recognize that government is not dealing with the problems that are uppermost in their lives: crime and drugs and war and inflation and unfair tax loads and fear of unemployment and family budgets that do not stretch to meet the housing and education and medical and recreational needs of their families. . . .

Today it is not just . . . minority-group "outsiders" who are frustrated by the inequities of our society and the laggard performance of our political-governmental system. Millions of middle-aged, middle-class white working Americans are coming to understand that they have been victimized by the irresponsible politics of the recent era. No one asked them if they wanted their sons sent to fight in Vietnam; no one asked them if they wanted to gamble their family security on their ability to keep one step ahead of inflation; no one asked them if they wanted to swap token cuts in their income taxes for walloping hikes in the property taxes on their homes. Yet all these things have been done to them, by their government, and they are not going to take it lying down. Failing any means of registering their views through the political system, they will follow the blacks and the students and the other minority groups into the streets. And confrontation politics—with its constant threat of violence and repression—will increase.

Is there not a better way to resolve our differences, to move ahead on our common problems? I believe there is. I have argued . . . that the instrument that is available to us—little used in the last sixteen years, at least—is the instrument of responsible party government. The alternative to making policy in the streets is to make it in the voting booth.

But, if that is to be more than a cliche answer, there must be real choices presented at election time—choices involving more than a selection between two sincere-sounding, photogenic graduates of some campaign consultant's academy of political and dramatic arts. The candidates must come to the voters with programs that are comprehensible and relevant to our problems; and they must have the kind of backing that makes it possible for them to act on their pledges once in office.

The instrument, the only instrument I know of, that can nominate such candidates, commit them to a program and give them the leverage and alliances in government that can enable them to keep their promises, is the political party.

But, even as I say that, I recognize that the notion will be greeted with enormous skepticism. The parties, it will be said, have been around for years; if they are the answer, then why do we have the problems we have now? My reply, of course, is that we have not seen responsible party government in this country—in Washington or in most states and cities—in the sixteen years I have been covering national politics. Instead, we have had fractured, irresponsible, nonparty government, and we have paid a fearful price for it.

I have dwelled . . . on the domestic consequences of our long period of governmental stalemate: the unmet needs of our major public services, the deteriorated condition of our governmental machinery. My emphasis was natural; it is in this area that my own reporting has concentrated and on which public attention now centers.

2. WHAT GOOD ARE POLITICAL PARTIES?

But I do not want to leave the impression that the most serious or costly consequences of the breakdown of responsible party government are in the domestic field. Still less do I want to leave unchallenged the argument, so often made, that politics should stop at the water's edge. For it is my firm conviction that if one wants to sum up in one word what can happen in the absence of responsible party government, that word is Vietnam.

For twenty-five years, respectable opinion in this country has held that the great questions of foreign policy should be kept sacred and inviolate, far removed from the sordid considerations of partisan advantage. The notion had a specific historic justification. In 1946, when Democrat Harry Truman was President, the Republicans captured Congress in an election that represented a strong public reaction against the wartime controls associated with the Democratic Administration.

The Republican congressional victory made responsible party government impossible. Faced with the necessity of securing support from a Republican Congress for major postwar international policies—including the Marshall Plan—Truman entrusted his foreign policy to a group of successful lawyers and businessmen, many of them liberal Republicans from the New York Establishment. The prominence given such men as Robert Lovett, Paul Hoffman, John McCloy, Allen and John Foster Dulles facilitated the course of bipartisanship that

was necessary under the historical circumstances.

Unfortunately, the notion became permanently enshrined that such nonpolitical men had a natural right to manage the nation's foreign policy. Dwight D. Eisenhower, . . . [who] was imbued with the myth of bipartisanship, let the Dulles brothers run foreign policy for him. And, as John Kenneth Galbraith has noted, even when the Democrats returned to power in 1961, "instead of Adlai Stevenson, W. Averell Harriman or J. W. Fulbright, with their Democratic party associations," John Kennedy gave the key international security jobs to such nonpolitical Establishment men as Dean Rusk, Robert McNamara, Roswell Gilpatric and the Bundy brothers, McGeorge and William.

"Foreign policy was thus removed from the influence of party politics . . . from the influence of men who had any personal stake in the future of the Democratic party, the President apart," Galbraith noted. Elections are held and party control of the presidency shifts, but the technicians and "experts"—the Walt Rostows and Henry Kissingers—never seem to lose their grip on the foreign policy machinery.

When protest over foreign policy arises from the ranks of the President's party, as it did from some Democratic senators in the Lyndon Johnson years and from some Republican legislators since Richard Nixon has been in office, it is the nonpolitical "experts" in the key foreign policy jobs who always rush forward to defend existing policies. It is these men, with their marvelous self-confidence and their well-developed contempt for politicians and public opinion, who wrote the clever scenarios and the cynical memoranda that comprise the history of Vietnam policy under three administrations contained in the Pentagon Papers. It is they who stand ready to advise a President how he can dupe the Congress and the public and maneuver the nation into war without disclosing his intentions.

How have they been able to maintain their control over foreign policy? Because the political parties, at critical junctures, have failed to meet their responsibilities. In none of the national elections during the whole course of the escalation and de-escalation in Vietnam were the American people given a choice of defined, coherent policies toward the struggle in Indochina. Either the issue was ignored entirely or smothered in a blanket of bipartisan generalities. For six long years—between 1964 and 1970—the leadership of both parties in Congress failed to try to bring to a vote a policy declaration on Vietnam. Vietnam is a classic instance of the costliness of isolating a basic foreign policy question from examination in partisan, political debate. It is a terrible measure of the failure of responsible party government in our time.

Letting the Parties Go

I am not optimistic about the prospects of reviving responsible party government in the near future.

The momentum of current trends, the drift of the public mood seem to me to point in the opposite direction: toward the further fracturing of the already enfeebled party structure in this decade. The survey that Haynes Johnson and I did at the time of the 1970 election convinced us that "not only are voters splitting their tickets and moving back and forth from election to election, but their perception of party differences is growing visibly weaker." That habit of partisanship, once lost, may be very difficult to regain.

If that proves to be the case, and if the young people entering the electorate remain as independent of the party system as they now appear to be, the major parties may no longer enjoy a monopoly in high office. Three or four or half-a-dozen serious presidential candidates may run each election year, posing a constitutional crisis whether we are operating under the existing electoral college system or a plan for direct election of the President. More minor party or independent candidates may find their way into Congress, weakening the existing party structure there.

If the distrust of politicians and parties continues to grow, it may be reflected in the deliberate crippling of responsible leadership, by dividing the branches of government between the parties and by turning officeholders out as soon as they show signs of amassing any significant power. While the masses of alienated voters use these tactics to cripple government, the activists for one cause or another may continue to press their demands through confrontation tactics—lawsuits, demonstrations, strikes, boycotts and the other weapons in their arsenal. The result would be an increase of domestic turbulence and violence. . . .

Taking the Political Option

Where do we turn? To ourselves. Obviously, that must be the answer. There is no solution for America except what we Americans devise. I believe that we have the instrument at hand, in the party system, that can break the long and costly impasse in our government. But it is up to us to decide whether to use it.

What would it entail on our part if we determined to attempt responsible party government? First, it would mean giving strong public support to those reform efforts which in the recent past have been carried on entirely by a small group of concerned political insiders, aimed at strengthening the machinery of political parties and government.

We should seek to strengthen the liaison between the presidency and Congress, on a mutual basis, and between the presidency and the heads of state and local government. We should elect the President in the same way we elect all other officials, by direct vote of his constituents, with high man winning.

We should expand the role and responsibilities of the party caucuses and the party leaders in Congress. The caucus should choose the floor leaders and policy committee members, the legislative committee chairmen and committee members, not on the basis of seniority but on the basis of ability and commitment to the party program. That leadership ought to be held accountable for bringing legislation to which the party is committed to a floor vote in orderly and timely fashion, with adequate opportunity for debate and particularly for consideration of opposition party alternatives. But procedures for due consideration should not justify devices like the filibuster, which prevent the majority party from bringing its measures to a final vote.

In state government, we need to reduce the number of elected officials, to provide governors with adequate tenure and staff to meet their responsibilities, and particularly to strengthen the legislatures, by limiting their size and by improving their pay, their facilities and their staffing, and to recognize they have a full-time job to do each year.

In local government, too, we need to reduce drastically the number of elected officials and make sure the jurisdictions they serve are large enough to provide a base for two-party competition and to bring resources together with problems along a broad enough front to give some hope of effective action.

We need to take every possible measure to strengthen the presidential nominating convention as the key device for making the parties responsible. The current effort to open the Democratic delegate-selection process to wider public participation is a promising start, and its emphasis on the congressional-district nominating convention offers corollary benefits for integrating congressional and presidential constituencies. Both parties should experiment with devices for putting heavier emphasis on the platform-writing phase of the convention's work, including the possibility of a separate convention, following the nomination, where the party's officeholders and candidates debate the program on which they pledge themselves to run and to act if elected.

Most important of all the structural reforms, we need to follow through the effort to discipline the use of money in politics, not only by setting realistic limits on campaign spending and by publicizing individual and organizational gifts, but also by channeling much more of the money (including, in my view, all general election spending) through the respective party committees, rather than through individual candidates' treasuries.

We need to strengthen the party organizations and their staffs, and recapture for them the campaign management functions that have been parceled out to independent firms which tend to operate with a fine disdain for the role of party and policy in government. We need to devise ways to make television—the prime medium of political communication—somewhat more sensitive to the claims of the parties to be a regular part of the political dialogue, and to protect the vital institution of the nominating convention from being distorted by the demands of the television cameras.

All these reforms would help, I believe, but they would not accomplish the invigoration of responsible party government unless they were accompanied by a genuine increase in the participation by the public in party affairs. The cure for the ills of democracy truly is more democracy; our parties are weak principally because we do not use them. To be strong and responsible, our parties must be representative; and they can be no more representative than our participation allows. Millions more of us need to get into partisan political activity.

We need also to become somewhat more reflective about what we do with our votes. We need to ask ourselves what it is that we want government to accomplish, and which candidate, which party comes closest to espousing that set of goals. That may sound so rationalistic as to be unrealistic. But this nation has more education, more communication, more leisure available to it than ever before. In the nineteenth century, James Bryce wrote of us, "The ordinary citizens are interested in politics, and watch them with intelligence, the same kind of intelligence (though a smaller quantity of it) as they apply to their own business.... They think their own competence equal to that of their representatives and office-bearers; and they are not far wrong." Are we to think less of ourselves today?

2. WHAT GOOD ARE POLITICAL PARTIES?

Finally, we need to examine some of our habits. It seems to me we should ask, before splitting a ticket, what it is we hope to accomplish by dividing between the parties the responsibility for government of our country, our state or our community. Do we think there is no difference between the parties? Do we distrust them both so thoroughly that we wish to set them against each other? Do we think one man so superior in virtue and wisdom that he must be put in office, no matter who accompanies him there? Why are we splitting our tickets? My guess is that, if we asked those questions, we would more often be inclined to give a temporary grant of power to one party at a time, rather than dividing responsibility so skillfully between the parties that neither can govern. If we were willing to risk this strategy, knowing that we would be able to throw the rascals out if they failed, we might even discover to our amazement that they are not always rascals. . . .

In such times of turbulence as our own, De Tocqueville advised relying on the "patriotism of reflection," which, he said, "springs from knowledge . . . is nurtured by the laws . . . grows by the exercise of civil rights, and, in the end . . . is confounded with the personal interests of the citizen."

And then he wrote the sentence that I think might well serve as the keynote of our search for a solution to the terrible impasse in which we find ourselves. "I maintain," he said, "that the most powerful and perhaps the only means that we still possess of interesting men in welfare of their country is to make them partakers in the government."

To make them partakers in the government. That is the challenge that now faces our political parties. That is ultimately the test of responsible party government—to make all citizens feel they are partakers and participants in the government.

(Cont. from p. 23, Shapiro, "Parties Undermined Democracy")

On the unchallenged assertion that parties are organized to win elections, representative government in the Republic is held to rest. On that same fact the entire ideology of "responsible party government" has been erected. There is only one thing wrong with the ideology and it is suggested by a simple question which nobody seems to ask. Are our political parties really governed by a desire to win elections and is the characteristic relation between the parties ceaseless competition for office? The answer to that question is, quite simply, that if parties competed for office nothing that actually happens in our political life can be understood at all.

The truly unquestionable fact about the parties is that between

1896 and around 1960, more than three quarters of the states in the Union have been virtually one-party states, states in which the minority party as of the turn-of-the-century has rarely, if ever, gained control of the dominant governmental body in their state, namely the state legislature. In three quarters of the states the minority party has been a permanent minority for sixty years and more.

Democratic one-party states are those of the South: Alabama, Georgia, Florida, South Carolina, North Carolina, Louisiana, Mississippi, Virginia, Tennessee, Arkansas; the southern border states of West Virginia, Kentucky, Maryland and Missouri; the southwestern states of Oklahoma, Texas, Arizona and, since 1932, New Mexico. The hegemony of the Democratic party has been strictly confined to the southern half of the country.

States controlled by the Republicans include: Maine, New Hampshire, Vermont, Massachusetts, Connecticut, Rhode Island, New York, New Jersey, Pennsylvania, Ohio, Indiana, Michigan, Illinois, Kansas, Iowa, Wisconsin, Wyoming, Montana, North Dakota, South Dakota, Oregon and California—the entire northern half of the country. It is as if the Democrats and the Republicans had split the Union into two separate party domains the way Spain and Portugal once split their world between their respective empires. Among the very few states where control of the legislature has shifted between parties fairly frequently are Colorado, Washington, Utah, Idaho and recently Delaware.

This freezing of the parties into permanent winners and permanent losers in the overwhelming majority of states for sixty years is—or ought to be—a truly remarkable fact. In that time, America has fought four major wars, undergone a hideous economic depression, witnessed the growth of huge cities, the enormous expansion of industry, an influx of several million foreign immigrants and vast shifts of population across state lines, yet the state parties have retained their domains *almost as if nothing had happened.*

Even the widespread turning away from the Republicans in the 1930s cost the Republicans their state hegemony in but a handful of states—New Mexico, for example. One reason for this was the state Democratic parties' curious unwillingness to exploit the party's sudden national popularity. As V.O. Key, the leading academic student of party politics, observed of the New Deal era: "The easy rewards of national politics certainly did not intensify efforts by the professionals to capture state governments"— curious conduct for parties bent on winning elections. By 1934, the majority of registered voters in Republican California were Democrats, yet the Democratic party did not succeed in winning even one house of the state legislature until 1956, partly for the reason that they let many of the seats in the legislature go to Republicans *without* a contest.

31

The Unexplained Prevalence of One-Party States

All kinds of *ad hoc* self-contradictory explanations are piled up to explain away one-party states in our allegedly competitive two-party system. It is said that Republicans are strong in rural states because rural people vote Republican. Yet Arizona, Texas and Oklahoma are rural and here the Republicans have been permanent losers. It is said that the Democrats are strong in highly industrialized areas, yet there is not *one* industrialized state whose legislature this century has been controlled by the Democrats as much as 20% of the time. It is said that the Democrats are only strong in the big cities, but Philadelphia, Cincinnati and St. Louis were long ruled by Republican administrations.

It is said that Democrats appeal strongly to ethnic minorities, yet in Michigan the Democrats were a hapless rump organization for decades, despite the fact that 41% of the population *outside* Detroit had immigrant backgrounds. It is said that the Democrats have a natural appeal to Catholic voters. Yet the Democrats run New York City and are moribund outside it, despite the fact that there is a higher percentage of Catholics outside New York City than in it. Indeed if Democrats really did monopolize the Catholic, immigrant vote, then Massachusetts, Connecticut and Rhode Island would have been one-party *Democratic* states since around 1920. Yet, in fact, Massachusetts Democrats did not gain control of the state legislature until 1958—after 100 years of allegedly trying.

Sometimes these "sociological" explanations are discarded and we are told, for example, that Republican state strongholds are such because the voters are "traditionally" Republican and the Democrats are a permanent minority party through the sheer abiding preference of the voters. Or to put it simply: parties are what they are because the voters are what they are.

Obviously, this "explanation" begs the question of democratic politics: Is any political unit so close to perfect harmony that a serious opposition party can find nothing to oppose for 60 years? What is more it flies in the face of the voters' actual preferences. In California, as was seen, the Democrats remained a minority party long after the majority of voters called themselves Democrats. In almost every other Republican stronghold (Vermont, for one, excepted) the perennially losing Democrats *regularly* poll from 40% to 50% of the vote in elections for governor. (In Democratic Oklahoma, the losing Republicans regularly poll 45% of the governorship vote).

Why Collusion, Not Competition Prevails Between Parties

So even in these one-party strongholds, almost half the voters regularly oppose the ruling party.

Indeed it is not the voters who are content with the ruling party, but the opposition party leaders, for in many one-party states the "opposition" manifests its opposition by putting up status quo candidates—surely a prescription for non-victory. In Minnesota, for example, a powerful statewide insurgent movement found the Democratic "opposition" so little opposed to the Republican regulars, its leaders had to form a third party, the Farmer-Labor party, to contest the G.O.P. Did the California Democratic party, or the Minnesota Democratic party or any permanent minority party really want to gain control over the legislature?

It is time to make the point explicit. Political parties are not governed by an exclusive desire to win elections. Far from it; they often try very hard to *lose* elections. Insofar as parties are *strong*, insofar as the party organization is controlled by a few party bosses—this is the key proviso—the goal of a political party is to protect the bosses' power over the destinies of the party. Winning and losing elections are but means to other ends.

To state the case in a general way: At any given moment, one party in a state is stronger than the other and strongly controls the state legislature. The minority party is a winning party, perhaps, in a single large city, or in a small bloc of counties, or among minority blocs of voters— union members, Catholics—more or less dispersed. If such a party is in the hands of organization bosses who can control the nominations of candidates, the party bosses have

almost no reason to build up their organizational strength elsewhere in the state in order to contest for control of the legislature.

To do so, the bosses would have to build up a statewide organization of independent local party organizations each bent on winning local election victories for its candidates. Such an extended party becomes a coalition of so many independent local units that the party bosses would cease to control the party and its nominations with all the enormous political influence that control implies. On the other hand the advantages of not building up a state wide competitive party are immediate, automatic and compelling. By preventing the party from organizing throughout the state, the bosses hand over control of the state legislature—and often enough, the governorship—to the current majority party. The leaders of that party, therefore, become not the competitors but the allies of the minority party's leaders. The reason is obvious. It is the power of the party bosses over their party which makes it a fake opposition and ensures the majority party its permanent hegemony.

If the minority party is merely a small, patronage organization, the ruling party will help see to it that the bosses have sufficient jobs, judgeships and state appointments to distribute in order to maintain control over the party organization. In Democratic Kentucky, as a political scientist has written, "The Republicans in their avidity for spoils invite the Democratic governor to attend their caucus for a reiteration of their bargains." If the minority party is entrenched in a city or a region, the majority party will not challenge it there, for the last thing it wishes to do is topple the bosses of the fake opposition. In short, between the bosses of the minority party and the leaders of the majority party there is an almost perfect *identity of interests* and the name of the relation between such parties is not competition but *collusion.*

The abiding common policy of the two collusive parties is the maintenance of the status quo; the abiding relation between the parties and the electorate is the parties' immunity to it. The abiding result for representative government is misrepresentative government and the corrupt rule of irresponsible power. Under two-party collusion, the men whom the citizens elect to office are controlled, not by those who elected them, but by the party leaders who nominated them, for thanks to the dummy opposition, it is the mere party label of the ruling party which insures a candidate's victory. If the voters are dissatisfied with the administration or the legislature, they must resort to a dummy opposition candidate. If the insurgent portion of the electorate forms a third party then the two collusive parties will combine against it, for the emergence of a competitive party would destroy the whole system of two-party collusion. Indeed it is only the fact of collusion which explains why the two "major" parties combine against a third

party. It explains that and much else besides.

How else can we explain what is otherwise inexplicable—that despite the turbulence of sixty years, the vast majority of states remained in command of a permanent ruling party? How else can we explain why in Democratic Missouri (not to mention Oklahoma, Ohio and Pennsylvania) the Republicans often fail to put up legislative candidates in the Democratic areas and the ruling Democrats fail to put up candidates in Republican areas, "including districts," as V.O. Key writes, "in which the minority legislative candidates would poll quite respectable votes and even on occasion win"? How else can we explain why the bosses of the California Democratic party, using the state's system of cross-filing candidates in primaries, regularly turned out a vote for *Republican* legislative candidates in their own primary elections? Or why it is that only *after* the party bosses lost control of the party through the upsurge of hundreds of grass-roots Democratic "clubs" around 1952, that the Democratic [sic] suddenly found they could elect a governor and win control over a house of the legislature? Obviously the party's candidates began winning when the party bosses lost their power to ensure defeat.

The System of Collusion at Work in the States

It is because only a boss-led party can be a collusive party that where competition between the parties prevails, the characteristic of the state parties is precisely that they are "weak" boss-less coalitions of independent local party organizations.

How else can we explain why in a dozen western states swept by insurgent movements the opposition Democratic party manifested its opposition to the Republicans by opposing the *insurgent*? What else besides two-party collusion explains why, when Wisconsin insurgents put up a candidate for governor in the 1922 Republican primary, the Democratic bosses urged their followers to vote in the Republican primary for the "regular" Republican candidate? What else explains why the Democrats of New York and Massachusetts retained their minority status by turning their backs on the huge number of Catholics, ethnic, city and factory worker votes outside New York City and Boston, whereas the minority Democrats of neighboring Maine, New Hampshire and Vermont retain their minority status by appealing only to urban and ethnic voters, who just happen to be a minority in those states.

The two-party collusion in the great industrial states of the Northeast are so decisive for national politics that it merits a more than passing mention here.

In New York State, the most revealing political fact is that in "upstate" New York the Democratic party organization is a mere inactive rump, despite the fact that the allegedly "rural Republicans"

there make up less than 15% of the upstate vote. By keeping the party defunct outside New York City, the New York City Democratic bosses turn the state legislature over to the Republicans. In return the Republicans do their best to preserve the rule of the Democratic bosses in New York City, an alliance which the Democratic bosses need for their very survival since they are, in fact, a minority party in New York City. Whenever anti-Tammany voters and Republicans can unite around a mayoral candidate the Democrats usually lose.

Two-Party Collusion Tammany Style

It is the permanent policy of the Republican state leaders to prevent, among other things, such a "fusion" from occurring, by keeping the city Republican party in the hands of "regulars" who know that their business is not to win elections but to put up candidates distinguished chiefly by their lack of appeal. Occasionally, an ambitious city Republican, more concerned with his career than the good of the party (i.e. collusion) will win the mayoralty of New York as a Republican-"Fusion" candidate. When this happens, the Republicans will harass him, withhold any legislative aid that might gain him popularity, and throw up a primary challenger when he seeks re-election. When the Republicans put up State Sen. John Marchi against Republican mayor John Lindsay, it was the first contested Republican mayoral primary since 1944—which just happened to be the last time New York had a Republican mayor.

In Massachusetts, the most revealing political fact this century is the Democratic party bosses' forty-year war against Democratic party organizations outside of Boston. By the second decade of the century it was becoming clear to the Boston machine that Democratic strength was growing throughout the state. In 1910 a Democrat from the western part of the state was elected governor and by 1920 some 68% of the entire state population consisted of ethnic voters. The Boston machine's control over the party was jeopardized and the only recourse of "Boss" Curley was to destroy the party organization outside the city. Instead of uniting the Democrats' massive Catholic vote in the state, Curley worked masterfully to split it, partly by putting up only Boston Irishmen for office and partly by keeping Italians out of the party ranks. Instead of giving local party organizations campaign money he systematically starved them of funds; the Boston machine making it a state party rule that local organizations get only what they can raise logically. If they are weak, they stay weak. In 1954, for example, the Republicans gave their state central executive $623,000 in campaign funds to distribute to local office seekers. The Democrats gave their state chairman $15,000—Boston keeping 95% of the funds. Is it any wonder that the Democrats succeeded in not controlling the legislature for 100 years?

Lest anyone think that the Boston Irish machine was at least beneficial to Boston, or to Irishmen it is worth pointing out here that Irishmen are among the poorest people in the city and that the city is not even governed by the Boston machine, since all real power over Boston is vested in the state legislature. The machinations of the Boston machine (or any machine for that matter) has nothing to do with Boston, with government or with people.

In Illinois the Cook County machine of Mayor Richard Daley works in collusion with the state Republicans in much the same manner as New York's Tammany has done. The Republicans give Daley Cook County and he in turn tries to confine the Democrats to that county. The Cook County machine, however, faces an obstacle peculiar to Illinois, namely the rural southern part of the state is both anti-Daley *and* Democratic. Under certain conditions, a popular Democratic governor could build up an independent party following and weaken Daley's control (and with it his collusion with the Republicans). Daley, therefore, is not anxious for a Democrat to win the governorship.

If so many state party organizations are in the hands of corrupt, collusive party bosses, what of the national parties, whose constituent members they are? The answer in general is that the national parties are not very different from the state parties, or, more precisely, they are exactly like the big-state party organizations which form the preponderant voice in the national parties.

Among the Democrats the big northeastern state parties are completely controlled by the big city bosses, whose sole political motive is to protect their position as big city bosses. A second powerful bloc of state parties are the southern state oligarchies, whose shaky rule over their states depends chiefly on the disenfranchisement of black people and poor whites, the maintenance of general poverty and whatever help they can get from the national party in keeping down rural insurgency. The southern Bourbons, in short, are more devoted to the status quo in more phases of public life than any other political parties in the country. For a century, therefore, they have been the allies and dependents of the big city machines.

United, the big city bosses and the Bourbons control the Democratic party, indeed they *are* the Democratic party. Only one thing has ever threatened their hegemony: the western states, principal home of political insurgency and of opposition to boss-rule in this Republic for several generations. If all the states from Ohio to Oregon were represented in the national Democratic party by vigorous state parties bent on winning elections—rather than by self-serving dummy oppositions and corrupt little patronage organizations—the power of the bosses and Bourbons would long ago have been broken and with it the whole system of collusion and irresponsible power. It is for this reason that the

bosses of the national party have made sure for so long that the Democratic parties in these states *remain* dummy oppositions and patronage machines.

Why the Democratic Party Withdrew from the West

The Democratic party failed to become the dominant party in the states of the North during the New Deal or in the 1930s, 1940s, and 1950s because the party as a collection of city machine bosses and the minority party in the various state systems of two-party collusion, could not expand without breaking up two-party collusion and state party bureaucracy, as it existed, and, thus, destroying itself. The Democratic party could not grow, therefore, without destroying the very foundations of its existence as a collection of city Tammany machines.

The Republican party in the Border South, in turn, failed to become the dominant party in these states or conceded the states to the Democrats because the party, as a collection of "mountain" machine bosses and the minority party in the state systems of two-party collusion, could not expand without breaking up the two-party collusion and state party bureaucracy in the Border South, as it existed, and, thus, destroying itself, as it existed.

That danger arose in its most imminent form in 1896 and it is the Democratic party's response to it which explains why for so many years since that date, the relative positions of state parties were frozen. The danger came with the great democratic insurgence known as the Populist revolt, which broke out of the Democratic party in the south and out of the Republican party in the West. To defeat the Populist *party* was one thing, but what was to prevent Western populists and quasi-populists from surging into the Democratic parties of their states, ousting its regulars and threatening the eastern bosses' hegemony? The Democrats had a ready answer; destroy the Democratic party in the western states. What the Democratic party did after 1896 was, quite literally, to withdraw the party back to its eastern bastions, the big cities and the South, in order to preserve boss-rule.

The Democrats were so successful in making their western state organizations into feeble nullities that whenever an insurgent movement rose in a western state, insurgent leaders had to fight within the Republican party or else form third parties.

By 1924, the Democratic bosses, in their total self-serving corruption, had brought the party so low that it was on the verge of ceasing to be the second major party. That year Robert La Follette, running for president as an independent Republican, got more votes west of the Mississippi than the Democratic candidate did. What was even more startling, he almost out-polled the Democrats in the northeastern quarter of the country, the Demo-

cratic candidate getting three million votes to La Follette's 2.6 million. Bent for so long on destroying the western half of the party nationally and on destroying their out-of-city organizations in the states, the city bosses were losing even their urban immigrant vote.

This fact, it might be said, was the sole public event that penetrated into the self-contained world of the Tammany machines since the Populist revolt itself. To repair their fortunes, the Democrats in 1928 nominated for president Alfred E. Smith, Catholic, Irish, immigrant background, city man and "wet"—a complex symbolism designed to restore loyalty to the national party where the bosses needed it, and to repel it where they didn't want it, namely almost everywhere else. The trick worked so well that in 1932, when the entire nation was stricken with economic disaster and fifteen million men were idle on the streets, the old guard at the national Democratic convention wanted to make repeal of prohibition the *chief* plank in the platform.

Cooler heads prevailed of course, and the New Dealers responded to the crisis by giving control of the currency back to the banks, by restoring and re-legalizing the trusts, by creating non-regulating "regulatory agencies," by driving the small farmer off the land, by restoring the Southern oligarchs, by keeping the Western parties safely in the hands of hacks, by pouring shaky big city machines and so restoring the corrupt political status quo as far as was humanly possible.

So much and more than enough for "responsible party government."

The chief point should be clear by now: political parties are not and can never be instruments of representative government, the ideal, never achieved goal of party leaders is to render themselves, through their mutual cooperation, utterly immune to the citizenry and to reduce all politics to the self-serving machinations of party bureaucracies—which means the death of politics and the permanent rule of irresponsible power.

Minimizing the Danger of Political Parties

The real question concerning the political parties is how we can *minimize* the threat they pose to representative government. There are three means available.

First, party usurpation of power is minimized in proportion as party organizations are weak and no ruling clique, no bosses, no disciplined band of "regulars" can monopolize control over the nomination of candidates. State parties are weak when each is a statewide coalition of local geographical entities, each trying to elect state legislators from their districts, each voicing the concerns of a local political unit in the deliberations over suitable candidates for statewide and national office. When state parties approximate this condition—as they do in some western states—no bosses can control the party for long, no permanent collusion is possible and elected officials

become free to represent the citizens who elected them.

Secondly, the threat of party usurpation is minimized by putting as much power as possible out of the reach of the parties, namely in political bodies below the state level, where non-partisan politics is not only possible, but in fact is quite common.

Thirdly, the danger of party politics is minimized when citizens understand that parties are a danger to their liberties, and represent at best a necessary evil.

All three means are supplied by one general republican measure: the establishment of local self-governing communities in the cities, and the restoration of local power to existing self-governing townships where local power has been usurped by state governments. The augmentation of local self-government—the foundation of republican government—obviously puts power below the reach of the parties, for in these "schools of the Republic" local citizens understand well enough that parties are not instruments of representative government. That's why they demand and get non-partisan local elections. So the second and third conditions are met.

By breaking up the huge urban concentrations of political impotence, self-governing communities within the cities will break up citywide party organizations, for a single boss-led machine cannot dictate terms to self-governing citizens represented by their own elected officials. When no single party leader can rule over a

2. WHAT GOOD ARE POLITICAL PARTIES?

metropolitan bailiwick, no city-based party faction can dominate the state party and use it to protect its own power. With citizens finding their interests represented in their own local communities, no party boss can control a state party by organizing his party strength around statewide "ethnic blocs," for only impotent politically rootless men can be persuaded that the only common interest they share with their fellows is their common interest with fellow Poles, or Jews or Irishmen hundreds of miles away.

Where local self-governing communities exist across each state and within each city, parties will become what they must be if representative government is to be assured: namely coalitions of independent local organizations honestly organizing the competition for state and Federal office. When they do, the republic of free and equal citizens will begin to reemerge from under the sham and corruption of a party system which has not only obscured and perverted it, but which has posed for so long and so successfully as the very substance of republican politics.

POSTSCRIPT

WHAT GOOD ARE POLITICAL PARTIES?

Broder and Shapiro obviously have different attitudes toward American political parties, yet their views may not be utterly irreconcilable. Broder is concerned here with what parties *can be,* while Shapiro is providing a report about what parties *have been.* Without abandoning his argument about the potential of parties, Broder could agree with Shapiro that parties, too often, have not been competitors but partners in collusion. It is less likely that Shapiro could agree with much of what Broder has to say without undermining his position. Shapiro, after all, is not merely citing examples of collusion; he is arguing that parties are *inherently* boss-driven organizations.

Are they? Broder is convinced that parties can be "reformed," though it is not entirely clear what he means by "reform." At times he equates it with "strengthening" parties. If that is what he means, couldn't it be argued that parties were stronger back in the old days of unchallenged boss rule? But boss-imposed discipline is not the kind of strength Broder has in mind. His real hope is that party unity will come as a result of shared convictions among party members. In other words, Broder is calling for more "programmatic" parties, parties which stand for clearly defined goals.

A number of writers have discussed the possibility of making parties more programmatic. One of the best-known of these is James MacGregor Burns, who developed his argument at length in *The Deadlock of Democracy* (Prentice-Hall, 1963). A more recent book by Judson L. James, *American Political Parties in Transition* (Harper & Row, 1974), refines and brings up to date what is essentially Burns' argument. On the other hand, Evron M. Kirkpatrick of the American Political Science Association argued in 1970 that neither the American party system nor the American electorate is ready for the kind of sharp distinctions between platforms which the advocates of "programmatic" parties advocate. (His argument was published in the *American Political Science Review* in December, 1971.) George Reedy, in Chapter 9 of *The Twilight of the Presidency* (New American Library, 1970), takes much the same position.

One other question, which we touched upon in the introduction to this Issue, is whether there is going to be much of parties left to reform in America. That political parties have lost prestige and influence is undeniable. Whether they will "wither away," and what could possibly replace them, are questions which can only be answered by time. For the present, even Shapiro is ready to concede that parties may be "a necessary evil."

ISSUE 3

DO
PRESSURE GROUPS SERVE
OR SUBVERT DEMOCRACY?

The very term "pressure group" has a negative connotation. If we do not always picture pressure groups in terms of lobbyists bribing congressmen, we do invariably think of them as "special interests" which subordinate the public good to their private advantage.

This way of thinking has deep roots in the United States. In the preceding issue we referred to James Madison's term "factions" in connection with political parties, but an even more direct application of the term is to what we call pressure groups. Madison defined "faction" as a group

> united and actuated by some common impulse of passion, or of interest, adverse to the rights of other citizens, or to the permanent and aggregate interests of the community.

Today as in Madison's time opposing interests righteously contend that they alone support the interests of the community, while their opponents stand for special (read selfish) interests.

Some observers have wondered whether the distinction between community interests and special interests is real or simply rhetorical. Isn't every interest a special interest? Can any group speak for the interests of the whole community? Indeed, what is the community interest? Perhaps the community is merely the aggregate of special interests, so that no single interest or combination of interests is entitled to be called the community interest.

One possibility is simply to let every group participate in government—indeed, to welcome the broadest participation of interest groups—and then enact into law whatever series of agreements these groups have been able to reach as they interact. If the groups broadly represent the spectrum of political positions in the society, their compromises and collective conclusions comprise for all practical purposes the community or national interest.

Insofar as Madison himself inclined toward such a view, he favored large republics over small ones because large republics "take in a greater variety of parties and interests," and he believed that the best society was one which was

42

"broken into so many parts, interests and classes of citizens" that nobody's rights could be endangered. Nevertheless, Madison at the same time implied the existence of a transcendent community interest and therefore considered "factions" as political forces to be tolerated but not welcomed.

Interest groups were more highly regarded by John C. Calhoun, a South Carolina Senator whose fear of an overbearing Northern majority in the 1840s led to his defense of interest-group participation as the only hope of constitutional government. Significant minority interests (Calhoun had the slave South in mind) had a right to veto majority acts which were contrary to their fundamental interests.

More than a century after Calhoun, "pluralist" political scientists emphasized the crucial role of pressure groups in making government work. Although they eschewed value judgments (they professed not to advocate the pluralist model, but rather to describe the way American politics works), it is hard to escape the conclusion that they liked what they saw, and considered government by interest groups to be the most practical (and perhaps the only possible) form of government for the United States.

The theoretical debate is essential if we are to put into perspective current controversies over fair and unfair pressure group activity, but we should not forget that the debate is not academic. The issues are important and controversial. Current concern over the influence of oil and gas interests, labor and farm interests, minority-group interests, and so on, prompts many questions: Are these groups exerting too much influence over legislation? Are their opponents getting an equal hearing? Is there an overriding *national* interest which needs to be represented? Or is pluralism inescapable in a society as variegated as ours?

Editor John Fischer candidly and vividly states the case for pluralism in an essay that has been widely read since its 1948 publication. Professor Robert Paul Wolff is one of the more recent critics who have charged that pluralism inhibits change, overlooks all interests except the established and powerful ones, and lacks vision and humanity.

John Fischer

IN DEFENSE
OF PRESSURE GROUPS

Perhaps it is the very subtlety of the American political tradition which is responsible for the almost universal misunderstanding of it abroad. Every practicing American politician grasps its principles by instinct; if he does not, he soon retires into some less demanding profession. Moreover, the overwhelming majority of citizens have a sound working knowledge of the system, which they apply every day of their lives—though many of them might have a hard time putting that knowledge into words. There are almost no foreigners, however (except perhaps D. W. Brogan), who really understand the underlying theory. Even the editors of the London *Economist*—probably the most brilliant and well-informed group of journalists practicing anywhere today—display their bewilderment week after week. To them, and to virtually all other European observers, our whole political scene looks arbitrary, irrational, and dangerous.

Another reason for this misunderstanding lies in the fact that surprisingly little has been written about the roles of American politics during our generation. The newspapers, textbooks, and learned journals are running over with discussions of tactics and mechanics—but no one, so far as I know, has bothered to trace out the basic tradition for a good many years.

In fact, the most useful discussion of this tradition which I have come across is the work of John C. Calhoun, published nearly a century ago. Today of course he is an almost forgotten figure, and many people take it for granted that his views were discredited for good by the Civil War. I know of only one writer—Peter F. Drucker of Bennington College—who has paid much attention to him in recent years. It was he who described Calhoun's ideas as "a major if not the only key to the understanding of what is specifically and uniquely American in our political system"; and I am indebted to Mr. Drucker for much of the case set forth here.

Calhoun summed up his political thought in what he called the Doctrine of the Concurrent Majority. He saw the United States as a nation of tremendous and frightening diversity—a collection of many different climates, races, cultures, religions, and economic patterns. He saw the constant tension among

Continued on p. 46

From "Unwritten Rules of American Politics," by John Fischer, *Harper's Magazine*, November, 1948.

44

Robert Paul Wolff

SPECIAL INTERESTS *VERSUS* THE NATIONAL INTEREST

[There exist] two principal "pluralist" theories of the relationship between group and government.

The first, or "referee" theory, asserts that the role of the central government is to lay down ground rules for conflict and competition among private associations and to employ its power to make sure that no major interest in the nation abuses its influence or gains an unchecked mastery over some sector of social life. The most obvious instance is in the economic sphere, where firms compete for markets and labor competes with capital. But according to the theory a similar competition takes place among the various religions, between private and public forms of education, among different geographic regions, and even among the arts, sports, and the entertainment world for the attention and interest of the people.

The second theory might be called the "vector-sum" or "give-and-take" theory of government. Congress is seen as the focal point for the pressures which are exerted by interest groups throughout the nation, either by way of the two great parties or directly through lobbies. The laws issuing from the government are shaped by the manifold forces brought to bear upon the legislators. Ideally, congress merely reflects these forces, combining them—or "resolving" them, as the physicists say—into a single social decision. As the strength and direction of private interests alters, there is a corresponding alteration in the composition and activity of the great interest groups—labor, big business, agriculture. Slowly, the great weathervane of government swings about to meet the shifting winds of opinion.... The weaknesses of pluralism lie not so much in its theoretical formulation as in the covert ideological consequences of its application to the reality of contemporary America. The sense of "ideological" which I intend is that adopted by Karl Mannheim in his classic study *Ideology and Utopia*, Mannheim defines ideology as follows:

> The concept 'ideology' reflects the one discovery which emerged from political conflict, namely, that ruling groups can in their thinking become so intensively interest-bound to a situation that they are simply no longer able to see certain facts which would undermine their sense of domination. There

Continued on p. 55

3. PRESSURE GROUPS

(Fischer, cont. from p. 44)

all these special interests, and he realized that the central problem of American politics was to find some way of holding these conflicting groups together.

It could not be done by force; no one group was strong enough to impose its will on all the others. The goal could be achieved only by compromise—and no real compromise could be possible if any threat of coercion lurked behind the door. Therefore, Calhoun reasoned, every vital decision in American life would have to be adopted by a "concurrent majority"—by which he meant, in effect, a unanimous agreement of all interested parties. No decision which affected the interests of the slaveholders, he argued, should be taken without their consent; and by implication he would have given a similar veto to every other special interest, whether it be labor, management, the Catholic church, old-age pensioners, the silver miners, or the corngrowers of the Middle West.

Under the goad of the slavery issue, Calhoun was driven to state his doctrine in an extreme and unworkable form. If every sectional interest had been given the explicit, legal veto power which he called for, the government obviously would have been paralyzed. (That, in fact, is precisely what seems to be happening today in the United Nations.) It is the very essence of the idea of "concurrent majority" that it cannot be made legal and official. It can operate effectively only as an informal, highly elastic, and generally accepted understanding. . . .

Moreover, government by concurrent majority can exist only when no one power is strong enough to dominate completely, *and then only when all of the contending interest groups recognize and abide by certain rules of the game.*

These rules are the fundamental bond of unity in American political life. They can be summed up as a habit of extraordinary toleration, plus "equality" in the peculiar American meaning of that term which cannot be translated into any other language, even into the English of Great Britain. Under these rules every group tacitly binds itself to tolerate the interests and opinions of every other group. It must not try to impose its views on others, nor can it press its own special interests to the point where they seriously endanger the interests of other groups or of the nation as a whole.

Furthermore, each group must exercise its implied veto with responsibility and discretion; and in times of great emergency it must forsake its veto right altogether. It dare not be intransigent or doctrinaire. It must make every conceivable effort to compromise, relying on its veto only as a last resort. For if any player wields this weapon recklessly, the game will break up—or all the other players will turn on him in anger, suspend the rules for the time being, and maul those very interests he is trying so desperately to protect. That was what happened in 1860, when the followers of Calhoun carried his doctrine to an unbearable extreme. Much the same thing, on a less violent scale, happened to American business interests in 1933 and to the labor unions in 1947.

This is the somewhat elusive sense, it seems to me, in which Calhoun's theory has been adopted by the American people. But elusive and subtle as it may be, it remains the basic rule of the game of politics in this country—and in this country alone. Nothing comparable exists in any other nation, although the British, in a different way, have applied their own rules of responsibility and self-restraint.

It is a rule which operates unofficially and entirely outside the Constitution—but it has given us a method by which all the official and Constitutional organs of government can be made to work. It also provides a means of selecting leaders on all levels of our political life, for hammering out policies, and for organizing and managing the conquest of political power.

The way in which this tradition works in practice can be observed most easily in Congress. Anyone who has ever tried to push through a piece of legislation quickly discovers that the basic units of organization on Capitol Hill are not the parties, but the so-called blocs, which are familiar to everyone who reads a newspaper. There are dozens of them—the farm bloc, the silver bloc, the friends of labor, the business group, the isolationists, the public power bloc—and they all cut across party lines.

They are loosely organized and pretty blurred at the edges, so that every Congressman belongs at different times to several different blocs. Each of them represents a special interest group. Each of them ordinarily works hand-in-hand with that group's Washington lobby. In passing, it might be noted that these lobbies are by no means the cancerous growth which is sometimes pictured in civics textbooks. They have become an indispensable part of the political machine—the accepted channel through which American citizens make their wishes known and play their day-to-day role in the process of government. Nor is their influence measured solely by the size of the bankrolls and propaganda apparatus which they have at their disposal. Some of the smallest and poorest lobbies often are more effective than their well-heeled rivals. For example, Russell Smith, the one-man lobby of the Farmers Union, was largely responsible for conceiving and nursing through Congress the Employment Act of 1946, one of the most far-reaching measures adopted since the war.

Now it is an unwritten but firm rule of Congress that no important bloc shall ever be voted down—under normal circumstances—on any matter which touches its own vital interests. Each of them, in other words, has a tacit right of veto on legislation in which it is primarily concerned. The ultimate expression of this right is the institution—uniquely American—of the filibuster in the Senate. Recently it has

3. PRESSURE GROUPS

acquired a bad name among liberals because the Southern conservatives have used it ruthlessly to fight off civil rights legislation and protect white supremacy. Not so long ago, however, the filibuster was the stoutest weapon of such men as Norris and the LaFollettes in defending many a progressive cause. . . .

Naturally no bloc wants to exercise its veto power except when it is absolutely forced to—for this is a negative power, and one which is always subject to retaliation. Positive power to influence legislation, on the other hand, can be gained only by conciliation, compromise, and endless horse-trading.

The farm bloc, for instance, normally needs no outside aid to halt the passage of a hostile bill. As a last resort, three or four strong-lunged statesmen from the corn belt can always filibuster it to death in the Senate. If the bloc wants to put through a measure to support agricultural prices, however, it can succeed only be enlisting the help of other powerful special interest groups. Consequently, it must always be careful not to antagonize any potential ally by a reckless use of the veto; and it must be willing to pay for such help by throwing its support from time to time behind legislation sought by the labor bloc, the National Association of Manufacturers, or the school-teachers' lobby.

The classic alliance of this sort was formed in the early days of the New Deal, when most of the Roosevelt legislation was shoved onto the statute books by a temporary coalition of the farm bloc and urban labor, occasionally reinforced by such minor allies as the public power group and spokesmen for the northern Negroes. Mr. Roosevelt's political genius rested largely on his ability to put together a program which would offer something to each of these groups without fatally antagonizing any of them, and then to time the presentation of each bill so that he would always retain enough bargaining power to line up a Congressional majority. It also was necessary for him to avoid the veto of the business group, which viewed much of this legislation as a barbarous assault upon its privileges; and for this purpose he employed another traditional technique, which we shall examine a little later.

This process of trading blocs of votes is generally known as log-rolling, and frequently it is deplored by the more innocent type of reformer. Such pious disapproval has no effect whatever on any practicing politician. He knows that log-rolling is a sensible and reasonably fair device, and that without it Congress could scarcely operate at all.

In fact, Congress gradually has developed a formal apparatus—the committee system—which is designed to make the log-rolling process as smooth and efficient as possible. There is no parallel system anywhere; the committees of Parliament and of the Continental legislative bodies work in an entirely different way.

Obviously the main business of

Congress—the hammering out of a series of compromises between many special interest groups—cannot be conducted satisfactorily on the floor of the House or Senate. The meetings there are too large and far too public for such delicate negotiations. Moreover, every speech delivered on the floor must be aimed primarily at the voters back home, and not at the other members of the chamber. Therefore, Congress—especially the House—does nearly all its work in the closed sessions of its various committees, simply because the committee room is the only place where it is possible to arrange a compromise acceptable to all major interests affected.

For this reason, it is a matter of considerable importance to get a bill before the proper committee. Each committee serves as a forum for a particular cluster of special interests, and the assignment of a bill to a specific committee often decides which interest groups shall be recognized officially as affected by the measure and therefore entitled to a hand in its drafting. "Who is to have standing before the committee" is the technical term, and it is this decision that frequently decides the fate of the legislation.

Calhoun's principles of the concurrent majority and of sectional compromise operate just as powerfully, though sometimes less obviously, in every other American political institution. Our cabinet, for example, is the only one in the world where the members are charged by law with the representation of special interests—labor, agriculture, commerce, and so on. In other countries, each agency of government is at least presumed to act for the nation as a whole; here most agencies are expected to behave as servants for one interest or another. The Veterans' Administration, to cite the most familiar case, is frankly intended to look out for Our Boys; the Maritime Board is to look out for the shipping industry; the National Labor Relations Board, as originally established under the Wagner Act, was explicitly intended to build up the bargaining power of the unions.

Even within a single department, separate agencies are sometimes set up to represent conflicting interests. Thus in the Department of Agriculture under the New Deal the old Triple-A became primarily an instrument of the large-scale commercial farmers, as represented by their lobby, the Farm Bureau Federation; while the Farm Security Administration went to bat for the tenants, the farm laborers, and the little subsistence farmers, as represented by the Farmers Union.

This is one reason why federal agencies often struggle so bitterly against each other, and why the position of the administration as a whole on any question can be determined only after a long period of inter-bureau squabbling and compromise. Anyone who was in Washington during the war will remember how these goings-on always confused and alarmed our British allies.

Calhoun's laws also govern the selection of virtually every candidate for public office. The mystery of "eligibility" which has eluded most foreign observers simply means that a candidate must not be unacceptable to any important special interest group—a negative rather than a positive qualification. A notorious case of this process at work was the selection of Mr. Truman as the Democrats' Vice Presidential candidate in 1944. As Edward J. Flynn, the Boss of the Bronx, has pointed out in his memoirs, Truman was the one man "who would hurt . . . least" as Roosevelt's running mate. Many stronger men were disqualified, Flynn explained, by the tacit veto of one sectional interest or another. Wallace was unacceptable to the businessmen and to the many local party machines. Byrnes was distasteful to the Catholics, the Negroes, and organized labor. Rayburn came from the wrong part of the country. Truman, however, came from a border state, his labor record was good, he had not antagonized the conservatives, and—as Flynn put it—"he had never made any 'racial' remarks. He just dropped into the slot."

The same kind of considerations govern the selection of candidates right down to the county, city, and precinct levels. Flynn, one of the most successful political operators of our time, explained in some detail the complicated job of making up a ticket in his own domain. Each of the main population groups in the Bronx—Italians, Jews, and Irish Catholics—must be properly represented on the list of nominees,

and so must each of the main geographical divisions. The result was a ticket which sounded like the roster of the Brooklyn Dodgers: Loreto, Delagi, Lyman, Joseph, Lyons, and Foley.

Comparable traditions govern the internal political life of the American Legion, the Federation of Women's Clubs, university student bodies, labor unions, Rotary Clubs, and the thousands of other quasi-political institutions which are so characteristic of our society and which give us such a rich fabric of spontaneous local government.

The stronghold of Calhoun's doctrine, however, is the American party—the wonder and despair of foreigners who cannot fit it into any of their concepts of political life.

The purpose of European parties is, of course, to divide men of different ideologies into coherent and disciplined organizations. The historic role of the American party, on the other hand, is not to divide but to unite. That task was imposed by simple necessity. If a division into ideological parties had been attempted, in addition to all the other centrifugal forces in this country, it very probably would have proved impossible to hold the nation together. The Founding Fathers understood this thoroughly; hence Washington's warning against "factions."

Indeed, on the one occasion when we did develop two ideological parties, squarely opposing each other on an issue of principle, the result was civil war. Fortunately, that was our last large-scale experiment with a third party formed on an ideological basis—for in its early days that is just what the Republican party was.

Its radical wing, led by such men as Thaddeus Stevens, Seward, and Chase, made a determined and skillful effort to substitute principles for interests as the foundations of American political life. Even within their own party, however, they were opposed by such practical politicians as Lincoln and Johnson—men who distrusted fanaticism in any form—and by the end of the Reconstruction period the experiment had been abandoned. American politics then swung back into its normal path and has never veered far away from it since. Although Calhoun's cause was defeated, his political theory came through the Civil War stronger than ever.

The result is that the American party has no permanent program and no fixed aim, except to win elections. Its one purpose is to unite the largest possible number of divergent interest groups in the pursuit of power. Its unity is one of compromise, not of dogma. It must—if it hopes to succeed—appeal to considerable numbers on both the left and the right, to rich and poor, Protestant and Catholic, farmer and industrial worker, native and foreign born.

It must be ready to bid for the support of any group that can deliver a sizable chunk of votes, accepting that group's program with whatever modifications may be necessary to reconcile the other members of the party. If sun worship, or Existentialism, or the nationalization of industry should ever attract any significant following in this country, you can be sure that both parties would soon whip up a plank designed to win it over.

This ability to absorb new ideas (along with the enthusiasts behind them) and to mold them into a shape acceptable to the party's standpatters is, perhaps, the chief measure of vitality in the party's leadership. Such ideas almost never germinate within the party itself. They are stolen—very often from third parties.

Indeed, the historic function of third parties has been to sprout new issues, nurse them along until they have gathered a body of supporters worth stealing, and then to turn them over (often reluctantly) to the major parties. A glance at the old platforms of the Populists, the Bull Moosers, and the Socialists will show what an astonishingly high percentage of their once-radical notions have been purloined by both Republicans and Democrats—and enacted into law. Thus the income tax, child-labor laws, minimum wages, regulation of railroads and utilities, and old-age pensions have all become part of the American Way of Life. . . .

While each major party must always stand alert to grab a promising new issue, it also must be careful never to scare off any of the big, established interest groups. For as soon as it alienates any one of them, it finds itself in a state of crisis.

3. PRESSURE GROUPS

For sixteen years the Republicans lost much of their standing as a truly national party because they had made themselves unacceptable to labor. Similarly, the Democrats, during the middle stage of the New Deal, incurred the wrath of the business interests. Ever since Mr. Truman was plumped into the White House, the Democratic leadership has struggled desperately—though rather ineptly—to regain the confidence of businessmen without at the same time driving organized labor out of the ranks. It probably would be safe to predict that if the Republican party is to regain a long period of health, it must make an equally vigorous effort to win back the confidence of labor. For the permanent veto of any major element in American society means political death—as the ghosts of the Federalists and Whigs can testify.

The weaknesses of the American political system are obvious—much more obvious, in fact, than its virtues. These weaknesses have been so sharply criticized for the past hundred years, by a procession of able analysts ranging from Walter Bagehot to Thomas K. Finletter, that it is hardly necessary to mention them here. It is enough to note that most of the criticism has been aimed at two major flaws.

First, it is apparent that the doctrine of the concurrent majority is a negative one—a principle of inaction. A strong government, capable of rapid and decisive action, is difficult to achieve under a system which forbids it to do anything until virtually everybody acquiesces. In times of crisis, a dangerously long period of debate and compromise usually is necessary before any administration can carry out the drastic measures needed. The depression of the early thirties, the crisis in foreign policy which ended only with Pearl Harbor, the crisis of the Marshall program all illustrate this recurring problem.

This same characteristic of our system gives undue weight to the small but well-organized pressure group—especially when it is fighting *against* something. Hence a few power companies were able to block for twenty years the sensible use of the Muscle Shoals dam which eventually became the nucleus of TVA, and—in alliance with the railroads, rail unions, and Eastern port interests—they [held] up development of the St. Lawrence Waterway. . . .

The negative character of our political rules also makes it uncommonly difficult for us to choose a President. Many of our outstanding political operatives—notably those who serve in the Senate—are virtually barred from a Presidential nomination because they are forced to get on record on too many issues. Inevitably they offend some important interest group, and therefore become "unavailable." Governors, who can keep their mouths shut on most national issues, have a much better chance to reach the White House. Moreover, the very qualities of caution and inoffensiveness which make a good candidate—Harding and Coolidge come most readily to mind—are likely to make a bad President.

An even more serious flaw in our scheme of politics is the difficulty in finding anybody to speak for the country as a whole. Calhoun would have argued that the national interest is merely the sum of all the various special interests, and therefore needs no spokesmen of its own—but in this case he clearly was wrong.

In practice, we tend to settle sectional and class conflicts at the expense of the nation as a whole— with results painful to all of us. The labor troubles in the spring of 1946, for instance, could be settled only on a basis acceptable to *both* labor and management: that is, on the basis of higher wages *plus* higher prices. The upshot was an inflationary spiral which damaged everybody. . . . Countless other instances, from soil erosion to the rash of billboards along our highways, bear witness to the American tendency to neglect matters which are "only" of national interest, and therefore are left without a recognized sponsor.

Over the generations we have developed a series of practices and institutions which partly remedy these weaknesses, although we are still far from a complete cure. One such development has been the gradual strengthening of the Presidency as against Congress. As the only man elected by all the people, the President inevitably has had to take over many of the policy-making and leadership functions which the Founding Fathers originally as-

signed to the legislators. This meant, of course, that he could no longer behave merely as an obedient executor of the will of Congress, but was forced into increasingly frequent conflicts with Capitol Hill.

Today we have come to recognize that this conflict is one of the most important obligations of the Presidency. No really strong executive tries to avoid it—he accepts it as an essential part of his job. If he simply tries to placate the pressure groups which speak through Congress, history writes him down as a failure. For it is his duty to enlist the support of many minorities for measures rooted in the national interest, reaching beyond their own immediate concern—and, if necessary, to stand up against the ravening minorities for the interest of the whole.

In recent times this particular part of the President's job has been made easier by the growth of the Theory of Temporary Emergencies. All of us—or nearly all—have come around to admitting that in time of emergency special interest groups must forego their right of veto. As a result, the President often is tempted to scare up an emergency to secure legislation which could not be passed under any other pretext. Thus, most of the New Deal bills were introduced as "temporary emergency measures," although they were clearly intended to be permanent from the very first; for in no other way could Mr. Roosevelt avoid the veto of the business interests.

Again, in 1939 the threat of war

3. PRESSURE GROUPS

enabled the President to push through much legislation which would have been impossible under normal circumstances. . . .

Because we have been so preoccupied with trying to patch up the flaws in our system, we have often overlooked its unique elements of strength. The chief of these is its ability to minimize conflict— not by suppressing the conflicting forces, but by absorbing and utilizing them. The result is a society which is both free and reasonably stable—a government which is as strong and effective as most dictatorships, but which can still adapt itself to social change.

The way in which the American political organism tames down the extremists of both the left and right is always fascinating to watch. Either party normally is willing to embrace any group or movement which can deliver votes—but in return it requires these groups to adjust their programs to fit the traditions, beliefs, and prejudices of the majority of the people. The fanatics, the implacable radicals cannot hope to get to first base in American politics until they abandon their fanaticism and learn the habits of conciliation. As a consequence, it is almost impossible for political movements here to become entirely irresponsible and to draw strength from the kind of demagogic obstruction which has nurtured both Communist and Fascist movements abroad.

The same process which gentles down the extremists also prods along the political laggards. As long as it is in a state of health, each American party has a conservative and a liberal wing. Sometimes one is dominant, sometimes the other— but even when the conservative element is most powerful, it must reckon with the left-wingers in its own family. At the moment the Republican party certainly is in one of its more conservative phases; yet it contains . . . men . . . who are at least as progressive as most of the old New Dealers. They, and their counterparts in the Democratic party, exert a steady tug to the left which prevents either party from lapsing into complete reaction.

The strength of this tug is indicated by the fact that the major New Deal reforms have now been almost universally accepted. In the 1930s the leading Republicans, plus many conservative Democrats, were hell-bent on wiping out social security, TVA, SEC, minimum-wage laws, rural electrification, and all the other dread innovations of the New Deal. Today no Presidential aspirant would dare suggest the repeal of a single one of them. In this country there simply is no place for a hard core of irreconcilable reactionaries, comparable to those political groups in France which have never yet accepted the reforms of the French Revolution.

This American tendency to push extremists of both the left and right toward a middle position has enabled us, so far, to escape class warfare. This is no small achievement for any political system; for class warfare cannot be tolerated by a modern industrial society. If it seriously threatens, it is bound to be suppressed by some form of totalitarianism, as it has been in Germany, Spain, Italy, Russia, and most of Eastern Europe.

In fact, suppression might be termed the normal method of settling conflicts in continental Europe, where parties traditionally have been drawn up along ideological battle lines. Every political campaign becomes a religious crusade; each party is fanatically convinced that it and it alone has truth by the tail; each party is certain that its opponents not only are wrong, but wicked. If the sacred ideology is to be established beyond challenge, no heresy can be tolerated. Therefore it becomes a duty not only to defeat the enemy at the polls, but to wipe him out. Any suggestion of compromise must be rejected as treason and betrayal of the true faith. The party must be disciplined like an army, and if it cannot win by other means it must be ready to take up arms in deadly fact. . . .

Because this sort of ideological

politics is so foreign to our native tradition, neither Socialists, Communists, nor Fascists have ever been accepted as normal parties. So long as that tradition retains its very considerable vitality, it seems to me unlikely that any third party founded on an ideological basis can take root. The notion of a ruthless and unlimited class struggle, the concept of a master race, a fascist elite, or a proletariat which is entitled to impose its will on all others—these are ideas which are incompatible with the main current of American political life. The uncompromising ideologist, of whatever faith, appears in our eyes peculiarly "un-American," simply because he cannot recognize the rule of the concurrent majority, nor can he accept the rules of mutual toleration which are necessary to make it work. Unless he forsakes his ideology, he cannot even understand that basic principle of American politics which was perhaps best expressed by Judge Learned Hand: "The spirit of liberty is the spirit which is not too sure that it is right."

(Cont. from p. 45, Wolff, "Special Interests")

is implicit in the word "ideology" the insight that in certain situations the collective unconscious of certain groups obscures the real condition of society both to itself and to others and thereby stabilizes it.

Ideology is thus systematically self-serving thought, in two senses. First,

and most simply, it is the refusal to recognize unpleasant facts which might require a less flattering evaluation of a policy or institution or which might undermine one's claim to a right of domination. For example, slave-owners in the antebellum South refused to acknowledge that the slaves themselves

3. PRESSURE GROUPS

were unhappy. The implication was that if they were, then slavery would be harder to justify. Secondly, ideological thinking is a denial of unsettling or revolutionary factors in society on the principle of the self-confirming prophecy that the more stable everyone believes the situation to be, the more stable it actually becomes.

One might think that whatever faults the theory of pluralism possessed, at least it would be free of dangers of ideological distortion. Does it not accord a legitimate place to all groups in society? How then can it be used to justify or preserve the dominance of one group over another? In fact, I shall try to show that the application of pluralist theory to American society involves ideological distortion in at least three different ways. The first stems from the "vector-sum" or "balance-of-power" interpretation of pluralism; the second arises from the application of the "referee" version of the theory; and the third is inherent in the abstract theory itself.

According to the vector-sum theory of pluralism, the major groups in society compete through the electoral process for control over the actions of the government. Politicians are forced to accommodate themselves to a number of opposed interests and in so doing achieve a rough distributive justice. What are the major groups which, according to pluralism, comprise American society today? First, there are the hereditary groups which are summarized by that catch-phrase of tolerance, "without regard to race, creed, color, or national origin." In addition there are the major economic interest groups- among which—so the theory goes, a healthy balance is maintained: labor, business, agriculture, and—a residual category, this—the consumer. Finally, there are a number of voluntary associations whose size, permanence, and influence entitle them to a place in any group-analysis of America, groups such as the veterans' organizations and the American Medical Association.

At one time, this may have been an accurate account of American society. But once constructed, the picture becomes frozen, and when changes take place in the patterns of social or economic grouping, they tend not to be acknowledged because they deviate from that picture. So the application of the theory of pluralism always favors the groups in existence against those in process of formation. For example, at any given time the major religious, racial, and ethnic groups are viewed as permanent and exhaustive categories into which every American can conveniently be pigeonholed. Individuals who fall outside any major social group—the non-religious, say—are treated as exceptions and relegated in practice to a second-class status. Thus agnostic conscientious objectors are required to serve in the armed forces, while those who claim even the most bizarre religious basis for their refusal are treated with ritual tolerance and excused by the courts. Similarly, orphanages in America are so completely dominated by the three major faiths that a non-religious or religiously-mixed couple simply cannot adopt a child in many states. The net effect is to preserve the official three-great-religions image of American society long after it has ceased to correspond to social reality and to discourage individuals from officially breaking their religious ties. A revealing example of the mechanism of tolerance is the ubiquitous joke about "the priest, the minister, and the rabbi." A world of insight into the psychology of tolerance can be had simply from observing the mixture of emotions with which an audience greets such a joke, as told by George Jessel or some other apostle of "interfaith understanding." One senses embarrassment, nervousness, and finally an explosion of self-congratulatory laughter as though everyone were relieved at a difficult moment got through without incident. The gentle ribbing nicely distributed in the story among the three men of the cloth gives each member of the audience a chance to express his hostility safely and acceptably, and in the end to reaffirm the principle of tolerance by joining in the applause. Only a bigot, one feels, could refuse to crack a smile!

Rather more serious in its conservative falsifying of social reality is the established image of the major economic groups of American society. The emergence of a rough parity between big industry and organized labor has been paralleled by the rise of a philosophy of moderation and cooperation between them, based on mutual understanding and respect, which is precisely similar to the achievement of interfaith and ethnic tolerance. What has been overlooked or suppressed is the fact that there are tens of millions of Americans—businessmen and workers alike—whose interests are completely ignored by this genial give-and-take. Non-unionized workers are worse off after each price-wage increase, as are the thousands of small businessmen who cannot survive in the competition against great nationwide firms. The theory of pluralism does not espouse the interests of the unionized against the non-unionized, or of large against small business; but by presenting a picture of the American economy in which those disadvantaged elements do not appear, it tends to perpetuate the inequality by ignoring rather than justifying it.

The case here is the same as with much ideological thinking. Once pluralists acknowledge the existence of groups whose interests are not weighed in the labor-business balance, then their own theory requires them to call for an alteration of the system. If migrant workers, or white-collar workers, or small businessmen are genuine *groups*, then they have a legitimate place in the system of group-adjustments. Thus pluralism is not explicitly a philosophy of privilege or injustice—it is a philosophy of equality and justice whose *concrete application* supports inequality by ignoring the existence of certain legitimate social groups.

3. PRESSURE GROUPS

This ideological function of pluralism helps to explain one of the peculiarities of American politics. There is a very sharp distinction in the public domain between legitimate interests and those which are absolutely beyond the pale. If a group or interest is within the framework of acceptability, then it can be sure of winning some measure of what it seeks, for the process of national politics is distributive and compromising. On the other hand, if an interest falls *outside* the circle of the acceptable, it receives no attention whatsoever and its proponents are treated as crackpots, extremists, or foreign agents. With bewildering speed, an interest can move from "outside" to "inside" and its partisans, who have been scorned by the solid and established in the community, become presidential advisers and newspaper columnists.

A vivid example from recent political history is the sudden legitimation of the problem of poverty in America. In the post-war years, tens of millions· of poor Americans were left behind by the sustained growth of the economy. The facts were known and discussed for years by fringe critics whose attempts to call attention to these forgotten Americans were greeted with either silence or contempt. Suddenly, poverty was "discovered" by Presidents · Kennedy and Johnson, and articles were published in *Look* and *Time* which a year earlier would have been more at home in the radical journals which inhabit political limbo in America. A

social group whose very existence had long been denied was now the object of a national crusade.

A similar elevation from obscurity to relative prominence was experienced by the peace movement, a "group;' of a rather different nature. For years, the partisans of disarmament labored to gain a hearing for their view that nuclear war could not be a reasonable instrument of national policy. Sober politicians and serious columnists treated such ideas as the naive fantasies of bearded peaceniks, communist sympathizers, and well-meaning but hopelessly muddled clerics. Then suddenly the Soviet Union achieved the nuclear parity which had been long forecast, the prospect of which had convinced disarmers of the insanity of nuclear war. Sober reevaluations appeared in the columns of Walter Lippmann, and some even found their way into the speeches of President Kennedy— what had been unthinkable, absurd, naive, dangerous, even subversive, six months before, was now plausible, sound, thoughtful, and— within another six months—official American policy.

The explanation for these rapid shifts in the political winds lies, I suggest, in the logic of pluralism. According to pluralist theory, every genuine social group has a right to a voice in the making of policy and a share in the benefits. Any policy urged by a group in the system must be given respectful attention, no matter how bizarre. By the same token, a policy or principle which lacks legitimate representation has no place in the society, no matter how reasonable or right it may be. Consequently, the line between acceptable and unacceptable alternatives is very sharp, so that the territory of American politics is like a plateau with steep cliffs on all sides rather than like a pyramid. On the plateau are all the interest groups which are recognized as legitimate; in the deep valley all around lie the outsiders, the fringe groups which are scorned as "extremist." The most important battle waged by any group in American politics is the struggle to climb onto the plateau. Once there, it can count on some measure of what it seeks. No group ever gets all of what it wants and no *legitimate* group is completely frustrated in its efforts.

Thus, the "vector-sum" version of pluralist theory functions ideologically by tending to deny new groups or interests access to the political plateau. It does this by ignoring their existence in practice, not by denying their claim in theory. The result is that pluralism has a braking effect on social change; it slows down transformation in the system of group adjustments but does not set up an absolute barrier to change. For this reason, as well as because of its origins as a fusion of two conflicting social philosophies, it deserves the title "conservative liberalism."

According to the second, or "referee," version of pluralism, the role of the government is to oversee and regulate the competition among interest groups in the society. Out of the applications of this theory have grown not only countless laws, such as the antitrust bills, pure food and drug acts, and Taft-Hartley Law, but also the complex system of quasi-judicial regulatory agencies in the executive branch of government. Henry Kariel, in a powerful and convincing book entitled *The Decline of American Pluralism*, has shown that this referee function of government, as it actually works out in practice, systematically favors the interests of the stronger against the weaker party in interest-group conflicts and tends to solidify the power of those who already hold it. The government, therefore, plays a conservative, rather than a neutral, role in the society.

Kariel details the ways in which this discriminatory influence is exercised. In the field of regulation of labor unions, for example, the federal agencies deal with the established leadership of the unions. In such matters as the overseeing of union elections, the settlement of jurisdictional disputes, or the setting up of mediation boards, it is the interests of those leaders rather than the competing interests of rank-and-file dissidents which are favored. In the regulation of agriculture, again, the locally most influential farmers or leaders of farmers' organizations draw up the guidelines for control which are then adopted by the federal inspectors. In each case, ironically, the unwillingness of the government to impose its own standards or rules results not in a free play of competing groups, but in the enforcement of the preferences of the existing predominant interests.

3. PRESSURE GROUPS

In a sense, these unhappy consequences of government regulation stem from a confusion between a theory of interest-conflict and a theory of power-conflict. The government quite successfully referees the conflict among competing *powers*—any group which has already managed to accumulate a significant quantum of power will find its claims attended to by the federal agencies. But legitimate *interests* which have been ignored, suppressed, defeated, or which have not yet succeeded in ˉorganizing themselves for effective action, will find their disadvantageous position perpetuated through the decisions of the government. It is as though an umpire were to come upon a baseball game in progress between big boys and little boys, in which the big boys cheated, broke the rules, claimed hits that were outs, and made the little boys accept the injustice by brute force. If the umpire undertakes to "regulate" the game by simply enforcing the "rules" actually being practiced, he does not thereby make the game a fair one. Indeed, he may actually make matters worse, because if the little boys get up their courage, band together, and decide to fight it out, the umpire will accuse them of breaking the rules and throw his weight against them! Precisely the same sort of thing happens in pluralist politics. For example, the American Medical Association exercised a stranglehold over American medicine through its influence over the government's licensing regulations. Doctors who are opposed to the A.M.A.'s political positions, or even to its medical policies, do not merely have to buck the entrenched authority of the organization's leaders. They must also risk the loss of hospital affiliations, specialty accreditation, and so forth, all of which powers have been placed in the hands of the medical establishment by state and federal laws. Those laws are written by the government in cooperation with the very same A.M.A. leaders; not surprisingly, the interests of dissenting doctors do not receive favorable attention.

The net effect of government action is thus to weaken, rather than strengthen, the play of conflicting interests in the society. The theory of pluralism here has a crippling effect upon the government, for it warns against positive federal intervention in the name of independent principles of justice, equality, or fairness. The theory says justice will emerge from the free interplay of opposed groups; the practice tends to destroy that interplay.

Finally, the theory of pluralism in all its forms has the effect in American thought and politics of discriminating not only against certain social groups or interests, but also against certain sorts of proposals for the solution of social problems. According to pluralist theory, politics is a contest among social groups for control of the power and decision of the government. Each group is motivated by some interest or cluster of interests and seeks to sway the government toward action in its favor. The typical social problem according to pluralism is therefore some instance of distributive injustice. One group is getting too much, another too little, of the available resources. In accord with its modification of traditional liberalism, pluralism's goal is a rough parity among competing groups rather than among competing individuals. Characteristically, new proposals originate with a group which feels that its legitimate interests have been slighted, and the legislative outcome is a measure which corrects the social imbalance to a degree commensurate with the size and political power of the initiating group.

But there are some social ills in America whose causes do not lie in a maldistribution of wealth, and which cannot be cured therefore by the techniques of pluralist politics. For example, America is growing uglier, more dangerous, and less pleasant to live in, as its citizens grow richer. The reason is that natural beauty, public order, the cultivation of the arts, are not the special interest of any identifiable social group. Consequently, evils and inadequacies in those areas cannot be remedied by shifting the distribution of wealth and power among existing social groups. To be sure, crime and urban slums hurt the poor more than the rich, the Negro more than the white—but fundamentally they are problems of the society as a whole, not of any particular group. That is to say, they concern the general good, not merely the aggregate of private

goods. To deal with such problems, there must be some way of constituting the whole society a genuine group with a group purpose and a conception of the common good. Pluralism rules this out in theory by portraying society as an aggregate of human communities rather than as itself a human community; and it equally rules out a concern for the general good in practice by encouraging a politics of interest-group pressures in which there is no mechanism for the discovery and expression of the common good.

The theory and practice of pluralism first came to dominate American politics during the depression, when the Democratic party put together an electoral majority of minority groups. It is not at all surprising that the same period saw the demise of an active socialist movement. For socialism, both in its diagnosis of the ills of industrial capitalism and in its proposed remedies, focuses on the structure of the economy and society as a whole and advances programs in the name of the general good. Pluralism, both as theory and as practice, simply does not acknowledge the possibility of wholesale reorganization of the society. By insisting on the group nature of society, it denies the existence of society-wide interests—save the purely procedural interest in preserving the system of group pressures—and the possibility of communal action in pursuit of the general good.

A proof of this charge can be found in the commissions, committees, institutes, and conferences

3. PRESSURE GROUPS

which are convened from time to time to ponder the "national interest." The membership of these assemblies always includes an enlightened business executive, a labor leader, an educator, several clergymen of various faiths, a woman, a literate general or admiral, and a few public figures of unquestioned sobriety and predictable views. The whole is a microcosm of the interest groups and hereditary groups which, according to pluralism, constitute American society. Any vision of the national interest which emerges from such a group will inevitably be a standard pluralist picture of a harmonious, cooperative, distributively just, *tolerant* America. One could hardly expect a committee of group representatives to decide that the pluralist system of social groups is an obstacle to the general good!

POSTSCRIPT

DO PRESSURE GROUPS SERVE
OR SUBVERT DEMOCRACY?

Neither Fischer nor Wolff may have finally resolved the question of whether pressure groups should be considered sinister or benign forces in America, but both have shed light on it. Wolff, while vigorously criticizing the theory and practice of "pluralism," does admit that it allows for reform, that it is not absolutely rigged against change. Once "out" groups—he cites the examples of anti-war and anti-poverty groups—get themselves recognized as legitimate participants in the "system," they can exert great leverage over government. The problem, of course, lies in getting up to the "plateau" of respectability, a process which, in his opinion, takes much too long. Fischer, for his part, is ready to concede a point made by Wolff: in the scramble for particularized benefits by self-interested groups, the national good may be neglected. Fischer's solution to this problem is to leave the national interest to the President, on the assumption that he stands above the clash of pressure groups. There is something to be said for that assumption—the President, after all, is elected by a national constituency—but Americans are still haunted by the memory of the Nixon years when White House staffers actually went on the initiative and extorted huge amounts of money from special interests.

For a book which paints pressure groups—and particularly their representatives in Washington—in extremely lurid colors, see Robert N. Winter-Berger, *The Washington Pay-Off* (Dell, 1972). The style is sensational, but, since the author was once a lobbyist and claims to write from first-hand experience, the content cannot be dismissed out of hand. At the other extreme, see Lester Milbrath, *The Washington Lobbyists* (Rand McNally, 1963), a book which pays homage to "the ordinary, honest lobbyist and his workaday activities." On a more theoretical level, a defense of pressure-group politics is found in David B. Truman, *The Governmental Process* (Knopf, 1951), while a broad-scale critique is supplied by Theodore J. Lowi in *The End of Liberalism* (Norton, 1969).

Those who, like John Fischer, defend interest-group politics are often criticized for failing to distinguish between "public," or common, interests—interests which are supposed to be good for the nation as a whole—and strictly "private" interests, such as the interest of business groups in securing tax advantages or protective tariffs. The reply of those defending interest-group politics is that it is impossible to make a valid distinction between "public" and "private" interests, since virtually every group can rationalize its interests as being beneficial to all.

ISSUE 4

PRESIDENTIAL ELECTION: ELECTORAL COLLEGE OR POPULAR VOTE?

The Electoral College might qualify paradoxically as being, at least in presidential election years, the most talked-about and least-understood feature of American government. Most Americans have only a dim idea of who the electors are or what they do. On the ballot usually appear not the names of the electors but those of the presidential and vice-presidential candidates for whom corresponding "slates" of electors are pledged to vote.

The number of electors allotted to each state varies with population. Each state has one elector for each Representative, plus two for each state's two Senators. Thus New York State has 41 electoral votes, Alaska has three (one for its single House seat plus two for its Senators), and so on. The winning slate of electors, no matter how small the margin of its victory, casts all of that state's electoral votes for the candidates to whom they are pledged. And that is all they do. Despite an occasional "faithless elector" who votes for someone other than the candidates on that ticket, the electors may be characterized as party robots who exercise no discretion. The original idea was that the electors would be wise and prudent citizens who would exercise their own judgment in deciding whom to vote for, but the early rise of the party system confined the electors to being more or less automatic reflectors of party sentiment.

In each state, the electoral vote is won on a "winner-take-all" basis. The voter casts his ballot for an entire slate of presidential electors, so that either all the electors pledged to one candidate or all those pledged to another will be elected. For example, all 41 of New York State's electoral votes went to Carter in 1976, even though Ford won 47 percent of the state's popular vote. Winning a state by one vote is as good as winning by a million. The normal effect is for the electoral vote to exaggerate the result of the popular vote. In 1976, Carter received only 51.05 percent of the popular vote, but he won 55.2 percent of the electoral vote. A shift of a few percent of the popular vote could have created an electoral vote landslide for either major party candidate. If Carter had obtained one percent more of the vote in every state, he would have received 87 more electoral votes; if Ford had received one percent more, he would have won the election.

4. PRESIDENTIAL ELECTION

Critics argue that this demonstrates the undemocratic character of the electoral college system, because it does not accurately reflect the popular vote and can even result in the election of a candidate who lost in the popular balloting. It has happened, in 1824, 1876 and 1888, and although the first and second incidents are complicated by other factors, the last presents a clear-cut case of the election of a President who received 100,000 fewer votes than his opponent. The 1824 election reminds us of another difficulty of the electoral college system. When there are more than two significant candidates, and none receives an electoral college majority, the election is thrown into the House of Representatives, with each state casting one vote, giving the least populous states the same weight as the most populous.

Given the antiquated and risky features of the Electoral College, the question arises: Why bother? Why not eliminate it and institute the direct popular election of the President? The suggestion is appealing in a nation which takes pride in its democratic elections, but it raises difficult questions. Would the candidate receiving the most votes in the nation be elected President irrespective of how small a plurality that candidate received? Might this not induce more candidates to run, increasing the possibility of electing a President with a very small percentage of the total vote? Should we require that the winning candidate receive a pre-determined proportion of the vote: an absolute majority, or, as pending proposals urge, 40 percent? Would this be likely to result in runoff elections, with all the complications, delay and disruption that such a procedure would entail?

Beyond these hypothetical questions, defenders of the present system can point to its long survival as a working mechanism, its contribution to the maintenance of the two-party system, and the extreme rarity of elections in which the candidate with fewer votes than an opponent wins. All of these and other positions are analyzed in the following selections, in which William T. Gossett urges abolition and Martin Diamond urges retention of the Electoral College method of presidential election.

William T. Gossett

THE ELECTORAL COLLEGE IS UNDEMOCRATIC AND UNDESIRABLE

There is no more vital issue facing the Nation today than that of electoral reform. Our most recent presidential election surely demonstrated that the electoral college is potentially hazardous to our nation. It also confirms the conclusion of the American Bar Association Commission on Electoral College Reform that "the electoral college method of electing a President of the United States is archaic, undemocratic, complex, ambiguous, indirect, and dangerous."

If [in 1968] there had been a shift of a relatively few popular votes in Ohio and Missouri, or if President Nixon had lost California, or if Mr. Wallace had carried three border states, no presidential candidate would have had a majority of the electoral votes. The choice of President would then have shifted to the electoral college, in which the electors pledged to George C. Wallace would have held the balance of power. Mr. Wallace certainly would have been tempted to play the role of a President-maker during the forty-one day period between election day and the meeting of the electors. If Mr. Wallace should have decided against any such role and his electors had voted for him, then the choice of President would have shifted to the House of Representatives under an inequitable one state—one vote formula susceptible to political wheeling and dealing and frustration of the popular will. One can only speculate as to the outcome of an election by the House. The twenty-six populated states, representing sixteen percent of the nation's total population, would have had the power to elect the President. It is conceivable that no candidate might have been able to obtain the votes of twenty-six states by Inauguration Day and that in consequence a Vice President selected by the Senate would have had to assume the powers and duties of the President that day. It is also conceivable that the House and Senate might have selected a split ticket by Inauguration Day. It is also conceivable that neither House might have been able to make a choice, in which event the Speaker of the House of Representatives would have become the Acting President.

Had a deadlock occurred in the 1968 election, it could have had the most perilous of consequences for our country and the office of President. Yet,

Continued on p. 68

From Statement of William T. Gossett, President of the American Bar Association. U.S. Congress, House of Representatives, Committee on the Judiciary, *Hearings, Electoral College Reform*, 91st Congress, 1st Session, 1969, pp. 198-209. Footnotes have been omitted.

Martin Diamond

THE ELECTORAL COLLEGE EMBODIES THE AMERICAN IDEA OF DEMOCRACY

In 1967, a distinguished commission of the American Bar Association recommended that the Electoral College be scrapped and replaced by a nationwide popular vote for the President, with provision for a runoff election between the top two candidates in the event no candidate received at least 40 percent of the popular vote. This recommendation was passed by the House in 1969, came close to passage in the Senate in 1970, and is now once again upon us. It is this proposal that has just been endorsed by President Carter and that is being pressed upon Congress under the leadership of Senator Bayh.

The theme of this attack upon the Electoral College is well summarized in a much-quoted sentence from the 1969 ABA Report: "*The electoral college method of electing a President of the United States is archaic, undemocratic, complex, ambiguous, indirect, and dangerous.*" These six charges may seem a bit harsh on a system that has worked well for a very long time, but they do provide a convenient topical outline for a brief defense of the basic principles and procedures of the Electoral College.

An "Archaic" System?

The word *archaic* evokes all those Herblock and other cartoons that portray the Electoral College (or any other feature of the Constitution that is being caricatured) as a deaf, decrepit, old fogey left over from the colonial era. This is the characteristic rhetoric and imagery of contemporary criticism of our now nearly two-centuries old Constitution. But we ought not (and perhaps lawyers, especially, ought not) acquiesce too readily in the prejudice that whatever is old is archaic, in the ABA's pejorative use of that word. On the contrary, it may be argued that the proper political prejudice, if we are to have one, ought to be in favor of the long-persisting, of the tried and true—that our first inclination in constitutional matters ought to be that old is good and older is better. We should remind ourselves of some Aristotelian wisdom reformulated by James Madison in *The Federalist,* Number 49, when he warned that tinkering with the Constitution would deprive the system of government of "that veneration which time bestows on everything, and without which perhaps the wisest and freest governments would not possess the requisite stability."

Continued on p. 77

Martin Diamond, *The Electoral College and the American Idea of Democracy,* © Washington: American Enterprise Institute for Public Policy Research, 1977, pp. 1-3, 6-9. Reprinted with permission.

4. PRESIDENTIAL ELECTION

(Gossett, cont. from p. 66)

unless our system is changed, we will suffer the risk of such consequences in every future presidential election. . . . No sooner was the Constitution adopted than proposals were introduced in Congress to reform the electoral college. The first proposal was introduced in 1797, and since then more than 500 proposals have been offered. The major plans of reform—the district, proportional, automatic and direct vote plans—have their roots in proposals introduced in Congress during the nineteenth century. . . .

The workings of the electoral college over the past 190 years show that it is something completely different from that envisioned by the Framers. Thanks to the extraordinary notes of James Madison, we know that the Framers of the Constitution encountered much difficulty in deciding on a method of electing the President. More than fifteen different methods were proposed at the Constitutional Convention, including election by the Congress, the state legislatures, and the people. Some of these proposals were first adopted and then reconsidered and rejected. Among the supporters of popular vote were James Madison, "the master-builder of the Constitution," James Wilson, one of the great lawyers of his age, Gouverneur Morris of Pennsylvania, John Dickinson of Delaware and Daniel Carroll of Maryland.

Not until the final weeks of the Convention was the electoral college adopted. Election by Congress was rejected because it was felt that the President would be subservient to the Legislative Branch and it opened the door for "intrigue, cabal or faction." A direct vote by the people was criticized on the grounds that the people were too "uninformed" and would be "misled by a few designing men." One delegate said that an election by the people would be like referring a "trial of colours to a blind man." What seemed to move the delegates to accept the electoral system were certain practical considerations, dictated not by political ideals but by the social realities of the time— realities that no longer exist. These were centered largely in the limited communications and relatively low literacy of the period, which made it virtually impossible for the people to know the candidates, rendered them subject to deception and would have inclined them to vote only for someone from their own state. This made it likely that the largest state, having the largest vote, usually would elect its candidate. On the other hand, the delegates assumed that the electors, to whom the people would delegate their franchise, would be the wise men of the community, with their disinterested role protected by the requirement that they not be officeholders or candidates.

The Electoral College was thus envisioned by the Framers as a kind of elite gathering in which the most distinguished and talented persons in the various states would participate. These electors would deliberate and cast an informed and independent vote for President.

Since it was felt that the large states would have considerable influence in the electoral voting, the Framers, in an effort to allay the fears of the small states, provided for the House of Representatives to choose the President, with each state having the same influence, where no candidate received a majority of the electoral votes. The Convention debates indicate that many of the Framers were of the view that most elections would be thrown into Congress.

We know that the design of the Framers in creating the electoral college was not fulfilled. Political parties appeared and the electors' role became a purely mechanical one of voting for their party's candidate. As they became partisan functionaries, their names and reputations became far less known to the citizens than those of the candidates. As a Committee of the Congress noted in 1826, electors "have degenerated into mere agents, in a case which requires no agency, and where the agent must be useless, if he is faithful, and dangerous if he is not."

Participation by the American people in presidential elections has come slowly. Since the Constitution left it to the states to determine the manner of selecting the electors, in the first eleven elections a number of states gave the right of choice to the members of their legislatures rather than to the people. It was not until late in the Nineteenth Century that every state had entrusted the

right of choice to the people. Today, of course, due to state law, the people choose the electors, who are expected to register the will of their constituents in the electoral college.

Experience has shown, however, that the electoral college is riddled with defects which could operate to frustrate the will of the people.

First, it can happen that the popular will of the majority of the nation can be defeated by mathematical flukes. Under the winner-take-all or unit vote rule for allocating a state's electoral votes a candidate could win an electoral victory and yet receive fewer popular votes than his opponent. Success in twelve key states alone would give a candidate an electoral majority, regardless of his margin of victory in those states and regardless of whether he received any votes in the other thirty-eight states. Three times in our history—1824, 1876 and 1888—the popular vote loser was elected President. In fifteen elections a shift of less than one percent of the national vote cast would have made the popular-vote loser President. I think it would be tragic for the popular-vote winner to be rejected again, particularly since the people have come to measure a President's success by his popular vote margin. This aspect of the electoral college allowing for the election of the popular-vote loser violates our most fundamental principle of government by consent of the governed.

Second, it can happen that the choice of the President is thrown into the House of Representatives,

4. PRESIDENTIAL ELECTION

where each state has but a single vote. While it has been 144 years since the House of Representatives has had to choose a President, we have had seven narrow escapes since then, including the elections of 1968, 1960 and 1948. A shift of less than one percent of the popular vote in a few key states would have thrown those elections into Congress with the consequent risk of political deals and possibly the election of a President who was rejected by a majority of the voters. This feature of our system is clearly a political monstrosity, fully distorting the most elementary principles of self-government.

Third, presidential electors can take matters into their own hands and reject the will of the people who chose them. The so-called constitutional independence of electors can take various forms. It can take the form of pledged electors defecting, as in our most recent election, 1960, and 1956: of unpledged elector movements, as in 1960: or third party electors being instructed by their presidential candidate to vote for one of the major candidates. Under the electoral college system, the decision of the people is meaningless unless it is approved by, in effect, another body of government. Such a barrier between the people and their President is both anachronistic and abhorrent.

The electoral college system violates fundamental democratic principles in other ways:

The winner-take-all feature of the system suppresses at an intermediate stage all minority votes cast in a state. The winner of the most popular votes in a state, regardless of his percentage of the votes cast, receives all of that state's electoral votes. The votes for the losing candidates are in effect discarded while those for the winner are multiplied in value. As Senator Thomas Hart Benton stated in 1824: "To lose their votes, is the fate of all minorities, and it is their duty to submit; but this is not a case of votes lost, but of votes taken away, added to those of the majority, and given to a person to whom the minority is opposed."

The present system discriminates among voters on the basis of residence. While a small state voter might seem to enjoy an electoral vote advantage because his state receives two electoral votes regardless of size, a large state voter is able to influence more electoral votes, and it is in the large industrial states that presidential elections are usually won or lost. There is no sound reason why every citizen should not have an equal vote in the election of our one official who serves as the symbol and spokesman for all the people.

The electoral college system fails to reflect the actual strength of the vote turnout in each state. Under the system each state casts its assigned electoral votes regardless of voter turnout. Thus, voters in states where the turnout is small are given a premium. It is not uncommon to find a great disparity in the vote turnout in states having the same number of electoral votes.

To remedy these evils, the

American Bar Association proposes a system of direct popular election, with the following major features:

A candidate must obtain at least forty percent of the popular vote to be elected President or Vice President. The ABA Commission felt that a majority vote requirement was not desirable because it would frequently happen that no candidate had a majority and therefore a second election would be required to decide the outcome. In this regard, it should be noted that one-third of our Presidents received less than a majority of the total popular vote cast. Additionally, the Commission felt that a majority vote requirement might encourage proliferation of the parties, since a small group might have the potential to cause the election to be resolved under the machinery established for a contingent election. In arriving at a forty percent plurality, the Commission was of the view that it was high enough to furnish a sufficient mandate for the Presidency and low enough so that the first election would decide the contest.

The ABA recommends that in the event no candidate receives at least forty percent of the popular vote, a national runoff should be held between the top two candidates. The Commission felt that a runoff was preferable to an election by Congress because it would avoid the possibility of political wheeling and dealing and assure the election of the popular vote winner. The Commission also believed that a national runoff, together with a forty percent plurality requirement,

would operate to discourage proliferation of the parties. The Commission reasoned that it would rarely occur that no major candidate had at least forty percent, even with minor party candidates in the field. However, if that happened, the people would choose between the top two. As the Commission stated in its report:

A runoff between the highest two would seem to have the tendency to limit the number of minor party candidates in the field in the original election because it is improbable that a minor candidate would be one of the top two; and the influence of such a group would be asserted more effectively, as now, before the major party nominations and platforms are determined. . . .

The advantages of direct popular election over other proposals are numerous. It is the only method that would eliminate once and for all the principal defects of our system: the "winner-take-all" feature and its cancellation of votes: the inequities arising from the formula for allocating electoral votes among the states: the anachronistic and dangerous office of presidential elector: and the archaic method by which contingent elections are handled. There would no longer be "sure states" or "pivotal states" or "swing voters" because votes would not be cast in accordance with a unit rule and because campaign efforts would be directed at people regardless of residence. Factors such as fraud and accident could not decide the disposition of all a state's votes.

4. PRESIDENTIAL ELECTION

Direct election would bring to presidential elections the principle which is used and has worked well in elections for Senators, Representatives, governors, state legislators, mayors, and thousands of other officials at all levels of government. That principle, "one person, one vote," would make the votes cast by all Americans in presidential elections of equal weight. All votes would be reflected in the national tally. None would be magnified or contracted. All citizens would have the same chance to affect the outcome of the election. Finally, under a popular vote system, presidential elections would operate the way most people think they operate and expect them to operate. . . .

Now I will address myself to the main arguments raised against direct election. They may be grouped under three headings: (1) Large or small state advantage, (2) threats to the two-party system, and (3) vote counting procedures.

1. Will Either Large or Small States Lose a Present Advantage?

(a) The Small State Advantage Argument

. . . Direct election was recently opposed on the theory that it will deprive small states of a present advantage in a law journal article which was inserted in the Congressional Record. It was noted that Alabama casts 2% of the Nation's electoral votes, while casting less than .9% of the national popular

vote; and the writer computed that New York had only 4 times the electoral power of Alabama even though it had 10 times as many voters. Similar figures were shown for the 25 least populated states, and it was concluded that the American Bar Association's proposal "will not sell" to the less populated states. Reserving for a moment the mathematical issue, let's examine the view that small states' citizens cannot be sold on the principle of voter equality in Presidential elections.

First, this prophecy is not justified by the positions of their elected leaders. No public official has a higher duty to represent the interests of a state in national politics than does its United States Senator. It is noteworthy, therefore, that Senators from smaller states are increasingly prominent among those who are sponsoring direct election proposals. They include Senators Gravel of Alaska, Inouye of Hawaii, Magnuson and Jackson of Washington, Hatfield and Packwood of Oregon, Bible of Nevada, Church of Idaho, Mansfield and Metcalf of Montana, Burdick of North Dakota, McGovern of South Dakota, Pearson of Kansas, Bellmon of Oklahoma, Randolph and Byrd of West Virginia, Ribicoff of Connecticut, Pell of Rhode Island, Aiken of Vermont, McIntyre of New Hampshire, and Smith and Muskie of Maine.

But what of the legislatures of these small states? Here, too, we are not left to speculation. In 1966 Senator Burdick of North Dakota

Electoral College Is Undemocratic

polled state legislators on their preferences among the various proposals for Electoral College reform. A surprisingly high return, 2,500 of 8,000 polled, showed 58.8% in favor of direct election. It was supported by 50% or more of the legislators replying from 44 states. Most significantly, there was little variation between large and small states. Among the most heavily populated states, California legislators voted 73.5% for direct election; New York legislators, 70.0%; Pennsylvania, 55.8%; Michigan, 52.4%; and Ohio, 57.1%. In the five smallest states—those with only 3 electoral votes— Vermont voted 60.9% for direct election; Nevada, 62.5%; Wyoming, 55.5%; Delaware, 53.8%; and Alaska, 50.0%.

The House of Delegates of the American Bar Association, a cross-section of American lawyers, approved our Commission's report by a 3 to 1 margin. Direct election has also been endorsed by other organizations representing wide segments and sections of American life, including the AFL-CIO, the U.S. Chamber of Commerce, the United Auto Workers, and the National Federation of Independent Business. Public opinion polls show that 79 to 81% of people throughout the country favor our proposal. Thus, those who accept the principle of popular election of the President should not assume that citizens of small states do not also accept it.

The small state advantage argument is diametrically opposed by a plausible theory that it is large states who profit from the present system.

(b) The Large State Advantage Argument

In a curious cross fire, direct election is also opposed by some champions of large states' interests. They claim that the small state advantage in ratio of electors to population is more than offset by the advantages accruing to large states from the winner-take-all laws. One such observer recently wrote that the features of the present system "have bred in modern times the decisive influence in Presidential elections of the large, populous, heterogeneous states, where bloc voting, as by ethnic or racial minorities or other interest groups, often determines the result. Much of the popular vote in the smaller, relatively homogeneous states, is simply wasted. Politicians and political scientists have at any rate long assumed that the Presidency is won or lost in the large states . . . we can now establish mathematically why modern Presidents have been particularly sensitive to urban and minority interests. . . . And only men who can be so responsive are generally nominated and elected.". . .

Without attempting to resolve the large versus small states issue, the ABA seeks to eliminate whatever unfair advantage either may have by virtue of the present system. Recent polls show that citizens of both types of state want no such advantage. As a matter of Constitutional structure, surely no

4. PRESIDENTIAL ELECTION

citizen's influence upon his President should depend upon his geographical location within the United States. Only direct election will achieve this voter equality.

This question occupied much of the ABA Commission's attention, and it adopted its position with confidence that direct election carries no risk of producing a multi-party system. Nonetheless, such objections have been raised. They are difficult to answer to the opposition's satisfaction because none of us can prophesy future political events with absolute certainty—including those who predict dire consequences to the two-party system. However, we can project probabilities upon the basis of relevant experience and expert opinion. This we did in 1967; and recent reappraisals in light of the 1968 election only strengthen our position.

Those who oppose direct election on third-party grounds labor a hard oar after the 1968 election. None has demonstrated more dramatically the potential for third-party leverage under our present system. I have mentioned three contingencies which in 1968 could have prevented any candidate from winning a majority of the electoral votes. The Wallace electors would have held a decisive balance of power when the Electoral College met on December 16th. We need not speculate further; the point was made that the present system offers special incentives to third-party candidates and can easily give them power disproportionate to their numbers.

Direct election would fully cure the defects in our system which the Wallace candidacy sought to exploit. It would also remedy other faults which can magnify third-party efforts. Close analysis proves that direct election will actually *strengthen* the two-party system—not weaken it—by removing special incentives to third parties and equalizing all voters throughout the Nation.

Analytically, there are three distinct types of third-party efforts—local, regional and national. The first two would undoubtedly be weakened by direct election. Local, or intra-state, parties, such as the Liberal and Conservative Parties in New York, now may sometimes have a pivotal power to tip a state's electoral bloc for or against one of the major candidates. An example is the Progressive Party vote for Henry Wallace in New York in 1948, whose main effect was to deny the state's electoral votes to Harry Truman. Under direct election the votes of such a splinter group would count only for what they are worth in numbers of persons; and votes for major candidates would always count nationally.

Regional or sectional parties include the States' Rights candidacy of Senator Thurmond in 1948 and, as it developed, the candidacy of Governor Wallace in 1968. Sectional feelings reflected by a plurality of popular votes in a few states can deliver large blocs of electoral votes and possibly produce a balance-of-power position in the Electoral College. The ruling of this Congress on the North Carolina elector who defected from Nixon to Wallace removes any doubt that the Wallace electors could have legally voted for a major candidate. Under direct election all votes will be counted as cast and a third candidate can receive no disproportionate leverage from being able to carry a few states.

The final type of third party, the national effort, is more difficult to analyze. Some argue that national third-party efforts would be encouraged by direct election merely because all state popular vote totals would be reflected in the national totals, whether or not any states were carried. This question was studied closely by our Commission. We found little evidence that elimination of the election is more likely to strengthen it. . . .

We have learned that no single factor accounts for the two-party system and that there is considerable disagreement as to its major causes. As stated by V. O. Key:

Explanations of the factors determinative of so complex a social structure as a party system must remain unsatisfactory. The safest explanation is that several factors conspired toward the development of the American dual party pattern. These included the accidents of history that produced dual divisions on great issues at critical points in our history, the consequences of our institutional forms, the clustering of popular opinions around a point of consensus rather than their bipolarization, and perhaps others. The assignment of weights to each of these is an enterprise too uncertain to be hazarded.

Among the causes listed by Key and others as accounting for our American commitment to the two-party system are: persistence of initial form; election of officials from single-member districts by plurality votes; the normal presence of a central consensus on national goals; cultural homogeneity; political maturity; and a general tendency towards dualism. Some of the experts list the Electoral College as a factor which may contribute; others ignore it; and some suggest that it is functionally opposed to two-partyism and that our party system may have survived *despite* the Electoral College rather than *because* of it.

The experts are virtually in agreement on one point, however. It is that election of legislators and executives by plurality votes from single-member districts is the chief cause of two-partyism. This is the one element which all two-party systems have in common. No one proposes to alter our practice of electing Members of Congress and State Legislators, Governors and Mayors on this basis. To the extent that these elections undergird our two-party system, that support will continue. Furthermore, our proposal essentially places Presidential elections on this same basis and thus perfects and extends that feature which best serves the two-party system. . . .

Nonetheless, we were sufficiently concerned by the possibility of weakening the two-party system that a major provision of our proposal is directed largely at supporting it. This is the provision requiring run-off elections when no candidate obtains 40% of the popular vote. This avoids peculiar evils of both majority and simple plurality requirements. A majority requirement would make run-offs the rule rather than the exception and positively encourage splinter candidacies. A simple plurality rule would enable a candidate to win with as little as one-fourth or one-third of the total vote—hardly a sufficient mandate to govern. This might encourage third and fourth parties. The 40% rule incorporates our historical experience as a future norm. In only the unique election of 1860 has a candidate failed to receive at least 40% of the vote, and Abraham Lincoln then received 39.79% despite his absence from the ballot in ten states. In a given election minor parties would have to win at least 20% of the national vote total in order even to cause a run-off, much less participate in it. This is unlikely and run-offs should occur rarely, if ever. . . .

3. Vote Counting Procedures

Another objection made to direct popular election is that it could delay the certification of a President for a long period of time due to vote counting procedures. This objection is addressed to the mechanics of a system of direct election and not to the principle. The vote counting problems which are likely to be encountered under such a system, such as recounts, fraud, challenged ballots and the like, are really no different in kind from those that exist in the election of a Governor or United States Senator. Any system of direct election requires an accurate, rapid and final vote count. These requirements have been satisfied in the direct election of officials at other levels of government, and I see no reason why they cannot be satisfied in a direct election for President. In the larger states millions of votes are now cast held in areas of thousands of square miles.

There are now procedures in the various states for certifying the results of popular elections for other offices which could be adapted to a system of direct election of the President. Under the ABA recommendations, the operation and regulation of presidential elections would be left to the states, with a reserve power in Congress to legislate in the field. The states thus would have the flexibility to adopt and change election procedures in the light of experience. It is foreseeable that the states might adopt a uniform state law standardizing the procedures for handling recounts and challenged ballots, and that Congress might create an Election Commission with responsibilities in the vote counting area.

The trend toward better regulated and more scientific vote counting has reduced and, in my opinion, will continue to reduce the possibilities of irregularities while expediting the final outcome. With a cooperative effort on the part of the states and federal government, I am confident that procedures and methods can be adopted to assure an effective system of direct popular election of the President.

Conclusion

The trend of our political system is toward direct democratic parti-cipation of the people at every level. That trend has been reflected in the Fifteenth, Seventeenth, and Nine-teenth Amendments to the Con-stitution. It should now be reflected in an amendment providing for popular election of the President, the last major office in the country on which the people do not have a direct voice.

(Cont. from p. 67, Diamond, "Electoral College")

In other words, a long-standing constitutional arrangement secures, by its very age, that habitual popular acceptance which is an indispen-sable ingredient in constitutional legitimacy, that is, in the power of a constitution to be accepted and lived under by free men and women. By this reasoning, we should preserve the Electoral College—barring truly serious harm actually experienced under it—simply on grounds of its nearly two-centuries long history of tranquil popular acceptance. We who have seen so many free constitutions fail because they proved to be mere parchment, unrooted in the hearts and habits of the people, should be responsive to Madison's understated warning; we should readily agree that it would not be a "superfluous advantage" even to the most perfectly devised constitution to have the people's habitual acceptance on its side.

But it is not necessary, in defense of the Electoral College, to rely on such sober (but startling nowadays) reasoning as that of Madison, because the Electoral College happens not to be an archaic element of our constitutional sys-tem. Not only is it not at all archaic, but one might say that it is the very model of up-to-date constitutional flexibility. Perhaps no other feature of the Constitution has had a greater capacity for dynamic historical adaptiveness. The electors became nullities; presidential elections became dramatic national contests; the federal elements in the process became strengthened by the general-ticket practice (that is, winner-take-all); modern mass political parties developed; cam-paigning moved from rather rigid sectionalism to the complexities of a modern technological society—and all this occurred tranquilly and legitimately within the original constitutional framework (as modified by the Twelfth Amend-ment). The Electoral College thus has experienced an immense his-torical evolution. But the remark-able fact is that while it now operates in historically transformed ways, in ways not at all as the Framers intended, it nonetheless still operates largely to the ends that they intended. What more could one ask of a constitutional provision? . . .

An "Undemocratic" System?

The gravamen of the "undemocratic" indictment of the Electoral College rests on the possibility that, because votes are aggregated within the states by the general-ticket system, in which the winner takes all, a loser in the national popular vote may nonetheless become President by winning a majority of the electoral votes of the states. This is supposedly the "loaded pistol" to our heads, our quadrennial game of Russian roulette; indeed, no terms seem lurid enough to express the contemporary horror at this possibility. This is what shocks our modern democratic sensibilities and, once the issue is permitted to be stated in this way, it takes a very brave man or woman to defend the Electoral College. But, fortunately, courage is not required; it suffices to reformulate the issue and get it on its proper footing.

In fact, presidential elections are already just about as democratic as they can be. We already have one-man, one-vote—*but in the states.* Elections are as freely and democratically contested as elections can be—*but in the states.* Victory always goes democratically to the winner of the raw popular vote—*but in the states.* The label given to the proposed reform, "direct popular election," is a misnomer; the elections have already become as directly popular as they

can be—*but in the states.* Despite all their democratic rhetoric, the reformers do not propose to make our presidential elections more directly democratic, they only propose to make them more directly *national,* by entirely removing the states from the electoral process. Democracy thus is not the question regarding the Electoral College, federalism is: should our presidential election remain in part *federally* democratic, or should we make them completely *nationally* democratic?

Whatever we decide, then, democracy itself is not at stake in our decision, only the prudential question of how to channel and organize the popular will. That makes everything easier. When the question is only whether the federally democratic aspect of the Electoral College should be abandoned in order to prevent the remotely possible election of a President who had not won the national popular vote, it does not seem so hard to opt for retaining some federalism in this homogenizing, centralizing age. When federalism has already been weakened, perhaps inevitably in modern circumstances, why further weaken the federal elements in our political system by destroying the informal federal element that has historically evolved in our system of presidential elections? The crucial general-ticket system, adopted in the 1830s for reasons pertinent then, has become in our time a constitutionally unplanned but vital support for federalism. Also called the "unit rule" system, it provides that the state's entire electoral vote goes to the winner of the popular vote in the state. Resting entirely on the voluntary legislative action of each state, this informal historical development, combined with the formal constitutional provision, has generated a federal element in the Electoral College which sends a federalizing impulse throughout our whole political process. It makes the states as states dramatically and pervasively important in the whole presidential selection process, from the earliest strategies in the nominating campaign through the convention and final election. Defederalize the presidential election—which is what direct popular election boils down to—and a contrary nationalizing impulse will gradually work its way throughout the political process. The nominating process naturally takes its cues from the electing process; were the President to be elected in a single national election, the same cuing process would continue, but in reverse.

It is hard to think of a worse time than the present, when so much already tends toward excessive centralization, to strike an unnecessaary blow at the federal quality of our political order. The federal aspect of the electoral controversy has received inadequate attention; indeed, it is regarded by many as irrelevant to it. The argument has been that the President is the representative of "all the people" and, hence, that he should be elected by them in a wholly national way, unimpeded by

the interposition of the states. Unfortunately, the prevailing conception of federalism encourages this erroneous view. We tend nowadays to have a narrowed conception of federalism, limiting it to the reserved powers of the states. But by focusing exclusively on the division of power between the states and the central government, we overlook an equally vital aspect of federalism, namely, the federal elements in the central government itself. The Senate (which, after all, helps make laws for all the people) is the most obvious example; it is organized on the federal principle of equal representation of each state. Even the House of Representatives has federal elements in its design and mode of operation. There is no reason, then, why the President, admittedly the representative of all of us, cannot represent us and hence be elected by us in a way corresponding to our compoundly federal and national character. The ABA Report, for example, begs the question when it says that "it seems most appropriate that the election of the nation's only two national officers be by national referendum." They are our two *central* officers. But they are not our two *national* officers; under the Constitution, they are our two *partly federal, partly national* officers. Why should we wish to change them into our two *wholly* national officers?

Since democracy as such is not implicated in our choice—but only whether to choose our Presidents in a partly federally democratic or a wholly national democratic way—

we are perfectly free prudentially to choose the partly federal rather than the wholly national route. We need only strip away from the Electoral College reformers their democratic rhetorical dress in order to make the sensible choice with good conscience.

Our consciences will be further eased when we note that the abhorrence of the federal aspect of the Electoral College—which causes the potential discrepancy between electoral and popular votes—cannot logically be limited to the Electoral College. It rests upon premises that necessitate abhorrence of any and all *district* forms of election. What is complained about in the Electoral College is endemic to all districted electoral systems, whether composed of states, or congressional districts, or parliamentary constituencies. If population is not exactly evenly distributed in all the districts (and it never can be), both in sheer numbers and in their political predispositions, then the possibility cannot be removed that the winner of a majority of the districts may not also be the winner of the raw popular vote. Regarding the British Parliament and the American Congress, for example, this is not merely a speculative matter or something that has not happened since 1888 (when Cleveland narrowly won the popular vote but lost the electoral vote, and thus the presidency, to Harrison), as in the case of the American presidency. It has happened more often and far more recently in England, where popular-minority governments are as pos-

sible as popular-minority Presidents are here. It is a source of wonder that Electoral College critics, who are often partisans of the parliamentary system, regard with equanimity in that system what they cannot abide in the American case. There the whole power of government, both legislative and executive, is at stake in an election, while here only the executive power is involved. . . .

One more point may usefully be made regarding the charge that the Electoral College is undemocratic. I have already argued that our presidential elections under the Electoral College are thoroughly democratic, albeit partly federally democratic, and that democracy may profitably be blended with the advantages of districting. But even on the basis of purely national democratic terms, the potential popular-vote/electoral-vote discrepancy of the Electoral College may be tolerated with good democratic conscience.

Not only has the discrepancy not occurred for nearly a century, but no one even suggests that it is ever likely to occur save by a very small margin. The margin in the last actual occurrence, in 1888, was of minute proportions; and the imaginary "near misses"—those horrendous hypotheticals—are always in the range of zero to one-tenth of 1 percent. The great undemocratic threat of the Electoral College, then, is the possibility that, so to speak, of 80 million votes, 50 percent minus one would rule over 50 percent plus one. Now there really is something strange in escalating this popgun possibility into a loaded pistol. For one thing, the statistical margin of error in the vote count (let alone other kinds of errors and chance circumstances) is larger than any anticipated discrepancy; that is to say, the discrepancy might be only apparent and not real. But even granting the possibility that 50 percent minus one might prevail over 50 percent plus one, how undemocratic would that really be? The answer is suggested by the fact that, in the long history of democratic thought, the problem never even arose before the present, let alone troubled anyone. It took us to invent it. When we understand why, we will also see that it is a spurious problem or, at least, a trivial one.

Historically, the problem of democracy was not about minute margins of electoral victory, but about whether, say, 5 percent (the rich and wellborn few), should rule over 95 percent (the poor many), to use the classical terms. That is what the real struggles of democracy were all about. Only a severe case of doctrinaire myopia blinds us to that and makes us see, instead, a crisis in the mathematical niceties of elections where no fundamental democratic issues are involved. Democracy is not at stake in our elections, only the decision as to which shifting portion of an overall democratic electorate will temporarily capture executive office. What serious difference does it make to any fundamental democratic value if, in such elections, 50 percent minus one of the voters *might—very*

infrequently—win the presidency from 50 percent plus one of the voters? Only a country as thoroughly and safely democratic as ours could invent the 50 percent problem and make a tempest in a democratic teapot out of it.

The irrelevance of the potential popular-vote/electoral vote discrepancy to any important democratic value is illustrated if we consider the following question: Would the Electoral College reformers really regard it as a disaster for democracy if Franklin D. Roosevelt (or any liberal Democrat) had beaten Herbert Hoover (or any conservative Republican) in the electoral vote but had lost by a handful in the national popular vote? The question is not meant, of course, in any spirit of partisan twitting. Rather, it is intended to suggest that no sensible person could seriously regard it as a disaster for democracy if—to use the language of caricature—a coalition of the poor, of labor, of blacks, et al., had thus squeaked by a coalition of the rich, the powerful, the privileged, and the like. To point this out is not to depreciate the importance of such an electoral outcome for the course of public policy. It is only to deny that it would threaten or make a mockery of the democratic foundations of our political order. To think that it would is to ignore the relevant socioeconomic requisites of democracy, and to be panicked into wide-reaching constitutional revisions by the bogeyman of the 50 percent minus one possibility. To risk such revision for such a reason is to reduce democracy not only to a matter of mere numbers, but to minute numbers, and to abstract numbers, drained of all socio-economic significance for democracy.

A "Complex" System?

The ABA Report does not make clear what is "complex" about the Electoral College or why complexity as such is bad. Perhaps the fear is that voters are baffled by the complexity of the Electoral College and that their bafflement violates a democratic norm. It must be admitted that an opinion survey could easily be devised that shows the average voter to be shockingly ignorant of what the Electoral College is and how it operates. But, then, opinion surveys almost always show the average voter to be shockingly ignorant of whatever a survey happens to be asking him about. It all depends upon what kind of knowledge the voter is expected to have. I would argue that most voters have a solid working knowledge of what a presidential election is all about. They know that they are voting for the candidate of their choice and that the candidate with the most votes wins in their state. And when watching the results on television or reading about them in the papers, they surely discover how the election came out. However ignorant they may be of the details of the Electoral College, their ignorance does not seem to affect at all the intention and meaning of their vote, or their acceptance of the

electoral outcome. What more is necessary than that? What is the use of making the process less complex?

However, the animus against the complexity of the Electoral College surely goes deeper than a fear that voters are unable to explain it when asked. There seems to be a hostility to complexity as such. This hostility has a long history. It goes back at least to those French Enlightenment thinkers who scolded John Adams for the unnecessary complexity, for example, of American bicameralism. However such complexity had helped to mitigate monarchical severities, of what possible use could bicameralism be, they asked, now that America had established popular government? When the people rule, they insisted, one branch is quite enough; no complexity should stand in the way of straightforwardly recording and carrying out the popular will. The answer to them, and to all like-minded democratic simplifiers ever since, derives from the very essence of American democracy, which is precisely to be complex. The American idea of democracy, as argued above, is to take into account both local and national considerations, and also to moderate democracy and blend it with as many other things as are necessary to the public good. That blending necessitates complexity.

The Electoral College is, of course, only one example of the complexity that characterizes our entire political system. Bicameralism is complex; federalism is complex; judicial review is complex;

the suspensory executive veto is a complex arrangement; the Bill of Rights introduces a thousand complexities. Are these also to be faulted on grounds of complexity? If a kind of prissy intelligibility is to be made the standard for deciding what should remain and what should be simplified in American government, how much would be left in place? In all fairness, the question is not whether our political system or any part of it is complex, but whether there is a good reason for any particular complexity. The skeptical, self-doubting American idea of democracy does not assume that the rich complexity of democratic reality is exhausted by mere national majoritarianism, nor does it assume that all good things automatically flow from democracy. It therefore asks of any institution not only whether it is democratic, but also whether, while leaving the system democratic enough, it contributes to fulfilling the complex requirements of democracy and to securing some worthwhile purpose not secured simply by democracy itself. That is the only appropriate question regarding the complexity of the Electoral College. . . .

An "Ambiguous" System?

This charge is rather puzzling. It is so far off the mark that a rebuttal is hardly required; rather, it supplies the opportunity to point out a particular advantage of the Electoral College in comparison with its proposed substitute. Far from speaking unclearly or confusingly, the Electoral College has delivered exceptionally prompt and unequivocal electoral pronouncements. This is not to say that there have never been any delays or uncertainties. Whenever an election is closely divided, as ours often have been and are likely to be, no election system can deliver prompt and absolutely certain verdicts, free of the ambiguity that inheres in the electorate's own behavior. But when a realistic rather than an utopian standard is applied, the Electoral College has to be rated an unqualified success. To deny this betrays a reluctance to credit the Electoral College with any merit at all. Or, perhaps, it is another instance of the human propensity, remarked on by Hobbes, to attribute all inconveniences to the particular form of government under which one lives, rather than to recognize that some inconveniences are intrinsic to government as such regardless of its form. This propensity seems to explain the finding of ambiguity in the way the present system works.

To judge fairly the charge of ambiguity, then, the Electoral College must be compared in this regard with other electoral systems and ,especially, with the 40 percent plus/runoff system proposed by President Carter and Senator Bayh as its replacement. Under the proposed system, the nation forms a single electoral district; the candidate who gets the most popular votes wins, provided the winning total equals at least 40 percent of the total number of votes cast; failing that, there would be a runoff election between the two candidates who had the most votes. Let us consider the prospects for ambiguity under this proposed system, in comparison with the actual experience under the Electoral College.

The American electorate has a fundamental tendency to divide closely, with "photo finish" elections being almost the rule rather than the exception. The Electoral College almost always announces these close election outcomes with useful amplification. In purely numerical popular votes, an election outcome might be uncertain and vulnerable to challenge; but the Electoral College replaces the numerical uncertainty with an unambiguously visible constitutional majority that sustains the legitimacy of the electoral result. If this magnifying lens is removed, the "squeaker" aspect of our presidential elections will become more visible and, probably, much more troubling. For example, the problem of error and fraud, no doubt endemic in some degree to all electoral systems, could very well be aggravated under the proposed national system, because every single precinct polling place could come under bitter scrutiny as relevant to a close and disputed national outcome. In contrast, under the Electoral College, ambiguity of outcome sufficient even to warrant challenge is infrequent and is always limited to but a few states. Indeed, the massive and undeniable fact is that, for a whole century, the Electoral College has produced unambiguous outcomes in every single presidential election, accepted by the losing candidate and party and by the whole American people with unfaltering legitimacy.

Not only is it extremely unlikely that the proposed replacement could match this record of unambiguity, but the 40 percent plus plurality provision could very well introduce a different and graver kind of ambiguity into our political system. This would not be uncertainty as to who is the winner, but a profounder uncertainty as to whether the winner is truly the choice of the American people. Under the modern Electoral College, we have elected popular-majority Presidents about half the time, and plurality Presidents with close to 50 percent of the vote the rest of the time, save for three who received less than 45 percent of the popular vote. This is a remarkable record of unambiguity in regard to public support compared with the history of most other democratic systems. But, given the dynamics of American political behavior, the proposed 40 percent plus plurality provision might very well *typically* produce winners at or just above the 40 percent level. . . .

A "Dangerous" System?

"Dangers" of the Electoral College

It is not possible here to discuss all the dangers that alarm critics of the Electoral College, for example, the faithless electors, or a cabal of them, or the problem of the contingency election in the House of Representatives. Some post real enough problems and would have to be dealt with in a fuller discussion. But the present remarks are limited to the main danger that the reformers fear, namely, the popular-vote/electoral-vote discrepancy. This is the loaded pistol pointed to our heads, the threat that necessitates radical constitutional revision. Now the funny thing about this loaded pistol is that the last time it went off, in 1888, no one got hurt; no one even hollered. As far as I can tell, there was hardly a ripple of constitutional discontent, not a trace of dangerous delegitimation, and nothing remotely resembling the crisis predicted by present-day critics of the Electoral College. But it must be sadly acknowledged that, the next time it happens, there might well be far greater public distress. It would be due, in large part, to the decades of populistic denunciation of the Electoral College; a kind of self-confirming prophecy would be at work.

All that is needed to defuse this danger is for the undermining of the moral authority of the Electoral College to cease. The American people will not, on their own initiative, react with rage if one of the near-misses actually occurs. As after 1888, they will go about their business and, perhaps, straighten things out in the next election, as when they elected Cleveland in 1892. They will go about their business as they did in a parallel instance, after Vice President Agnew's resignation and Watergate,

when the provisions of the Twenty-fifth Amendment went doubly into effect. The democratic foundations of our political system, and even the vigor of the presidency, were not weakened by the temporary absence of the majority or plurality popular support that normally undergirds the presidency. There need be no dangerous weakening should the Electoral College again produce a temporary shortfall in popular support—if only the reformers cease to cry havoc, and if those who ought to speak up do so and help the American people learn to enjoy the compatibility of the Electoral College with the American idea of democracy.

Dangers of Direct Election

Not every danger alleged to inhere in our present electoral system could thus be made to evaporate merely by the exercise of our own common sense; like every political institution, the Electoral College contains dangerous possibilities. But this much may be said about them: all the dangers critics claim to see in the Electoral College are entirely matters of speculation. Some have never actually occurred, and others have not occurred for nearly a century. Nothing whatever has actually gone wrong with the Electoral College for a very long time. Experience has demonstrated that the dangers incident to the present system are neither grave nor likely to occur. But what of the dangers incident to the proposed reform? It is as important to speculate about them as to frighten ourselves with imaginary pos-

4. PRESIDENTIAL ELECTION

sibilities under the Electoral College. Three dangers seem seriously to threaten under the proposed reform: weakening the two-party system, weakening party politics generally, and further imperializing the presidency.

Many have warned that the 40 percent plus/runoff system would encourage minor parties and in time undermine the two-party system. The encouragement consists in the runoff provision of the proposed reform, that is, in the possibility that minor parties will get enough votes in the first election to force a runoff. Supporters of the proposed change deny this likelihood. For example, the ABA Report argues that a third party is unlikely to get the 20 percent of the popular vote necessary to force a runoff. Perhaps so, and this has been very reassuring to supporters of the reform. But why does it have to be just "a" third party? Why cannot the runoff be forced by the combined votes of a half dozen or more minor parties that enter the first election? Indeed, they are all there waiting in the wings. The most powerful single constraint on minor-party presidential candidacies has always been the "don't throw your vote away" fear that caused their support to melt as election day approached. Norman Thomas, who knew this better than anyone, was certain that a national popular election of the kind now proposed would have immensely improved the Socialist electoral results. Now this is not to say that the Electoral College alone is what prevents ideological parties like that of the Socialists from winning elections in America. Obviously, other and more powerful factors ultimately determine that. But what the electoral machinery can determine is whether such parties remain electorally irrelevant, minuscule failures, or whether they can achieve sufficient electoral success to fragment the present two-party system. The relevant question is not whether the proposed reform of the Electoral College would radically change the ideological complexion of American parties, but whether it would multiply their number.

Moreover, not only ideological parties would be encouraged by the proposed change, but also minor parties and minor candidacies of all sorts. Sectional third parties would not be weakened by the 40 percent plus/runoff arrangement; they would retain their sectional appeal and pick up additional votes all over the country. The threat that dissident wings might bolt from one of the two major parties would instantly become more credible and thereby more disruptive within them; sooner or later the habit of bolting would probably take hold. Would there not also be an inducement to militant wings of ethnic, racial, and religious groups to abandon the major party framework and go it alone? And, as the recent proliferation of primary candidacies suggests, would-be "charismatics" might frequently take their case to the general electorate, given the inducements of the proposed new machinery.

All this might not happen immediately. The two-party habit is strong among us, and many factors would continue to give it strength. But the proposed reform of the Electoral College would remove or weaken what is generally regarded as the most powerful cause of the two-party system, namely, the presidency as a "single-member district." There would, of course, still be a single office finally to be won or lost, but *not in the first election.* That is the key. If runoffs become the rule, as is likely, the first election would become in effect a kind of two-member district. There would be two winners in it; we would have created a valuable new electoral prize—a second place finish in the preliminary election. This would be a boon to the strong minor candidacies; needing now only to seem a "viable" alternative for second place, they could more easily make a plausible case to potential supporters. But, more important, there would be something to win for nearly everyone in the first, or preliminary, election. Minor party votes now shrink away as the election nears and practically disappear on election day. As is well known, this is because minor-party supporters desert their preferred candidates to vote for the "lesser evil" of the major candidates. But the proposed reform would remove the reason to do so. On the contrary, as in multiparty parliamentary systems, the voter could vote with his heart because that would in fact also be the calculating thing to do. There would be plenty of time to vote for the lesser evil in the eventual runoff election. The trial heat would be the time to help the preferred minor party show its strength. Even a modest showing would enable the minor party to participate in the frenetic bargaining inevitably incident to runoff elections. And even a modest showing would establish a claim to the newly available public financing that would simultaneously be an inducement to run and a means to strengthen one's candidacy. . . .

It is clearly likely that the two-party system would be dangerously weakened by the proposed reform, whereas it is certain that it has been created and strengthened under the Electoral College. Most Americans agree that the two-party system is a valuable way of channelling democracy because that mode of democratic decision produces valuable qualities of moderation, consensus, and stability. It follows then that the proposed reform threatens a serious injury to the American political system.

Not only might the change weaken the two-party system, but it might well also have an enfeebling effect on party politics generally. The regular party politicians, which is to say, the state and local politicians, would become less important to presidential candidates. This tendency is already evident in the effect the presidential primaries are having; regular party machinery is becoming less important in the nominating process, and the individual apparatus of the candidates more important. The defederalizing of the presidential election seems likely to strengthen this tendency. No longer needing to carry states, the presidential candidates would find the regular politicians, who are most valuable for tipping the balance in a state, of diminishing importance for their free-wheeling search for popular votes. They probably would rely more and more on direct-mail and media experts, and on purely personal coteries, in conducting campaigns that would rely primarily on the mass media. The consequence would seem to be to disengage the presidential campaign from the party machinery and from the states and to isolate the presidency from their moderating effect. If "merchandising" the President has become an increasingly dangerous tendency, nationalizing and plebiscitizing the presidency would seem calculated only to intensify the danger.

This raises, finally, the question of the effect of the proposed reform on the presidency as an institution, that is, on the "imperial presidency." The populistic rhetoric that denounces the Electoral College as undemocratic has had, since the time of the New Deal, a corollary inclination to inflate the importance of the presidency. In recent years, however, we have all learned to be cautious about the extent of presidential power. Yet the proposed change could only have an inflating effect on it. The presidency has always derived great moral authority and political power from the claim that the President is the only representative of all the people. Why increase the force of that claim by magnifying the national and plebiscitary foundations of the presidency? This would be to enhance the presidential claims at just the moment when so much fear had been expressed about the "imperial presidency."

Many who deal with the Electoral College are concerned chiefly with its consequences for partisan purposes. They support or oppose it because of its alleged tendency to push the presidency in a liberal direction. As for myself, I am not at all sure what those partisan effects used to be, are now, or will become in the future. Accordingly, it seems a good time to rise above party considerations to the level of constitutional principle. On that level, it seems quite clear to me that the effects of the proposed change are likely to be quite bad. And it likewise seems quite clear to me that the Electoral College is easy to defend, once one gets the hang of it. It is a paradigm of the American idea of democracy. Thus to defend it is not only to help retain a valuable part of our political system, but also to help rediscover what the American idea of democracy is.

POSTSCRIPT

PRESIDENTIAL ELECTION:
ELECTORAL COLLEGE OR POPULAR VOTE?

The Electoral College was designed for a nation which did not have universal suffrage, rapid communications, and national political parties. Its critics consequently consider it to be an anachronism, and call for its replacement by direct popular election of the President, or dividing the electoral vote of each state among the candidates, or some other change designed to reflect the popular will more surely and accurately than the Electoral College. Yet the constitutional system's supporters insist that it has worked well in adapting to changing circumstances, and if some reform might remove the remote possibility of the election of a minority-choice President, all reforms raise more serious problems than they resolve.

The debate has been fueled by President Carter's recommendation of a constitutional amendment to institute direct election of the President. That position is also taken by Lawrence D. Longley and Alan G. Braun in *The Politics of Electoral College Reform* (Yale, 2nd ed., 1975). Longley and Braun contend that a direct popular vote would not favor any special interests. In *Voting for President* (Brookings, 1970), Wallace S. Sayre and Judith H. Parris surveyed all of the proposed reforms and concluded that we should leave well enough alone and retain the Electoral College. In a different analysis, Judith Best has also made *The Case against Direct Election of the President* (Cornell, 1971). Recent *Hearings* and *Reports* of congressional committees contain anlyses drawing upon recent electoral experience.

How have so many political participants and interest groups expended so much thought and passion for so many years on what may be considered a fairly technical feature of our constitutional system? Part of the reason lies in opposed political instincts, one of which gives the highest priority to democratizing every feature of our politics that does not maximize the will of the people, while the other values most the preservation of those historical practices which have worked successfully and which therefore will resist any tampering with the system.

But, on this issue as on so many others, political principles are colored by the prospects of political advantage. Some political analysts and participants believe that retention of the Electoral College or its elimination will benefit particular interests, either the populous states or the smaller states, urban or rural areas. Inevitably, such perceptions, whether right or wrong (and they are likely never to be conclusively tested) will influence our assessment of the Electoral College.

PART II

DOES AMERICAN GOVERNMENT GOVERN PROPERLY?

ISSUE 5

IS CONGRESS STRONG ENOUGH?

Can Representative Government Do the Job? was the question posed in the title of a thoughtful 1945 book, and many Americans remain uncertain as to the answer. Putting the question another way, we may bluntly ask: Is Congress strong enough?

There is a widespread feeling that Congress isn't strong. The structure of Congress impresses—or depresses—its critics as being a horse-and-buggy vehicle in a jet age. Power is fragmented among many committees in the absence of national parties which might impose discipline on legislators and coherence on legislation. Within the committees, power is concentrated in the chairmen who, until recently, were chosen strictly on the basis of seniority (length of service) rather than leadership capacities. Woodrow Wilson called it "a government by the chairmen of standing committees of congress," and if much power has shifted since to the President, within Congress the chairmen remain subject to few checks.

President Truman campaigned against what he characterized as a Do-Nothing Congress. The criticism that Congress doesn't do much good leads even incumbent congressmen to run against Congress's record and to promise reform.

Perhaps the decline of Congress in this century is partly due to its outmoded structure, but it is easy enough to see the cause in two World Wars, Korea and Vietnam, the Great Depression, and economic and other issues that transcend national boundaries. Increasingly, we have looked to the President rather than to Congress for inspiration, initiative, and leadership. He is after all an individual and we can personalize his power; we can identify him and identify *with* him, while Congress remains a faceless abstraction.

The President can act with promptness and decisiveness not available to two houses with 535 members. He alone is nationally elected and may therefore come closer to being a tribune of the people. He alone possesses life-and-death power as the negotiator of international relations and Commander-in-Chief of the armed forces.

It was not surprising therefore that liberals looked to the President for the bold action that was not forthcoming from a lethargic and leaderless Congress. But many who had prayed for presidential dominance remained to scoff the Imperial Presidency as a result of Watergate, the abuse of power, the evidence of unnecessary presidential secrecy and calculated deceit, and a new awareness of unchecked presidential decision-making.

The fear that presidential power may be abused has kindled the hope that representative government can be improved. To that end, the iron-clad seniority rule has been abandoned by the House Democratic caucus and undermined by its Senate counterpart, the requirement of open committee meetings and increased access to once-confidential files has increased public (and particularly press) scrutiny of governmental behavior, Congress has set up its own budget committees, and the War Powers Act was designed to inhibit presidential war-making in the absence of a congressional declaration of war.

Perhaps what is necessary is not technical reform but political will, that is, a public desire to have Congress exercise its power more vigorously. Reformers cannot fairly criticize Congress for not adopting programs which most Americans have not indicated they want Congress to adopt. On the other hand, it might be argued that reformers are simply incapable of strengthening Congress, even if they have the American people behind them, because the presidency today is beyond the reach of legislative checks and balances.

Neither of these positions rules out sensible procedural reforms, but both urge that we assess what is desirable and what is possible before we undertake change for change's sake. In the readings that follow, two Brookings Institution analysts reach opposed conclusions. While James L. Sundquist believes that there isn't much that Congress can do to redress the predominance of presidential power in the constitutional system, Gary Orfield argues that there isn't much that Congress cannot do, at least domestically, if it really wants to.

Gary Orfield

CONGRESS IS AS GOOD
AS WE WANT IT TO BE

Popular Stereotypes of Congress

Americans continually proclaim their pragmatic flexibility and realism. Yet they maintain the oldest set of stable political institutions in the world and repeatedly describe the operations of that structure in terms of seldom challenged myths. These myths include a view of Congress as a declining and hopelessly fragmented body trying with little success to cope with the expansive and even dangerous power of a stronger institution, the Presidency.

Even in early 1974, when, with the deepening of the Watergate crisis, respect for Presidential authority approached its modern low point Congress was seen in an even more intensely unfavorable light. While the polls showed that only a fourth of the public approved of the job President Nixon was doing, they also showed that Congress had the respect and approval of only one American in five. Even Congress's impressive performance in the impeachment proceedings, which forced President Nixon's resignation, has produced little confidence that Congress can play a major positive role in the formation of national policy.

The assumptions about the sorry state of Congress have often been so pervasive that observers don't even bother to look at the evidence. This book will argue that the popular stereotype is fundamentally wrong. Congress is alive and well, at least in the field of domestic policy. If it is not progressive, it is usually reasonably representative and responsive. As public opinion changes, as Presidents define their constituency in different ways, and political circumstances gradually alter the membership of the House and Senate, Congress has been moving away from its traditional conservative or passive role in the development of national policy. This change became quite apparent with the beginning of the Nixon Administration. As the President moved sharply to the right on social policy, and the Supreme Court was largely neutralized by a series of four conservative appointments, Congress often remained the most progressive of the three branches in dealing with social policy issues.

The early 1970s did not see Congress become a seedbed for liberal activism. Although the legislative branch was now often more responsive to new social

Continued on p. 96

James L. Sundquist

CONGRESS CAN'T
CHECK THE PRESIDENT

The question "What has happened to our system of checks and balances?" is a difficult one to answer because there are so many different kinds of checks and balances and different things have happened to them under different circumstances. It is difficult to put together any neat generalization as to what has happened, but I won't let that deter me from trying a couple of neat opening generalizations.

The first one is that not much has happened to the system of checks and balances. There has been a bit of erosion here and there, but it has had only a marginal effect on the system. The second generalization is that the system never did amount to very much.

The reason we *think* something has happened to it is that we have discovered, as a result of Watergate and other recent events, that the system of checks and balances is inadequate. My thesis is that the system was never really there in the first place—and that fact is just now coming to light.

Confusion arises because we are accustomed to see the President and the Congress in a state of deadlock—at each other's throats. And we look at that and say, "Isn't that wonderful; they are really checking and balancing each other." But if we look closely, we will see that that situation applies only to the field of legislation, where the President and Congress share the power. As written in the Constitution, in fact, each branch of the government has a veto over the other. But most of the things that have upset people lately are not legislative matters at all.

I assume the reason for this conference is the concern people have expressed over Vietnam and Watergate. And the question is: Why hasn't our checks and balances system prevented those episodes from occurring?

Well, the reason it didn't prevent them is that these are not legislative matters, but questions of how the President uses the power that is assigned to the head of the executive branch. And the executive power under the Constitution is not shared; it is all assigned to the President. He is responsible under the Constitution for the faithful execution of the laws. The other branches only get in in a marginal way—occasionally, to some extent—on the

Continued on p. 105

"What Happened to Our Checks and Balances?" by James L. Sundquist in *Has the President Too Much Power*, Charles Roberts, ed. Copyright © 1974 by the Washington Journalism Center. Reprinted by permission of Harper & Row Publishers, Inc.

5. IS CONGRESS STRONG ENOUGH?

(Orfield, cont. from p. 94)

needs than the other principal institutions of government, there were still very broad and important areas of inaction and stalemate in domestic policy. This analysis will show that there is nothing in the institutional structure of Congress which renders the legislative branch either weak or conservative .In fact, Congress regularly exercises more power than it is credited with, and the ideological impact of its participation shifts from issue to issue and from political circumstance to political circumstance.

Our political system's lack of responsiveness to some of the very real social crises that preoccupy many intellectuals is not inherent in the Congressional process. Congressional reformers are simply wrong when they claim that institutional changes will produce "good" responses to the environmental problem, to inequitable taxation, irrational urban policies, and other major difficulties. The basic problem is more fundamental, and arises from the fact that the major progressive political force in this society, the activist liberal wing of the Democratic Party, is almost always a minority. Reformers spread the illusion that different procedures within Congress would produce answers to problems most Americans simply don't want to face. So long as Congress is a representative body, it is highly unlikely to produce decisive answers to controversial questions before public opinion accepts the necessity of action. . . .

The Changing Presidency

The Presidency, political scientists have often said, is inherently progressive because the Presidential election system has a built-in liberal bias, while Congressional power grows out of an electoral structure that magnifies local concerns. A number of Presidential campaigns during the past several decades have been organized around competition for the big blocks of electoral votes in the large urbanized states. At the same time Congressional malapportionment overrepresented rural areas in the House, while the lightly populated nonindustrial states have always been greatly overrepresented in the Senate.

Most political scientists have argued that the great importance of the big, closely divided states in Presidential elections has magnified the political influence of the urban minorities concentrated in these states. The political situation, analysts argued, made the President the natural spokesman for minority and urban needs. This very argument was used by some Congressional liberals in 1969 against adoption of a Constitutional amendment for direct election of the President.

Whatever the historical validity of these assertions, they no longer hold. In the 1964, 1968, and 1972 Presidential campaigns the GOP candidates wrote off the black vote and operated on the assumption that the real swing vote was in the suburbs. The Republican nominees saw the black vote, not as a swing vote, but as an integral locked-in element of the Democratic Party base. Turning their backs on the declining central-city electorate, they looked to the suburbs. In dramatic contrast to previous elections, the GOP adamantly refused to concede the South to the Democrats. By following a strategy that ignored the urban ghettos and put primary importance on the Southern and Border states, the Republicans were altering the Presidential political base from a source of liberal leverage to a collection of forces desiring to slow and reverse social changes already underway. . . .

The Decline of Conservative Power in Congress

While a new interpretation of the Presidential constituency was taking hold in the minds of many, something quite the opposite was beginning to become evident in Congress. As the 1970s began, the big cities enjoyed reasonable representation and growing seniority power within Congress. As political competition in the South spread and produced real challenges in former one-party districts, a growing proportion of the safe, stable, one-party districts that remained were located in the central cities, where Democratic voters frequently constitute overwhelming majorities. Given the continuing decline in central city population and the ten-year time lag before a new reapportionment, the relatively

liberal central-city constituencies were destined to have increasing overrepresentation in the House as the 1970s advanced. . . .

The Senate was now seldom in the control of the old, rigidly conservative coalition of Southern Democrats and Republicans. On a number of issues it was now possible to form a moderate-liberal majority in support of social policy proposals.

The Unchanging Criticism of Congress

Congress was changing, but perceptions of Congress remained largely fixed. Denunciations of Congressional ineptitude and legislative stalemate continued to proliferate. Inside and outside of Congress, critics said that only basic reforms could preserve Congress's intended role as a major force in American government. Even while they were sending their local incumbents back to Washington in great numbers, the American people expressed extremely low regard for Congress as an institution.

Characteristically, both the criticisms of Congress and the proposed cures are usually stated in institutional terms. We are told that the Congressional structure is inefficient or unresponsive, or that the rules screen out the competent and stifle innovation. Implicitly, however, the criticisms are political. When a critic says that Congress is not responsive, he obviously has in mind some set of national needs he believes Congress should respond to. Often these are the needs of an oppressed social group or of important decaying public institutions like the central cities and their school systems. The reform proposals often implicitly assume that procedural changes would release a suppressed progressive majority, likely to take a far more activist role in the provision of governmental services. This assumption may well be incorrect.

While the claim that certain major institutional features of Congress imposed a conservative bias on the legislative process has considerable historic validity, the recent picture is unclear. With a few notable exceptions, which run in both liberal and conservative directions, recent Congresses have rather accurately reflected the values and the confusion of the public in dealing with major issues of social change.

If the interpretation offered here is correct, liberals are unlikely to accomplish much by reforming Congressional procedures. The sobering reality is that the real obstacles are not so much on Capitol Hill as in the society as a whole. While tinkering with legislative arrangements may permit some minor improvements, basic social reforms probably require a political movement able to change public values.

Most of the time, we have the Congress we really want and the Congress we deserve. We send the same members back to Washington time after time. Congress is inherently neither liberal nor conservative. Its political tendencies change with the times, with political circumstances, with the delayed responses of the seniority system, and with tides of public opinion. In social policy battles of the early 1970s, Congress became relatively more progressive and activist than the Presidency.

Recent Areas of Confrontation

The interplay of Presidential and Congressional influences can be examined by closely looking at the development of policy in three broad areas—civil rights, education, and employment—during the period from the late Johnson Administration through the early portion of President Nixon's second term. These issues, analyzed in the central portion of this study, and others discussed in less detail thereafter, obviously cannot adequately represent the whole sweep of domestic social policy. Each, however, is a prominent and long standing political question on which there were relatively clear progressive and conservative positions. By looking at the development of several issues through a large number of legislative battles spanning several years, one obtains a more realistic portrait of the policy process than by merely examining the legislative history of one or a few bills.

The civil rights section will underline the limits of Presidential authority and the power of the Congressional veto when the President tries to reverse reforms that are already part of established law. Though he invested considerable time and prestige and intensely pressured his Congressional supporters, the President met a series of costly defeats. Even though he drew on his leadership role to deepen and exploit racial polarization, the President encountered successive frustrations.

In education policy the President's main objectives were to reduce the federal support for education and to renounce most of the existing federal leverage on state and local school systems. Congress, on the other hand, pressed each year for higher funding and retention of the federal requirements in the Great Society legislation. It was Congress that prevailed—only modestly in the financial struggle, but much more clearly in the protection of the legislative framework.

While the civil rights and school policy battles often involved legislative vetoes of conservative White House initiatives, the development of a new jobs policy is best seen as an important Democratic Party effort to initiate a new domestic policy from a Congressional base, in the face of strong Presidential opposition. Study of this effort provides an opportunity to reflect on both the possibilities and the limitations of Congressional policy initiation during a period of executive hostility. . . .

The Need for Reassessment of Congress

We must stop thinking in terms of institutional stereotypes and un-examined assumptions. Both scholars and activists need to devote more attention to reassessing the contemporary reality and future possibilities of Congressional policy initiatives. They need to think less in terms of a handful of visible new bills, and more in terms of the whole array of Congressional influences that help shape policy in a given area. It is time for critics to rethink their wildly overoptimistic promises about Congressional reform, and to recognize that Congress often only reflects the indecision or contradictory desires of the local publics and the local political structures.

It is a delusion for liberals to think that there is a hidden majority for basic social reform somewhere inside Congress that could be liberated by a few institutional reforms. Activist liberals must begin with the realization that they have only a minority in Congress, particularly in the House. On some issues, in fact, a more democratic House might be an even less progressive House. If strong progressive programs are to prevail in Congress, their supporters must first prevail in elections.

Congress and Social Policy: A Summary

The United States has been passing through a period of massive social and economic change during the past decade. Congress has played an extremely important role in shaping the uneven governmental responses to those changes. Contrary to popular cliches, the nation has not entered a period of an

5. IS CONGRESS STRONG ENOUGH?

imperial Presidency and a passive Congress, nor has deadlock totally paralyzed action in most areas of policy.

The past decade has brought profound changes in the position of blacks, women, and young people in the social and political system. The major civil rights laws were a powerful response to the central shame of American democracy, governmental enforcement of the racial caste system of the South. After decades of resistance, Congress not only passed these laws, but strengthened them and then protected them from a hostile President. Congressional action has been crucial to the women's movement's attack on concepts of female status ingrained in Western culture. Congressional action making eighteen-year-olds full citizens has had little visible immediate impact, but will surely make the political system more open and responsive to young people.

After Congress approved the vast expansion of the federal role in domestic programs in the 1960s, the determined efforts of a conservative President to reverse the trend tested the real dispositions of the Democratic Congress. The period found even the more conservative elements of the legislative branch operating more progressively than the President. This was very apparent, for example, in the massive Social Security boosts approved by the Ways and Means and the Senate Finance committees, and in the continual rejection of the President's meager education and health budgets by both Appropriations committees. In most cases Congress led the executive branch in responding to new ecological issues and in creating new tools for control of the economy.

The period of the late 1960s and early 1970s witnessed simultaneously the advance of sweeping claims of Presidential powers, and the decline of the real strength of the Presidency. During the period between the end of the Second World War and the late 1960s, Presidents enjoyed great latitude in the conduct of foreign policy and military affairs. This freedom of action, and the bipartisan Congressional support that sustained it, began to erode when rising opposition to the Vietnam War destroyed the Johnson Presidency. At first it affected the margins of international power, such as foreign military assistance, but by the early 1970s it had produced serious Congressional pressures to restrain the military apparatus and to subject Presidential action to legislative control. War powers legislation—passed over a Presidential veto—and some reductions in the defense and foreign aid budgets began to cut into the muscle of executive leadership; 1973 saw the extraordinary spectacle of Congress forcing the end of military action in Cambodia by cutting off funds, and Congress rejecting trade legislation central to the policy of detente with the U.S.S.R.

The Nixon period witnessed the resurgence of some long neglected legislative powers in domestic affairs, and the most striking Congressional rejection of a President's domestic program in decades. In the major Supreme Court nomination fights, Congress resumed an active role in the constitution of the highest Court, a power that had lain dormant for most of the twentieth century. When the early phases of the Watergate scandal indicated grave improprieties in the executive branch, Congress acted both through a massive investigation and through insistence on an independent special prosecutor to force revelation of the most serious corruption in American history. When the investigation came under Administration attack, very heavy Congressional pressure persuaded the President to retreat. Eventually he was forced to leave office.

The success of the legislators in resisting a sustained, intense White House fight against serious investigation of the scandals and in helping the press educate the public, and forcing the President to yield unprecedented personal records was a tribute to the vitality of Congress. The experience seemed certain to increase both Congressional power and Congressional vigilance for some time to come. Anyone who doubts the continuing reality of Congressional power need only read the transcripts of the extraordinary White House tapes that President Nixon was forced to release by pressure from the House Judiciary Committee. Amid all the plots and the bitter, candid criticisms of men and institutions, it is evident that President Nixon and his chief advisors

retained a fear of Congressional power. While their discussions are full of plans to thwart the independence and manipulate the operations of various governmental institutions, the mass media, and the criminal justice system, there is a continual recognition of the limited power the White House can exercise over Congress.

In 1974 the House Judiciary Committee began the impeachment process for the second time in American history. The process had been virtually forgotten since Congress failed to impeach Andrew Johnson after the Civil War, but now it worked. Only when impeachment and conviction seemed certain did the President resign. The revival of Congress's ultimate weapon surely lends strength to the legislative branch, and diminishes the power and autonomy of future Presidents.

Presidential power rests to a substantial degree on the sense of respect and legitimacy accorded to the office of President. One certain effect of the Watergate scandal and the President's resignation has been to weaken that respect for some time to come, thus increasing the relative power of Congress.

While the Watergate disaster dramatized Congress's investigatory power and resurrected the idea of impeachment, its drama often obscured more mundane facts about the period. In the long and often unpublicized domestic policy struggles of the period, Congress responded to intense and single-minded White House pressure without yielding its role.

The period of Presidential reaction on social policy under President Nixon showed that the close tie between Congress and various organized constituencies could have liberal as well as conservative consequences. Coming to office with the belief that he had a mandate to reverse many of the domestic innovations of the Great Society, the President encountered determined resistance from Congress. Congress responded by rejecting a higher portion of Nixon legislative proposals than those of any recent President, even though Nixon presented a relatively slim set of innovations. Only by stretching executive powers and spending his political authority in bitter confrontations with Congress over vetoes and impoundments was the President able to slow the momentum of those programs. Eventually, the price to be paid was strong Congressional attempts to cut back on the powers of the executive branch.

In arguing that Congress possesses a substantial capacity to initiate new national policies, and that those policies may well be more "progressive" or "responsive" than positions taken by a President, this book certainly does not mean to support another false view of Congress. While Congress may be *relatively* more activist than a conservative President, it can hardly be described as a liberal institution. The major liberal force in American politics is the Northern and Western wing of the Democratic Party. Only when political circumstances give that wing of the party an operating majority in Congress (a rare circumstance) or predominant influence in the executive branch (a more common occurrence) does that institution become the primary focus for policy innovation.

During the Nixon Administration Congress succeeded in putting a few major new social issues on the national agenda, and in protecting much of the Great Society framework. On many other issues, however, its record was far more mixed. Design of new housing policies, for example, was long stalled by a stalemate within Congress, as well as by one between Congress and the White House. Congress delegated vast powers over the economy to the executive branch without making basic policy decisions. Congress preserved existing civil rights laws, aimed primarily at the classic Southern forms of discrimination, but proved incapable of developing policies to cope with the intensifying racial separation of the urban North. There were few significant new ideas in education policy in the legislation of the early 1970s, and the intense national discussion of health care needs yielded little on Capitol Hill. Efforts to reform the tax structure or to alter the basic assumptions of welfare policy were largely barren. The list goes on and on.

Judged against the national goals of activist liberal groups, or even against the Democratic Party platform, the record of Congress was fundamentally inadequate. Congress has not responded forcefully to a number of evident social needs. The obstacle has been sometimes the President, and sometimes Congress itself.

The important thing to remember is that the failings criticized by activists are usually not failings produced by the structure or procedures of Congress, but by the vision of its members. The short-comings—and many of the achievements—result from reasonably effective Congressional representation of widely held and often contradictory values of the public and of the members' active and important constituents. The unwillingness to move forward in some significant areas of social policy reflects far less the inadequacies of Congress as an organization than the failure of middle-class Americans to recognize that any social crisis exists. The basic reason why neither Congress nor the President is truly liberal is that liberalism normally represents a minority position in the United States—a fact often obscured by the assumption that the Democratic Party is a liberal party, rather than an exceedingly broad coalition.

Much of the national movement for extensive Congressional reform is based on false assumptions. Reform and rationalization of committee jurisdiction, chairmen's powers, the budget process, Congressional staff capacity, etc., may produce a more efficient legislative body, more equitable to individual members, and perhaps better able to compete with the executive branch. These are worthwhile goals,

but they are not likely to transform the substance of Congressional decisions. Reformers who promise an institutional answer to a political question are likely to be disappointed. There are no shortcuts. Probably the only way to build a new Congress is to undertake the hard political work necessary to send new men and women to Capitol Hill.

Although Congress is neither the liberal institution some would wish, nor the conservative institution many believe it to be, it is a powerful force in the construction of national policy. While the political circumstances of depression, wars and international crises, and a burgeoning executive branch have often served to magnify the Presidency, the remarkable fact is that Congress has preserved the Constitutional model of fragmented power through an era of serious parliamentary decline in most Western nations. If anything, the political scandals of the early 1970s have only reinforced this model, increasing public support for the assertion of Congressional authority.

The difficulty of weighing the role of Congress in the policy process is magnified by the complex and often obscurely indirect nature of Congressional influence. Fortunately for this analysis, the rare circumstance of clear and frequently harsh ideological and partisan differences between the President and Congress during the Nixon Administration brought out into the open much of the continuing but often subliminal contest for power. This makes possible a more accurate

5. IS CONGRESS STRONG ENOUGH?

perception of the policy process, and a growing awareness of the largely unused reservoirs of Congressional authority that can be drawn upon : when a President neglects the tradition of consultation and compromise with the legislative branch.

In a society experiencing rapid social and political change, the major democratic institutions reflect shifting constituencies and evolving political alliances. At the present time these forces tend to be moving Congress away from its very conservative past, and the Presidency away from the historical circumstances that once made the White House the powerful spokesman for urban minorities. The very heavy dependence of GOP Presidential candidates on Southern support and the growing power in the House of liberal Democrats from safe one-party urban seats are two signs of these changes. Nothing suggests, however, that there is anything permanent or historically inevitable about these changes. The time has come for students of American politics to recognize the limits of institutional generalizations based on the political circumstances of the recent past.

The abuses of Presidential power revealed by the Watergate scandals have tended to replace the popular image of the beneficience of Presidential power with a popular fear of the abuse of executive authority. The long-established tendency of progressives to look to the White House for responsive leadership is being replaced by a judgment that

the President is excessively powerful, and by a tendency to look to Congress for salvation. Both images assume that the President possesses vast, even excessive, powers. While this is surely true in the fields of foreign policy, military affairs, and national security, it is not true in the development of the nation's social policy. Thus, for example, institutional changes intended to reduce the power of a corrupt executive branch may have the consequence of constricting the already limited power of a future liberal President to initiate and implement major social reforms.

It has been a disservice—and one currently conducive to a crushing disillusionment with politics—for academics to spread the belief that Presidential power is better than Congressional power. (What they actually meant was that during the period between the early 1930s and the mid-1960s, the Presidency was usually controlled by the Democratic Party, and that the President tended to respond to a more liberal constituency than that of the Congressional leadership.) It would, of course, be equally misleading to assume that Congressional power is better, more progressive, or less corrupt.

It is vital to realize that the making of national domestic policy takes place in a context of genuinely divided power, and that the Congress as well as the President possesses both the ability to initiate and the power to veto major policy changes. The system works well when there is a clear consensus in the country, or clear control of both branches by the dominant wing of either party. Usually these conditions are not present and the system is biased either toward compromise and incremental change, or toward confrontation and inaction. The Nixon period clearly shows that the modern Presidency can be quite as efficient an engine of negative social policy as was Congress during certain earlier progressive Administrations.

It is only fair to recognize that much of the criticism that has been aimed at Congress has been misdirected. It is really criticism of the inefficiencies and delays built into the American Constitutional system, and of the nebulous and often contradictory ideological bases of the alliances that constitute the national political parties. Failure to

correctly identify these underlying causes leads one to misjudge the solutions.

The people of the United States generally have the kind of legislative body they want and deserve. It is a Congress that has the power to take decisive action, but most of whose members rarely believe the public demands such change. It is an evolving institution and an increasingly representative one. It has great power but rarely selects leaders who use that power with energy, skill, and imagination. With a few significant exceptions, the altering of its internal rules will not change its decisions much. Congress is likely to be a moderately progressive institution in the next years. If it is to be much more than that—or less—its membership must be significantly changed.

(Cont. from p. 95, Sundquist, "Congress Can't Check the President")

question of how the President uses the executive power. I have broken that down into six ways.

The first is the intervention by the judicial branch. The courts can blow the whistle if the President acts illegally.

Then, there are five categories of checks and balances that the Congress exercises.

The first is the power to confirm appointments.

The second is legislative control. If the President uses his power in a way that the Congress doesn't like,

it can act through the legislative process.

And the third is the power of the purse. If the President acts in a way the Congress doesn't like, it can take budgetary action.

Fourth, there is a generalized function called Congressional oversight, which is really an implied power growing out of the legislative and budget powers.

And, finally, there is impeachment.

To answer the question of what has happened to checks and

5. IS CONGRESS STRONG ENOUGH?

balances, let's look at each one of these in turn and see what has happened to it.

First, the check by the courts. I think we can say there that nothing has happened, but that this has always been a very limited power in terms of checking the kind of abuses we are talking about. It only operates after the fact, after the damage has been done. There is no real power in this particular check and balance to prevent anything illegal from happening.

And second, probably more important, it has no bearing at all on decisions that are legal but simply unwise. The President can use his powers improperly in lots of perfectly legal ways.

And then there is a third problem: In very many cases you can't effectively get into the courts. There were a number of litigants who tried to take the Vietnam War to court, including the State of Massachusetts. But it turned out to be a very ineffective way of exercising a check upon Presidential power.

Now, impeachment is much the same as the judicial process—a trial process. It has all the same weaknesses except that since it is the most extreme form of check it can be used only under the most extreme circumstances—again after the fact, again only after serious crimes have been committed. So it doesn't operate as an effective check either.

So on these two checks and balances I think my two generalizations apply. Nothing much has happened to these powers. They still exist and are still being used as

effectively as ever. The Watergate proceedings show that the judicial process is still an important check after the fact. But they have those weaknesses that I have enumerated.

Now, the power of confirming appointments. If the two checks that I have mentioned operate only after the fact, the confirmation of appointments operates much too much before the fact. In a confirmation proceding, there is really no way for the Senate to know who is going to abuse the power of the office it is confirming the man for. Some of the leading figures in the Watergate affair, we know, were confirmed back in 1969—Attorney General Mitchell and Secretary of Commerce Stans. Even as late as 1973, Bud Krogh was confirmed as Under Secretary of Transportation. And I suspect if Haldeman, Ehrlichman, and Colson, E. Howard Hunt, James McCord, anybody you wanted to name, had had their names submitted in 1969 for confirmation as members of the White House staff, they all would have been confirmed because nobody then had the foggiest idea what they were going to do.

If the Senate could unconfirm a man in office, that would be a real check and balance, but that power is denied—for a very good reason—by the Constitution. Once in, they stay in. So the two generalizations seem also to apply here: Confirmation power is still being used as it always has been, but it is really not much of a check and balance in terms of preventing something unwise or even illegal from happening.

The fourth check is the power to correct the President by formal legislative action. It is true that if the President does something Congress doesn't like, it can write a law outlawing his action. But this has very severe limitations, too. The most obvious one is that the President can veto the correction that the Congress makes. And that can be sustained if the President has support of as much as one-third plus one member of either house. And it is very rare that a President's veto can be overridden. His own party, which always has more than one-third of one house, is very hesitant about voting no-confidence in the President on a really serious Constitutional question.

Moreover, the law being abused is in most cases—presumably in the view of Congress in all cases—a good law, or it wouldn't be on the books in the first place. Take a case like the President raising the price of milk right after big cash contributions were received by the Committee to Reelect the President. If the Congress considers that as an abuse, what can they really do about it through legislation? They can repeal the milk law, but they want the milk law on the books. They can't set the price of milk in the statute because it has got to be handled flexibly. There is really no way they can alter the law to prevent the President from misusing his discretionary power.

The power of the purse, the budget control, is very much the same because the budget is enacted through the legislative process; it is written in appropriation bills which have to be passed by both houses and are subject to veto. So all the same limitations that apply to legislation apply to the power of the purse. It operates only after the fact. If the President abuses his power in using this year's money, all the Congress can do is take away next year's money. But they would have to take the money away from programs that they believe in and want properly executed. So it would be a case of throwing the baby out with the bath.

If, for example, the FBI were to abuse its functions in the eyes of Congress, what can it do? Can it abolish the FBI? That is not going to serve its purposes. Taking away the bureau's funds isn't going to serve its purpose either. What Congress wants is for the money to be properly expended. And if it attaches a legislative rider on an appropriation bill putting certain restrictions on the use of the money, that applies only to the future, not the past. And, again, it is subject to veto.

It is commonly said that the Congress should have and could have cut off the funds for the Vietnam War and controlled the President that way. But it is easier said than done. Suppose they put in a rider saying that the money could not be used for purposes of prosecuting the Vietnam War beyond a certain date. All the President has to do is veto that and then the onus is back on the Congress. Should Congress let the Defense Department go without any funds—in

5. IS CONGRESS STRONG ENOUGH?

effect abolish the Defense Department? Since that is inconceivable, the Congress is bound sooner or later to capitulate and write something in there that the President will accept. There is a lot of bluffing back and forth, but in the end, it turns out to be a very, very limited kind of power.

And, finally, there is the Congressional oversight function which, as I said, is really an implied power. If Congress has the power to legislate and the power to enact the budget, then it presumably has the power to collect information and hold hearings and so on.

This is only the power, however, of publicity. Congressional committees can hold hearings, they can expose, threaten, they can bulldoze and they can intimidate, but they can't command. A committee of Congress can bring the spotlight of public opinion to focus on an issue and this is important. It is very much like what the media do. And they often work in tandem. The press exposes something and the Congress then holds hearings and dramatizes the situation—which is the case in Watergate. Or it can operate the other way around. The Congressional committee can expose something which then the press picks up. And if between the two of them they can influence public opinion, then they can have a bearing on the way the President uses his power. But it is very indirect, and it takes a long time to take effect.

But nothing has happened to this power. I think we see it used, in the

case of the Watergate hearings, probably as effectively as it has ever been used.

So that goes through the six types of checks and balances that we can identify. And, to come back to my generalizations, they are all still there, they all are operating about as effectively as ever. Nothing has been changed fundamentally. But taken all together, the checks don't amount to very much. Essentially, the executive remains unchecked unless he does something illegal or unless Congress chooses to change laws or cut off funds after the fact and has enough votes to override a veto.

If the President simply acts unwisely within legal limits and one-third plus one of either house sustains him, there are no checks and balances, and there never have been. There is only the recourse on the part of Congress to public opinion to try to right the situation.

Now, having said all this, I would say that there has been some erosion even in these weak checks and balances which has rendered them even weaker. And I will make a generalization about this, too. It is that the forces that have brought about this weakening are really not reversible. These shifts have happened for very good reasons which I think would be sustained by public opinion.

The first weakening we can see is a gradual shift in the boundary between what is legislative and what is executive. Some of this shift has taken place with the consent of Congress. For instance, one of the most conspicuous shifts was the power delegated in about 1935 to the President to negotiate trade agreements. Congress used to have the tariff-making power, but it discovered that if it made a tariff in a given year it couldn't do anything else, and it couldn't do the job well, that it was the kind of process that was subject to infinite corruption. And they really had to turn it over to the President and let him handle it after that.

A similar kind of legislation passed for the reorganization of the executive branch. Reorganization powers were delegated to the President subject to the right of either house of Congress to reject what the President did. We have a current example in price and wage control. This is obviously a power that the Congress quite properly feels that it can't exercise itself. It can't legislate price and wage standards.

The budget appears to be going in the same direction. The Congress is struggling valiantly right now to reorganize itself so that it can keep control ultimately of the budget process. But last year both houses of Congress passed bills in effect delegating to the President the right to cut the budget and make the ultimate decisions as to what the appropriations should be. They failed to become law only because the two houses couldn't agree on the form of the law. Anyway, this function also appears in the second category of movement of boundary that has occurred—without Congressional consent, the President

has accomplished the same result through impoundment of funds.

In the movement of the boundary without explicit consent of Congress, the biggest area is in the foreign affairs, war-making power area. It may have been the intent of the founders that Congress should have the real say about whether the country gets into war or not. But in this century, that power has gradually shifted. That, I suppose, is basically because the world moves much faster these days.

While President Wilson could talk about open covenants openly arrived at, none of the other countries think seriously in those terms, and we have discovered that in international affairs we have got to play the game the same way. The President has got to have the power to give ultimatums and respond to ultimatums and, as John Foster Dulles said, take us to the brink of war. The Congress can't conduct foreign relations and, well, war is an element of foreign relations, after all.

It is significant, when we talk about reversing these trends, that the Congress in its current legislation has not even seriously proposed to take the war-making powers back. All it has put in the Javits-Zablocki bill is that the President can go ahead and get us into a war, but he has to consult Congress afterward within a specified time period. Well, after the damage is done, it is going to be pretty hard for the Congress to extricate the country.

It is a bit like when Theodore

5.   IS CONGRESS STRONG ENOUGH?

Roosevelt asked Congress for the authority to send the Navy around the world and they said no. So he sent it halfway around the world and said to Congress, "You bring it back." They came up with the funds.

The same thing is true, really, of the economy. It is necessary if we are having an inflationary period or are on the verge of recession that the President act quickly and decisively with price and wage controls or whatever else it might be. And here, I think, we are going to conclude sooner or later that the boundary hasn't shifted far enough, that the President really has got to have discretionary power over the tax rate so that he can impose fiscal action quickly and decisively at the time when fiscal action will have its greatest effect.

You may recall President Kennedy's comparison of our government with the British government, when he pointed out he and Prime Minister Macmillan reached the decision about the same time they had to have a big tax cut in order to stimulate their respective economies. Prime Minister Macmillan got his tax cut through in six weeks. And at the end of three years, when President Kennedy was assassinated, his hadn't gone through Congress yet. But it was needed three years earlier. By the time it was enacted, it could very well have been the wrong kind of fiscal medicine.

In the case of impoundment, it may be that the trend will be reversed and that power, or part of it, will be taken away from the President. We will have to see what the courts do. But in any case, I do not believe that we are going to see any decisive reversal of the general drift of powers from the Congress to the President through conversion of legislative matters to executive-type action.

The second trend that has weakened the control of Congress is the sheer expansion of the government. I can remember when I was in the Bureau of the Budget, the budget was $50 billion. It is now five times as large. Within the last decade, it has increased from $100 billion to $250 billion.

It is not so much the size of those numbers as the diversity and character of the programs that make the difference. The scope of government has expanded immeasurably. And yet the Congress is still a single institution with the same number of members and the same potential for committee work. There is just a limit on how much an individual member of Congress or a Congressional committee can oversee. And the Congress has been slow to equip itself with staff which would extend its reach, while the President has expanded his staff from practically nothing only thirty-five years ago to several hundred people. But no matter how Congress reorganizes itself, it depends on the members. And they can extend themselves only so far.

The oversight is divided among committees and subcommittees. If the chairman of a particular committee happens to be interested and zealous and has time for it and has the temperament for it and does his homework, and has the staff, he can do a good job of oversight. But it is bound to be pretty spotty because assignments are somewhat random. And it often happens that the man in charge of overseeing a particular agency—like the Commodity Exchange Authority in the Department of Agriculture, say—really isn't interested in commodity exchanges. And if he were to master the subject to the point where he could do an effective job of oversight, he wouldn't be able to do anything else, because it is that complicated a subject.

As for staff, well, staff on Capitol Hill is not usually much of a match for the staff in the executive branch. Again, they are spread terribly thin. You have got thousands of executives and policy-making people working in the executive branch. You really can't match them on the Hill on anything close to a one-for-one basis. But beyond that, there is no merit system covering employment on the Hill. And there is no tenure. The result is that a very high percentage of amateurs is appointed in the first place—many for patronage reasons rather than reasons of professional competence. And the turnover is high. So about the time that a Congressional staff man learns the job, he is apt to be in the process of leaving.

It is not a very satisfying job anyway. Oversight is essentially a dull occupation unless something is happening. It is a rare bird who can really keep a close watch on an executive agency unless his boss happens to be equally interested in it. There are a few rare birds on Capitol Hill who do this job and don't go to seed on it, but they *are* rare.

And, finally, the third trend is the trend toward secrecy. There has always been secret diplomacy, but it has become much more the standard. The big new development is the extension of secrecy in domestic affairs through the doctrine of executive privilege. That, too, is being tested in the courts. And this is an obvious area where something conceivably could happen to the checks and balances system, strengthening the position of Congress to get information. But I suspect when it is all over, the area of executive privilege will still be very extensive, particularly in anything pertaining to foreign affairs.

So I would say that none of these things are going to be changed much. We are not going to change the basic nature of Congress, which makes it difficult for it to do an oversight job under any circumstances. We are not going to move the boundary back, putting things back in the legislative area that are in the executive area now. We are not going to give up secret diplomacy. If we curtail impoundment and curtail executive privilege through the judgments of the courts, that will be about all, and that won't change the balance between the President and Congress very much.

One reason for the widespread impression that the system of checks and balances has been changed drastically is not because of the power that the President has taken away from the Congress, but because of another kind of power, the power that he has pulled up from elsewhere in the executive branch, primarily from the Cabinet.

Nothing in the Constitution ever said the President had to share power with a Cabinet. The Cabinet was not mentioned in the Constitution. The habit of sharing power grew up somewhat by accident and from the tendency to copy what was being done in Britain. This continued to a considerable extent right into the twentieth century. But it was bound to happen sooner or later that a President would realize he didn't have to do that. He didn't have to offset himself with people who had independent power bases, who could cause him real trouble, who could act independently and serve as a check on him. After all, what President really wants to be checked? It wasn't long before somebody discovered he could have a Cabinet of yes-men—in the immortal words of John Ehrlichman, the kind of men who when the White House asked them to jump would ask only, "How high?"

Power never really existed in the Cabinet anyway, even when its members had political standing and could defy the President. When they did defy the President, there was nothing they could do but resign. Bryan as Secretary of State was opposed to what Wilson was doing in foreign policy at the time of our entry into the First World War. All Bryan could do was protest and resign. Wilson still had the power. You also remember the famous Lincoln statement at the Cabinet meeting when he took the poll on the Emancipation Proclamation: "Seven nays and one aye. The ayes have it."

Now, the putting of lesser men in the Cabinet—which has reached its climax right now in men responsive to the President's bidding—has coincided with two other trends: first, the building up of a staff in the White House so that the President can make his will known; and, second, the planting of people in the agencies so that if the Cabinet members are not responsive the President and his staff can go around the members of the Cabinet and deal with people who are compliant.

As for the growth of the White House staff, I doubt if this trend is going to be reversed, because the development of White House power arises from a very real need. The government does have to be coordinated, and you really can't have every department head as an independent satrap running his own principality and going his own way. The programs of the government have got to be interrelated in all kinds of ways. The President is the only elected person responsible to the people, and he does come in with a mandate, and he does have the right to have people who will carry out his mandate. You do have to have at the head of the government something like a general staff. That may shift in its composition somewhat from time to time, but it is not going to be dismantled.

When the appropriation bill for the Executive Office of the President came up this last time around Senator Mondale proposed a couple of token cuts just to indicate that the members of Congress thought that the Executive Office of the President was overbuilt and was aggrandizing itself. It is significant that even these token cuts were defeated. And nobody has proposed any serious cuts.

So that is where we stand, it seems to me. We can't move the boundary and give powers back to Congress. Checks and balances in Congress have always been weak, and there isn't really any way to strengthen them. Checks and balances that were in the Cabinet have been destroyed, and we really can't expect to see them revived, except occasionally for short periods. In other words, the day of the strong President is here to stay. It is a necessity of the times. People want it that way. Ask the people who the great Presidents were, and they don't name any weak Presidents; they name the strong Presidents. They name Jackson and Lincoln, Jefferson and Washington, Franklin Roosevelt and Teddy Roosevelt. They are the men who built the Presidency and made a practice of kicking the Congress around. People don't even remember the names of the weak Presidents of the nineteenth century who thought as a matter of principle the Presidency should be weak.

I don't mean I am happy about this, but I think that is realistically what the situation is.

POSTSCRIPT

IS CONGRESS STRONG ENOUGH?

Between Gary Orfield's contention that Congress has the power to be coequal with the President, and James Sundquist's view that Congress cannot be given that power, there are those who hold that a stronger Congress is possible only if we undertake the necessary constitutional or statutory change. There is one question that might be asked before we consider whether Congress can provide effective leadership and whether it can check the President. That question is: Should it?

Perhaps the difference in prevailing attitudes toward and expectations of Congress and the President is reflected in the abundant and exciting books on the presidency. Almost every major presidential adviser seems inclined to add to the list. By contrast, books on Congress are far fewer and too often are pedestrian and pedantic. Among the more stimulating and insightful recent books on Congress are David Mayhew, *Congress: The Electoral Connection* (Yale, 1974), which begins its analysis with the assumption that the congressperson's principal motive is reelection, and Eric Redman, *The Dance of Legislation* (Simon and Schuster, 1973), which, in focusing upon a single Senate bill (the National Health Service Corps Act of 1970) gives a vivid and particularized portrait of the legislative process. Mark Green, *Who Runs Congress?* (Bantam/Grossman, revised 1975), is a muckraking survey that dwells upon what's wrong with Congress, and depressingly concludes that there is a great deal of that. A student new to the subject might enjoy a lively, unfootnoted journalistic account, such as Warren Weaver, a *New York Times* correspondent, has provided in a readable and anecdotal book, *Both Your Houses* (Praeger, 1972).

Can Congress occupy a constitutional role comparable to that envisioned by the Framers? Or has its function been diminished by irreversible circumstances resulting in the ascendancy of the President? It is easy to lose sight of these questions when we consider the details of congressional procedure: the continuing, although diminishing, influence of seniority, the unrepresentativeness of committee power, the delaying tactic of the Senate filibuster, and what impresses so many Americans as the cumbersomeness of congressional operation. Dealing with congressional procedure is important; however, a Congress that cannot function efficiently is not likely to play its best role in the constitutional system.

ISSUE 6

IS THE
PRESIDENT TOO POWERFUL?

"Energy in the executive," said Alexander Hamilton in 1787, "is a leading character in the definition of good government." Hamilton dreamed of a vast American "empire" of manufacturing and commerce. An energetic executive was to be the lynchpin of the empire. Defense against foreign and domestic enemies would require "decision, activity, secrecy, and dispatch," which only a single, powerful executive could provide. The President was to be "the bulwark of national security."

Nearly two centuries later, Hamilton's vision seems to have acquired a life of its own, growing into something which Hamilton himself could not have dreamed of. As chief executive and commander-in-chief, the President today commands six million employees and carries a sword which would surely startle a Caesar or a Bonaparte. He has also been called our chief legislator, chief of state, chief diplomat, chief of party, and manager of our prosperity. But even this litany does not take the full measure of his powers. Hamilton was deeply suspicious of popular government, but it has turned out to be the greatest spring of all for "energy in the executive." Today's President is more than just a manager; he has become an embodiment of popular sovereignty, a "steward of the people," as President Theodore Roosevelt called himself—or, in the words of a more recent admirer of the office, a "republican king."

After Vietnam and Watergate some Americans became less sanguine about the powers of the presidency. Hamilton considered "decision, activity, secrecy, and dispatch" to be the unique virtues of the executive, but some observers now wondered whether "decision" could not at times resemble arrogance, "dispatch" recklessness, and "secrecy" furtiveness. Hamilton's invocation of "national security" also sounded hollow to those who remembered how far that claim was stretched during the Johnson and Nixon administrations—far enough to cover everything from uinilateral warmaking to domestic spying and burglary.

Some of the more recent critics of the executive branch had once been promoters of the activist presidency. From the early days of the New Deal to the middle of the 1960s American liberals tended to regard the President as the people's tribune, and the Congress as a patchwork of special interests. But as President Johnson led the nation deeper into Vietnam, many of these same liberals began to worry about "the arrogance of power" in the White House. And by the time of the Watergate revelations it was Congress, not the presidency, which seemed to them the authentic voice of the American people. The President, formerly the people's tribune,was now an ominous "imperial" figure.

Gerald Ford's presidency may have quieted these fears to some extent. Liberals had no love for his policies, but as a person he seemed totally free of imperial pretensions. Nevertheless, the White House which Jimmy Carter inherited in January of 1977 was charged with enormous powers. The question of whether those powers are excessive should not turn upon our opinion of President Carter's personality, or even on our reaction to his behavior in office.

In the selections which follow, Theodore Sorensen, a former top aide to President Kennedy, and Michael Novak, a social analyst, try to construct their arguments upon more objective considerations. Novak builds his case for modifying the President's powers on the need for constitutional balance. Sorensen, on the other hand, holds fast to his pre-Vietnam position that the health of the nation requires a strong presidency.

Michael Novak

REFORMING
THE PRESIDENCY

Every four years, Americans elect a king—but not only a king, also a high priest and a prophet. It does not matter that we are a practical and sophisticated people, no longer (we think) influenced by symbols, myths, or rituals. To what our president represents, we react with passion.

The president of the United States is no mere manager of an insurance firm. The way he lives affects our image of ourselves. His style and his tastes weigh upon our spirits. Eisenhower encouraged a "silent" generation, Kennedy an "activist" decade. Nixon at first made some feel solid and appreciative and others, even in the beginning, heavy and ashamed. Intimate and personal feelings are affected by our experience of various presidents.

The symbolic power of the president is real. Ten million police officers, heads of boards of education, lawyers, judges, realtors, union leaders, and local officials calibrate their daily decisions according to the support or the resistance they expect from the White House. What will the Justice Department do, or fail to do? The president is able to make his own views felt in every town and village of the nation, by compulsion and enforcement, by imitation and antipathy. On the local level, if ultimately one expects support far up the line, great risks can be taken. If one is left to one's own resources merely, one must confront the local balance of powers.

Some speak of the "moral leadership" of the presidency as though what we need is a moral man out in front, like a cavalry officer lowering his saber. Yet moral leadership in the presidency is not something habitually "out in front" of us, but something that infiltrates our imaginations and our hearts. The president, whoever he is, affects our *internal* images of authority, legitimacy, leadership, concern. By his actions, he establishes a limit to national realism. What he *is* drives us away from America and makes us feel like exiles—or attracts our cooperation. Cumulatively, the presidents under whom we happen to live influence our innermost attitudes.

For this reason, the election of a president is an almost religious task; it intimately affects the life of the spirit, our identity. Who the man is determines in real measure who we are. Thus, the swirling, otherwise inexplicable passions

Continued on p. 120

Theodore Sorensen

THE DANGER
OF AN IMPOTENT PRESIDENCY

The weak Nixon Presidency, masquerading as a strong and powerful Presidency, obscured the fact that this country today requires strong presidential leadership. Not unaccountable leadership, not a monopoly on leadership, but strong leadership nevertheless. Our only nationally elected executive must possess the flexibility and strength necessary to provide this country with responsible direction. We have survived caretaker Presidents in the past, but the price of those deceptively quiet periods in our history has always had to be paid later.

It is not altogether bad and certainly not coincidental that the flow of power to the Presidency has accelerated at times of major international crisis. Within his lawful authority, the Executive—and only the Executive—can move with the speed, energy and flexibility such crises usually require. Now the problems we face are global, affecting all peoples: the critical shortages of food, fertilizer, fuel, and certain other basic commodities; the twin failures of arms control and population control; the spread of world-wide inflation and the spectre of world-wide depression. Within the last two years the leaders of virtually every major democracy on earth found themselves replaced or in political trouble because of their inability to cope effectively with these and other problems. I would not go as far as Senator J. William Fulbright (of all people) went in the 1961 Stevens Memorial Lecture at Cornell, when he argued:

> that the price of democratic survival in a world of aggressive totalitarianism
> is to give up some of the democratic luxuries of the past . . . [through] the
> conferral of greatly increased authority on the President.

But the present critical hour of mounting crises and leadership vacuum is a most unlikely time to seek a passive or powerless President in the most powerful nation on earth.

Nor was it coincidental that the other quantum leap in permanent presidential power was spurred by the Great Depression. A single point of responsibility, speaking for the whole people, representing in egalitarian fashion the interests of the powerless as well as the powerful, was indispensable in the 1930s to pull this country through spiritually as well as economically.

Continued on p. 127

6. IS THE PRESIDENT TOO POWERFUL?

(Novak, cont. from p. 118)

of many presidential elections. Not only power or money are at stake, important as these are, but our own inner life. The presence of one man rather than another, the ascendance of Nixon (say) rather than the ascendance of McGovern, has great power to depress or to elate, to liberate energies or to shrink them.

Eugene McCarthy said we must "depersonalize" the presidency, "demystify" the office. Without separating kingship from administration, that can scarcely be accomplished. Today the symbolic role inheres in the office. It is enhanced by the nation's bigness, diversity, and tightening networks of power.

Dostoevsky once wrote that an invisible filament of humble charity covers the entire earth. An act at any one point on the earth, he imagined, reverberates until it touches every other person. In our day, on television, a single act simultaneously inhabits the fantasy of millions of humans everywhere, *becomes* them, obliges them to accept or to reject, enters immediately into the structures of their psyche. We do not know what the truth is, but if on television the president says our ships were attacked in the Gulf of Tonkin, then that attack (even if it did not occur) occupies our attention and demands that we refute it or accept it or dismiss it. Whatever we do, there stands the president's assertion, solid until painstakingly disproved. This power over our attention, over our power to structure issues, is so enormous that it dwarfs all others.

The president of the United States is one of the great symbolic powers known to human history. His actions seep irrepressibly into our hearts. He dwells in us. We cannot keep him out. That is why we wrestle against him, rise up in hatred often, wish to retch—or, alternatively, feel good, feel proud, as though his achievements were ours, his wit the unleashing of powers of our own.

Hands are stretched toward him over wire fences at airports like hands extended toward medieval sovereigns or ancient prophets. One wonders what mystic participation our presidents convey, what witness from what other world, what form of cure or heightened life. The president arouses waves of "power," "being," "superior reality," as if where he is is history. It is true that the president's hand is on the button of destruction. Life and death are in his hands; honor and dishonor too. What he does affects the daily life of each of us in ways witch doctors could scarcely even dream. His office is, in quite modern and sophisticated form, a religion in a secular state. It evokes responses familiar in all the ancient religions of the world. It fills a perennial vacuum at the heart of human expectations. . . . It would be much easier for the president if he were a prime minister, called simply to manage the affairs of government in as practical and unadorned a way as possible. Yet, in American politics what critics refer to as "the cult of personality" arises. It arises not because it is willed either by the citizenry or by the presidents themselves, but because of the nature and the limits of the human imagination.

Causes, institutions, and administrative processes must be personified before humans can passionately engage them. Humans are flesh and blood, and they understand best what is flesh and blood. Thus, Martin Luther King made black civil rights a cause that it has ceased to be since his death. Thus, Eugene McCarthy in 1968 observed that antiwar sentiment in the United States needed to be personified in order to be a political force, and he agreed to step forward as the person. McCarthy's deed was a great one and it catalyzed a great new force in American politics, the new politics of the "new class." Yet, great as that force is in American life, it is no stronger than its ability to personify itself in a leader able to command the dedication of a wide range of people. Leaderless, it is ineffective . . . .

Thus, talk about "doing away with the cult of personality" or "demythologizing the presidency" must be taken as gestures toward an unrealistic rationalism. The president dominates not only the news, but also the language of policy, the shape and pace of legislation, and the spirit of appointments to the federal courts. His idiosyncrasies, ambitions, and failures dominate more conversations than those of any other citizen—as truly if he is unpopular as if he is popular. Let us be as skeptical as may be, we are living in a symbolic world over which the president has unparalleled power. To cease believing in his power will not make it go away. To say we must not vest our hopes or fears in him runs counter to the plain fact that he has nuclear power at his fingertips, more police power than any sovereign in history, more power to dominate the organs of public opinion than any other human, more power in defining who are the nation's enemies, more power over the military and the making (if not the declaring) of war than any citizen or group of citizens.

Thus, the president is rather more like a shaman than we might wish. Our lives *do* depend on him. A person with power over life and death is raised above a merely pragmatic level. He is surrounded, as it were, with a nimbus of magic. He necessarily lives on a level that must seem to him "above" that of other humans. The fact that he *is* human gives a sort of reassurance about which we endlessly read— that he eats breakfast food, prefers mysteries, listens to Bach or Lawrence Welk. But our survival is linked to his deeds. Our lives participate in his. His nerves, his wisdom, his panic, his steadiness make us vulnerable. Even if we have contempt for him, he has power over the shape and direction of our lives. If he decides that the great moral conflict of our time is permissiveness or the need for individual selfishness, not only must those who disagree fight against the ordinary tides of evil, they must also fight against the respectability the president gives their opponents. If he symbolizes an America we despise, he divides our own hearts against themselves.

6. IS THE PRESIDENT TOO POWERFUL?

The president also affects the cultural tone of the entire nation. It makes a difference if he prefers Bach to Welk or John Wayne to Dustin Hoffman or enjoys the company of Pablo Casals rather than Bob Hope and Billy Graham. Such choices on his part send out a signal either that discrimination is worth an effort, or else that it is well to glory in what happens to be popular.

Thus, the president enters into the innermost symbols by which we identify ourselves. We do not think about him all the time; on many days we give him not a thought. It is the property of basic symbolic forms to influence us even when we are not conscious of them. When the president acts as president, he acts in our name. He is us. If he goes by a way we do not approve, he uses us against ourselves. This alone is a remarkable power. . . .

The presidency has in recent decades acquired symbolic power far beyond that of Congress. Television, above all, places at his disposal a highly personal medium. It magnified individuals, picking them out from crowds, lifting out a single face for intense and gripping presentation. Television cannot do equal justice to the Congress. Humans participate easily in the drama of persons; we have only a pale comprehension of social forces and institutional processes. To this fundamental human imbalance, television adds the harsh individualism of the camera.

The camera is metaphysically biased. It cannot reveal everything about human life. It selects only those features that suit its nature: personal drama rather than abstract, underlying causes; facial surfaces rather than movements of the spirit and the mind. It is a powerful instrument, often unsparing and ruthless in its revelations, suggestive, quick to capture certain quicksilver movements of emotion behind the texture of a face or the radiance of an eye. But it is not a good instrument for rendering those kinds of complexity that require many words.

Television fixes on the president and makes him the main symbolic representative of government. Symbolically, it dwarfs the Congress and the courts. There may be a balance of powers in the government; but no such balance exists on television.

Thus, television places in the president's hands enormous metaphysical powers not provided for in the Constitution—powers over reality, powers over appearances, powers over perception, powers over the imaginative matrix within which issues are presented. The Constitution did not intend for the president to have powers of speech and presence beyond that of other citizens. It envisaged that he would argue as a man among men. Now television takes his face, as it takes no other face in politics, into every living room. Not merely his *words*— in a speech barely audible to a distant audience or on the cold printed page—but his *presence* dominates the attention of citizens who sit in silence and only listen.

For nine months after June, 1972, the vast majority of newsmen assigned to Washington merely reported what the White House told them regarding Watergate, with little further inquiry. One reason they were comfortable in doing so is that television lets the president establish the underlying sense of reality within which all citizens live and move. The medium is insidious. It is a holistic medium, a purveyor of "wholes." It sets "facts" in "contexts." It provides images which block necessary insights and prompt misleading ones. It deflects attention. It sets up appearances as persuasive as reality itself. Television is not a good instrument for complicated, remote investigative reporting. It requires the "big sto-ry." It lacks the patience available to a daily newspaper, and it cannot accommodate the mass of tiny details by which a lengthy investigation proceeds. Most profoundly of all, it silently suggests what is the "reasonable," "calm," "moderate" attitude to assume. Television is a *total* guide. That is why watching it is effortless.

If we are to reform the presidency, the heart of the matter is the president's power over reality, his symbolic power. The social reality of the United States cannot be left to definition by one man alone. Whoever names a problem gains power over it; to set the terms of debate is to narrow possible resolutions. There are at least four reforms that might be taken, by Constitutional amendment if necessary, in order to restore a balance of powers in symbolic realities.

First, Congress, and in particular the opposition party in the Con-gress, must have a single spokesman who can personify the Congress of the United States, just as the president personifies the executive branch. . . . He (or she) need not be the *leader* of the opposition, although obviously the public prominence he or she would gain would yield considerable power. He or she need not supplant the majority leaders of the Senate or the House, for example. It would not necessarily follow, either, that the Opposition Spokesman would be the next presidential nominee of his party. He might be selected, indeed, precisely because he could not or would not be the nominee. His utterances would then be uniquely free of the taint of personal ambition. . . .

Second, the range of executive power has such enormous sweep that the president should be obliged on a biweekly basis to come before leaders of the opposition for a public, hour-long accounting of his policies. These conferences would be in addition to press conferences. Their purpose would be to allow opposition leaders to bring questions of fact, goals, priorities, and procedures into public view. Without such power, how will the Congress and the people learn in what entanglements the 2 million 500 thousand employees of the executive branch are involving them? Agents of the executive branch have often implicated the United States in unexamined military and commercial practices. Executive policies, out of public view, mired the nation in Vietnam long before the people knew how deeply. Executive impenetrability encased President Nixon in the scandals of his election campaign more foolishly and for a longer time than the public should have endured.

The executive branch does not come *under* the Congress. But it is accountable to the people. As representatives of the people, the leaders of the opposition party in Congress would function as public interrogators of the president. In such a forum, the separation of powers would not be impugned. The obligatory question periods would not be "hearings." They would not be official functions of the Congress, *qua* Congress. They would be modeled on press conferences, except that elected officials of the opposition rather than newsmen would raise the questions. The site could be alternated between the White House and the Senate caucus room. Congressmen would here be functioning as surrogates of the people's right to facts and information. The president might bring with him various cabinet officers, to help him with precise replies. It would not be permissible for him to absent himself. The president is at present accountable to the people almost solely on election day. 'He would now become so on a regular basis, in respect to truthfulness and fact, under questioning, at such biweekly conferences. . . .

Third, the president's cabinet should always, perhaps by force of law, include a proportion of members of the opposition party. A paramount need of the president is a unified executive branch. But a second, indispensable need is for counselors close at hand who have a political base outside his own party. Better that he should know in his own councils the questions troubling the opposition than face them only *ex post facto* and across Capitol Hill. Telling the truth to the president is difficult for persons around him, even in the best of times. In the worst of times, an institutional device for providing the president with a built-in opposition may well be his salvation, as it might have been at several junctures in the last three administrations.

Fourth, we must begin to think of a step we have for two centuries avoided—the separation of the presidency into two functions: the head of state and the chief executive. I realize that this suggestion is not immediately practical; it is too radical, too shocking to our tradition. But thinking about it illuminates our present dilemma. And perhaps one day it will seem obvious and practical. For our present arrangement flies in the face of human nature. Human beings are symbolic animals. We are not "rational," in the sense that we respond, or should respond, solely to pragmatic calculation.

A president may hold all the powers and responsibilities for foreign affairs and domestic management now in his possession, while being stripped of his role as personifier of the national identity, and be greatly liberated, not impeded, in his performance of his daily duties. It is true that he would lose some of the magic and mysticism surrounding his present office. It is true that, living outside the White House and working in closer proximity to the working offices of the Senate and the House, he would not be held in quite the awe his present eminence now affords him. But his actual administrative authority would remain clear and untrammeled; his access to radio, television, and the press would be uninhibited; his capacity to conduct foreign affairs—even his authority over nuclear weapons—would remain intact.

There would be one change in the presidency, and one only; but it would be a substantive one. No longer would the president be the personification of the nation and no longer could he derive from that personification a cloak for his administrative failings, a moral stature to which his deeds did not entitle him. His stewardship of government, naked and undisguised, would be easier to measure. His pretenses would necessarily be fewer.

"Moral leadership" would still be open to him. For on him would still fall the task of defining what in each season is significant for the nation's attention, and what commands its capacity for action. He would define the goals, priorities, and practices of political administration. He would take to the people the courses of action he felt they should embrace. He would wrestle with the Congress even as he does now.

He would lose, it is true, that

power to tame men and to awe them by the honors he can bestow; for he would no longer bestow such honors. But he would not lose his capacity to telephone private persons for advice or to invite them to his offices or to be photographed with them—so that some sense of central importance and proximity to power might be shared with them.

A chief of state, meanwhile, would be elected at the beginning of each decade. By his prior career and his personality he would furnish to that decade part of its symbolic character. He would be charged with reinforcing ceremonially all those qualities among citizens that make a nation civilized, accomplished, and creative. He would be the organizer of scientific academies and prizes, of artistic performances and certificates of honor, of such studies and commissions—on violence or urban needs or pornography or education—as national perplexities might make appropriate. A sizable budget would be available to him for these activities. Although he had no powers of military command, the chief of state would be the Ceremonial Marshal of the Armed Forces, charged with review of their fitness and their readiness. He would preside at launchings and reentries of ventures into outer space and other scientific-technical initiatives. His intellectual creativity and personal enthusiasms would become a major source of public dialogue about national priorities.

Chief of state and president would compete in the public mind as symbols of prestige, as establishers of trends, and as directors of opinion. A chief of state of one political party and a president of the other might, quite subtly, wage war for the support of public opinion, not so much over individual policies (over which the chief of state would have no jurisdiction) but rather over the "tone" and "style" and "direction" of the government. Each would no doubt find it to his advantage not openly to bait the other; for each would need the other's support, a divided public not being of assistance to either. The longer term of office of the chief of state would yield him some independence from the president; the actual Constitutional powers of the presidency would yield the president more than sufficient independence of the chief of state. Yet for symbolic reasons it would be to the interests of both to work in significant harmony. By conferring honors, by speeches, by establishing official commissions, the chief of state could strengthen— or weaken—the authority of the president. By opposing in the Congress the budget requests (beyond a fixed base) the chief of state would annually present to pay for his cultural activities, the president would have a weapon in reply.

Suppose, for example, that from 1960 to 1970, Averell Harriman or Adlai Stevenson or Dwight D. Eisenhower or Margaret Mead or Loren Eisely or Kingman Brewster or John D. Rockefeller III had been chief of state. In electing a chief of state, the people would be electing a person to represent them to the world and to preside over their cultural life. The election could be held after a national primary. The two candidates who finished highest in the primary would then oppose one another in the general election, such election being held in the odd-numbered year before a new decade opens (an anniversary year of the Constitutional convention of 1789).

The main point of this proposal is not to suggest that the roles of chief of state and head of government can in fact be separated with maximum practical gain both for the presidency and for the nation. The main point is to emphasize the unforeseen aggrandizement of the office of the president, when television and the course of world affairs exalted his symbolic power without providing any safeguards for the people's liberty and free perception of reality. If this proposal does not provide a way to restrain the president's swollen symbolic power, while keeping intact an energetic executive power, some other proposal will have to be better designed to meet the same two purposes.

The path of dictatorship lies through symbolic power—through propaganda. If once a president gains monistic power over the nation's symbols, his ability to override and circumvent and dominate the Congress seems now quite evident. If a president is restrained by symbolic pluralism, the danger of dictatorship is largely overcome. For a president not supported by the citizenry can scarcely intimidate the Congress, the courts, and other centers of opposition.

Power flows from the energy of symbols. A wall of separation to block the president's power over the nation's symbols is the most important self-defense we must . . . now erect.

(Cont. from p. 119, Sorensen, "Danger of an Impotent Presidency")

Now our economic crisis again requires someone willing to make tough, unpleasant, and unprecedented decisions. Solutions to the problems of unemployment and laggard economic growth were never easy. But they were child's play in comparison with the search for politically acceptable and effective answers to our current problems—inflation in the midst of recession, quadrupled energy prices, a series of shortages—answers that are also consistent with our democratic framework, our global responsibilities, and our simultaneous need to reduce poverty and racial discrimination.

The President may in fact have *too little* power today to tackle fast-changing economic problems effectively. He cannot adjust taxes or spending without long congressional debate and approval, and by then it is often too late to apply a slow-acting fiscal stimulus or brake. He cannot openly control the Federal Reserve Board's policies on money and credit. He cannot veto excessive items in an appropriations bill or (as of this writing, with some cases still pending) impound the funds authorized thereunder. His powers over exports, imports, stockpiles, prices, wages, housing, debt, and government employment are all strictly limited by Congress and by the willingness of the bureaucracy to accept and implement his policies. He has few facilities for effective, long-range economic planning. He has no power to put into one enforceable package a "social contract" on taxes, wages, prices, interest rates, and spending that could enlist the support of all elements of the economy—as distinguished from merely holding an economic summit meeting.

A dozen years ago President Kennedy pointed out that he and Prime Minister Macmillan both sought the fiscal stimulus of a tax cut at about the same time. Macmillan's was enacted in six weeks. Kennedy's was still pending months later at his death.

Even the *New York Times,* recently in the forefront of those favoring a dispersal of White House powers, advised President Ford, with regard to inflation:

> Successful prosecution of the job will require vigorous Presidential command of his own department and agency heads (who too often behave like interest-group representatives and spokesmen, rather than as servants of all the people).

Unfortunately only editorial writers can enjoy the luxury of calling for more "vigorous Presi-

6. IS THE PRESIDENT TOO POWERFUL?

dential command" of the executive branch one day and a more rapid dispersal of presidential power the next. There is no doubt that any increase in presidential discretion to meet the increased complexity and pace of our economic problems would involve an increased risk. There is always risk in giving any official any power. But there is also risk in denying ourselves the machinery to master our economic problems.

By definition, inclination, and long training, Congress cannot provide executive leadership. An issue such as the 1973 Middle East oil embargo produced separate legislative hearings in 40 separate committees, several inconsistent "emergency" bills to cope with the embargo—some not enacted until months after the embargo was ended—frequent statements of goals that had no prospect of ful-fillment, and little in the way of meaningful congressional policy initiatives or in-depth research. Even while loudly protesting the practice of impoundment in late 1972, both houses passed bills leaving it to the President to decide which programs beyond his arbi-trary budget ceiling would be cut.

While the role of Congress should be strengthened to restore con-stitutional balance, that cannot be accomplished by weakening the Executive. Pennsylvania Avenue, it has been rightly said, is not a see-saw.

Nixon's abuse of the power to grant clemency, or to hire and fire employees, or to set milk support prices—to cite only three minor examples from the Watergate annals—does not mean that those powers could be better exercised by Congress. When the legislative branch tried to run the executive branch after the Andrew Johnson-Ulysses Grant era, it was not a period of greatness in Washington.

Those liberals, soured by Vietnam and Nixon, who desire a transfer of authority from the Presidency to Congress, appear to be acting on the basis of one or more assumptions—that most members of Congress are consistently less "hawkish" than the President on matters of war and peace, or less subject to the influence of the military-industrial complex, or more liberal on civil rights and civil liberties, or less responsive to the pressures of special-interest elites and short-term politics, or more ethical, open, nonpartisan, credible, and pure in deed and motivation. The overall record does not support a single one of those assumptions.

Nor can a collective legislative body, any more than a weak and passive President, convey the sense of dedication needed to redirect our energies and restore our sense of discipline and worth, and thus end our national crisis of the spirit, as Franklin Roosevelt did in 1933.

The single largest difficulty with curbing executive authority is that the power to do great harm is also the power to do great good.

● To have denied, as some would deny, any "implied consti-tutional authority" in the Presi-dency might have blocked some of

Nixon's wiretaps; but such an approach would also have blocked Kennedy's first Executive Order in which, without express statutory authority, he expanded the surplus food distribution program for the poor, using funds from Customs reserves.

● To have eliminated, as some would eliminate, all secrecy in presidential foreign affairs operations unrelated to troop movements and intelligence sources might have prevented not only Nixon's bombing of Cambodia, but also his opening of relations with China.

● To have required, as some would require, advance congressional approval of any Executive Order which resembled legislative rule-making might have stopped both the Huston covert intelligence program and certain LBJ civil rights directives on housing and employment.

● Permitting the effectuation of no international agreements or understandings other than those submitted to the Senate, as recently proposed, might have blocked not only dubious deals with South Vietnam, but also the resolution of the Cuban missile crisis.

● A recently suggested constitutional or statutory amendment might have made possible a new presidential election when a firestorm of protest greeted Nixon's firing of Archibald Cox; but, under such an amendment, Truman might have lost his post for firing Douglas MacArthur.

● Had there been no White House Special Projects Fund providing every President since 1956 with $1.5 million for contingencies (and Congress has recently considered its abolition), Nixon would have had to look elsewhere to finance some of the plumbers' activities, but Kennedy would have been unable to establish in the face of an unconcerned Congress an emergency guidance counselor program to ease youth unemployment in the summer of 1962.

We cannot endlessly add to the powers of the Presidency with a Lincoln in mind without increasing a Nixon's opportunity to do harm. But we cannot unduly weaken the office with a Nixon in mind without hampering a law-abiding President's power to do good.

Proposed Structural Changes

With the aforementioned parallels in mind, I see no merit in the various structural and institutional changes in presidential power arrangements proposed or revived as suggested statutes or constitutional amendments in the wake of the Nixon Presidency. Most are Maginot lines designed to fight the last "war," the last crisis to confront the country, Watergate, without any thought as to their effect on the next one. These proposals will be only briefly mentioned here.

Some are merely gimmicks substituting ill-considered action for thought, thrown onto the floor in response to the cry of "do some-

6. IS THE PRESIDENT TOO POWERFUL?

thing." Those voiced to me, not all seriously, range from the perennial suggestion of a national ombudsman with no power base in the system, to an unworkably rigid apparatus for greater Cabinet participation, to novelties such as prohibiting public relations men in political campaigns or having the President periodically travel about listening in disguise like the ancient caliphs of Baghdad. . . .

Such thoughtful observers as Michael Novak would have us imitate those countries which separate the head of state from the head of government, enabling our President as latter to avoid both the burden and the glory that come with ceremonial duties. I want to see less pomp and grandeur surrounding our Presidents. But neither our traditions, our politics, nor our concepts of efficiency neatly divide the head of state and head of government functions. The President would still need to dine with foreign leaders. He would still want to meet the 4-H Club chairmen whose parents are voters. He would still be revered for his power, even if a head of state lived in the White House and gave out the medals. And in the light of justifiable concern over every President's isolation, we should not now cut back on the speech-making, delegation-greeting, and dam-dedicating that may keep him at least in some slight contact with the citizenry. It is a mistake to exaggerate the amount of time wasted by Presidents in needless ceremonial functions that they have no wish to attend.

This is only one of many proposals borrowed from other systems of government, with no evidence that those systems have proven more successful than our own in stemming the flow of power to the executive. The parliamentary system with merged legislative and executive power, and all members of Parliament including the Prime Minister and other ministers standing for office simultaneously, appears to have worked best in smaller, less diverse countries than ours—countries where the states are creatures of the national government, centralized national parties can discipline errant legislators, and senior civil servants dominate the ministries. None of these conditions applies here or is likely to be adopted here. Nor do all proponents of our accepting such a system realize the extent, under most parliamentary systems, to which a Prime Minister is becoming more and more a chief executive with centralized powers and can generally dominate Parliament for legislative purposes more readily than many an American President can dominate Congress.

In this country, the power to bring the executive branch down with a legislative vote of "no confidence" would introduce utter confusion. Many congressmen, fearful of the cost of campaigning, would not support such a motion when merited. But many with safe seats who are about to seek reelection anyway would support it regardless of merit; and given the recently volatile nature of the electorate's emotions and pressures, Presidents might be shuffled in and out before they could rearrange the furniture in the Green Room. At the very least, every President would be forced, far more than at present, to gratify the demands of a variety of special factions, cliques, and pork barrel interests. . . .

Like the vote of no confidence, other recent proposals are aimed at a quicker gratification of the public desire to get rid of an unpopular President: special elections, recall elections, or a less rigid standard for impeachment. Without doubt our system is slower than many others in responding even to legitimate needs to change Chief Executives; and the ordeal of Richard Nixon struck many as unnecessarily prolonged and traumatic. Yet in the end it is clear that quicker ouster would have left questions of guilt unresolved and the country bitterly divided.

It is best that Presidents, like containers, not be too easily disposable. Some unpopular acts (like John Adams' refusal to go to war) may turn out to be in the long-run national interest; some serious mistakes (like the Bay of Pigs) may constitute the experience from which wisdom comes; and, in the absence of some extraordinary occurrence such as a dual vacancy in the Presidency and Vice Presidency, fixed elections are a stabilizing tradition we should not quickly cast aside. As previously noted, tampering with the system conceived by the framers has not always been successful.

The final group of proposed structural curbs would, in various forms, pluralize presidential decision-making: require him to obtain the concurrence of an Executive Council, the Cabinet, or of Congress or its leaders; or divide his duties, with separate executives for foreign and domestic affairs, or for policy and administration; or substitute government by Cabinet or committee. "The only way to defuse the Presidency," wrote Barbara Tuchman, "is to divide the power and spread the responsibility."

But making the President less responsible is not an answer to irresponsible Presidents. Plural bodies can, after some delay and fragmentation, produce a legislative decision acceptable to the lowest common denominator. But they cannot produce the kind of executive leadership this nation's problems require.

No matter whom a President is formally required to consult, he can still informally meet with a "kitchen cabinet" of his own choosing. Adding another structural layer of advice can increase delay and indecisiveness, but rarely safety. Advice is cheap, but it can be expensive for the country. For it is the President, because he is the one held responsible if policies go wrong, who is likely to be more cautious. Advisers, as JFK observed, can always "move on to new advice." (The Joint Chiefs of Staff recommended new military initiatives to him, he said, "the way one man advises another one about whether he should marry a girl. He doesn't have to live with her.")

Moreover, foreign and domestic, or policy and administrative, burdens are less separable now than ever. There is no need to reopen the framers' deliberate decision that a single Executive is best.

None of these structural or institutional reorganizations would have prevented Watergate. All would provide corrective action, if at all, only after the fact—as our present system already does. None would solve the political and operational problems at the heart of the matter. . . . Many would carelessly curb or reshape an office that over the long haul has served us well.

Unfortunately these ill-considered if well-motivated proposals that would harm the Presidency are part of the Nixon legacy. "Support the Presidency" proclaimed the buttons his organized devotees distributed during the impeachment proceedings. Support the Presidency. I still do. He did not.

By now, my basic conclusion should be clear: instead of punishing or weakening the Presidency for the sins of Richard Nixon, its powers should be renewed but held accountable—more closely watched, more precisely defined, more carefully kept within constitutional bounds, and more clearly answerable to the electorate, Congress, and our other institutions.

POSTSCRIPT

IS THE PRESIDENT TOO POWERFUL?

Once again it is the task of Americans to weigh the considerations on both sides. Do we need further checks on the executive branch, or is the risk too great that such checks will not only weaken the presidency but the nation itself? As President Lincoln framed the question: "Must a government of necessity be too strong for the liberties of its own people, or too weak to maintain its own existence?"

Arthur Schlesinger, Jr., once a rather uncritical promoter of the activist presidency, later recanted and offered his *mea culpa* in The Imperial Presidency (Houghton Mifflin, 1973). George Reedy, former press secretary to President Johnson, wrote a small classic on the "monarchical" White House and what it does to its chief occupant (*The Twilight of the Presidency,* New American Library, 1970.) In defense of the presidency, Clinton Rossiter argued in *The American Presidency* (Harcourt Brace Jovanovich, 1960) that the President is adequately checked but hardly needs to be, since only decent men are elected to the office. This last contention may raise some eyebrows today, but Rossiter's basic theme—"Leave your presidency alone!"—is still arguable. One who does argue it, and who is now serving as President Carter's Secretary of Health, Education, and Welfare, is Joseph Califano, Jr. See his *A Presidential Nation* (W.W. Norton, 1975).

Our last words are not intended to resolve any issue but simply to remind the reader that the presidency and its power are subject to changing fortunes. In 1885 Woodrow Wilson wrote: "The presidential office . . . has fallen from its first estate of dignity because its power has waned; and its power has waned because the power of Congress has become predominant." In 1908 Wilson reached a radically different conclusion: "If he [the President] rightly interprets the national thought and boldly insists upon it, he is irresistible . . . . His office is anything he has the sagacity and force to make it."

ISSUE 7

THE SUPREME COURT: SHOULD JUDICIAL REVIEW BE LIMITED?

Although the Supreme Court has declared fewer than one hundred Acts of Congress unconstitutional, judicial review (the power to exercise this judgment) is a critical feature of American government. It extends to all law, not simply federal law, and not only statutes, but the actions of all agents of governmental power.

The power of judicial review consists not only of a negative power to invalidate acts contrary to the Constitution but equally, and far more frequently, of a positive power to give meaning and substance to constitutional clauses and the laws enacted in accordance with constitutional power. Finally, individual cases have impact and reverberation which may profoundly influence the future direction of law and behavior. To take a prominent example, when the Supreme Court reinterpreted the equal protection clause of the Constitution's Fourteenth Amendment in 1954, it changed forever the legal and social patterns of race relations in the United States.

Awed by the remarkable power of judicial review—compelling the states to redraw legislative districts so that they contain nearly equal population, requiring specific safeguards for persons accused of crimes, spelling out whether and when seditious speech exceeds the bounds of First Amendment protection, requiring the busing of school children or the hiring of minority-group members to achieve a desired constitutional result—we are likely to acknowledge that the Court is supreme. We should not however forget that it is always a court. It does not render advisory opinions in the absence of a real case before it. A case may take years or decades to proceed through the state or federal courts, and the Supreme Court's judgment may not be rendered until the practical issue has disappeared.

Some limitations on judicial review are self-imposed, such as the Court's refusal to consider "political questions," that is, questions better decided by the elective branches rather than the courts, but it is the Supreme Court which decides which questions are political. The Supreme Court has been notably reluctant to curb a President's extraordinary use of emergency power in wartime, and has done so rarely.

Still other limitations on judicial review derive from the judicial process, such as the requirement that the party bringing a case to court (any court) must have sufficient "standing" as an aggrieved party to be heard. Some laws do not appear to give any contesting party the basis for bringing a suit. Other laws rarely present themselves in an appropriate form for judicial decision, such as the ordinary exercise of presidential power in foreign relations. These exceptions qualify yet do not really negate the spirit of Alexis de Tocqueville's observation nearly a century and a half ago that "scarcely any political question arises in the United States that is not resolved, sooner or later, into a judicial question."

Judicial review is exercised by state courts and inferior federal courts as well as by the U.S. Supreme Court, but the last word is reserved to it. When a power so vast is exercised in areas so controversial as those cited, the judiciary cannot claim immunity from criticism, and it does not receive it. Critics have argued that the Framers of the Constitution did not intend that so great a power should be possessed by so unrepresentative (i.e., unelected) an organ of government. The Court has been chided for going too far too fast (law-enforcement agencies on the rights of accused persons) and for not going far enough fast enough (civil rights activists on racial equality). In the 1930s, liberals castigated the Nine Old Men for retarding social progress in invalidating major New Deal measures. In the 1950s, conservatives pasted "Impeach Earl Warren" (Warren was then Chief Justice) stickers on their car bumpers, and they bemoaned the Court's coddling of communists and criminals. In the 1970s, four more-or-less conservative Nixon appointees may have turned the tide again, and critics view the Court headed by Chief Justice Warren Burger as being less sympathetic to enforced integration, women's rights, the defense of accused persons, and the protection of socially disapproved expression.

Whether the Framers intended that the courts exercise this power or not, they now possess it, they are not going to relinquish it, and it is unimaginable that Congress will ever take it away. But is it democratic for a five-four division of nine life-tenure judges to reverse the will of the elected branches? Or does judicial review fulfill a democratic purpose in upholding the rights of minorities (which are ultimately the rights of all) even against the power of a majority?

In the following selections former U.S. Supreme Court Justice Arthur Goldberg urges that the courts employ judicial review in defense of liberty, while U.S. Circuit Court of Appeals Judge Arlin M. Adams warns that the excessive use of judicial power endangers liberty.

135

Arthur Goldberg

JUDICIAL REVIEW IS
ESSENTIAL TO CIVIL LIBERTY

"Judicial restraint"—the basic attitude that makes a court most reluctant to overturn legislative judgments—is in some respects a sound philosophy. Review of the constitutionality of acts of other branches of the government is "the gravest and most delicate duty that [the] Court is called on to perform." And, as I indicated for the Court in *Kennedy v. Mendoza-Martinez*, such a review must be conducted with all respect for the powers of other branches. Yet, I still believe that a proper view of judicial restraint applies with far greater force to laws that regulate economic and social matters than to laws that inhibit the exercise of basic personal liberty. In the latter area, where the Court's critics seem most anxious for the Court to exercise "restraint," the Court should be most reluctant to do so. . . .

The rationale for judicial restraint rests in part on basic democratic theory. Justices, after all, are not responsible to the electorate; they are appointed to their posts for life; and their personal views of the merits of legislation may differ radically from popular beliefs of the day. Legislators, on the other hand, are directly responsible to the public; they are democratically elected; and they are more likely to be moved by popular sentiment.

The value judgment implicit in the argument—that popular, democratic judgment is to be preferred to that of the judge—makes good sense when economic regulation is at issue. It is difficult to see why, if a majority of the electorate wishes to regulate aspects of the economic system under which it lives, it should not be free to do so. Nor is there any reason to believe that the judiciary is more capable than a legislature in determining the means appropriate to meet various economic and social ills.

Still, insofar as judicial restraint is rooted in democratic theory, its application is limited. A preference for democratic decision-making will not, by itself, justify restraint when the functioning of that decision-making process is faulty or when the legislation at issue would weaken the democratic decision-making process. Let me illustrate what I mean by describing four, often overlapping, sets of circumstances in which strict judicial scrutiny of

Continued on p. 138

From Arthur Goldberg, *Equal Justice* (Evanston, Ill.: Northwestern University Press, 1971).

136

Arlin M. Adams

JUDICIAL ACTIVISM UNDERMINES DEMOCRACY

Although we Americans date our independence from July 4, 1776, it is not to the Declaration of Independence but to the Constitution that we owe our present strong and flexible government. Without the adoption of a strong federal Constitution the noble experiment undertaken in 1776 probably would have degenerated into disarray, foreign intrigue, and perhaps even armed conflict.

What was the genius that made our Constitution possible in the first place, and made it so effective over these last 200 years? I suggest that it was the spirit of compromise and accommodation, as well as a sense of moderation.

The founding fathers were content to preserve the balance between governmental authority and individual liberty in terms of broad outlines, leaving the details to the wisdom and experience of future generations. Painting with broad strokes rather than engraving with fine lines allowed for the same type of accommodation and moderation in the future that made the Constitution possible in the first place. The far-sighted handiwork of that brilliant group of statesmen has proved fully equal to meeting the needs of the nation in periods of domestic tranquility and in periods of unrest, in times of peace and in times of war.

Now we are again in an era of international disquiet and domestic uncertainty. Our system is under assault from abroad, and strident demands of one kind and another confront us at home.

Times of testing produce temptations and pressures to depart from the traditional constitutional distribution of authority and responsibilities. One current notion much in vogue that holds subtle capacity for serious mischief is a cosmic view of the judicial function. The practical effect of that view is the expectation that all deficiencies in our society that have gone uncorrected in other forums may find a cure in the courts of law.

Such a thesis, it seems to me, is associated with three attitudes: First, doubt that the federal system is still adequate to meet the needs of modern society; second, impatience with the slowness of political solutions; and third, desire for instant panaceas. It is these attitudes which we must examine.

Continued on p. 141

Reprinted with permission of the American Judicature Society.

7. THE SUPREME COURT

(Goldberg, cont. from p. 136)

governmental action is not only mandated by the Constitution but also is perfectly consistent with that respect for democracy inherent in the notion of judicial restraint.

First, the Court has always more strictly examined legislative enactments that adversely affect those who are not represented in the legislature. A court, for example, might exercise Holmesian restraint in examining an Illinois statute requiring all milk sold within the state to be pasteurized; but surely its suspicions would be aroused were that statute to require that all milk sold must be pasteurized *in Illinois*. In the latter case, courts past and present have examined with some care the importance of the local interest that the law serves, weighed it against the burden that it imposes upon interstate commerce, and looked for a less restrictive means to attain the locally desired end. Why such extensive scrutiny? Fundamentally because the Constitution mandates the maintenance of a nationwide free market. And, as the commerce clause envisaged, Wisconsin farmers have no voice in the Illinois legislature. Thus, a democratic legislative process which offers Illinois residents some hope of defending themselves against unfair treatment offers no such opportunity to the Wisconsin farmer. And it is just where the democratic check falters that the Court must stand ready to examine closely the purpose of and need for the governmental action in relation to the extent to which it impinges upon a constitutionally protected right. . . .

Second, we should expect a Court, concerned that the unrepresented cannot secure fair treatment through the legislative process, to be equally sensitive to threats to the integrity of that process itself. It was natural, then, for the Constitution's framers to desire strong protection for freedom of speech, of the press, and of expression, as well as close judicial examination of any restriction of those freedoms. Democratic theory requires that those potentially in the minority on any issue have the opportunity to convince others of their point of view. Thus, if ideas cannot circulate with perfect freedom, the effectiveness of the democratic check upon unwise, unfair governmental action is weakened. . . .

Third, certain legislative enactments force the Court to face squarely what might be called the problem of the "permanent minority." Democratic theory suggests that democracy works best when majorities are formed from continually shifting coalitions. That is to say, each and every citizen who finds himself in the minority on some issues should find himself in the majority on others. As long as minorities can float in this way, majorities will hesitate to treat them unfairly. For he who votes to exploit another today may find himself in a minority subject to exploitation tomorrow.

Democracy will not work well, however, to protect from exploitation an easily identifiable group, say a racial group, that has difficulty forming political alliances and, as a result, finds itself in the minority on many, if not most, important legislative issues. An ill-spirited majority might easily treat such a group unjustly with only limited fear of political reprisal. Thus, one might be particularly reluctant to rely upon the democratic political process to protect such a group from unfair legislation. . . .

The "permanent minority" problem suggests a fourth, and related, set of circumstances in which consistency with the purposes of the Constitution requires a departure from an attitude of judicial restraint. When legislators consider laws that would restrict the freedom of particularly feared or hated individuals, such as political dissenters or criminal suspects, they may not, and on occasion do not, take adequate account of the long-term harm caused society by setting restrictive authoritarian precedents. But legislators, like the rest of us, swayed by feelings of the moment, tend to react emotionally to news of rising crime rates. Moreover, we cannot rely upon the few unpopular individuals likely to be affected by restrictive laws to organize politically to fight their passage; nor can or should we rely upon potential criminal defendants to do so. As a practical matter they cannot easily influence legislation. Neither the executives nor the legislatures are noted for their sensitivity to the views or interests of criminal defendants or political dissenters. It was fear that a legislature, swayed

by momentary emotion and political pressure, would be unable to take long-term societal harm into account that led the Constitution's framers to embed protection for fundamental personal liberties and scrupulously fair criminal procedure in the Bill of Rights. For the Court to substitute "restraint" for close scrutiny when such liberties are at stake would make the legislature or the executive their ultimate guardian, thereby undermining the purposes of embodying them in a Bill of Rights. . . .

In sum, I have tried to show that proper respect for the democratic process—the philosophy that underlies "judicial restraint"—is perfectly consistent with "activism" in some areas, particularly when the rights of minorities or fundamental individual liberties or the health of the democratic process itself are at issue.

My analysis of "judicial restraint" would be incomplete without recognition of one other element that discussions of that doctrine contain. It is often argued that the Court should strike down enactments of the legislature only with the utmost reluctance lest the Court overextend itself politically and invite public opprobrium and legislative retaliation. The Court's decisions are politically, as well as legally, controversial, it is pointed out. But, since the Court is not popularly elected, it lacks the political support needed to withstand sustained legislative attack from the other branches of government. Thus, it should not provoke the legislative or executive branches by declaring their acts unconstitutional. . . .

I subscribe unhesitatingly to [this view:] . . . Throughout its history the Court that has resolutely applied the law without regard to political popularity has survived any resulting political storm, though occasionally, as in the "Court-packing" controversy, it has been forced to trim its sails. . . . On the other hand, when the Court has made decisions or refrained from making decisions for political reasons, it more often than not has inflicted a shameful wound upon itself. . . .

Perhaps the most unfortunate retreat in the Court's history was that taken during the Reconstruction years to accommodate what the Court conceived to be the "political realities." In *Plessy v. Ferguson* and other cases, the Court undermined the intent of the framers of the Civil War amendments and the Civil Rights acts. It was then that the Court erected the totally discredited doctrine of "separate but equal."

How different the subsequent history of the races in this country might have been had the Court in *Plessy v. Ferguson* adopted the position of Justice Harlan, who in dissent argued wisely that no "legislative body or judicial tribunal may have regard to the race of citizens when the civil rights of those citizens are involved." If only the majority of the Court had heeded the warning of Justice Harlan, the Elder, who, dissenting from the "separate but equal" doctrine, predicated the following:

In my opinion, the judgment this day rendered will, in time, prove to be quite as pernicious as the decisions made by this tribunal in the Dred Scott case. . . . The present decision . . . will not only stimulate aggressions, more or less brutal and irritating, upon the admitted rights of colored citizens, but will encourage the belief that it is possible, by means of state enactments, to defeat the beneficent purposes which the people of the United States had in view when they adopted the recent amendments of the Constitution. . . . The destinies of the two races, in this country, are indissolubly linked together, and the interests of both require that the common government of all shall not permit the seeds of race hate to be planted under the sanction of law. What can more certainly arouse race hate, what more certainly create and perpetuate a feeling of distrust between these races, than state enactments, which, in fact proceed on the ground that colored citizens are so inferior and degraded that they cannot be allowed to sit in public coaches occupied by white citizens.

These words of Justice Harlan are well known to us today when the name of the author of the majority opinion in *Plessy* has fled the memory of all but the historian. Yet, tragically, it is the majority's legacy of distrust and racial bitterness which today we must attempt to overcome.

On the other hand, I believe that Courts that have unflinchingly [done] their duty—Courts that have not hesitated to apply the provisions of the Constitution for fear of political opposition—have and will be remembered in history as great Courts. And I do not believe they will suffer politically from having done so.

(Cont. from p. 137, Adams, "Judicial Activism")

Division of Power

Our federal arrangement, though born of economic, military, and diplomatic necessity, has proved to be a protector of liberty as well. We are accustomed to speaking of the Bill of Rights and the Fourteenth Amendment as the principal guarantees of our personal freedom. Yet it would be short-sighted not to realize that it is our political structure that accounts, in large measure, for our free society.

It was upon the division of powers that the founders primarily focused. Because of their confrontation with the Crown, they were suspicious of a central authority that would be absolute, and sought to ensure that such a government would never exist in this country. The federal establishment was fashioned in such a way as to diffuse power among the executive, legislative, and judicial branches. The allocation of responsibility between federal and state authority serves the same end, and assumes added significance with the increasing size of the federal bureaucracy.

A system of divided and shared powers is, of course, difficult to operate, demanding political skills of the highest order. It requires accommodations that may often seem irksome or inefficient. But out of that very necessity come pragmatic solutions of more lasting value than those that emanate from the pens of theoretical planners.

When courts blur the distinctions between the spheres of the federal government and the states by broad but not fully thought-out ideas of constitutional rights, they do a great disservice to our philosophy of ordered liberty. Many well-meaning people suppose that the judges are more likely than the politicians to provide solutions to pressing social questions. Perhaps, in a way, this is a compliment to the judiciary. It is, however, untrue to democratic principles.

Confidence that the judiciary can produce better and quicker solutions to political problems is sometimes difficult for judges to resist, particularly when the solutions seem to carry the hallmarks of authentic judicial activity: statutory construction and constitutional review. When a judge is struck by the injustice, harshness, or lack of wisdom of a statute, he may be tempted to revise the law by judicial construction or to abrogate it as contrary to the due process or equal protection clauses. Should the court misconstrue the intention of the legislature, the judge may reason, its ruling can be undone by legislative enactment or by constitutional amendment.

Such reasoning is attractive but deceptive. In the end, this judicial improvisation transfers a substantial law-making power to the courts. Judges are ill-suited to law-making, because judicial authority depends, in part, upon aloofness from the political arena. Judges, who should be beholden to no one for their conscientious conduct, lack the day-to-day responsibility to the electorate that is the real basis of workable reform. Judicial activism also erodes the legislative process, because it tends to relieve legislators from accountability for social reconstruction and constitutional propriety.

Judicial Initiative

Many constitutional experts trace the recent trend toward intervention by the courts to the school desegregation cases of the 1950's. Having overcome a perhaps too-rigid adherence to substantive due process, the Supreme Court had at the midpoint of this century learned to appreciate what the late Alexander Bickel described as the "passive virtues." But litigation does not permit abstention from the passions of the times.

After many unheeded decisions that forewarned of its intention, the Supreme Court, in 1954, unanimously declared it unconstitutional for states to operate racially segregated school systems. A year later, *Brown v. Board of Education* and its companion cases were sent back to the trial level so that decrees could be designed to achieve compliance with the historic ruling.

At this point, the courts still showed considerable deference to state and local officials. The mandate was a negative one: "Don't operate segregated schools." And the Supreme Court's timetable was indefinite, ordering only that desegregation be accomplished "with all deliberate speed."

However, after many years of delay, courts began to require "affirmative action" from school boards, particularly those in the South. The judges slipped into the initiative as the other branches of government appeared to abdicate their responsibilities. The assumption by the courts of the position of superintendent of schools, as it were, was silently sanctioned by the presidents, a considerable portion of the Congress, and many local officials as well.

Once the first bad taste of this unaccustomed power had dissipated, the second swallow did not seem so unpalatable. The later reapportionment cases also occasioned a considerable number of mandatory injunctions. After years of hesitation and admonitions, the "one-man, one-vote" rule was applied initially to Congressional districts and then to state legislative districts. Once again, upon encountering legislative recalcitrance the courts began to structure affirmative relief. Some judges even hired their own election experts and drew up their own electoral district maps.

Emboldened by these forays into activism, judges began to discover for the first time Constitutional mandates for judicial initiative in other areas:

● In one jurisdiction, a program requiring school districts to offer instruction for the mentally handicapped was decreed, even though it meant appropriating millions of dollars—a course never debated and never enacted into law by any legislative body.

● Expansive interpretation of the "cruel and unusual punishment" clause put many courts into the prison business. States were ordered to either spend substantial funds for additional penal facilities or to shut down the prisons that existed and release those confined. In St. Louis, a court imposed on the city jail a limit of 228 inmates, directed the hiring of additional staff, required the spending of more money for recreation, and mandated two correctional officers at all times for each jail floor.

● Courts have begun to insist that prison authorities must hold disciplinary hearings before they may deprive inmates of a large variety of privileges. Indeed, some courts have gone so far as to require the provision of counsel, the opportunity to call witnesses, and the right of cross-examination before a prisoner may be transferred to another institution.

● Courts have also begun to enter the domain of administrative detail in both mental and general hospitals. An Alabama court recently issued an order requiring that for every 250 patients, each state mental hospital be staffed with two psychiatrists, seven physicians, eighteen nurses, four psychologists, and seven social workers.

Misgivings

Misgivings about this course of adjudication have been expressed by Archibald Cox, Williston professor of law at Harvard Law School. In his new book, *The Role of the Supreme Court in American Government,* he stated:

> I would support nearly all these |rules| as important reforms if proposed in a legislative chamber or a constitutional convention. In appraising them as judicial rulings, however, I find it necessary to ask whether an excessive price was paid by enlarging the sphere and changing the nature of constitutional adjudication.

Professor Louis Jaffe, also of Harvard Law School, has likewise warned of the dangers of "self-conscious activism" that expands "each right to the limits of its logic with only the most casual concern for countervailing claims of other groups and society in general." Recognizing that many decisions are the angry response to unending abuses and persistent failures of government, he reminds us that nonetheless,

> |J|udges when laying down constitutional rules must do more than react . . . they must allow for the working out of a system . . . Nor can they justify over-rigid rules as the inevitable dictate of the

Constitution . . . . [T]he propositions of the Constitution are rarely so strict as to exclude choice . . . .

Democracy—and the judicial system in our democracy—will not, in my view, succumb to assassination. But it may succumb to an erosion of confidence from the disruptive and unwise arrogation of legislative power by institutions not suited to its exercise.

All this is not to say that courts should never intervene in social issues, or that judges should confine themselves to a rigid course of strict adherence to narrow statutory construction. If courts cannot be the engines of progress, neither can they ignore their role as facilitators of change. Indeed, judicious adjustments of social interests within the broad outlines set by democratic decision-making is of no small consequence to the success of legislative statesmanship.

But even where the courts are competent to intervene and issues are present that call for constitutional resolution, there is a natural temptation, sometimes, to travel too far too fast. A judicial decision that is founded simply on the impulse that something should be done, or which looks no further than the justice or injustice of a specific case, is not likely to have a lasting influence.

Oliver Wendell Holmes, a man of unsurpassed judicial sensitivity, once remarked that he had told his colleagues many times that if a man begins to talk about justice, for one reason or another, he is no longer thinking in legal terms.

Our legal system is grounded, like the common law, on enlightened and uniformly applied legal principles, not on *ad hoc* notions of what is right or wrong in a particular instance. The judge must certainly administer justice, but it is not to be the personal justice of a Louis IX, seated beneath the oak tree at Vincennes. Rather, it is to be the justice described on the lintel of the Supreme Court Building: "Equal Justice Under Law."

The stability and flexibility of our constitutional system are largely a result of carrying into constitutional adjudication the common-law approach to legal development. Woodrow Wilson epitomized that approach in these eloquent words:

> Not all change is progress, not all growth is a manifestation of life. Let one part of the body be in haste to outgrow the rest and you have malignant disease. The growth that is a manifestation of life is equable. It draws its springs gently out of the old fountains of strength, builds upon old tissue, and covets the old airs that have blown upon it time out of mind.

Respect for Law

There is further concern about judicial activism, however, which goes beyond the doubts about the attitudes that underlie intervention. It is the fear that the activist philosophy in the courts is one that eventually leaches away respect for the law—the very mortar which holds our society together.

Too frequent invocation of the Constitution tends to debase it. Popular respect for judicial decisions stems, to a considerable extent, from the belief that the decisions represent the practical application of neutral principles of adjudication. But frequent recourse to the Constitution may render it a convenient weapon for partisan debate, and may cast judges into the role of interested manipulators of that document. If that is to be the status of the Constitution and the courts, it becomes more difficult to see them as arbiters in time of crisis and guardians of liberty in time of need.

A parallel concern is that the invocation of the Constitution may sometimes polarize political discourse. The text is rich in connotations, and each person comes to it from a different origin, bearing different hopes. The Constitution is, from one perspective, the sacred scroll of what some have called our "civil religion." It evokes powerful feelings. Thus, the repeated appeal to its vaguest provisions—the very ones which are most susceptible to deeply-felt and divergent interpretations—tends to engage the strongest emotions. I am not convinced that this is healthy for the courts or for the country.

The soul of a government of laws is the judicial function, and that function can endure only if adjudication is understood by our people to be an essentially disinterested, considered, and rational element in our society. Even reinforced by a most carefully crafted Constitution, the fabric that binds society is a delicate one, in need of constant attention. Improvident stretching can be as damaging as taut resistance to all movement. The care of the social fabric, however, is not for the judges alone, although they have a vital role. Their assumption of responsibilities that have been entrusted to others may rend the fabric and rupture the constitutional design.

More and more, litigants and lawyers seek to thrust the judiciary into a position of importance in connection with many of the troubling controversies of the day. Swept up in the immediacy of the case at hand, it is sometimes hard to maintain perspective. The readjustments that these overriding questions call for, however, will never be satisfactorily accomplished by a single institution. Nor will answers be found in the demands of pressure groups, on whichever side of the matter they may be.

Judicial office calls for objectivity, patience, an inclination to reckon with the just demands of history, and a willingness to compromise, accommodate and moderate. Perhaps above all, it calls for an insistence upon the steadfastness to orderly processes.

POSTSCRIPT

THE SUPREME COURT:
SHOULD JUDICIAL REVIEW BE LIMITED?

The opposed positions on the scope of judicial power are customarily defined as judicial activism and judicial self-restraint, the former seeking to use judicial power to fulfill constitutional purposes, the latter yielding to the popularly elected branches of the government and to the people. Neither position should be pushed too far. None are so activist as to allow judicial initiative in areas where the courts have not been asked to render decisions, and few are so self-restraining as to withdraw entirely the power of the courts to declare unconstitutional the acts and actions of elected officials.

In *The People and the Court* (Macmillan, 1960), Charles L. Black, Jr. carefully developed the argument that judicial review is compatible with, and the best safeguard of, constitutional government. Eugene V. Rostow, in *The Sovereign Imperative* (Yale, 1962), has gone further, maintaining that judicial review serves to keep the other branches democratic. The late Alexander Bickel was possibly the most influential and profound critic of judicial review in recent times. In *The Least Dangerous Branch* (Bobbs-Merrill, 1962), and *The Morality of Consent* (Yale, 1975), Bickel has argued that relying too much on judicial power increases the risk of committing injustice in the name of moral duty.

Debate on the scope of judicial power does not deter judges from continuing to render decisions in cases involving such controversial issues as compulsory busing, preferential treatment for minorities, the right of abortion and the power of the states to outlaw it, women's rights, unions' rights, and the President's right of executive privilege. Tocqueville's observation on judicial power in 1835 will not seem to be an overstatement today: "Scarcely any political question arises in the United States that is not resolved, sooner or later, into a judicial question." But a Supreme Court that boldly entertains bitterly divisive issues cannot escape becoming a subject of political controversy itself.

PART III

WHAT GOALS AND STRATEGIES SHOULD WE PURSUE?

ISSUE 8

HOW CAN WE DETER CRIME?

Crime is a major social problem in America, and most Americans suspect that it is becoming greater. There is little disagreement on objectives; everyone, except perhaps the criminals themselves, wants to eliminate crime. The question is: how?

The problem is serious and complex. The fact is that even the federal crime index does not give a precise idea of the incidence of major crime. (Major crimes are identified by the Federal Bureau of Investigation as criminal homicide, forcible rape, robbery, aggravated assault, burglary, larceny over $50, and auto theft.) We cannot even be certain whether the incidence of major crimes has increased strikingly in recent decades or whether more crimes are being reported by victims (the increase in personal, automobile, and home insurance has probably led to an increase in reported crimes) and better recorded by police.

There are, however, some aspects of crime in the United States that are indisputable. Crime is widespread but more concentrated in urban areas. It is disproportionately committed by the young, the poor, and members of minority groups. The commission of some crimes (those that require public knowledge of the activity, such as prostitution, drug selling, and gambling) will involve the corruption of law-enforcement officials. The rates for some crimes, particularly violent crimes, are much higher in the United States than in many other countries. For example, there are more criminal homicides in New York City (whose *rate* of homicide is lower than that of a number of other American cities) than in all of Great Britain or Japan, which have respectively nine and fifteen times the population of New York.

150

One more aspect of crime about which there is little dispute is the increased public awareness of the problem, and the widespread fear which people, particularly parents and older people, feel in high-crime areas. Something needs to be done, but what? Reform society? Reform criminals? There are those who would deal with what they describe as root causes, but our knowledge of aberrant behavior is too slight to give us confident belief that we know what the root causes of crime are. Others think that the solution lies in the severity of punishment. One often hears the slogan, "Lock them up and throw away the keys!" Short of such constitutionally (and morally?) questionable action, imprisonment raises questions even as it resolves others. Imprisonment for whom, for how long, and for what crimes? Most of the Watergate criminals, whose offenses endangered the American electoral process, were sent to country-club prisons for a matter of months. Lower-class criminals usually do their more-considerable time in much bleaker surroundings. Is our system of justice biased in favor of white-collar and well-connected criminals? Even if it is not, or even if the bias is corrected, are most prisons serving the purposes they are supposed to serve? Do they really deter crime, or do they serve as schools for criminals, making them more hardened? Are there perhaps more "enlightened" ways of dealing with crime in America?

These are some of the questions touched upon by U.S. Court of Appeals judge David Bazelon and political scientist James Q. Wilson in the selections following. It will be seen that their answers are quite different from one another.

151

David L. Bazelon

REFORM SOCIETY

There has been a good deal of inflamed, get-tough rhetoric about crime from politicians seeking votes. This rhetoric is echoed by some academicians, who are asked—and funded—to advise us what we must do to keep the lid on. The public and the press are demanding that we hired hands in the criminal justice system—police, prosecutors, courts, and corrections—sweep away this disturbing problem. But can we—without dealing with the social injustice that breeds this behavior?

For many years, it was widely believed that the solution to crime was to rehabilitate the offender. Now we are told by those who have studied recidivism rates that this expectation is beyond our abilities. The guiding faith of corrections—rehabilitation—has been declared a false god.

Of course, not everyone concedes that rehabilitation cannot work. Many corrections officials have argued that we have never really supported it enough to judge its possibilities and limitations. But I do not wish to rehash this debate with you here. For now, let us assume that a man's soul cannot be reformed by coercion or by the enticement of early release from prison. And let us assume that no one has the professional expertise to "cure" the people from the bottom of the socio-economic ladder who commit street crimes.

Conceding all this, should we strip our prisons of all nonessential services and settle for mere warehousing? If we cannot show that a particular program has lowered recidivism rates, should we toss it on the garbage heap?

The answer, I submit, is emphatically no. Rehabilitation—by which I mean educational, counseling, and social service—should never have been sold on the promise that it would reduce crime. Recidivism rates cannot be the only measure of what is valuable in corrections. Simple decency must count too. It is amoral, if not immoral, to make cost-benefit equations our lodestar in corrections. Neither the costs nor the benefits of providing or withholding vital human services can be objectified. Whether in prison or out, every person is entitled to physical necessities, medical and mental health services, and a measure of privacy. Beyond these requisites of decent custodial care, prisoners should be given the opportunity to make their time in prison

Continued on p. 154

Reprinted with permission from *The Center Magazine,* a publication of the Center for the Study of Democratic Institutions, Santa Barbara, California.

James Q. Wilson

PUNISH CRIMINALS

I argue for a sober view of man and his institutions that would permit reasonable things to be accomplished, foolish things abandoned, and utopian things forgotten. A sober view of man requires a modest definition of progress. A 20 percent reduction in robbery would still leave us with the highest robbery rate of almost any Western nation but would prevent about sixty thousand robberies. A small gain for society, a large one for the would-be victims. Yet a 20 percent reduction is unlikely if we concentrate our efforts on dealing with the causes of crime or even if we concentrate on improving police efficiency. Were we to devote those resources to a strategy that is well within our abilities—namely, to incapacitating a larger fraction of the convicted serious robbers—then not only is a 20 percent reduction possible, but even larger ones are conceivable.

Most serious crime is committed by repeaters. What we do with first offenders is probably far less important than what we do with habitual offenders. A genuine first offender (and not merely a habitual offender caught for the first time) is in all likelihood a young person who, in the majority of cases, will stop stealing when he gets older. This is not to say we should forgive first offenses, for that would be to license the offense and erode the moral judgments that must underlie any society's attitude toward crime. The gravity of the offense must be appropriately impressed on the first offender, but the effort to devise ways of reeducating or uplifting him in order to insure that he does not steal again is likely to be wasted—both because we do not know how to reeducate or uplift and because most young delinquents seem to reeducate themselves no matter what society does.

After tracing the history of nearly ten thousand Philadelphia boys born in 1945, Marvin Wolfgang and his colleagues at the University of Pennsylvania found that over one-third were picked up by the police for something more serious than a traffic offense, but that 46 percent of these delinquents had no further police contact after their first offense. Though a third started on crime, nearly half seemed to stop spontaneously—a good thing, because the criminal justice system in that city, already sorely taxed, would in all likelihood have

Continued on p. 159

Chapter 10, "Some Concluding Thoughts," from *Thinking About Crime*, by James Q. Wilson, © 1975 by Basic Books, Inc., Publishers, New York.

8. HOW CAN WE DETER CRIME?

(Bazelon, cont. from p. 152)

something other than dead time, time without hope. They need programs to provide relief from boredom and idleness, which are surely among the greatest cruelties and causes of violence in our prisons as they are in our streets. For those who are willing, there should be tools available for self-improvement—libraries, classes, physical and mental activities.

If society cannot expect to rehabilitate the offender, what can it expect? Some people argue that because prisons have been such complete failures at reforming offenders, society could expect at least as much as it is now getting from the corrections system if we bulldozed all the prisons in this country and relied instead on community-based programs of surveillance, restraint, and support. The abolitionists rest their case on studies showing that institutionalization frequently increases the probability of recidivism, just as it increases the anger and alienation of the inmate.

Community-based programs are probably our most humane hope in dealing with people who have already turned to crime. Yet, I believe we delude society if we bill any of these programs as more than after-the-fact treatments that never prevent, and only occasionally cure, criminal behavior. If our goal is to reduce street violence, more is needed than additional probation officers. Even one-on-one supervision will not suffice. We must look to the conditions that bred the crime in the first place, or else expect the offender to break the law again when we send him back to those conditions.

Also, as much as I long for the day when we can dynamite the bastilles of this nation, I fear that we will always need prisons to isolate dangerous offenders. The day Adam stepped from the garden, we had to begin worrying about protecting the sheep from the wolves. Some offenders simply must be locked up to protect society; otherwise, we face the prospect of escalating street violence, including lynchings, to avenge the victims. Everyone would probably agree that the dangerous offender must be imprisoned. The problem—the terrible problem—is to define "dangerous" and then find the tools to measure it. As it now stands, we are being pushed to lock up ten suspected of being dangerous in an effort not to miss one who actually is. I only note the questions. I could not begin to answer them here, even if I were able.

Where there is no alternative to incarceration, we should consider new approaches. The most basic change that can be made is to reduce the size of our prisons. Experience has shown that our super-fortresses housing thousands of inmates carry a built-in brutality. Control over these huge prison populations tends to come by harsh disciplinary measures, or not at all.

On the other end of the spectrum from the abolitionists there are growing numbers of criminologists and politicians who are promising society great victories in the war on crime by changing our sentencing policies. They speak of flat sentences, uniform sentences, mandatory sentences, presumptive sentences. Under one proposal, a new sentencing commission would set standards, and appellate courts would review sentencing decisions to insure that those standards are implemented.

Some of these proposals come from those who have given up on rehabilitation and indeterminate sentencing, which uses the unfixed release date to induce prisoners to reform themselves. Since prisons now seem to serve no purpose but punishment and isolation, they say, there is no reason that like crimes should not receive like sentences. These people rest their case for uniform sentences on fairness for prisoners themselves, who are too often kept ignorant of their release date or subjected to unequal treatment.

Perhaps it is true that "we have not achieved either the individual love and understanding or the social distribution of power and property that is essential if discretion is to serve justice." Yet, I still cling to the ideal of individualized justice. As others have recognized, in abandoning individualism here, we make it progressively easier to abandon it elsewhere. I fear that if we shift from concern for the individual to mechanical principles of fairness, we may cease trying to learn as much as possible about the circumstances of life that may have brought the particular offender to the bar of justice.

At present, sentencing discretion is shared by prosecutors, judges, parole boards, and others. Uniform and mandatory sentencing would merely transfer most of this discretion to prosecutors, who would in effect set sentences by their decisions about whom to charge with what crime and whether to plea bargain. Since prosecutors need not reveal their reasons, their exercise of discretion is not reviewable.

Of course, keeping discretion in judges' hands is preferable only if judges explain their decisions and make themselves accountable to the public. Sentencing discretion cannot appear fair or serve justice or teach anyone anything unless its exercise is fully explained. Unfortunately, most judges now give only boiler-plate reasons, if that, for their sentencing. I would guess that some judges—those who are moved by retribution and vengeance—would be ashamed to say so forthrightly. Others suppose there must be right and wrong sentences, so they are embarrassed to reveal their understandable dilemma in not knowing one from the other. And finally, there are those who can't be troubled; if they bothered to probe their own minds, who knows what useful insights or disturbing biases they would find?

All the proposals for sentencing reform are worthless unless trial judges clearly and honestly reveal in writing the reasons for the sentence imposed. Without such reasons, no review—judicial or otherwise— would have any basis for determining whether the judge abused his sentencing discretion. And without reasons, we would be denied the experience which would be essential for fixing sentencing standards and guidelines by any court, commission, or legislature.

I am also disturbed by the movement for mandatory and uniform sentencing because some people advertise it as a way of reducing crime. Led by Harvard University's James Wilson and New York University's Ernest van den Haag, this group argues that increasing the certainty of a prison sentence will decrease the crime rate, either by removing the more prolific criminals from the streets or by deterring others from yielding to temptation. Some politicians have told me that they are highly impressed with the theory, which they attribute to Wilson, that the current surge in crime is caused by the postwar baby boom. Apparently, the idea is that as this generation enters its crime-prone years, all that is required is essentially a holding action—put these people away until the population bulge passes, and eventually the problem of unacceptable crime statistics will largely solve itself.

What can society really expect from these proposals? Of course, all these proposals are almost certain to increase the number of prisoners, even if sentences are shortened. Most state systems are already overcrowded; many are operating at 130 percent or more of capacity. In one state, the Department of Corrections has stopped issuing a capacity figure "because

we keep passing it." New prison construction, totalling billions of dollars, is scheduled for the next few years; yet at a cost of thirty-five to fifty thousand dollars per cell, we can safely assume that overcrowding will get worse before it gets better.

Can society expect harsher sentences to deter crime? The white-collar offender may weigh the risks of punishment, but the street offender—the one who is the cause of our alarm—most probably does not. With no job, no opportunity, no close family ties, he may well believe he has more to gain than he has to lose. More than three percent of this nation's non-white male population between the ages of eighteen and thirty-four was imprisoned in 1970. This is six times the percentage for whites. Can anyone doubt the connection between these out-of-proportion figures and the out-of-proportion unemployment rates and lack of opportunity facing this country's non-white slum dwellers?

Also, even *if* it is true that we can reduce crime simply by locking up enough lawbreakers, we must ask, for how long and at what cost to them and to ourselves? Is the plan to keep them behind bars for life? Even if it succeeds, will this approach make our society more just, or merely more repressive?

Most disturbing, all these proposals fail to consider the social injustices that breed crime. Can it be true that this nation would rather build a new prison cell for every slum dweller who turns to crime than try to alleviate the causes of his lawlessness? I do not understand how politicians can have a clear conscience preaching repression as the solution to crime, unless, of course, they believe that despite the accident of birth everyone in this country is equally endowed, mentally and physically, and has the same opportunities they have had to get ahead.

If the present debates in corrections are aimed at making prisons less brutal and sentencing more fair, then the effort is worthwhile. But if they are aimed at reducing crime, they are dangerously off-target. They are dangerous because they risk repression and greater suffering. They are off-target because they encourage society to expect magic cures rather than facing the real causes of crime.

One of the few clues that we do have about the sources of street crimes is that a viable family structure is crucial for social integration. A child needs a family because that is where his roots and his education are. Mothers and fathers who spend time with their child are better at it than are most organized group-care arrangements. We are learning that the child-rearing practices of the poor do not differ markedly from the most affluent. Statistics show that with a rising income, the same mother spends more time with her child.

But many poverty-level parents have less time and energy for their families. They are easily overwhelmed simply by the struggle for survival. A frantic and harassed mother is not a real mother. A father filled with failure and exasperation is not a real father, and he may not even stay around long enough to try. A parent who cannot put food on the table cannot convey to a child a sense of order, purpose, or self-esteem. The poor are confronted by the same problems which confront the rich, and more of them. The difference is simply that they do not have the resources or the time to cope. And when they slip, they find it all the harder to come back.

I am not saying poverty equals crime. That would be silly. I am merely stating the obvious: that poverty—and the deprivation and discrimination that so often go with it—creates the conditions that make street crime more likely.

It doesn't take an expert to guess that too many children reared in the slums, where acknowledgment of one's own identity or worth is impossible, will develop at best a hard insensitivity to other humans. My own experience with delinquents and criminals is that they feel cut off from and hated by society, and they in turn feel nothing but hatred toward their victims. Presentencing reports call these youths "streetwise"—which means merely that they have the mental armor to survive in the streets. Almost every one of the thousands of criminal defendants that have come before me has had a long record reaching back to age ten, nine, or even younger. As the child is the father of the man, so is the juvenile delinquent the father of the hardened criminal.

8. HOW CAN WE DETER CRIME?

None of our providers of treatment services—psychiatrists, psychologists, or social workers—have the know-how to implant our middle-class sensibilities into youngsters who have been actively neglected twenty-four hours a day, every day. There is no magic humanizing pill for these youths.

One step we can take is to guarantee to every family an income sufficient to enable parents to provide the kind of home environment their children need. Of course, we cannot be sure that more money given directly to the family will prevent delinquency, but there is no chance of preventing delinquency without it. Most important, it is right for its own sake.

We must also have sufficient job opportunities to provide a real alternative to crime for youths and adults. Unemployment among black teenagers, aged sixteen to nineteen, is now at thirty-four percent. For the poverty areas of our cities, the figure is put at forty-five percent. The boredom of free time, the desire for money in the pocket, resentment about having no access, even by hard work, to the things that most of society enjoys—these are the ingredients of crime by youths.

Crime is not surprising. What amazes me is that so many deprived Americans accept their lot without striking out. Surely violent crimes among America's poor would be much more prevalent but for religion, welfare checks, and alcohol. I am stunned by those who point to the many docile poor and say, "Their poverty doesn't force them to break the law, so why should it force others to?"

Society should be as alarmed by the silent misery of those who accept their plight as it is by the violence of those who do not. I see no hope for reducing violent street crime in this country until our society reaches this level of concern and humanity.

Prison reform and tougher sentencing seem like hollow promises when we realize that it is *this* kind of crime with *these* causes that we are really talking about. At worst, the present attacks on crime are repressive. At best, they are mere nibbling.

Of the more humane reforms that I call "nibbling," Norval Morris argues that "it is a serious mistake to oppose any reform until all can be reformed." Of course I agree. Making sentences more fair and relieving overcrowding in prisons need not wait for the elimination of poverty in this country. Surely review of the sentencing judge's discretion—accompanied by a requirement that he give his reasons—could eliminate *wide* disarities in sentencing without ignoring differences in individual offenders that justify different treatment.

But what I reject is the notion we should strive to achieve *only* these changes in the criminal justice system. Instead, we must try to hold in mind the full picture. We must not forget that the people I have been speaking about in the criminal justice system are merely the end products of our failing social justice system.

What ultimately is at issue in the debate over alternative responses to the crime problem is a question of the goal to be pursued: repressive order or moral order. To choose to eliminate social injustice is to choose a long, painful, and costly process. The only option I can imagine that is less appealing is not to choose it. Creating order through repression will not be easy, and maintaining it, as the frustrations of the deprived grow, will be more and more difficult. As the poet Langston Hughes warned:

> What happens to a dream deferred?
> Does it dry up
> like a raisin in the sun?
> Or fester like a sore—
> And then run?
> Does it stink like rotten meat?
> Or crust and sugar over—
> like a syrupy sweet?
> Maybe it just sags
> like a heavy load.
> *Or does it explode?*

Everything I have said here you have heard somewhere, sometime before. I have given you no new data or new theories. My purpose in coming here was to deliver a simple message: in the growing debate about corrections and the rising hysteria about crime, we have lost sight of old truths and old priorities. I believe there is a desperate need to inform the nation that there are no nostrums for street crime apart from social reform, and that to put social order ahead of social justice is repressive.

The crux of the dilemma is this: it is easy to concede the inevitability of social injustice and find the serenity to accept it. The far harder task is to feel its intolerability and seek the strength to change it.

(Cont. from p. 153, Wilson, "Punish Criminals")

collapsed. Out of the ten thousand boys, however, there were six hundred twenty-seven—only 6 percent—who committed five or more offenses before they were eighteen. Yet these few chronic offenders accounted for *over half* of all the recorded delinquencies and about *two-thirds* of all the violent crimes committed by the entire cohort.

Only a tiny fraction of all serious crimes lead immediately to an arrest, and only a slightly larger fraction are ultimately "cleared" by an arrest, but this does not mean that the police function is meaningless. Because most serious crime is committed by repeaters, most criminals eventually get arrested. The Wolfgang findings and other studies suggest that the chances of a persistent burglar or robber living out his life, or even going a year, with no arrest are quite small. Yet a large proportion of repeat offenders. . . suffer little or no loss of freedom. Whether or not one believes that such penalties, if inflicted, would act as a deterrent, it is obvious that they could serve to incapacitate these offenders and thus, for the period of the incapacitation, prevent them from committing additional crimes.

We have a limited (and declining) supply of detention facilities, and many of those that exist are decrepit, unsafe, and overcrowded. But as important as expanding the supply and improving the decency of the facilities is the need to think seriously about how we wish to allocate those spaces that exist. At present, that allocation is hit or miss. A 1966 survey of over fifteen juvenile correctional institutions revealed that about 30 percent of the inmates were young persons who had been committed for conduct that would not have been judged criminal were it committed by adults. They were runaways, "stubborn children," or chronic truants—problem children, to be sure, but scarcely major threats to society. Using scarce detention space for them when in Los Angeles over 90 percent of burglars with a major prior record receive no state prison sentence seems, to put it mildly, anomalous.

Shlomo and Reuel Shinnar have estimated the effect on crime rates in New York State of a judicial policy other than that followed during the last decade or so. Given the present level of police efficiency and making some assumptions about how many crimes each offender commits per year, they conclude that the rate of serious crime would be only *one-third* what it is today if every person convicted of a serious offense were imprisoned for three years. This reduction would be less if it turned out (as seems unlikely) that most serious crime is committed by first-time offenders, and it would be much greater if the proportion of crimes resulting in an arrest and conviction were increased (as also seems unlikely). The reduction, it should be noted, would be solely the result of incapacitation, making no allowance for such additional reductions as might result from enhanced deterrence or rehabilitation.

The Shinnar estimates are based on uncertain data and involve assumptions that can be challenged. But even assuming they are overly optimistic by a factor of two, a sizable reduction in crime would still ensue. In other countries such a policy of greater incapacitation is in fact followed. A robber arrested in England, for example, is more than three times as likely as one arrested in New York to go to prison. That difference in sentencing does not account for all the difference between English and American crime rates, but it may well account for a substantial fraction of it.

That these gains are possible does not mean that society should adopt such a policy. One would first want to know the costs, in additional prison space and judicial resources, of greater use of incapacitation. One would want to debate the propriety and humanity of a mandatory three-year term; perhaps, in order to accommodate differences in the character of criminals and their crimes, one would want to have a range of sentences from, say, one to five years. One would want to know what is likely to happen to the process of charging and pleading if every person arrested for a serious crime faced a mandatory minimum sentence, however mild. These and other difficult and important questions must first be confronted. But the central fact is that *these are reasonable questions* around which facts can be gathered and intelligent arguments mustered. To discuss them requires us to make few optimistic assumptions about the malleability of human nature, the skills of officials who operate complex institutions, or the capacity of society to improve the fundamental aspects of familial and communal life.

Persons who criticize an emphasis on changing the police and courts to cope with crime are fond of saying that such measures cannot work so long as unemployment and poverty exist. We must acknowledge that we have not done very well at inducting young persons, especially but not only blacks, into the work force. Teenage unemployment rates continue to exceed 20 percent; though the rate of growth in the youthful component of the population has slowed, their unemployment shows little sign of abating. To a degree, anticrime policies may be frustrated by the failure of employment policies, but it would be equally correct to say that so long as the criminal justice system does not impede crime, efforts to reduce unemployment will not work. If legitimate opportunities for work are unavailable, many young persons will turn to crime; but if crimi-

nal opportunities are profitable, many young persons will not take those legitimate jobs that exist. The benefits of work and the costs of crime must be increased simultaneously; to increase one but not the other makes sense only if one assumes that young people are irrational.

One rejoinder to this view is the argument that if legitimate jobs are made absolutely more attractive than stealing, stealing will decline even without any increase in penalties for it. That may be true provided there is no practical limit on the amount that can be paid in wages. Since the average "take" from a burglary or mugging is quite small, it would seem easy to make the income from a job exceed the income from crime. But this neglects the advantages of a criminal income. One works at crime at one's convenience, enjoys the esteem of colleagues who think a "straight" job is stupid and skill at stealing is commendable, looks forward to the occasional "big score" that may make further work unnecessary for weeks, and relishes the risk and adventure associated with theft. The money value of all these benefits—that is, what one who is not shocked by crime would want in cash to forego crime—is hard to estimate, but is almost certainly far larger than what either public or private employers could offer to unskilled or semiskilled young workers. The only alternative for society is to so increase the risks of theft that its value is depreciated below what society can afford to pay

161

in legal wages, and then take whatever steps are necessary to insure that those legal wages are available.

Another rejoinder to the "attack poverty" approach to crime is this: The desire to reduce crime is the worst possible reason for reducing poverty. Most poor persons are not criminals; many are either retired or have regular jobs and lead conventional family lives. The elderly, the working poor, and the willing-to-work poor could benefit greatly from economic conditions and government programs that enhance their incomes without there being the slightest reduction in crime—indeed, if the experience of the 1960s is any guide, there might well be, through no fault of most beneficiaries, an increase in crime. Reducing poverty and breaking up the ghettoes are desirable policies in their own right, whatever their effects on crime. It is the duty of government to devise other measures to cope with crime, not only to permit antipoverty programs to succeed without unfair competition from criminal opportunities, but also to insure that such programs do not inadvertently shift the costs of progress, in terms of higher crime rates, onto innocent parties, not the least of whom are the poor themselves.

One cannot press this economic reasoning too far. Some persons will commit crimes whatever the risks; indeed, for some, the greater the risk the greater the thrill, while others—the alcoholic wife beater, for example—are only dimly aware that there are any risks. But more important than the insensitivity of certain criminal activities to changes in risks and benefits is the impropriety of casting the crime problem wholly in terms of a utilitarian calculus. The most serious offenses are crimes not simply because society finds them inconvenient, but because it regards them with moral horror. To steal, to rape, to rob, to assault—these acts are destructive of the very possibility of society and affronts to the humanity of their victims. It is my experience that parents do not instruct their children to be law abiding merely by pointing to the risks of being caught, but by explaining that these acts are wrong whether or not one is caught. I conjecture that those parents who simply warn their offspring about the risks of crime produce a disproportionate number of young persons willing to take those risks.

Even the deterrent capacity of the criminal justice system depends in no small part on its ability to evoke sentiments of shame in the accused. If all it evoked were a sense of being unlucky, crime rates would be even higher. James Fitzjames Stephens makes the point by analogy. To what extent, he asks, would a man be deterred from theft by the knowledge that by committing it he was exposing himself to one chance in fifty of catching a serious but not fatal illness—say, a bad fever? Rather little, we would imagine—indeed, all of us regularly take risks as great or greater than that when we drive after drinking, when we smoke cigarettes, when we go hunting in the woods. The criminal sanction, Stephens concludes, "operates not only on the fears of criminals, but upon the habitual sentiments of those who are not criminals. A great part of the general detestation of crime . . . arises from the fact that the commission of offenses is associated . . . with the solemn and deliberate infliction of punishment wherever crime is proved."

Much is made today of the fact that the criminal justice system "stigmatizes" those caught up in it, and thus unfairly marks such persons and perhaps even furthers their criminal careers by having "labeled" them as criminals. Whether the labeling process operates in this way is as yet unproved, but it would indeed be unfortunate if society treated a convicted offender in such a way that he had no reasonable alternative but to make crime a career. To prevent this, society ought to insure that one can "pay one's debt" without suffering permanent loss of civil rights, the continuing and pointless indignity of parole supervision, and frustration in being unable to find a job. But doing these things is very different from eliminating the "stigma" from crime. To destigmatize crime would be to lift from it the weight of moral judgment and to make crime simply a particular occupation or avocation which society has chosen to reward less (or perhaps more!) than other pursuits. If there is not stigma attached to an activity, then society has no business making it a crime. Indeed, before the invention of the prison in the late eighteenth and early nine-

teenth centuries, the stigma attached to criminals was the major deterrent to and principal form of protection from criminal activity. The purpose of the criminal justice system is not to expose would-be criminals to a lottery in which they either win or lose, but to expose them in addition and more importantly to the solemn condemnation of the community should they yield to temptation.

Anyone familiar with the police stations, jails, and courts of some of our larger cities is keenly aware that accused persons caught up in the system are exposed to very little that involves either judgment or solemnity. They are instead processed through a bureaucratic maze in which a bargain is offered and a haggle ensues at every turn—over amount of bail, degree of the charged offense, and the nature of the plea. Much of what observers find objectionable about this process could be alleviated by devoting many more resources to it, so that an ample supply of prosecutors, defense attorneys, and judges were available. That we do not devote those additional resources in a country obsessed with the crime problem is one of the more interesting illustrations of the maxim, familiar to all political scientists, that one cannot predict public policy simply from knowing popular attitudes. Whatever the cause, it remains the case that in New York County (Manhattan) there were in 1973, 31,098 felony arrests to be handled by only 125 prosecutors, 119 public defenders, and 59 criminal court judges. The result was predictable: of those arrested, only 4130 pleaded guilty to or were convicted on a felony charge.

One wonders whether the stigma properly associated with crime retains much deterrent or educative value. My strong inclination is to resist explanations for rising crime that are based on the alleged moral breakdown of society, the community or the family. I resist in part because most of the families and communities I know have not broken down, and in part because, had they broken down, I cannot imagine any collective action we could take consistent with our civil liberties that would restore a moral consensus, and yet the facts are hard to ignore. Take the family: Over one-third of all black children and one in fourteen of all white children live in single-parent families. Over two million children live in single-parent (usually father absent) households, almost *double* the number of ten years ago. In 1950, 18 percent of black families were female-headed; in 1969 the proportion had risen to 27 percent; by 1973 it exceeded 35 percent. The average income for a single-parent family with children under six years of age was, in 1970, only $3100, well below the official "poverty line."

Studies done in the late 1950s and the early 1960s showed that children from broken homes were more likely than others to become delinquent. In New York State, 58 percent of the variation in pupil achievement in three hundred schools could be predicted by but three variables—broken homes,

overcrowded housing, and parental educational level. Family disorganization, writes Urie Bronfenbrenner, has been shown in thousands of studies to be an "omnipresent overriding factor" in behavior disorders and social pathology. And that disorganization is increasing.

These facts may explain some elements of the rising crime rate that cannot be attributed to the increased number of young persons, high teenage unemployment, or changed judicial policies. The age of persons arrested has been declining for more than fifteen years and the median age of convicted defendants (in jurisdictions for which data are available) has been declining for the last six years. Apparently, the age at which persons begin to commit serious crime has been falling. For some young people, thus, whatever forces weaken their resistance to criminal activity have been increasing in magnitude, and these forces may well include the continued disorganization of the family and the continued deterioration of the social structure of inner city communities.

One wants to be objective, if not optimistic. Perhaps single-parent families today are less disorganized or have a different significance than such families in the past. Perhaps the relationship between family structure and social pathology will change. After all, there now seem to be good grounds for believing that, at least on the East Coast, the heroin epidemic of the 1960s has run its course; though there are still thousands of addicts, the rate of formation of new addicts has slowed and the rate of heroin use by older addicts has dropped. Perhaps other aspects of the relationship among family, personality, and crime will change. Perhaps.

No one can say how much of crime results from its increased profitability and how much from its decreased shamefulness. But one or both factors must be at work, for population changes alone simply cannot account for the increases. Crime in our cities has increased far faster than the number of young people, or poor people, or black people, or just plain people who live in those cities. In short, objective conditions alone, whether demographic or economic, cannot account for the crime increase, though they no doubt contributed to it. Subjective forces—ideas, attitudes, values—played a great part, though in ways hard to define and impossible to measure. An assessment of the effect of these changes on crime would provide a partial understanding of changes in the moral structure of our society.

But to understand is not to change. If few of the demographic factors contributing to crime are subject to planned change, virtually none of the subjective ones are. Though intellectually rewarding, from a practical point of view it is a mistake to think about crime in terms of its "causes" and then to search for ways to alleviate those causes. We must think instead of what it is feasible for a government or a community to do, and then try to discover, by experimentation and observation, which of those things

will produce, at acceptable costs, desirable changes in the level of criminal victimization.

There are, we now know, certain things we can change in accordance with our intentions, and certain ones we cannot. We cannot alter the number of juveniles who first experiment with minor crimes. We cannot lower the recidivism rate, though within reason we should keep trying. We are not yet certain whether we can increase significantly the police apprehension rate. We may be able to change the teenage unemployment rate, though we have learned by painful trial and error that doing this is much more difficult than once supposed. We can probably reduce the time it takes to bring an arrested person to trial, even though we have as yet made few serious efforts to do so. We can certainly reduce the arbitrary and socially irrational exercise of prosecutorial discretion over whom to charge and whom to release, and we can most definitely stop pretending that judges know, any better than the rest of us, how to provide "individualized justice." We can confine a larger proportion of the serious and repeat offenders and fewer of the common drunks and truant children. We know that confining criminals prevents them from harming society, and we have grounds for suspecting that some would-be criminals can be deterred by the confinement of others.

Above all, we can try to learn more about what works, and in the process abandon our ideological preconceptions about what *ought* to

165

8. HOW CAN WE DETER CRIME?

work. Nearly ten years ago I wrote that the billions of dollars the federal government was then preparing to spend on crime control would be wasted, and indeed might even make matters worse if they were merely pumped into the existing criminal justice system. They were, and they have. In the next ten years I hope we can learn to experiment rather than simply spend, to test our theories rather than fund our fears. This is advice, not simply or even primarily to government—for governments are run by men and women who are under irresistible pressures to pretend they know more than they do—but to my colleagues: academics, theoreticians, writers, advisers. We may feel ourselves under pressure to pretend we know things, but we are also under a positive obligation to admit what we do not know and to avoid cant and sloganizing. The government agency, the Law Enforcement Assistance Administration, that has futilely spent those billions was created in consequence of an act passed by Congress on the advice of a presidential commission staffed by academics, myself included.

It is easy and popular to criticize yesterday's empty hopes and mistaken beliefs, especially if they seemed supportive of law enforcement. It is harder, and certainly most unpopular, to criticize today's pieties and pretensions, especially if they are uttered in the name of progress and humanity. But if we were wrong in thinking that more money spent on the police would bring down crime rates, we are equally wrong in supposing that closing our prisons, emptying our jails, and supporting "community-based" programs will do any better. Indeed, there is some evidence that these steps will make matters worse, and we ignore it at our peril.

Since the days of the crime commission we have learned a great deal, more than we are prepared to admit. Perhaps we fear to admit it because of a newfound modesty about the foundations of our knowledge, but perhaps also because the implications of that knowledge suggest an unflattering view of man. Intellectuals, although they often dislike the common person as an individual, do not wish to be caught saying uncomplimentary things about humankind. Nevertheless, some persons will shun crime even if we do nothing to deter them, while others will seek it out even if we do everything to reform them. Wicked people exist. Nothing avails except to set them apart from innocent people. And many people, neither wicked nor innocent, but watchful, dissembling, and calculating of their opportunities, ponder our reaction to wickedness as a cue to what they might profitably do. We have trifled with the wicked, made sport of the innocent, and encouraged the calculators. Justice suffers, and so do we all.

POSTSCRIPT

HOW CAN WE DETER CRIME?

It may be said of crime, as Mark Twain said of the weather, that everyone talks about it, but no one does anything about it. Perhaps this is because the easy solutions only sound easy. We could lock up the criminals, but where would we put them? And would society be prepared to pay the staggering cost? We could remedy the poverty, inequality, and discrimination that purportedly lead to crime, but where and how do we begin? And, again, is society willing to foot the bill?

If we separate out the superficial and hysterical accounts of crime on the one hand and the technical and statistical studies by criminologists on the other, there is a paucity of thoughtful reading. Former U.S. Attorney General Ramsey Clark takes a position strongly opposed to James Wilson's in *Crime in America* (Simon and Schuster, 1970). Clark urges not only sweeping social reform, but the reform of human character. Two recent studies have sought to deal thoroughly with the causes and prevention of major categories of crime. Yong Hyo Cho, *Public Policy and Urban Crime* (Ballinger Publishing Co., Cambridge, 1974) and Stuart Palmer, *The Prevention of Crime* (Behavioral Publications, New York, 1973) both contain a wealth of factual information as well as assessments of the proposed solutions. The most far-reaching governmental study is that of the President's Commission on Law Enforcement and Administration of Justice, *The Challenge of Crime in a Free Society* (U.S. Government Printing Office, 1967).

It is unlikely that objective analysis will have much influence on most people's thinking about crime. Fear, compassion, religious teaching, and generalized morality are not easily altered by statistics. The man or woman in the street suspects that "facts" on the incidence of crime are not altogether reliable, and "facts" on the causes of crime are almost entirely lacking. Yet, reasoning need not be abandoned. Judge Bazelon and Professor Wilson provide powerful reasons to support opposed approaches. Where Bazelon is convinced that we must do what is necessary, Wilson insists that it is futile to attempt to do more than is possible. Both criticize prevailing practices toward crime and punishment as unjust, and both urge reform, but they differ in their assessment of the injustice as they do in their prescriptions for reform. Society may never definitively resolve these issues, but it cannot escape them.

ISSUE 9

IS CAPITAL PUNISHMENT JUSTIFIED?

Although capital punishment (the death penalty) is ancient, both the definition of capital crimes and the legal methods of putting convicted persons to death have changed. In eighteenth-century Massachusetts, there were fifteen capital crimes, including blasphemy and the worship of false gods. Slave states often imposed the death sentence upon blacks for crimes that, when committed by whites, were punished by two or three years' imprisonment. It has been estimated that in this century approximately ten percent of all legal executions have been for the crime of rape, one percent for all other crimes (robbery, burglary, attempted murder, etc.), and nearly 90 percent for the commission of murder.

Although the number of murders has increased, the number of executions has declined in recent decades, from 1667 in the 1930s to 717 in the 1950s. Seven persons were executed in 1965, one in 1966, and two in 1967, when the last legal executions took place before the execution of Gary Gilmore in 1977. Put another way, in the 1930s and 1940s, there was one execution for every sixty or seventy homicides committed in states which had the death penalty; in the first half of the 1960s, there was an execution for every 200 homicides; and by 1966 and 1967, there were only three executions for approximately 20,000 homicides.

Despite the sharp decline in the administration of the death penalty, many hundreds of convicted persons were sentenced to death, and "death rows" swelled in numbers during the years after the U.S. Supreme Court suspended carrying out the death penalty in 1972. The constitutional issue was and remains whether the death penalty is cruel and unusual punishment, which is prohibited to the federal government by the Eighth Amendment to the Constitution, and prohibited to the states by interpretation of the Fourteenth Amendment. Two Justices, in separate opinions, concluded that the death penalty is too severe, although both alluded to the arbitrary and discriminatory manner of its exercise. Three other Justices, each in a separate opinion, stressed the rarity of the death penalty, its arbitrariness, and the fact that executed persons were disproportionately likely to be black, poor, uneducated, and young. The four dissenters together and separately deplored the use of the death penalty but defended the right of the states to impose it.

9. IS CAPITAL PUNISHMENT JUSTIFIED?

Some Americans prematurely concluded that the Supreme Court had abolished capital punishment, but what the Court had done was forbid its unfair exercise without judicially resolving the basic constitutional issue. When the Court returned to examine new state laws involving capital punishment in 1976, seven Justices concluded that it was within the power of a state to take the life of a convicted murderer. (Internal analysis of the 1972 and 1976 opinions suggests that capital punishment will not be upheld for crimes other than murder.) On the other hand, states are forbidden to exercise this power in an arbitrary or discriminatory manner. One of the ways in which many states hoped to overcome the Supreme Court's 1972 objections to the rarity and capriciousness of the exercise of the death penalty was to mandate death sentences for first-degree murder and certain other categories. This, the Court said in 1976 and again in 1977, was unduly harsh.

The debate still rages, although for most Americans the constitutional considerations are only some of the factors to be considered. Is society entitled to retribution, an eye for an eye? Does the death penalty deter the commission of certain crimes, particularly murder? Is the death penalty unjust because of its finality and the fact that an error cannot be rectified? (Can the error ever be rectified if an innocent person has unjustly spent most of his life in prison?) Gary Gilmore, facing execution in Utah, compelled the American people to consider still another question: Does a person condemned to life in prison have a right to prefer death?

When an issue such as the death penalty involves considerations of justice, morality, and public safety, it is unlikely that debate will be rational. Although many nations have abolished the death penalty, its abandonment in the United States seems unlikely in the foreseeable future, given the nation's high homicide rate and the power of the fifty states individually to decide upon penalties. Legislatures will continue to alter their laws to meet what they · conceive to be the prevailing judicial standards, and those standards will be set by the U.S. Supreme Court.

In the readings which follow, Donal E. J. MacNamara sums up virtually every widely used argument against the death penalty, while Ernest van den Haag focuses his defense upon the argument of deterrence.

Donal E. J. MacNamara

THE DEATH PENALTY
IS UNJUSTIFIED

The infliction of the death penalty is becoming less frequent and the actual execution of the sentence of death even more rare, both in the United States and in foreign countries. Not only is this trend apparent in those nations and states which have formally repudiated the *lex talionis* and have eliminated capital punishment from their penal codes but it is almost equally clear in many of the jurisdictions which still retain the ultimate sanction for from one to fourteen crimes. This diminished frequency is a reflection of the popular distaste for executions and of the recognition by many criminologically and psychiatrically oriented judges, juries, prosecutors, and commuting and pardoning authorities that capital punishment is as ineffective as a special capital crimes deterrent as it is ethically and morally undesirable.

The case against the death penalty is supported by many arguments—with the order of their importance or precedence dependent upon the orientation of the proponent or the composition of the audience to whom the argument is being addressed. The late Harold Laski, in opening his series of lectures to one of my graduate seminars in political theory, suggested that a lecturer or writer was under obligation to his audience to define both the articulate and inarticulate basic premises upon which his theoretical structure, and its practical application to the matters under discussion, rested. This writer, then, is a practicing criminologist with both administrative and operational experience in police and prison work over a period of more than two decades; he was brought up in a Catholic household, went to parochial schools for twelve years, and then took degrees from two non-sectarian institutions. He is a "convert" to abolition, for during his active police and prison career he not only accepted the death penalty pragmatically as existent, necessary, and therefore desirable but participated in one or another formal capacity in a number of executions.

The case against capital punishment is ten-fold:

1. *Capital punishment is criminologically unsound.* The death penalty is the antithesis of the rehabilitative, non-punitive, non-vindictive orientation of twentieth century penology. It brutalizes the entire administration of criminal

Continued on p. 172

Printed by permission of Office for Church in Society, United Church of Christ.

Ernest van den Haag

THE DEATH PENALTY
DETERS CRIME

If rehabilitation and the protection of society from unrehabilitated offenders were the only purposes of legal punishment, the death penalty could be abolished: it cannot attain the first end, and is not needed for the second. No case for the death penalty can be made unless "doing justice," or "deterring others," are among our penal aims. Each of these purposes can justify capital by itself; opponents, therefore, must show that neither actually does, while proponents can rest their case on either.

Although the argument from justice is intellectually more interesting, and, in my view, decisive enough, utilitarian arguments have more appeal: the claim that capital punishment is useless because it does not deter others is most persuasive. I shall, therefore, focus on this claim. Lest persuasiveness suffer, I shall show, nonetheless, that claims of injustice have no independent standing: their weight depends on the weight given to deterrence.

Capital punishment is regarded as unjust because it may lead to the execution of innocents or because the guilty poor (or disadvantaged) are more likely to be executed than the guilty rich.

Regardless of merit, these claims are relevant only if "doing justice" is among the purposes of punishment. Unless one regards it as good, or at least better, that the guilty be punished rather than the innocent and that the equally guilty be punished equally, unless, that is, one wants penalties to be just, one cannot object to them because they are not. However, if one does include justice among the purposes of punishment, it becomes possible to justify any one punishment—even death—on grounds of justice. Yet, those who object to the death penalty because of its alleged injustice usually deny not only the merits, or the sufficiency, of specific arguments based on justice but the propriety of justice as an argument: they exclude "doing justice" as a purpose of legal punishment. If justice is not a purpose of penalties, injustice cannot be an objection to the death penalty (or to any other); if it is, justice cannot be ruled out as an argument for any penalty.

Continued on p. 179

From Ernest van den Haag, "On Deterrence and the Death Penalty" in *Ethics*, volume 78 (July 1968), pp. 280–288. Copyright © 1968. Reprinted by permission of the University of Chicago Press.

9. IS CAPITAL PUNISHMENT JUSTIFIED?

(MacNamara, cont. from p. 170)

justice. No criminologist of stature in America or abroad gives it support. And those "arm-chair" and so-called "utilitarian" criminologists who plead its necessity (never its desirability or morality) do so in terms of Darwinian natural selection and/or as a eugenics-oriented, castration-sterilization race purification technique, an economical and efficient method of disposing of society's jetsam. Those who advance these arguments are probably not aware that they are rationalizing a residual lust for punishment or propagating an immoral, virtually paganistic, philosophy.

2. *Capital punishment is morally and ethically unacceptable.* The law of God is "Thou shalt not kill," and every system of ethics and code of morals echoes this injunction. It is well recognized that this Commandment (and the laws of man based upon it) permit the killing of another human being "in the lawful defense of the slayer, or of his or her husband, wife, parent, child, brother, sister, master or servant, or of any other person in his presence or company" when there is "imminent danger" and in "actual resistance" to an assault or other criminal act. It is equally well recognized that society, organized as a sovereign state, has the right to take human life in defending itself in a just war against either internal or external unjust aggression. But the individual citizen has no right in law or morals to slay as punishment for an act, no matter how vile, already committed; nor has he legal or moral justification to kill when—his resistance to an attempted criminal act having proved successful short of fatal force—the imminent danger is eliminated and the criminal attack or attempt discontinued.

Individuals in groups or societies are subject to the same moral and ethical codes which govern their conduct as individuals. The state, through its police agents, may take human life when such ultimate measure of force is necessary to protect its citizenry from the imminent danger of criminal action and in actual resistance to felonious attempts (including attempts forcibly to avoid arrest or escape custody). Once, however, the prisoner has been apprehended and either voluntarily submits to custody, or is effectively safeguarded against escape (maximum security confinement), the right of the state to take his life as punishment, retribution, revenge, or retaliation for previously committed offenses (no matter how numerous or heinous) or as an "example" to deter others, or as an economical expedient, does not exist in moral law.

I argue this despite the fact that it is a position which is contrary to that expounded by a number of eminent theologians, notably Thomas Aquinas. Writing in times long past and quite different, and expressing themselves in terms of conditions, logic and experiences of those times, such theologians have defended the right of the state to take human life as a punishment "when the common good requires it." Moreover, they have held that, under certain conditions, the state is morally bound to take human life and that not to take it would be sinful. Although I am philosophically opposed to war whether as an extension of diplomacy or an instrument of national policy, I recognize the right of a nation, through its armed forces and in accord with the rules of civilized warfare, to take human life in defense of its sovereignty, its national territory, and its citizens. Such recognition is in no way inconsistent with my views anent the death penalty, for the Geneva Convention makes it clear that the killing of one's enemy (no matter how many of one's troops he has slaughtered in battle) after he has laid down his arms, surrendered, or been taken prisoner, will not be countenanced by civilized nations.

3. *Capital punishment has demonstrably failed to accomplish its stated objectives.* The proponents of the death penalty base their support largely on two basic propositions: (1) that the death penalty has a uniquely deterrent effect on those who contemplate committing capital crimes; and (2) that the provision of the death penalty as the mandatory or alternative penalty for stated offenses in the statute books removes for all time the danger of future similar offenses by those whose criminal acts have made them subject to its rigors.

Neither of these propositions will stand logical or statistical analysis. Proposition 1 is dependent upon acceptance of the repudiated "pleasure-pain" principle of past-century penology. This theory presupposes a "rational man" weighing the prospective profit or pleasure to be derived from the commission of some future crime against the almost certain pain or loss he will suffer in retribution should he be apprehended and convicted. That many persons who commit crimes are not "rational" at the time the crime is committed is beyond dispute. Avoiding the area of psychiatric controversy for the moment, let it be sufficient to report that Dr. Shaw Grigsby of the University of Florida in his recent studies at the Raiford (Florida) State Penitentiary found that more than seventy-five per cent of the males and more than ninety per cent of the females then in confinement were under the influence of alcohol at the time they committed the offenses for which they were serving sentence; and that Dr. Marvin Wolfgang's studies of the patterns in criminal homicide in Philadelphia in large measure lend support to Dr. Grigsby's findings.

While perhaps the theological doctrine of "sufficient reflection and full consent of the will" as necessary prerequisites to mortal sin is somewhat mitigated by the mandate to "avoid the occasions of sin" in the determination of moral responsibility, we are here discussing rationality in terms of weighing alternatives of possible prospective deterrence rather than adjudicated post-mortem responsibility. Proposition 1 further presupposes knowledge by the prospective offender of the penalty provided in the penal code for the offense he is about to commit—a knowledge not always found even among lawyers. It further assumes a non-self-destructive orientation of the offender and, most importantly, a certainty in his mind that he will be identified, apprehended, indicted, convicted, sentenced to the maximum penalty, and that the ultimate sanction will indeed be executed. When one notes that of 125 persons indicted for first degree murder in the District of Columbia during the period 1953–1959, only one (a Negro) was executed despite the mandatory provision of the law; and further that, despite the fact that more than three million major felonies were known to the police in 1960, the total prison population (federal and state) at the January 1961 prison census (including substantially all the convicted felons of 1960 and many from prior years) stood at a miniscule 190,000, the rational criminal might very well elect to "play the odds."

The second part of the proposition assumes that all or a high proportion of those who commit crimes for which the death penalty is prescribed will in fact be executed—an assumption, rebutted above, which was false even in the hey-day of capital punishment when more than two hundred offenses were punishable on the gallows. It shows no awareness that the mere existence of the death penalty may in itself contribute to the commission of the very crimes it is designed to deter, or to the difficulty of securing convictions in capital cases. The murderer who has killed once (or committed one of the more than thirty other capital crimes) and whose life is already forfeit if he is caught would find little deterrent weight in the prospect of execution for a second or third capital crime—particularly if his victim were to be a police officer attempting to take him into custody for the original capital offense. The suicidal, guilt-haunted psychotic might well kill (or confess falsely to a killing) to provoke the state into imposing upon him the punishment which in his tortured mind he merits but is unable to inflict upon himself.

Prosecutors and criminal trial lawyers have frequently testified as to the difficulty of impanelling juries in capital cases and the even greater difficulty of securing convictions on evidence which in non-capital cases would leave little room for reasonable doubt. Appeals courts scan with more analytical eye the transcripts in capital cases, and error is located and deemed prejudicial which in non-capital cases would be overlooked. The Chessman case is, from this viewpoint, a monument to the determination on the part of American justice that no man shall be executed while there is the slightest doubt either as to his guilt or as to the legality of the process by which his guilt was determined. Criminologists have pointed out repeatedly that the execution of the small number of convicts (fewer than fifty each year in the United States) has a disproportionately brutalizing effect on those of us who survive. Respect for the sanctity and inviolability of human life decreases each time human life is taken. When taken formally in the circus-like atmosphere which unfortunately characterizes twentieth century trials and executions (both here and abroad), emotions, passions, impulses and hostilities are activated which may lead to the threshold of murder many who might never have incurred the mark of Cain.

4. *Capital punishment in the United States has been and is prejudicially and inconsistently applied.* The logic of the retentionist position would be strengthened if the proponents of capital punishment could demonstrate that an "even-handed justice" exacted the supreme penalty without regard to race or nationality, age or sex, social or economic condition; that all or nearly all who committed capital crimes were indeed executed; or, at least, that those pitiful few upon whom the sentence of death is carried out each year are in fact the most dangerous, the most vicious, the most incorrigible of all who could have been executed. But the record shows otherwise.

Accurate death penalty statistics for the United States are available for the thirty-year period, 1930–1959. Analysis of the more than three thousand cases in which the death penalty was exacted discloses that more than half were Negroes, that a very significant proportion were defended by court-appointed lawyers, and that few of them were professional killers. Whether a man died for his offense depended, not on the gravity of his crime, not on the number of such crimes or the number of his victims, not on his present or prospective danger to society, but on such adventitious factors as the jurisdiction in which the crime was committed, the color of his skin, his financial position, whether he was male or female (we seldom execute females), and indeed oftentimes on what were the character and characteristics of his victim (apart from the justifiability of the instant homicidal act).

It may be exceedingly difficult for a rich man to enter the Kingdom of Heaven but case after case bears witness that it is virtually impossible for him to enter the execution chamber. And it is equally impossible in several states to execute a white man for a capital crime against a Negro. Professional murderers (and the directors of the criminal syndicates which employ them) are seldom caught. When they are arrested either they are defended successfully by eminent and expensive trial counsel; or they eliminate or intimidate witnesses against them. Failing such advantages, they wisely bargain for a plea of guilty to some lesser degree of homicide and escape the death chamber. The homicidal maniac, who has massacred perhaps a dozen, even under our archaic M'Naghten Rule, is safely outside the pale of criminal responsibility and escapes not only the death penalty but often even its alternatives.

5. *The innocent have been executed.* There is no system of criminal jurisprudence which has on the whole provided as many safeguards

against the conviction and possible execution of an innocent man as the Anglo-American. Those of us who oppose the death penalty do not raise this argument to condemn our courts or our judiciary, but only to underline the fallibility of human judgment and human procedures. We oppose capital punishment for the guilty; no one save a monster or deluded rationalist (e.g., the Captain in Herman Melville's *Billy Budd*) would justify the execution of the innocent. We cannot however close our minds or our hearts to the greater tragedy, the more monstrous injustice, the ineradicable shame involved when the legal processes of the state, knowingly or unknowingly, have been used to take the life of an innocent man.

The American Bar Foundation, or some similar research-oriented legal society, might well address itself to an objective analysis of the factors which led to the convictions of the many men whose sentences for capital crimes have in the past few decades been set aside by appellate courts (or by executive authority after the courts had exhausted their processes), and who later were exonerated either by trial courts or by the consensus of informed opinion. Especial attention should be directed to the fortunately much smaller number of cases (e.g., the Evans-Christie case in England and the Brandon case in New Jersey) in which innocent men were actually executed. Perhaps, too, a reanalysis would be profitable of the sixty-five cases cited by Professor Edwin Borchard in his *Convicting the Innocent,* the thirty-six cases mentioned by U. S. Circuit Court of Appeals Judge Jerome Frank in *Courts on Trial,* and the smaller number of miscarriages of justice outlined by Erle Stanley Gardner in *Court of Last Resort.*

6. *There are effective alternative penalties.* One gets the impression all too frequently, both from retentionist spokesmen and, occasionally, from the statements of enthusiastic but ill-informed abolitionists, that the only alternative to capital punishment is no punishment; that, if the death penalty does not deter, then surely no lesser societal response to the violation of its laws and injury to its citizens will prove effective.

The record in abolition jurisdictions, some without the death penalty for more than one hundred years, both in the United States and abroad, in which imprisonment for indeterminate or stated terms has been substituted for the penalty of death, is a clear demonstration that alternative penalties are of equal or greater protective value to society than is capital punishment.

In every instance in which a valid statistical comparison is possible between jurisdictions scientifically equated as to population and economic and social conditions, the nations and states that have abolished capital punishment have a smaller capital crimes rate than the comparable jurisdictions that have retained the death penalty. Further, the capital crimes rate in those jurisdictions which, while retaining the death penalty, use it seldom or not at all is in most instances lower than the capital crimes rates in the retentionist jurisdictions which execute most frequently.

And, finally, comparing the before, during, and after capital crimes rates in those jurisdictions (nine in the United States) which abolished capital punishment and then restored it to their penal codes, we find a consistently downward trend in capital crimes unaffected by either abolition or restoration. Startling comparisons are available. The United States Navy has executed no one in more than 120 years; yet it has maintained a level of discipline, effectiveness, and morale certainly in no sense inferior to that of the United States Army which has inflicted the death penalty on more than 150 soldiers in just the last three decades.

Delaware, most recent state to abolish the death penalty, experienced a remarkable drop in its capital crimes rate during the first full year of abolition. No criminologist would argue that abolition will necessarily reduce capital crimes; nor will he attempt to demonstrate a causal connection between absence of the death penalty and low capital crimes rates. In point of fact, homicide is the one major felony which shows a consistent downward trend in both capital punishment and abolition jurisdictions—indicating to the student of human behavior that the crime of murder, particularly, is largely an irrational reaction to a concrescence of circumstances, adventitiously related, wholly independent of and neither positively nor negatively correlat-

able with the legal sanction provided in the jurisdiction in which the crime actually took place. Dr. Marvin Wolfgang has pointed out with some logic that our decreasing murder rate is probably in no small part due to improved communications (ambulance gets to the scene faster), improved first aid to the victim, and the antibiotics, blood banks, and similar advances in medicine which save many an assault victim from becoming a corpse—and of course his assailant from being tagged a murderer. The consistent upward trend in assaultive crimes gives support to Dr. Wolfgang's thesis.

7. *Police and prison officers are safer in non-death penalty states.* The studies of Donald Campion, S.J., associate editor of *America,* and others indicate (albeit with restricted samplings) that the life of a police officer or a prison guard is slightly safer in the non-death penalty states, although the difference is so slight as to be statistically insignificant. Prison wardens overwhelmingly support abolition but large segments of the police profession support the retention of the death penalty both as a general crime deterrent (which it demonstrably is not) and as a specific safeguard to members of their own profession. Significantly, few of the police officers who serve in non-death penalty states are active in the fight to restore capital punishment and most of those who oppose abolition in their own jurisdictions have never performed police duties in an abolition state. It is a cri-

minological axiom that it is the certainty, not the severity, of punishment that deters. Improvements in the selection, training, discipline, supervision, and operating techniques of our police will insure a higher percentage of apprehensions and convictions of criminals and, even without the death penalty, will provide a greater general crime deterrent and far more safety both for the general public and for police officers than either enjoys at present.

8. *Paroled and pardoned murderers are no threat to the public.* Studies in New Jersey and California, and less extensive studies of paroled and pardoned murderers in other jurisdictions, indicate that those whose death sentences have been commuted, or who have been paroled from life or long-term sentences, or who have received executive pardons after conviction of capital crimes are by far the least likely to recidivate. Not only do they not again commit homicide, but they commit other crimes or violate their parole contracts to a much lesser extent than do paroled burglars, robbers, and the generality of the non-capital crimes convicts on parole. My own study of nearly 150 murderers showed that not a single one had killed again and only two had committed any other crime subsequent to release. Ohio's Governor Michael DiSalle has pointed out (as Warden Lewis Lawes and other penologists have in the past) that murderers are by and large the best and safest prisoners; and he has demonstrated his confidence by

employing eight convicted murderers from the Ohio State Penitentiary in and about the Executive Mansion in Columbus in daily contact with the members of his family.

9. *The death penalty is more costly than its alternatives.* It seems somewhat immoral to discuss the taking of even a murderer's life in terms of dollars and cents; but often the argument is raised that capital punishment is the cheapest way of "handling" society's outcasts and that the "good" members of the community should not be taxed to support killers for life (often coupled with the euthanasian argument that "they are better off dead"). The application of elementary cost accounting procedures to the determination of the differential in costs peculiar to capital cases will effectively demonstrate that not only is it not "cheaper to hang them"; but that, on the contrary, it would be cheaper for the taxpayers to maintain our prospective executees in the comparative luxury of first-rate hotels, with all the perquisites of non-criminal guests, than to pay for having them executed. The tangible costs of the death penalty in terms of long-drawn-out jury selection, extended trials and retrials, appeals, extra security, maintenance of expensive, seldom-used death-houses, support of the felon's family, etc., are heavy.

10. *Capital punishment stands in the way of penal reform.* Man has used the death penalty and other forms of retributive punishment throughout the centuries to control

and govern the conduct of his fellows and to force conformity and compliance to laws and codes, taboos and customs. The record of every civilization makes abundantly clear that punishment, no matter how severe or sadistic, has had little effect on crime rates. No new approach to the criminal is possible so long as the death penalty, and the discredited penology it represents, pervades our criminal justice system. Until it is stricken from the statute books, a truly rehabilitative approach to the small percentage of our fellowmen who cannot or will not adjust to society's dictates is impossible of attainment. That there is a strong positive correlation between advocacy of the death penalty and a generally punitive orientation cannot be gainsaid. Analysis of the votes for corporal punishment bills, votes against substitution of alternative for mandatory features in the few mandatory death penalty jurisdictions, votes against study commissions and against limited period moratoria, and comparison with votes for bills increasing the penalties for rape, narcotics offenses, and other felonies discloses a pattern of simple retributive punitiveness, characterizing many of our legislators and the retentionist witnesses before legislative committees.

Many church assemblies of America and individual churchmen of every denomination have underscored the moral and ethical nonacceptability of capital punishment. Church members have the responsibility to support the campaign to erase this stain on American society. Capital punishment is brutal, sordid, and savage. It violates the law of God and is contrary to the humane and liberal respect for human life characteristic of modern democratic states. It is unsound criminologically and unnecessary for the protection of the state or its citizens. It makes miscarriages of justice irredeemable; it makes the barbaric *lex talionis* the watchword and inhibits the reform of our prison systems. It encourages disrespect for our laws, our courts, our institutions; and, in the words of Sheldon Glueck, "bedevils the administration of criminal justice and is the stumbling block in the path of general reform in the treatment of crime and criminals."

(Cont. from p. 171, van den Haag, "Death Penalty Deters Crime")

Consider the claim of injustice on its merits now. A convicted man may be found to have been innocent; if he was executed, the penalty cannot be reversed. Except for fines, other penalties cannot be reversed either: time spent in prison cannot be returned. However, a prison sentence may be remitted once the prisoner is found innocent; and he can be compensated for the time served (although compensation ordinarily cannot repair the harm). Thus, though (nearly) all penalties are irreversible, the death penalty, unlike others, is irrevocable as well.

Despite all precautions, errors will occur in judicial proceedings: the innocent may be found guilty; or the guilty rich may more easily escape conviction, or receive lesser penalties, than the guilty poor. These injustices do not reside in the penalties inflicted but in their maldistribution. It is not the penalty—death or prison—which is unjust when inflicted on the innocent but its imposition on someone who is innocent. Inequity between poor and rich also involves distribution, not the penalty distributed. Thus injustice is not an objection to the death penalty but to the distributive process—the trial. Trials are more likely to be fair when life is at stake—the death penalty is probably less often unjustly inflicted than any other. It requires special consideration not because it is more, or more often, unjust than other penalties but because it is always irrevocable.

Can any amount of deterrence justify the possibility of irrevocable injustice? Certainly injustice is by definition unjustifiable in each actual individual case; it must be objected to whenever it occurs. But we are concerned here with the process that may produce injustice, and the penalty that would make it irrevocable—not with the actual individual cases produced, but with general rules that potentially produce them. To consider objections to a general rule (the provision of any penalties by law), we must compare the likely net result of alternative rules and prefer the rule (or penalty) likely to produce the least injustice, since, however one defines it, to favor justice may mean more but cannot mean less than to favor the least injustice. If the death of innocents because of judicial error is unjust, so is the death of innocents by murder. If some murders could be avoided by a possibly deterrent penalty—for example, the death penalty—then the question becomes: which penalty will minimize the total number of innocents killed (by law enforcement and by law violation)? It follows that some amount of deterrence could justify irrevocable injustice.

In general, the possibility of injustice argues against penalization only if the expected usefulness of penalization is less important than the probable harm (particularly to innocents) and the probable inequities. The possibility of injustice argues against the death penalty only inasmuch as the added usefulness (deterrence) expected from irrevocability is thought less important than the added harm. (Were my argument specifically concerned with justice, I could compare the injustice inflicted by the courts with the injustice—outside the courts— avoided by the judicial process. That is, "important" here may be used to include everything to which importance is attached.)

We must briefly examine now the

general use and effectiveness of deterrence to decide whether the death penalty adds enough deterrence to be warranted.

Does any punishment "deter others" at all? Doubts have been thrown on this effect because it is thought to depend on the incorrect rationalistic psychology of some of its eighteenth and nineteenth-century proponents. Actually deterrence does not depend on rational calculation, on rationality or capacity for it, or on rationalistic psychology. Deterrence depends on the regularity—not on the rationality—of human responses to danger and on the possibility of reinforcing internal controls by vicarious external experiences.

Responsiveness to danger is generally found in human behavior; the danger can, but need not, come from the law or from society; nor need it be explicitly verbalized. Unless intent on suicide, people do not jump from high mountain cliffs, however tempted they are to fly through the air; and they take precautions against falling. The mere risk of injury often restrains us from doing what is otherwise attractive; we refrain even when we have no direct experience, and usually without explicit computation of probabilities, let alone conscious weighing of expected pleasure against possible pain. One abstains from dangerous acts because of vague, inchoate, habitual, and, above all, preconscious fears. Risks and rewards are more often felt than calculated; one abstains without accounting to oneself because "it isn't done" or because one literally does not conceive of the action one refrains from.

Unlike natural dangers, legal threats are constructed deliberately by legislators to restrain actions which may impair the social order. Thus legislators try to transform *social* into *personal* dangers. I must forego elaboration here of the added element of moral obligation, which transforms external into internal danger. Though arising from the authority of rulers and rules, it is constantly reinforced by the coercive imposition of that authority on recalcitrants. Most people refrain from offenses because they feel an obligation to behave lawfully. This feeling of obligation internalizes social rules and social authority and is reinforced with the help of penalties.

Although the legislators may calculate their threats and the responses to be produced, the effectiveness of the threats neither requires nor depends on calculations by those responding. The predictor (or producer) must calculate, not the predicted (or produced). Hence, although legislation (and legislators) should be rational, subjects need not be, in order to be deterred as intended. They only need to be responsive.

Punishments deter those who have not violated the law for the same reasons—and in the same degrees (except for reinforcement and internalization: moral obligation)—as do natural dangers. Often natural dangers (all dangers not deliberately created by legislation—

for example, injury of the criminal inflicted by the crime victim) are insufficient. Thus, the fear of injury (natural danger) does not suffice to control city traffic; it must be reinforced by the legal punishment meted out to those who violate the rules. These punishments keep most people observing the regulations. However, where (in the absence of natural danger) the threatened punishment is so light that the advantage of violating rules tends to exceed the disadvantage of being punished (divided by the risk), the rule is violated (that is, parking fines are too light). In this case, the feeling of obligation tends to vanish as well. Elsewhere, punishment deters.

To be sure, not everybody responds to threatened punishment. Non-responsive persons may be (a) self-destructive or (b) incapable of responding to threats (or even of grasping them). Increases in the size, or certainty, of penalties would not affect these two groups. A third group (c) might respond to more certain or more severe penalties. If the punishment threatened for burglary, robbery, or rape were a five dollar fine in North Carolina, and five years in prison in South Carolina, I have no doubt that the North Carolina treasury would become quite opulent (until vigilante justice would provide the deterrence not provided by law). Whether to increase penalties (or improve enforcement) depends on the importance of the rule to society, the size and likely reaction of the group that did not respond before, and the added punishment and enforcement

required to deter it. Observation would have to locate the points—likely to differ in different times and places—at which diminishing, zero, and negative returns set in. There is no reason to believe that all present and future offenders belong to the a priori non-responsive groups or that all penalties have reached the point of diminishing, let alone zero, returns.

Even though its effectiveness seems obvious, punishment as a deterrent has fallen into disrepute. Some ideas which help explain this progressive heedlessness were uttered by Lester Pearson, then prime minister of Canada, when, in opposing the death penalty, he proposed that, instead, "the state seek to eradicate the causes of crime—slums, ghettos and personality disorders."

"Slums, ghettos and personality disorders" have not been shown, singly or collectively, to be "the causes" of crime.

1. The crime rate in slums is indeed higher than elsewhere; but so is the death rate in hospitals. Slums are no more "causes" of crime than hospitals are of death; they are locations of crime, as hospitals are of death. Slums and hospitals attract people selectively; neither is the "cause" of the condition (disease in hospitals, poverty in slums) that leads to the selective attraction.

As for poverty which pulls people into slums and, sometimes, into crime, *any* relative disadvantage may lead to ambition, frustration, resentment, and, if insufficiently restrained, to crime. Not all relative disadvantages can be eliminated; indeed, very few can be, and their elimination increases the resentment generated by the remaining ones; not even relative poverty can be removed altogether. (Absolute poverty—whatever that may be— hardly affects crime.) However, though contributory, relative disadvantages are not a necessary or a sufficient cause of crime: most poor people do not commit crimes, and some rich people do. Hence, "eradication of poverty" would, at most, remove one (doubtful) cause of crime.

2. Negro ghettos have a high crime rate; Chinese ghettos have a low one. Ethnic separation, voluntary or forced, obviously has little to do with crime. I can think of no reason why it should.

3. I cannot see how the state could "eradicate" personality disorders even if all causes and cures were known and available. Nor are personality disorders necessary or sufficient causes for criminal offenses, unless these be identified by means of (moral, not clinical) definition with personality disorders. In this case, Mr. Pearson would have proposed to "eradicate" crime by eradicating crime—certainly a sound, but not a very helpful, idea.

Mr. Pearson's views were voiced more vaguely but not less delusively by U.S. Attorney-General Ramsey Clark, when he told a congressional committee that "only the elimination of the causes of crime can make

a significant and lasting difference in the incidence of crime." Uncharitably interpreted, Mr. Clark revealed that only the elimination of causes eliminates effects—a sleazy cliche and wrong to boot. Given the benefit of the doubt, Clark probably meant that the causes of crime are social and that, therefore, crime can be reduced "only" by non-penal (social) measures.

The attorney-general's view suggests a fireman who declines fire-extinguishing apparatus by pointing out that "in the long run only the elimination of the causes" of fire "can make a significant and lasting difference in the incidence" of fire and that fire-fighting equipment does not eliminate "the causes"— except that such a fireman would probably not rise to fire chief. Actually, whether fires are checked depends on fire-fighting apparatus and on the efforts of the firemen using it no less than on the presence of "the causes": inflammable materials. So with crimes. Laws, court, and police actions are no less important in restraining them than "the causes" are in impelling them. If firemen (or attorneys-general) pass the buck, and refuse to use the means available, we may all be burned while waiting for "the long run" and "the elimination of the causes."

Whether any activity—be it lawful or unlawful—takes place depends on whether the desire for it, or for whatever is to be secured by it, is stronger than the desire to avoid the costs involved. Accordingly, people work, attend college, commit crimes, go to the movies—or refrain from any of these activities. Attendance at a theater may be high because the show is entertaining and because the price is low. Obviously, the attendance depends on both—on the combination of expected gratification and cost. The wish, motive, or impulse for doing anything—the experienced, or expected, gratification—is the cause of doing it; the wish to avoid the cost is the cause of not doing it. One is no more and no less "cause" than the other. In this sense, penalties (costs) are causes of lawfulness, or (if too low or uncertain) of unlawfulness, of crime. People do commit crimes because, given their conditions, the desire for the satisfaction sought prevails. They refrain if the desire to avoid the cost prevails. The crime rate increases if the cost is reduced or the desire raised. It can be decreased by raising the cost or by reducing the desire.

The cost of crime is more easily and swiftly changed than the conditions producing the inclination to it. Further, the costs are very largely within the power of the government to change, whereas the conditions producing propensity are often only indirectly affected by government action, and some are altogether beyond the control of the government. Our unilateral emphasis on these conditions and our undue neglect of costs may contribute to an unnecessarily high crime rate.

The foregoing suggests the question posed by the death penalty: is the deterrence added (return)

sufficiently above zero to warrant irrevocability (or other, less clear, disadvantages)? The question is not only whether the penalty deters but whether it deters more than alternatives and whether the difference exceeds the cost of irrevocability. (I shall assume that the alternative is actual life imprisonment so as to exclude the complication produced by the release of the unrehabilitated.).

In some fairly infrequent but important circumstances, the death penalty is the only possible deterrent. Thus, in case of acute coups d'etat, or of acute substantial attempts to overthrow the government, prospective rebels would altogether discount the threat of any prison sentence. They would not be deterred because they believe the swift victory of the revolution will invalidate a prison sentence and turn it into an advantage. Execution would be the only deterrent because, unlike prison sentences, it cannot be revoked by victorious rebels. The same reasoning applies to deterring spies or traitors in wartime. Finally, men who, by virtue of past acts, are already serving, or are threatened by, a life sentence, could be deterred from further offenses only by the threat of the death penalty.

What about criminals who do not fall into any of these (often ignored) classes? Professor Thorsten Sellin has made a careful study of the available statistics; he concluded that they do not yield evidence for the deterring effect of the death penalty. Somewhat surprisingly,

Sellin seems to think that this lack of evidence for deterrence is evidence for the lack of deterrence. It is not. It means that deterrence has not been demonstrated statistically—not that non-deterrence has been.

It is entirely possible, indeed likely (as Sellin appears willing to concede), that the statistics used, though the best available, are nonetheless too slender a reed to rest conclusions on. They indicate that the homicide rate does not vary greatly between similar areas with or without the death penalty, and in the same area before and after abolition. However, the similar areas are not similar enough; the periods are not long enough: many social differences and changes, other than the abolition of the death penalty, may account for the variation (or lack of it) in homicide rates with and without, before and after abolition; some of these social differences and changes are likely to have affected homicide rates. I am unaware of any statistical analysis which adjusts for such changes and differences.

Homicide rates do not depend exclusively on penalties any more than other crime rates. A number of conditions which influence the the propensity of crime, demographic, economic, or generally social, changes or differences—even such matters as changes in the divorce laws or in the cotton price—may influence the homicide rate. Wherefore variation or constancy cannot be attributed to variations or constancy of the penalties, unless we know that no other factor in-

fluencing the homicide rate has changed. Usually we do not. To believe the death penalty deterrent does not require one to believe that the death penalty, or any other, is the only, or the decisive, causal variable; this would be as absurd as the converse mistake that "social causes" are the only, or always the decisive, factor. To favor capital punishment, the efficacy of neither variable need be denied. It is enough to affirm that the severity of the penalty may influence some potential criminals and that the added severity of the death penalty adds to deterrence, or may do so. It is quite possible that such a deterrent effect may be offset (or intensified) by non-penal factors which affect propensity; its presence or absence, therefore, may be hard, and perhaps impossible, to demonstrate.

Contrary to what Sellin and others seem to presume, I doubt that offenders are aware of the absence or presence of the death penalty state by state or period by period. Such unawareness argues against the assumption of a calculating murderer. However, unawareness does not argue against the death penalty if by deterrence we mean a preconscious, general response to a severe but not necessarily specifically and explicitly apprehended or calculated threat. A constant homicide rate, despite abolition, may occur because of unawareness and not because of lack of deterrence: people remain deterred for a lengthy interval by the severity of the penalty in the past, or by the severity of penalties used in similar circumstances nearby.

I do not argue for a version of deterrence which would require me to believe that an individual shuns murder because of the death penalty while in North Dakota, and merrily goes to it in South Dakota, since it has been abolished there; or that he will start a murderous career, from which he had hitherto refrained, after abolition. I hold that the generalized threat of the death penalty may be a deterrent, and the more so, the more generally applied. Deterrence will not cease in the particular areas of abolition or at the particular times of abolition. Rather, general deterrence will be somewhat weakened, through local (partial) abolition. Even such weakening will be hard to detect owing to changes in many offsetting, or reinforcing, factors.

For all of these reasons, I doubt that the presence or absence of a deterrent effect of the death penalty is likely to be demonstrable by statistical means. The statistics presented by Sellin and others show only that there is no statistical proof for the deterrent effect of the death penalty. But they do not show that there is no deterent effect. Not to demonstrate presence of the effect is not the same as to demonstrate its absence; certainly not, when there are plausible explanations for the nondemonstrability of the effect.

It is on our uncertainty that the case for deterrence must rest.

If we do not know whether the death penalty will deter others, we are confronted with two uncertain-ties. If we impose the death penalty, and achieve no deterrent effect thereby, the life of a convicted murderer has been expended in vain (from a deterrent viewpoint). There is a net loss. If we impose the death sentence, and thereby deter some future murderers, we spare the lives of some future victims (the pros-pective murderers gain, too: they are spared punishment because they were deterred). In this case, the death penalty has led to a net gain, unless the life of a convicted murderer is valued more highly than that of the unknown victim, or vic-tims (and the non-imprisonment of the deterred non-murderer).

The calculation can be turned around, of course. The absence of the death penalty may harm no one and therefore produce a gain—the life of the convicted murderer. Or it may kill future victims of murderers who could have been deterred and thus produce a loss—their life.

To be sure, we must risk some-thing certain—the death (or life) of the convicted man, for something uncertain—the death (or life) of the victims of murderers who may be deterred. This is in the nature of uncertainty; when we invest, or gamble, we risk the money we have for an uncertain gain. Many human actions, most commitments—in-cluding marriage and crime—share this characteristic with the deter-rent purpose of any penalization, and with its rehabilitative purpose (and even with the protective).

More proof is demanded for the deterrent effect of the death penalty than is demanded for the deterrent effect of other penalties. This is not justified by the absence of other utilitarian purposes, such as protection and rehabilitation; they involve no less uncertainty than deterrence.

Irrevocability may support a demand for some reason to expect more deterrence than revocable penalties might produce but not a demand for more proof of deterrence, as has been pointed out. . . (above). The reason for expecting more deterrence lies in the greater severity, the terrifying effect inherent in finality. Since it seems more important to spare victims than to spare murderers, the burden of proving that the greater severity inherent in irrevocability adds nothing to deterrence lies on those who oppose capital punishment. Proponents of the death penalty need show only that there is no more uncertainty about it than about greater severity in general.

The demand that the death penalty be proved more deterrent than alternatives cannot be satisfied any more than the demand that six years in prison be proved to be more deterrent than three. But the uncertainty which confronts us favors the death penalty as long as by imposing it we might save future victims of murder. This effect is as plausible as the general idea that penalties have deterrent effects which increase with their severity. Though we have no proof of the positive deterrence of the penalty, we also have no proof of zero or negative effectiveness. I believe we have no right to risk additional future victims of murder for the sake of sparing convicted murderers; on the contrary, our moral obligation is to risk the possible ineffectiveness of executions. However rationalized, the opposite view appears to be motivated by the simple fact that executions are subject to more social control than murders. However, this applies to all penalties and does not argue for the abolition of any.

POSTSCRIPT
IS CAPITAL PUNISHMENT JUSTIFIED?

Opinion in the United States has always been sharply divided on the death penalty. While Massachusetts in 1785 defined nine capital crimes (that is, crimes punishable by death), and North Carolina as late as 1837 had more than twenty, other states early rejected the death sentence entirely. American sentiment has been so divided that at least eleven of the states have abolished the death penalty only to restore it some years later.

In the readings in this chapter, MacNamara acknowledges a variety of assertions made in defense of the penalty as well as his need to rebut each of them. By contrast, van den Haag emphasizes only one, the death penalty as a surer deterrent of future crime—at least by the murderer being executed. Neither of these closely reasoned examinations should obscure the fact that most consideration of capital punishment is not as rational. Deep emotional and moral convictions are not likely to be much influenced by statistics on murder and executions, the relationship between murder rates and frequency of executions, and the constitutional issue of whether or when the death sentence constitutes "cruel or unusual punishment."

The student who prefers evidence to emotion will find a wealth of historical and statistical material in William J. Bowers, *Executions in America* (Lexington Books, 1974). The movement that led to the abolition of the death penalty in Great Britain prompted the publication of several books, the most stimulating of which is Arthur Koestler and C. H. Rolph, *Hanged by the Neck* (Penguin, 1961). Probably the most reflective, and almost certainly the most engrossing, literature on the subject in the United States is to be found in the many books dealing with the executions of Sacco and Vanzetti (plays and films have also dealt with their case), the Rosenbergs, and Caryl Chessman. In each of these cases, deep feelings favoring and opposing their execution were aroused by political issues and questions regarding their guilt, as well as by divided sentiments on the exercise of capital punishment. Almost certainly, popular attitudes toward the death sentence in these cases were never entirely separable from other circumstances.

Apart from the constitutional issues, the debate is more narrowly drawn than in earlier times. Although the death penalty is sometimes urged as punishment for such acts as treason or skyjacking, it is principally considered in connecton with the crime of murder. There is little dispute with the proposition that the manner of execution should be least painful—no one is drawn and quartered in modern civilized society—although there is no unanimity of opinion as to whether death by electrocution, gas, or hanging best meets that test. However, it is neither the question of how or how often to impose capital punishment, but whether to take a life for a life that society is obliged to examine.

ISSUE 10

AFFIRMATIVE ACTION: IS IT EQUALITY OR IS IT REVERSE DISCRIMINATION?

Equality is as basic a political principle in America as liberty. "All men are created equal" is the most famous phrase in the Declaration of Independence. More than half a century later, Alexis de Tocqueville examined *Democracy in America* and concluded that its most essential ingredient was the equality of condition. We know it was not true, not for women, not for blacks, not for Indians and other racial minorities, and not for other disadvantaged social classes. Nevertheless the ideal persisted. When slavery was abolished after the Civil War, the Constitution's then-new Fourteenth Amendment proclaimed: "No State shall . . . deny to any person within its jurisdiction the equal protection of the laws."

Equality has been a long time coming. For nearly a century after the freeing of the slaves, American blacks were denied equal protection by law in some states and by social practice nearly everywhere. One-third of the states and the national capital either permitted or compelled racially segregated schools, and a similar result was achieved elsewhere through housing policy and social behavior. In 1954 the Supreme Court reversed a 58-year-old standard which had found "separate but equal" schools compatible with equal protection of the law. A unanimous Court held that separate is not equal for the members of the discriminated-against group when the segregation "generates a feeling of inferiority as to their status in the community that may affect their hearts and minds in a way unlikely ever to be undone." The 1954 ruling on public elementary education has been extended by many decisions since to other areas of both governmental and private conduct, including housing and employment.

Even if judicial decisions and congressional statutes could end all segregation and racial discrimination, would we have achieved equality—or merely an end to future inequality? The question requires examination of housing patterns which have both by design (unscrupulous realty practices and restrictive sales and rentals) and circumstance (public housing concentrated in the central cities, while new private home building has taken place in the growing suburbs) physically separated whites and blacks, including the children who cannot easily be integrated in the schools if they live far apart. The question posed above also compels consideration of whether non-discrimination achieves equality in employment if minority-group members do not meet the qualifications for particular jobs, and if a generation or more must pass before the proportion of blacks or women in a given occupation reflects their proportion in the total population.

The answer the courts have given is that government has a responsibility to insure equality now, but courts have divided on the issue of whether equality implies equal distribution and equal rewards now. Carried to its logical conclusion, the desire for equal results has led courts in school cases to order compulsory busing of children to schools far from home in order to establish a judicially determined racial balance. In employment cases a similar reasoning has resulted in controversial programs of affirmative action.

At the heart of the controversy is a profound difference regarding equality. To the advocates of affirmative action, treatment cannot be equitable unless it is preferential for those who have been subject to discrimination and disadvantages not of their own making. Whether we look upon the policy as society's repayment of a debt or its fulfillment of an obligation, equality must not only be proclaimed, it must be made unequivocally evident. This can happen only when racial and ethnic groups possess the jobs and privileges of society in proportion to their numbers.

To the critics, affirmative action is a euphemism for a different discrimination. The motive of compensatory treatment for centuries of prejudice may be noble, but the consequence is the same under the new as under the old discrimination, except that the tables have turned. A quota system, which critics of affirmative action often call it, violates equal protection and racial and ethnic equality just as surely as the racial exclusion which we   have banished.

There are technical problems, in the definition of those who are to receive favored treatment and in the determination of when to terminate a preferential program. But the overriding questions are moral and political. Does the new discriminate compensate for the old and create a society fairer not only in form but also in fact? Or does it establish new injustice, new bitterness, and new racial tensions?

The sides are clearly drawn in the following selections. Herbert Hill and Nathan Glazer both profess an unswerving commitment to equality, yet they find themselves diametrically opposed on the constitutional, moral, and political consequences of affirmative action.

Herbert Hill

"RACE-CONSCIOUS INJURIES REQUIRE RACE-CONSCIOUS REMEDIES"

The Civil Rights Act of 1964 was debated and eventually enacted into law during a time of turmoil and upheaval. For a brief period, a part of the white population joined with black Americans in expressing a vast outrage against the crimes of racism. During the mid-1960s, as a result of direct confrontation with the forces of segregation and discrimination, together with the emergence of a new body of constitutional law, a great hope was born—a hope that the legacy of centuries of slavery and racism would finally be abolished and that America, at long last, would become a just, decent, and compassionate society.

But that hope was not yet to be realized. In retrospect, it is evident that the high moral outburst of the 1960s was but a passing spasm. The memory of that period has already receded and diminished into a remote past, and black people, once again, are left to fight the battle alone. . . .

A major manifestation of the sharp turning away from the goal of racial equality is to be found in the shrill and paranoid attacks against affirmative action programs. The effort to eliminate the present effects of past discrimination, to right the wrongs of many generations was barely underway when it was aborted. And now, even the very modest gains made by black men and women through affirmative action are being erased, as powerful institutions turn the clock of history back to the dark and dismal days of "separate but equal."

Judging by the vast outcry, it might be assumed that the use of numerical goals and timetables to eliminate racist job patterns has become as widespread and destructive as discrimination itself. As with the much distorted subject of busing, the defenders of the racial status quo have once again succeeded in confusing the remedy with the original evil. The term "quota" like "busing" has become another code word for resistance to demands for the elimination of prevailing patterns of discrimination.

This issue is now a major national controversy and because it has become the focus of conflicting forces in current civil rights struggles, it is necessary to identify, within the limits of this paper, the leading opponents of affirmative action. The attack comes from many places, among these are the academic

Continued on p. 194

From Herbert Hill, "Affirmative Action and the Quest for Job Equality," in *The Review of Black Political Economy*, Spring 1976, pp. 263-276. Copyright © 1976 by The Review of Black Political Economy. Reprinted by permission. Footnotes have been omitted.

Nathan Glazer

"COMPENSATION FOR THE PAST IS A DANGEROUS PRINCIPLE"

A new course in dealing with the issues of equality that arise in the American multiethnic society has been set since the early 1970s. It is demonstrated that there is discrimination or at least some condition of inequality through the comparison of statistical patterns, and then racial and ethnic quotas and statistical requirements for employment and school assignment are imposed. This course is not demanded by legislation—indeed, it is specifically forbidden by national legislation—or by any reasonable interpretation of the Constitution. Nor is it justified, I have argued, by any presumed failure of the policies of nondiscrimination and of affirmative action that prevailed until the early 1970s. Until then, affirmative action meant to seek out and prepare members of minority groups for better jobs and educational opportunities. It still means only this much in the field of residential distribution. But in the early 1970s affirmative action came to mean much more than advertising opportunities actively, seeking out those who might not know of them, and preparing those who might not yet be qualified. It came to mean the setting of statistical requirements based on race, color, and national origin for employers and educational institutions. This new course threatens the abandonment of our concern for individual claims to consideration on the basis of justice and equity, now to be replaced with a concern for rights for publicly determined and delimited racial and ethnic groups.

The supporters of the new policy generally argue that it is a temporary one. They argue (or some do) that consideration of race, color, and national origin in determining employment and education is repugnant, but it is required for a brief time to overcome a heritage of discrimination. I have argued that the heritage of discrimination, as we could see from the occupational developments of the later 1960s, could be overcome by simply attacking discrimination. The statistical-pattern approach was instituted *after,* not before, the remarkably rapid improvement in the black economic and occupational position in the 1960s. I have argued that the claim that school assignment on the basis of race and ethnicity is only temporary is false, because the supporters of such an approach now demand it whatever the

Continued on p. 202

Excerpted from *Affirmative Discrimination: Ethnic Inequality and Public Policy,* by Nathan Glazer, © 1975 by Nathan Glazer, Basic Books, Inc., Publishers, New York.

10. AFFIRMATIVE ACTION

(Hill, cont. from p. 192)

community and the educational bureaucracy, big business and labor unions, white ethnic organizations and, of course, the federal government itself. Although worthy of a far more extensive examination, a few examples will suffice.

The clarion call in the ideological war against affirmative action was sounded by Professor Sidney Hook, . . . who denounced affirmative action programs in institutions of higher learning and called upon his colleagues to resist all such demands from civil rights groups. He was soon joined by many distinguished academicians and the Committee for a Rational Alternative emerged (later known as the University Center for Rational Alternatives) followed by the Committee on Academic Non-discrimination and Integrity. These groups, using the names of some of the most prestigious figures in academia and with virtually unlimited access to the media have conducted a steady drumbeat of attack against affirmative action programs in colleges and universities. . . .

The Anti-Defamation League of B'nai B'rith and the American Jewish Congress both condemned affirmative action requirements imposed by the federal government on educational institutions and on June 20, 1972 called on the Department of Health, Education and Welfare to repudiate "preferential treatment" in federally funded programs. On August 4, 1972, the American Jewish Committee in an open letter to President Nixon urged him to "reject categorically the use of quotas and proportional representation" in civil rights programs, and on January 12, 1973 six national Jewish organizations charging "reverse discrimination" against white males sent a protest to the Department of Health, Education and Welfare urging it to "prevent or eliminate preferential treatment."

Typical of the position of most labor unions is the resolution adopted by the AFL-CIO Building and Construction Trades Department which stated:

> Racial quotas, under any guise are repugnant to all Americans. When a proposal is made to establish racial quotas as public policy, honest men must protest. . . We prefer the free choice of free men and we are certain that the vast majority of Americans, white and nonwhite alike prefer such freedom.

Spokesmen for corporate enterprise issued equally sanctimonious expressions of outrage and in March of 1973 *Fortune* magazine further distorted the issue by warning against the dangers of job quotas. Its executive editor, Daniel Seligman, wrote, "For a democratic society to systematically discriminate against 'the majority' seems quite without precedent."

Another major source of organized opposition to the mandate of affirmative action developed in litigation under Title VII, comes from the newly emerging network of groups based on the ethnic working-class population. The undeniable fact that the white worker is exploited has in the recent past been solemnly rediscovered in a variety of books and articles. But those who engage in these idealized portrayals of the white proletariat conveniently forget that the black working-class is the most systematically discriminated against and exploited group in American society; that the victimization of Blacks has been different in kind from anything known by the white ethnics. Furthermore, the past and present deprivation experienced by white workers of various ethnic backgrounds cannot be accepted as justification for their intense opposition to black advancement, nor can their violence and racism be excused on the grounds that they too have suffered.

Michael Novak, a leading spokesman for the "unmeltable ethnics," to use his term, sought recently to warrant the intransigent response of these white workers to black demands for equality by blithely explaining that current racial problems are due to "special weaknesses in the culture of American blacks." This attempt to make the victims responsible for their condition while exonerating the actions of those who firebomb buses carrying black children and engage in other acts of racist violence is, of course, obscene but typical of the current attitude. Whatever lofty sentiments are spouted by those who try to excuse white working-class racism, the truth about the new ethnic revivalism is revealed on the streets of Boston, Brooklyn, Louisville, and

elsewhere. After all the pieties are stripped away, the real reason for the existence of these groups is made clear by their oft repeated cry "STOP THE NIGGERS."

The diverse forces united in their intense opposition to affirmative action programs deliberately distort the issue by equating affirmative action based upon numerical goals with a fiction called the "quota system" and "reverse discrimination." But there is a fundamental distinction between quotas and numerical goals. Quotas are used to exclude, while numerical goals are a means to include those workers who have been systematically excluded in the past. Quotas establish a ceiling—that is, a maximum. Numerical goals used in affirmative action establish only a minimum which can, and often should be exceeded. In short, quotas have been used as a limitation, while numerical goals represent the exact opposite.

Those who attack the use of numerical goals often argue that affirmative action programs will penalize innocent whites who are not responsible for past discriminatory practices. This argument turns on the notion of individual rights and sounds very moral and high-minded, indeed. But it ignores basic social reality. For example, black workers have not been denied jobs as individuals but as a class— no matter what their personal merits and qualifications. Women have not been denied training and jobs as individuals, but as a class regardless of their individual talent or lack of it.

Correspondingly, white males as a class have benefitted from this systematic discrimination. Wherever discriminatory employment patterns exist, hiring and promotion without affirmative action perpetuates injustice.

The federal courts have recognized in Title VII litigation that employment discrimination is by its nature class discrimination. . . . It was also established that relief must go to the entire injured class and the use of specified numerical goals can be most effective in achieving compliance with the law.

Common to most attacks upon affirmative action programs is the assumption that such approaches constitute "reverse discrimination" and that the quality of performance and work standards will be severely diminished as a result of the employment of non-whites and women. The *a priori* assumption that no "qualified" Blacks or women exist is implicit in this argument. Also implicit is the assuption that if Blacks and women were to be employed, the allegedly high standards now in force would be diminished. But in reality, the so-called merit system operates to give preference to mediocre or incompetent whites at the expense of highly talented Blacks, as well as at the expense of mediocre and incompetent Blacks.

In *Chance v. Board of Examiners* (in which the United Federation of Teachers, AFL-CIO, filed a brief *amicus curiae* against the black and Puerto Rican plaintiffs and against "infamous quota systems") a federal court ruled that New York City must stop using its traditional examinations for selecting school principals becuase the tests had the "effect of discriminating significantly and substantially against qualified black and Puerto Rican applicants." The court concluded that the procedures of the Board of Examiners, allegedly based upon the merit system, could not be justified as being reasonably related to job performance. . . .

To argue that the merit approach operates in the building trades, as spokesmen for organized labor frequently do, is to depart from all reason and sanity. As had been demonstrated in many lawsuits throughout the country, the worst forms of nepotism and favoritism prevail. . . .

In *U.S. v. Local 46, Lathers Union*, in New York City, the district court found that:

> There is a deep-rooted and pervasive practice in this Union of handing out jobs on the basis of union membership, kinship, friendship and, generally, 'pull.' The specific tactics, practices, devices and arrangements just enumerated have amounted in practical fact to varying modes of implementing this central pattern of unlawful criteria. The hirings at the site, the bypassing of the lists, the use of the hiring hall, when it was used at all, as a formality rather than as a place for legitimate and nondiscriminatory distribution of work—all reflected the basic evil of preferring Local 46 members, relatives, friends or friends of friends in job referrals.

And since the membership of this Local has for so long been almost exclusively white, the result could have been forecast: the jobs, and especially the more desirable jobs, have gone disproportionately to whites rather than blacks.

Commenting on the relationship between nepotism and racial discrimination, the Court added a sharply worded statement:

> Because courts may know what all the world knows, practices of nepotism and favoritism like those disclosed here could, and probably should, be condemned as inevitably discriminatory, . . . the Government has shown in case after case the preference of whites over blacks on grounds of nepotism or acquaintanceship. The officers of the Local did not merely acquiesce in this state of affairs; many, if not all, have been active participants in the pattern of favoritism and its inevitable concomitant, racial discrimination.

Under the guise of defending "merit systems" that in reality do not exist, the opponents of affirmative action are, in fact, attempting to maintain unstated but traditional discriminatory practices that result in the exclusion of Blacks, women, and others from desirable, high-paying, skilled jobs. A major factor in the resistance to new legal remedies is that white male expectations, based on the systematic denial of the rights of minorities, have become the norm. Thus any alteration of this norm is considered "reverse discrimination."

It should be evident that what is really involved in the debate over affirmative action programs is not that Blacks and women will be given preference over white males, but that a substantial body of law now requires that discriminatory systems which operate to favor white males at the expense of women and Blacks must be eliminated.

During the past quarter of a century, the federal courts have increasingly recognized the validity of numerical goals in eliminating traditional forms of discrimination. The courts have used this approach as a remedy to end systematic discrimination in the selection of juries and it has also been utilized in legislative reapportionment litigation, and in school segregation cases.

In *Swann v. Charlotte-Mecklenburg Board of Education,* the Supreme Court held that:

> Absent a constitutional violation there would be no basis for judicially ordering assignment of students on a racial basis. All things being equal, with no history of discrimination, it might well be desirable to assign pupils to schools nearest their homes. But all things are not equal in a system that has been deliberately constructed and maintained to enforce racial segregation. The remedy for such segregation may be administratively awkward, inconvenient and even bizarre in some situations and may impose burdens on some; but all awkwardness and inconvenience cannot be avoided in the interim period when remedial adjustments are being

made to eliminate the dual school systems.

Significantly, the Court ruled that mathematical racial ratios could be used as "a starting point in the process of shaping a remedy."

Although the courts have repeatedly spoken on this issue, the extensive public discussion of affirmative action programs has ignored the major legal interpretations of the validity of numerical goals and timetables in civil rights enforcement efforts. In the last half of the 1960s, as a result of an emerging body of law relating to employment discrimination, new forms of implementation were developed to obtain compliance with legal requirements. Among the most important of these was the concept of numerical goals to be achieved within stated time frames. The use of numbers expressed in the form of goals and timetables to enforce the legal prohibitions against job discrimination had its origin in a Fourteenth Amendment case, *Ethridge v. Rhodes.* . . .

In this case, the NAACP proposed the principle that state agencies require a contractual commitment from building contractors to employ a specific minimum number of black and other minority workers in each craft at every stage of construction. This concept, later incorporated in the Philadelphia Plan, was potentially the most effective means of achieving compliance with the law. The Philadelphia Plan, challenged in the federal courts, was a significant development in contract compliance efforts. It was to become the case that joined the issue and was most important in establishing the legality of the use of numerical goals in federal civil rights enforcement.

In response to the arguments of contractors and labor unions that the plan contained illegal racial quotas, the U.S. Court of Appeals for the Third Circuit stated, "Clearly the Philadelphia Plan color-conscious . . . In other contexts color-consciousness has been deemed to be an appropriate remedial posture."

The court further held that:

> The Philadelphia Plan is valid Executive action designed to remedy the perceived evil that minority tradesmen have not been included in the labor pool in which the Federal Government has a cost and performance interest. The Fifth Amendment does not prohibit such action.

In this important decision, the appellate court decisively rejected the argument that government imposed goals and timetables for the employment of Blacks and other minorities was unconstitutional. On the contrary, the court specifically validated the legality of this approach where necessary and the Supreme Court let it stand by refusing to review.

In a later case involving the Illinois state government, the Seventh Circuit Court of Appeals in 1972 affirmed the use of job ratios and held that:

> Numerical objectives may be the only feasible mechanism for defining with any clarity the obli-

gation of federal contractors to move employment practices in the direction of true neutrality.

As the courts perceive it, pledges of passive non-discrimination alter nothing and there is no meaningful measure of change other than numbers.

In this context, federal courts repeatedly recognized that race-conscious injuries require race-conscious remedies. In *Norwalk CORE v. Norwalk Redevelopment Agency,* a federal court stated:

> What we have said may require classification by race. That is something which the Constitution usually forbids, not because it is inevitably an impermissible classification, but because it is one which usually, to our national shame, has been drawn for the purpose of maintaining racial inequality. Where it is drawn for the purpose of achieving equality it will be allowed, and to the extent that it is necessary to avoid unequal treatment by race, it will be required. . . .

In *Associated General Contractors of Massachusetts, Inc. v. Altshuler,* a federal court validated a statewide affirmative action plan requiring building contractors to employ a specified minimum percentage of minority workers. In rather eloquent language the court explained the necessity for such approaches:

> It is by now well understood, however, that our society cannot be completely color-blind in the short term if we are to have a color-blind society in the long term. After centuries of viewing through colored lenses, eyes do not quickly

adjust when the lenses are removed. Discrimination has a way of perpetuating itself, albeit unintentionally, because the resulting inequalities make new opportunities less accessible. Preferential treatment is one partial prescription to remedy our society's most intransigent and deeply rooted inequalities. . . .

On the basis of these and other federal court decisions, it is evident that a substantial body of case law has established not only the permissibility, but indeed the necessity, of numerical goals and affirmative action programs to eliminate discriminatory employment patterns. But the opponents of affirmative action persist in their campaign of distortion, deliberately confusing goals with the pejoratively labeled "quotas" and denouncing affirmative action as "reverse discrimination."

It must also be noted that Title VII contains an affirmative action provision, 706(g), which authorizes federal courts, after a finding of unlawful employment practices, to "order such affirmative action as appropriate which may include but is not limited to . . . the hiring of employees . . . or any other equitable relief that the court deems appropriate." Ten years of active litigation under Title VII demonstrates that the normal operation of seniority structures, of testing procedures, and of so-called "merit" systems usually perpetuates the discriminatory pattern. Thus, litigation under Title VII has resulted in a new judicial perception of the nature of employment discrimination and in far-reaching decisions, such as that of the Supreme Court in *Griggs v. Duke Power Co.*, which held that it is consequences, not intent, that matters and that traditional job testing methods which result in the exclusion of Blacks and other minorities from desirable job classifications are unlawful.

A well-orchestrated nationwide propaganda operation, based upon systematic misrepresentation and the manipulation of racial fears among whites has succeeded in causing the federal government to retreat on these crucial issues. Administrative enforcement of affirmative action requirements contained in the comprehensive body of civil rights laws and executive orders has, for all practical purposes, ceased. . . .

The Office of Federal Contract Compliance, for example, has become functionally useless, and the less said about the Office for Civil Rights in HEW the better. The Report of the United States Commission on Civil Rights issued July 1975 sums up the matter:

> Instead of imposing sanctions on contractors who do not follow the affirmative action requirements, the compliance agencies and OFCC devote substantial resources to extended conciliation, which can often stretch out over several years.

The Commission's Report cites many examples of:

> the contract compliance program's widespread tolerance of violations of the Executive Orders and its virtual failure to impose any sanctions. The message com-

municated to government contractors is that there is no threat of debarment or other sanctions, and the effect is to obliterate any credibility in the program.

It is within this context that we must fight to preserve the integrity of the Equal Employment Opportunity Commission. Given a national administration hostile to civil rights progress, and the heightened racism of the society, civil rights advocates must do everything possible to prevent the EEOC from going the way of other civil rights administrative agencies. The disastrous rates of unemployment among the non-white populations and the continuing patterns of job discrimination make it imperative that the EEOC function as a vital and aggressive agency in carrying out the mandate of the Civil Rights Act of 1964.

Title VII is meant to operate in bad times as well as in good times, during periods of depression as well as during periods of prosperity, and we reject the argument that whites have a prior right to a job and that black people must wait until there is full employment before they too can work. Thus it may be anticipated that there will be intensified activity under Title VII and that the EEOC's burdens will increase. It is necessary to point out that the Commission's responsibility is not fulfilled by mechanically disposing of charges received. Its purpose under the Act is to eliminate racist and sexist employment patterns throughout the society.

There is every reason to believe

that the current unemployment crisis will last for a decade or more. A most important aspect of the long-term economic forecast is that at the same time that the nation is expected to experience a continuing high rate of unemployment many millions of workers will remain on the job. Not everyone will be unemployed. In fact, 85 million are now working. It is clear that the pattern of unemployment is unevenly distributed with black people, as usual, hurt the most. Therefore, the fundamental question now and for the next ten years and perhaps longer will be WHO WORKS? Industry-wide patterns of discrimination based on race and sex are a decisive factor in determining who does or does not work.

The EEOC, if it is to survive as a viable agency, must reject the pressures to retreat that are exerted upon it by other organs of the federal government, such as the Civil Service Commission, the Department of Labor, and the Department of Health, Education and Welfare, among others. These agencies have crippled civil rights enforcement in their respective jurisdictions and they have done this by rejecting the concept of affirmative action and substituting instead an abstraction called voluntary compliance. But programs based upon voluntarism, with their expressed or implied promise not to enforce the law, have failed to eliminate discriminatory employment practices.

Voluntary compliance programs avoid the concept that racial discrimination is illegal, that black workers and other minorities have fundamental rights which cannot be bargained away, and that the institutions which discriminate against them are required by law to change their conduct. This, of course, is the basic message delivered by the courts as a result of litigation under Title VII. Voluntary compliance and "good faith efforts" do not work in eliminating job discrimination, and years of experience have demonstrated that the piling of pledge upon pledge not to discriminate by employers and labor unions changes little or nothing.

The record of thirty years of fair employment practice laws and executive orders makes it absolutely clear that the concept of passive non-discrimination is totally inadequate and obsolete. A ritualistic policy of "nondiscrimination" in practice usually means perpetuation of the traditional discriminatory patterns or, at best, tokenism. Discrimination in employment is not the result of random acts of malevolence; it does not usually occur because of individual bigotry, but rather is the consequence of systematic institutionalized patterns that are rooted in the society. Thus sweeping measures are necessary if racial employment patterns are to be fundamentally changed and affirmative action based on numerical goals and timetables is an essential component in achieving this end.

If we realize the potential of Title VII, the broad application of af-

10. AFFIRMATIVE ACTION

firmative action programs will be necessary, where performance can be measured by tangible results, not by the proliferation of self-serving statements pledging "equal opportunity," an equal opportunity that always remains beyond the reach of those who are the victims of the dual racial labor system. Without affirmative action, Blacks will have to wait until the millennium to achieve equality with whites.

In the final analysis, affirmative action is an attempt at redistribution, an attempt to achieve a limited but necessary reallocation of jobs and income within the existing legal structure. It is part of a long-term civil rights strategy to make the law operate as an instrument of social change. When the law is permitted to function at its best, it fulfills its historic role of preserving public order while, at the same time, redressing collective grievances and thereby giving the institutions of society an opportunity to change without fatal trauma.

The history of the twentieth century teaches us that if those victimized by injustice are denied relief under law, then the alternative is violence; and violence, whatever its motivation, is certain to result in disaster. But the opponents of affirmative action are succeeding in nullifying the law, are confirming the belief that black people are indeed powerless in American society and it is certain that in the perspective of time, history will judge them most harshly.

(Cont. from p. 193, Glazer, "Compensation for the Past")

circumstances, and the Constitution is now so interpreted that it can be required permanently.

We have created two racial and ethnic classes in this country to replace the disgraceful pattern of the past in which some groups were subjected to an official and open discrimination. The two new classes are those groups that are entitled to statistical parity in certain key areas on the basis of race, color, and national origin, and those groups that are not. The consequences of such a development can be forseen: They are already, in some measure, upon us. Those groups that are not considered eligible for special benefits become resentful. If one could draw a neat line between those who have suffered from discrimination and those who have not, the matter would be simpler. Most immigrant groups have had periods in which they were discriminated against. For the Irish and the Jews, for example, these periods lasted a long time. Nor is it the case that all the groups that are now recorded as deserving official protection have suffered discrimination, or in the same way.

The Spanish-surnamed category is particularly confused. It is not at all clear which groups it covers, although presumably it was designed to cover the Mexican Americans and Puerto Ricans. But in San Francisco, Nicaraguans from Central America, who were neither conquered by the United States nor subjected to special legislation and who very likely have suffered only from the problems that all immigrants do, given their occupational and educational background, their economic situation, and their linguistic facility were willy-nilly swept up into one of the categories that had to be distributed evenly through the school system. The Cuban immigrants have done well and already have received special government aid owing to their status as refugees: Are they now to receive, too, the special benefit of being considered Spanish-surnamed, a group listed in the goals required in affirmative action programs?

The protected groups include variously the descendants of free immigrants, conquered peoples, and slaves, and a single group may include the descendants of all three categories (e.g., the Puerto Ricans). Do free immigrants who have come to this country voluntarily deserve the same protected treatment as the descendants of conquered people and slaves? The point is that racial and ethnic groups make poor categories for the design of public policy. They include a range of individuals who have different legal bases for claims for redress and remedy of grievances. If the cate-gories are designed to correct the injustices of the past, they do not work.

They do not work to correct the injustices of the present either, for some groups defined by race and ethnicity do not seem to need redress on the basis of their economic, occupational, and educational position. The Asian Americans have indeed been subjected to discrimination, legal and unofficial alike. But Chinese and Japanese Americans rank high in economic status, occupational status, educational status. (This does not prevent members of these groups from claiming the benefits that now accrue to them because they form a specially protected category under affirmative action programs.) If they were included in the protected category because they have faced discrimination, then groups in the unprotected categories also deserve inclusion. If they were included because they suffer from a poor economic, occupational, and educational positon, they were included in error. So if these ethnic and racial categories have been designed to group individuals with some especially deprived current condition, they do not work either. Just as the Chinese and Japanese and Indians (from India) do not need the protection of the "Asian American" category, the Cubans do not need the protection of the Spanish-surnamed category, and middle-class blacks the protection of the Negro category in order to get equal treatment today in education and employment. The inequalities created by the use of these categories became sharply evident in 1975 when many private colleges and universities tried to cut back on special aid for racially defined groups, who did indeed include many in need, but also included many in no greater need than "white" or "other" students. But the creation of a special benefit, whether needed or not, is not to be given up easily: Black students occupied school buildings and demanded that the privileges given on the basis of race be retained. This is part of the evil of the creation of especially benefited ethnic and racial categories.

The racial and ethnic categories neither properly group individuals who deserve redress on the basis of past discriminatory treatment, nor properly group individuals who deserve redress on the basis of a present deprived condition. The creation of such specially benefited categories also has inevitable and unfortunate political consequences. Groups not included wonder whether it would not be to their benefit to be included. . . . There are already cases of individuals who redefine themselves in this country for some benefit—the part American Indian who becomes an Indian for some public purpose, the person with a Spanish-surnamed mother who now finds it advantageous to change his or her name; conceivably the black who has passed as white and who may reclaim black status for an educational or employment benefit. We have not yet reached the degraded condition of the Nurem-

berg laws, but undoubtedly we will have to create a new law of personal ethnic and racial status to define just who is eligible for these benefits, to replace the laws we have banned to determine who should be subject to discrimination.

The gravest political consequence is undoubtedly the increasing resentment and hostility between groups that is fueled by special benefits for some. The statistical basis for redress makes one great error: All "whites" are consigned to the same category, deserving of no special consideration. That is not the way " whites" see themselves, or indeed are, in social reality. Some may be "whites," pure and simple. But almost all have some specific ethnic or religious identification, which, to the individual involved, may mean a distinctive history of past—and perhaps some present—discrimination. We have analyzed the position and attitudes of the ethnic groups formed from the post-1880 immigrants from Europe. These groups were not particularly involved in the enslavement of the Negro or the creation of the Jim Crow pattern in the South, the conquest of part of Mexico, or the near-extermination of the American Indian. Indeed, they settled in parts of the country where there were few blacks and almost no Mexican Americans and American Indians. They came to a country which provided them with less benefits than it now provides the protected groups. There is little reason for them to feel they should bear the burden of the redress of a past in which they had no or little part, or to assist those who presently receive more assistance than they did. We are indeed a nation of minorities; to enshrine some minorities as deserving of special benefits means not to defend minority rights against a discriminating majority but to favor some of these minorities over others.

Compensation for the past is a dangerous principle. It can be extended indefinitely and make for endless trouble. Who is to determine what is proper compensation for the American Indian, the black, the Mexican American, the Chinese or Japanese American? When it is established that the full status of equality is extended to every individual, regardless of race, color, or national origin, and that special opportunity is also available to any individual on the basis of individual need, again regardless of race, color, or national origin, one has done all that justice and equity call for and that is consistent with a harmonious multigroup society.

Each of the policies we have discussed of course raises special problems. Inclusion in employment goals and quotas is clearly a positive benefit for individuals in the benefited groups, an actual loss for the others. As a result, these benefits will be defended most fiercely. It is less clear what the benefit is in school desegregation. It is obviously considered no benefit at all but an actual loss by some of the populations involved, white and Asian American, may well be seen as a loss

by many of the Spanish-surnamed groups involved, and is even seen as a loss by many of the blacks. Residential distribution is an even more ambiguous case. It is a clear gain if it means access to better housing and communities with better services. But it may imply only the dubious benefit of housing in a project or low-income section of the suburbs, rather than a project or a low-income section in the central city; and if we consider this concrete reality, many for whom such a policy is designed may well see it as a disadvantage, too.

These policies are based on two equally inadequate views of the nature of racial and ethnic groups in the United States. First, they assume that these groups are so easily bounded and defined, and so uniform in the condition of those included in them, that a policy designed for the group can be applied equitably and may be assumed to provide benefits for those eligible. The fact is that, for many of the groups involved, the boundaries of membership are uncertain, and the condition of those included in the groups are diverse. Furthermore, it clearly does not serve the creation of an integrated nation for government to intervene in creating sharper and more meaningful ethnic boundaries, to subdivide the population more precisely than people in general recognize and act on. The fact is, a good deal of integration—taken in the fullest sense of the term—has gone on in this country. The process will not be aided by trying to fix categories for division and identification and then make them significant for people's fates by law. We are not a nation such as Belgium, which can draw a geographical line across the country and pronounce one side Flemish and the other French (and even Belgium has a serious problem in considering what to do about mixed—that is, "integrated"—Brussels). Nor do we want to become such a nation, in which our people live within ironclad ethnic and racial divisions defined by law.

These policies make a second and opposite error, and that is to ignore the reality that some degree of community and fellow-feeling courses through these groups and makes them more than mere assemblages of individuals. We have seen how school desegregation policies have taken a positively hostile attitude toward any expression of such a group reality, how residential distribution policies assume that any community is a "ghetto," imposed from without rather than chosen from within. Even statistically oriented employment policies also ignore certain realities of community. Racial and ethnic communities have expressed themselves in occupations and work groups. Distinctive histories have channeled ethnic and racial groups into one kind of work or another, and this is the origin of many of the "unrepresentative" work distributions we see. These distributions have been maintained by an occupational tradition linked to an ethnic community, which makes it easier for the Irish to become

policemen, the Italians fruit dealers, Jews businessmen, and so on. None of us would want these varied occupational patterns maintained by discrimination. Nor, however, should we want to see the strengths provided by an ethnic-occupational link—strengths for the group itself, and for the work it contributes to society—dissipated by policies which assumed all such concentrations were signs of discrimination and had to be broken up. A rigorous adherence to requirements of no discrimination on grounds of race, color, and national origin would weaken these concentrations and offer opportunities to many of other groups. A policy of statistical representation in each area of employment would eliminate them—but that would be to go beyond the demands of justice and equity.

Thus policies of statistical representation in employment, education, and residence insist that it is possible to divide the racial and ethnic groups with precision and assign them on the basis of past discrimination and present circumstance to a class for which a strict statistical parity must be required, and a class which does not warrant this protection (if protection it is—as we saw, in some cases, even the protected groups look dubiously on what is proposed for their putative benefit). But on the other hand, these policies insist that despite the precision with which these groups may be defined and discriminated, none of them may exist in any group or corporate form even if this is a matter of their own choosing. In contrast, the emergent American ethnic consensus we described in the first chapter of this book insisted that the group characteristics of an individual were of no concern to government, that it must take no account of an individual's race, color or national origin. And on the other side the consensus insisted that any individual could participate in the maintenance of a distinctive ethnic group voluntarily, and that government could not intervene to break up and destroy these voluntary communal formations. Finally, I |have earlier| argued, the American ethnic consensus would not accept these voluntary racial and ethnic formations as component parts of the American polity. There were to be no group political rights added to the rights of every individual and of the component states. This element, too, of the consensus is in process of being subverted by the emergence of a required statistical representation of some racial and ethnic groups in key areas of life, because to ascribe rights on the basis of ethnic group membership inevitably *strengthens* such groups and gives them a greater political role.

. . . We have a complex of education, culture, law, administration, and political institutions which has deflected us into a course in which we publicly establish ethnic and racial categories for differential treatment, and believe that by so doing we are establishing a just and good society. Behind it all stands, to my mind, a radical misunderstanding of how we in the United States

have attempted to deal with the problems of a multiracial and multiethnic society. The pattern we have developed is not easily summed up in slogans—which is perhaps its defect—for we have decided against both the forcible assimilation of all groups into one mold and the legal recognition of each group for the establishment of a formal parity between them. It is a pattern that has emerged from the complex interplay of constitutional principles, political institutions, American culture, and that has had, at times, to be reestablished through force and violence.

For ten years now, we have drifted in another direction, certainly in some ways an easier one to understand, and in some ways even easier to institute. Let us number and divide up (some of) the people into their appropriate racial and ethnic groups, and let equality prevail between them and the "others." But this has meant that we abandon the first principle of a liberal society, that the individual and the individual's interests and good and welfare are the test of a good society, for we now attach benefits and penalties to individuals simply on the basis of their race, color, and national origin. The implications of the new course are an increasing consciousness of the significance of group membership, an increasing divisiveness on the basis of race, color, and national origin, and a spreading resentment among the disfavored groups against the favored groups. If the individual is the measure, however, our public concern is with the individual's capacity to work out an individual fate by means of education, work, and self-realization in the various spheres of life. Then how the figures add up on the basis of whatever measures of group we use may be interesting, but should be no concern of public policy.

This, I believe, is what was intended by the Constitution and the Civil Rights Act, and what most of the American people—in all the various ethnic and racial groups that make it up—believe to be the measure of a good society. It is now our task to work with the intellectual, judicial, and political institutions of the country to reestablish this simple and clear understanding, that rights attach to the individual, not the group, and that public policy must be exercised without distinction of race, color, or national origin.

POSTSCRIPT

AFFIRMATIVE ACTION: IS IT EQUALITY OR IS IT REVERSE DISCRIMINATION?

As of December 1977, the U.S. Supreme Court had not decided the *Bakke* case, in which a young white man denied admission to a University of California medical school argued that preferential treatment on behalf of racial minorities violated his constitutional rights. The implications of preferential treatment and quota systems—or their rejection—extend far beyond admissions criteria for colleges and graduate schools, to many social and economic practices, including employment. In America in the late 1970s, feelings run deep on the opposing sides of this issue.

Robert M. O'Neil, in *Discriminating against Discrimination* (Indiana, 1975), studied preferential admissions to universities, and supported preferential treatment without racial quotas. Those critical of this distinction hold that preferential treatment necessarily implies racial quotas. Certainly, racial quotas are involved in most court-ordered compulsory school busing orders. This policy is examined and deplored by Lino A. Graglia, in *Disaster by Decree* (Cornell, 1976). There is likely to be a considerable outpouring of articles and books in the wake of the Supreme Court's decision in the *Bakke* case.

Whatever the Supreme Court's decision, the issue is not likely to be finally resolved. There are few issues on which opposing sides are more intransigent than on this. What is remedial action against past discrimination to the advocates of preferential treatment is reverse discrimination to its opponents. Conversely, what is the absence of discrimination to the critics of busing and preferential treatment is the perpetuation of discrimination to the supporters of compensatory treatment. It appears as if there is no satisfactory "solution," and, at the moment, no compromise that can long abate the passionate convictions on both sides. The continuing resentment and recrimination are unrelieved by any awareness that both sides profess an identical commitment to equality.

ISSUE 11

ELIMINATING POVERTY: AN UNWINNABLE WAR?

In 1964 President Lyndon Johnson declared an "unconditional war on poverty." Congress responded by passing the Equal Opportunity Act, an ambitious plan which tied together existing programs and launched new ones; its initial funding was set at an annual $2 billion. The goal was to eliminate poverty in the nation by the time of its bicentennial.

Something, obviously, went wrong. Whether we walk the streets of the inner city or drive through the rural hollows of America, it does not take long to realize that poverty is still with us.

To be sure, the optimist might argue that at least some measurable progress has been made. If we define poverty by using the official government standard for it (based upon the Department of Agriculture's estimate of a minimum nutritional diet), then the extent of poverty declined from 20 percent, at the time of Lyndon Johnson's declaration of "war," to 12 percent in 1970. The standard, however, is a dubious one at best. It is based upon the cost of an "emergency" diet, not one intended for normal or consistent use. What the official standard may be measuring is not poverty but outright desperation— the point where biological survival itself may be threatened. But surely poverty has a larger meaning than that. To be poor in contemporary America means more than to be starving. It also means: to live in bad housing, to send your children to bad schools, to live (especially in urban areas) surrounded by pimps, prostitutes, drunks, drug dealers and addicts, in constant fear of violent crime. Above all it means to live with the sense of having been left out and left back in a society which prides itself on newness and progress and affluence. Not all of these things can be measured by statistics, but it is probably safe to say that those who suffer them number more than 12 percent of the nation.

However defined, poverty remains with us today, and shows no sign of disappearing in the foreseeable future. Where, then, do we go from here?

In the broadest possible sense, two reactions are possible—activism and quietism. Activists come in several varieties, according to their diagnoses of and prescriptions for the social pathology which we call poverty. What they all have in common is the conviction that something, indeed a great deal, can be done to reduce or eliminate it. R. Sargent Shriver, the former director of the Office of Economic Opportunity, thinks that his program was never given enough money; the solution, then, is the simple quantitative one of providing more funds. Many in the anti-war movement in the 1960s thought that the poverty program was doomed to fail once President Johnson diverted his energies to the war in Southeast Asia; otherwise, presumably, it might have worked. Some of the participants in the poverty program thought that it failed because of sabotage from big-city mayors and other officials who resented its emphasis on "community action"; again, the implication is that it might have worked if Johnson had not knuckled under to the bosses. Still other critics have suggested that the "services" strategy of the war on poverty was a mistaken approach; instead of paying middle-class bureaucrats to "teach" or "motivate" the poor, it would be better simply to provide cash grants to them in some manner or another. All of these critics are, in a sense, optimists. The war on poverty is dead, they admit, but it might be revived. If we do it the right way, if we plan it properly, and protect it from sabotage, then . . .

To the quietist, these hopes seem naive. He (or she) would probably reject the label of "quietist," preferring instead to be called a realist. For his claim is to be guided by the facts—even if those facts are unpleasant or contrary to our cherished ideals. The Declaration of Independence says that "all men are created equal," but the harsh fact is that certain people have less foresight, less ambition, less willingness to forego immediate pleasures for the sake of future gains, than do others. Specifically, the lower classes carry with them a "culture," a set of values and attitudes, which militates against their rising out of poverty. Not all of the poor share these attitudes, but a large percentage of them do, and for them not much can be done—short of kidnapping their children—to break the attitudinal barriers to mobility which are passed down from generation to generation. To the activist, accustomed to answering problems with solutions, the quietist seems, at best, to be unwarrantedly pessimistic. Is he? Perhaps the following selections may be helpful in forming a judgment.

The first is from William Ryan's book, *Blaming the Victim,* in which Ryan, a psychologist and social activist, analyzes the problem of poverty in terms of the forces acting *upon* the poor, keeping them down. In the second selection, sociologist Edward Banfield argues that the root causes of poverty come from *within* the culture of the lower classes.

William Ryan

"BLAMING THE VICTIM"

... Zero Mostel used to do a sketch in which he impersonated a Dixiecrat Senator conducting an investigation of the origins of World War II. At the climax of the sketch, the Senator boomed out, in an excruciating mixture of triumph and suspicion, "What was Pearl Harbor *doing* in the Pacific?" This is an extreme example of Blaming the Victim. ... The same process has been going on every day in the arena of social problems, public health, anti-poverty programs, and social welfare. A philosopher might analyze this process and prove that, technically, it is comic. But it is hardly ever funny.

Consider some victims. One is the miseducated child in the slum school. He is blamed for his own miseducation. He is said to contain within himself the causes of his inability to read and write well. The shorthand phrase is "cultural deprivation," which, to those in the know, conveys what they allege to be inside information: that the poor child carries a scanty pack of cultural baggage as he enters school. He doesn't know about books and magazines and newspapers, they say. (No books in the home: the mother fails to subscribe to *Reader's Digest.*) They say that if he talks at all—an unlikely event since slum parents don't talk to their children—he certainly doesn't talk correctly. (Lower-class dialect spoken here, or even—God forbid!—Southern Negro. (*Ici on parle nigra.*) If you can manage to get him to sit in a chair, they say, he squirms and looks out the window. (Impulse-ridden, these kids, motoric rather than verbal.) In a word he is "disadvantaged" and "socially deprived," they say, and this, of course, accounts for his failure (*his* failure, they say) to learn much in school.

Note the similarity to the logic of Zero Mostel's Dixiecrat Senator. What is the culturally deprived child *doing* in the school? What is wrong with the victim? In pursuing this logic, no one remembers to ask questions about the collapsing buildings and torn textbooks, the frightened, insensitive teachers, the six additional desks in the room, the blustering, frightened principals, the relentless segregation, the callous administrator, the irrelevant curriculum, the bigoted or cowardly members of the school board, the insulting history

Continued on p. 214

Edward C. Banfield

THE CULTURE
OF THE LOWER CLASSES

A slum is not simply a district of low-quality housing; rather, it is one in which a squalid and wretched style of life is widespread. The logic of growth *does* require that, in general, the lowest-income people live in the oldest, highest-density, most run-down housing, which will be nearest to the factories, warehouses, stores, and offices of the inner, or downtown, part of the central city; however nothing in the logic of growth says that such districts must be squalid or crime-ridden.

To account for these and certain other features of metropolitan development in the United States, a second explanatory principle must, so to speak, be placed over the first. This is the concept of class. . . .

The lower-class individual lives from moment to moment. If he has any awareness of a future, it is of something fixed, fated, beyond his control: things happen *to* him, he does not *make* them happen. Impulse governs his behavior, either because he cannot discipline himself to sacrifice a present for a future satisfaction or because he has no sense of the future. He is therefore radically improvident: whatever he cannot consume immediately he considers valueless. His bodily needs (especially for sex) and his taste for "action" take precedence over everything else—and certainly over any work routine. He works only as he must to stay alive, and drifts from one unskilled job to another, taking no interest in the work. . . .

The lower-class individual has a feeble, attenuated sense of self; he suffers from feelings of self-contempt and inadequacy, and is often apathetic or dejected. (In her discussion of "very low-lower class" families, Eleanor Pavenstadt notes that "the saddest, and to us the outstanding characteristic of this group, with adults and children alike, was the self-devaluation.") In his relations with others he is suspicious and hostile, aggressive yet dependent. He is unable to maintain a stable relationship with a mate; commonly he does not marry. . . . He feels no attachment to community, neighbors, or friends (he has companions, not friends), resents all authority (for example, that of policemen, social workers, teachers, landlords, employers), and is apt to think that he has been "railroaded" and to want to "get even." He is a nonparticipant: he belongs to no voluntary organizations, has no political interests, and does not vote unless paid to do so.

Continued on p. 226

11 ELIMINATING POVERTY

(Ryan, cont. from p. 212)

book, the stingy taxpayers, the fairy-tale readers, or the self-serving faculty of the local teachers' college. We are encouraged to confine our attention to the child and to dwell on all his alleged defects. Cultural deprivation becomes an omnibus explanation for the educational disaster area known as the inner-city school. This is Blaming the Victim. . . .

The millionaire, freshly risen from the lower class, whose crude tongue and appalling table manners betray the newness of his affluence, is a staple of American literature and folklore. He comes on stage over and over, and we have been taught exactly what to expect with each entrance. He will walk into the parlor in his undershirt, gulp tea from a saucer, spit into the Limoges flowerpot, and, when finally invited to the society garden party, disgrace his wife by saying "bullshit" to the president of the bank. When I was growing up, we had daily lessons in this legend from Jiggs and Maggie in the comic strips.

This discrepancy between *class* and *status*, between possession of economic resources and life style, has been a source of ready humour and guaranteed fascination for generations. The centrality of this mythical strain in American thought is reflected again in the strange and perverse ideas emerging from the mouths of many professional Pauper Watchers and Victim Blamers.

In real life, of course, Jiggs' character and behavior would never remain so constant and unchanging over the decades. The strain between wealth and style is one that usually tends to be quickly resolved. Within a fairly short time, Jiggs would be coming into the parlor first with a shirt, then with a tie on, and, finally, in one of his many custom-made suits. He would soon be drinking tea from a Limoges cup, and for a time he would spit in an antique cuspidor, until he learned not to spit at all. At the garden party, he would confine his mention of animal feces to a discussion of the best fertilizer for the rhododendron. In real life, style tends to follow close on money, and money tends to be magnetized and attracted to power. Those who try to persuade us that the process can be reversed, that a change in style of life can lead backward to increased wealth and greater power, are preaching nonsense. To promise that improved table manners can produce a salary increase; that more elegant taste in clothes will lead to the acquisition of stock in IBM; that an expanded vocabulary will automatically generate an enlargement of community influence—these are pernicious as well as foolish. There is no record in history of any *group* having accomplished this wondrous task. (There may be a few clever individuals who have followed such artful routes to money and power, but they are relatively rare.) The whole idea is an illusion of fatuous social scientists and welfare bureaucrats. . . .

Although few would argue that issues of status and life style have no relationship at all to the production

214

of social problems, it is very hard—
after a close look—to evade the
conclusion that issues of class and
power are far more significant.
Consider some of the roles of money
in these processes. For example, it
has been demonstrated by a number
of researchers—most notably Pa-
tricia Sexton—that there is a high
correlation between the amount of
money spent in an educational
system and the quality and level of
educational achievement of students in the system. This is not
proof that more money causes
better education: indeed . . . there
are a number of other factors to be
considered. Still, it is hardly naive to
hypothesize that the reason subur-
banites tax themselves so readily for
their school budget is that they
believe—with good reason—that
they are buying better schooling for
their children. To those scientists
and educationists who belittle the
importance of money in education, I
would ask, "How would you feel
about a thirty percent cut in the
number of dollars spent on *your*
child in *your* suburban school system?"

And one can return to the simple
relationship between low income
and illegitimacy—a relationship
that is most readily explained by
lack of money (an explanation that
fits both common knowledge and
common sense). Is it possible that
the sociologists, in wealthy universities, who talk so wisely about the
sexual standards and behavior of
the poor, do not know that flocks of
their coed students swallow the Pill
every day? And that they do so
because they can afford to get the

prescription from their private
physicians? And that a poor single
working girl is not going to get that
service at a city hospital? And are
there any of these sociologists . . .
who don't know of at least one
woman who went away pregnant to
Jersey City, or Oakland, or San Juan
and came back with the fetus
removed from her belly and five
hundred dollars less in her pocket-
book? How many of them were poor?

No reasonable person could
spend five minutes in the outpatient
clinic or emergency room of a
general hospital—particularly a
public hospital—and another five
minutes in the waiting room of a
highly competent internist, or pe-
diatrician, or gynecologist, and
not come away with some pretty
strong hunches about why the rich
are healthier and longer-lived than
the poor.

It is highly unlikely that any of the
major issues I have covered—problems that affect a large proportion of
the population—could have their
causes rooted in the personal
qualities or individual characteristics of those who are suffering from
the problem. If a cholera epidemic is
raging in the town, only a lunatic
would study the victims to find out
what distinguishes them from their
healthy neighbors—to discover
their personal, hypothetical, chol-
era-catching characteristics. The
object of such a study would be to
find out in what way the victims
differ from the non-victims in the
ways they interact with their *environment*. What kind of food have
they eaten, and where do they get it?
Where does their water and milk

11. ELIMINATING POVERTY

come from? What is the state of their housing and plumbing? Where do they spend their time? Doing what? With whom?

A famous public health legend—the story of the Broad Street Pump—illustrates this approach precisely. The physician who conducted the investigation was a good physician; he was anxious to do and to help, but he was also a good social analyst. He discovered that a greatly disproportionate number of cholera victims got their water from the pump on Broad Street. He concluded that there was something about the *pump* (not those who drank the water) that was causing the disease. Now, the next part of the story is very crucial. What did he do? He did *not* apply for a research grant to study the characteristics of the pump and its water in order to develop a theory of the etiology of cholera. Nor did he publish a pamphlet urging people not to get their water from this pump. He *ripped the handle off the pump.* That particular cholera epidemic subsided.

The crucial criterion by which to judge analyses of social problems is the extent to which they apply themselves to the *interaction* between the victim population and the surrounding environment and society, and, conversely, the extent to which they eschew exclusive attention to the victims themselves—no matter how feeling and sympathetic that attention might appear to be. Universalistic analysis will fasten on income distribution as the basic cause of poverty, on dis-

crimination and segregation as the basic cause of racial inequality, on social stress as the major cause of the majority of emotional disturbances. It will focus, not on problem families, but on family problems; not on motivation, but on opportunity; not on symptoms, but on causes; not on deficiencies, but on resources; not on adjustment, but on change.

Slum housing, for example, is a problem that cannot be realistically attributed to most of the causes covered by conventional wisdom—such as lack of acculturation among tenants, or even, primarily, of some especially deviant brand of businessman called a slum landlord. The city planner's explanation—"blighting" influences such as mixed uses, excessive density, or poor traffic flow—is, at best, only of secondary significance. Slum housing is due to shortage of standard low-income housing. As has been demonstrated in several European countries, creating a sufficient supply of sound low-rent housing is not merely the *way* to eliminate slums, it is the *definition* of the elimination of slums.

Existing programs . . . have failed because they have not, and could not, increase the supply. What programs might be developed that would do so? In the predominantly private sphere of activity, there is the need to deal with such political and technological problems as: obsolete building construction codes; low productivity of craft union labor; development of new materials and methods of construction; and the fact that housing construction is carried out to a great extent as a high overhead, expensive small business. Just as government subsidies are used to develop new aircraft designs or new weapons designs, a similar effort could be made to subsidize research and development of less expensive housing. One or more universities might set up low cost housing institutes with governmental and foundation support. A semi-public corporation—analogous to COM-SAT—could be established to deal directly with developmental problems identified in the research institutes.

The primary aim of all such programs would be the stimulation of greater and cheaper construction by the private sector. Another, a governmental program aimed at stimulation of private activity, would be *direct* housing subsidies for the poor—as opposed to the present corruption-prone rent certificate program whereby local housing authorities lease dwelling units for selected tenants. For example, among housing economists, there appears to be agreement on two issues: that it is impossible to build new housing to rent for less than $100 a month, and that people with lower income should not budget more than about twenty percent of their net income for total housing costs. This means, as an example, that a family of four, in which the breadwinner earns $2 an hour, should not spend more than $65 a month for sound housing—an almost impossible ideal to achieve. If it were assumed, however, that

$100 was a minimum realistic budget, a direct $35 a month subsidy could be paid to that family in the form of a negotiable rent certificate. Administrative costs would be fairly inexpensive—eligibility being determined readily either by affidavit or, if necessary, by a copy of income tax returns; certificates being mailed directly to tenants; and redemption of the certificates being carried out for a fee by banks. This would create a realistic demand for decent new housing and, while there would doubtless be significant seepage—at least initially—by inflation of existing slum rents, the long-term effect should be a significant increase in the housing stock. Such a program should have a certain appeal to conservatives, since it is quite congruent with our growing pattern of a subsidized economy, and since the basic transactions would occur in the private sphere between tenants and landlords, rather than through massive government action.

Another kind of governmental policy action would be required to revise our present high-priority emphasis on ownership of single-family homes. FHA insurance, income tax deductions for homeowners on mortgage interest and real estate taxes, highway construction grants, planning and facilities grants, and other subsidization primarily from Federal funds—all have shaped our national housing program for the past twenty years and have given enormous advantages to the middle-income family that wants to own a single house in the suburbs. The low-income problem, on the other hand, requires an emphasis on multiple-unit housing in the cities. To encourage this, government policy must be turned around to provide income tax deduction for *rent* paid, construction grants for public rapid-transit facilities, and tax advantages to builders that would offset the temptation to reap the advantages of building suburban developments.

The direct public action solution to the low-income housing problem is public housing—but not the kind of public housing we have become used to as another form of slum. At first glance, our American public housing appears to fit the criteria of universalistic programs; however, at second glance, the differences become apparent. First, public housing is a commodity that is dealt out exactly as if it were a form of welfare: with means tests, eligibility requirements, and caste marks of suitability or unsuitability. Second, it is provided in tiny quantities—doled out in doleful trickles—with the result that the enormous unmet need and the long waiting lists reinforce the idea that admission to such housing is a rare privilege rather than a right. Third, it is managed essentially as a custodial institution for second-class citizens. It is these characteristics, rather than design factors, or issues of high-rise or low-rise, or even issues of location, that completely vitiate the theoretically universalistic characteristics of public housing.

An effective public housing program could provide for both pub-licly-operated housing and housing that was publicly subsidized but operated by non-profit corporations. It would provide for rental fees based on a proportion of income (with no upper- or lower-income limits). And it would eliminate all the means tests, eligibility checks, and other screening procedures. In other words, public housing would be just that—housing that was public rather than private. The only significant distinction would be the difference between fixed rents geared to the market and rents based on a proportion of income. To have any effect on the slum problem, however, billions of dollars would have to be spent for hundreds of thousands of public housing units; public housing in tiny quantities, administered as a quasi-charity, has a seemingly inevitable tendency to be assimilated into the slum housing stock. A substantial output of this kind of public housing would also have a stabilizing effect on the private housing market—it would serve the kind of yardstick function that was originally envisioned for public electrification projects like TVA. If families entered such public housing when their income was $5,000 and their rent was $100 a month, a crucial question would be: how much would they be willing to pay to stay there? When their income rose to $7,500, would they be willing to pay $150 for the same apartment? (This would probably mean that they were then paying *more* than cost, and were helping to subsidize other tenants.) The answer to that question would be dependent on the state of the private market—whether or not there was an equivalent apartment that was either materially more attractive, or was at least of sufficient attractiveness that, coupled with that particular family's motivation to move into private housing, it would pull the family out of the public market and into the private market.

The final and most complete kind of governmental action that could be taken to solve the housing problem would require a massive redefinition of the place of housing in American life—legislation defining housing as a public utility (just as water, gas, electricity, telephones, freight movement and passenger travel are defined as public utilities). Of course, housing is a more complex matter than any of these public utilities. It has more variability—lacking the simple unidimensional structure of electricity or water supply, and is a more local issue—unlike regional or national transportation networks. As such, it would require regulation at a much lower governmental level—the level of the municipality or even the neighborhood.

Singly and in combination, all these proposed programs and devices would contribute to the overall goal of solving the slum housing problem by producing more low-income housing.

The question of inner-city education can be approached in a similar way: providing for limited private enterprise solutions and broad public action programs, all of which would be directed at changing the *schools* rather than the children.

The problem is how do we encourage, motivate, or even, if need be, *force* the schools to educate the children?

One private enterprise program has been proposed by persons as various as Christopher Jencks and Milton Friedman. This is the idea of rearranging the whole basis of the commitment to public education: making the basic unit of fiscal administration the student rather than the school system. This would be accomplished through educational vouchers attached to the child—in somewhat the same fashion that the G.I. Bill of Rights attached a financial voucher to the veteran himself, which he could use in any college, or university, or vocational training program that would accept him. *Public* education would then be carried out through a mixture of public *and* private institutions competing in a classical free-enterprise situation for the business of the student with the voucher. It would be up to the schools themselves to initiate changes and improvements—on a voluntary basis—that would make them more attractive. It would be up to the student—or, more accurately, the student's parents—to evaluate those schools and to choose which one was best.

There are, of course, obvious drawbacks to this idea. Such a laissez-faire approach to elementary education would invite efforts to exploit schooling for profit, for example, and would provide a convenient method of perpetuating racial segregation. For many conservatives, this potential should add appeal to the scheme. Moreover, the advocates of progressive education and of community schools and free schools, I suppose, would be willing to pay the price: the abandonment of the goal of integration.

I would like to propose another possible private enterprise solution to the slum school problem that, as far as I know, has not been put forth previously. Why not pay teachers on the basis of production? The task of education is to teach—to teach children to read and write, to know something about history and geography, to be able to use our arithmetical system. To apply an unfamiliar term to the situation, the *productivity* level of teachers in slum schools is abominably low. They teach very little. What if we attached a direct incentive to effective teaching? Suppose we paid substantially more money to those teachers who performed their task more effectively? Might this not have an effect on the level of ghetto education?

How might such a system work? A fourth-grade teacher is confronted with the task of teaching thirty children one year's worth of, for example, reading. Her effectiveness can be measured through standardized tests of reading achievement. (These tests are now administered under highly variable conditions, by teachers or guidance counselors or psychologists with minimal investment, and with highly diversified expectations; what if the results of these tests were the basis for fellow professionals' salary levels?) Under the terms of my proposal, the teach-

er's salary would be tied to the results of the achievement tests. If, on the average, each of her thirty pupils advanced by an increment of ten months over the previous year's testing, she would get the standard salary for her grade, education, and years of experience. If she had been an especially productive teacher, and this was evidenced by, say, an average advance in achievement test scores of *eleven* months—substantially above the norm—she would be rewarded by an appropriate bonus. If her productivity level had been low, and the pupils had advanced in their reading levels by only nine months or even eight months, her salary would be sharply reduced by an appropriate percentage. Different formulas would have to be worked out for different grade levels, weighing achievement in reading, writing, arithmetic, social studies, science, and so forth; but this would represent no insuperable problem. The two major obstacles to such a program would be the problem of differential ability and the problem of the accuracy of achievement tests. To the latter problem, my own response would be that schools are not now concerned, to any uproarious degree, about the validity of these tests. Does this mean that teachers now accept their validity but would not do so if it affected their own material well-being? What about the present and future material well-being of millions of students who, on the basis of these tests, are being labeled, packaged, tracked, and channeled year after year? If prudence dictated that the whole practice of achievement testing must be reevaluated before attaching to it the presumably far more important question of teachers' salaries, I would heartily concur. Then there is the problem of differential abilities and similar issues. What if a teacher—by unlikely chance—were confronted with thirty students who had, on the average, lesser or greater natural ability? Or, in a similar vein, what if a teacher were teaching in a particular school that—because of the administration, the principal, the atmosphere engendered by other teachers—was in itself detrimental to learning? Would it be fair to penalize a teacher for matters that were outside her control? Or conversely, to reward her for matters that were none of her doing? This might be handled by using, as the norm of the teacher's productivity, each pupil's previous average achievement through his total school experience. If it did nothing else, such an arrangement might slow down the *rate* of deterioration of academic performance in ghetto schools.

The public action style of solution would involve two components: an equalization of investment of resources for each student, and an appreciable measure of influence on the course of a child's education by the child himself, and by his parents. This formula can be translated into an increase of both centralization and decentralization. Such issues as teacher performance, curriculum *goals*, and funding would have to be drastically more centralized. We would have to work out arrangements so that the student in Scars-

dale, the student in Harlem, the student in Hough, the student in Shaker Heights, the student in Newton, and the student in Roxbury would have essentially the same quantity of financial resources invested in his education (*not* in the administration of his education); and the results of his education would have to be evaluated by the same yardstick, and the *worth* of his teachers (as measured by salary) would have to be equivalent. This would have to mean extensive centralization—at least at the state level, perhaps at the Federal level. At the same time, on day-to-day issues, on questions of teacher attitude, on problems of student morale, on all the questions that might be termed operational, the school system would have to be drastically *decentralized*. Which teachers, principals, and local administrators should be hired would have to be determined by parents— or, more appropriately, by representatives of parents; detailed questions of school programs, curriculum variations, and so forth would be determined in the same way. In such a manner, the solutions of money and power could be brought to bear simultaneously on the social problem of inferior ghetto education.

Examples of both private enterprise and public action programs could be cited for all the social problems that have been discussed. On the general problem of health care a private enterprise solution would be to extend Medicare so as to cover the total population, and to include preventive services, inoc-

11. ELIMINATING POVERTY

ulations, periodic checkups, etc. A public action solution would be to institute a publicly-run National Health Service (what we shudder about when we say "socialized medicine!").

The income maintenance problem falls into two large universalistic segments: unemployment and underemployment, on the one hand, and, on the other hand, financial assistance to those who should not work—such as children, the aged, husbandless mothers, the physically and mentally disabled. (There are several small corners of the income problem where exceptionalistic analysis and programming is appropriate—for example, the functionally illiterate adult, whose inability to read prevents him from working, would need a program to teach him to read. Occupants of such corners are relatively small in number.)

Poverty that is the result of unemployment, underemployment, or very low-wage employment is obviously a universalistic problem. For example, in 1940, eight million were out of work, while in 1942, only a little more than one million were out of work. The seven million who went from a jobless status to drawing a weekly paycheck in that two year period were no different in 1940 than in 1942. When the war began, it wasn't that millions of people suddenly developed the ability to run a calculator, or a drill press, or a truck, or a riveting hammer. The situation changed, not the people. Jobs were suddenly created by the demands of the war economy, and millions of people (who were very likely identified previously as "untrained," "unmotivated," etc.) went to work. The current unemployment rate, as I write,* is approximately 3.5 percent, compared with 6.7 percent in 1961. Over two million persons are working now who were not working then. The reason is that the economy was heated up, and more jobs became available.

The great bulk of the low-income problem reflected in an unemployment rate of more than one or two percent, then, can be logically analyzed only in terms of the state of the economy and the consequent availability of jobs; and the solution to unemployment is not "manpower development," or "job training" (although they may be desirable or necessary supplemental programs), but *jobs*. The federal government should take ultimate responsibility for making sure that sufficient jobs are available—through fiscal policy, through subsidizing New Careers programs in the public sector, and, if necessary, as a last resort, by acting as the employer—in such direct governmental programs as housing construction, construction of health and educational facilities, water pollution abatement projects, etc.

As to low-wage employment in marginal industries and commercial activity: the income must be raised directly. The public action approach would be a universal high minimum wage (at today's prices, about $2.50 an hour). The private enterprise

*Editor's note: This was in 1971. The early 1978 rate of unemployment was above 7 percent.

approach would be to subsidize low-wage industries by a direct government grant to workers—such as a family allowance with monthly payments to families determined by the number and age of children. This would, on the one hand, preserve the supply of cheap labor from the employers' point of view; but it would raise substantially the total income of the underpaid laborer.

To supply income to the "dependent"—that is, those who *should* not work—is a different matter. The occasions that produce these needs—death, desertion, divorce, illegitimate birth, accidents, prolonged illness, birth defects, mental retardation, etc.—although they occur to individuals under specific circumstances, are wholly predictable. They occur in substantial numbers year after year because we make no social provisions to prevent or minimize their occurrence. For example, there are tens of thousands of automobile accidents every year because we are very lax about safety and repair service standards for both cars and highways. Consequently, we know that many thousands of family breadwinners are going to be killed each year in this way, leaving widows and orphans in need of income. A substantial number of them will be ineligible for social security payments and will have to turn to public assistance. Because of the deprivation of contraceptive information, we know—we can predict—that tens of thousands of illegitimate children will be born to mothers who

will turn to public assistance for income.

It is a waste of time, energy, and the skills of dedicated workers to deal with all these situations as remarkable, unexpected, unusual circumstances that must be investigated and evaluated to determine eligibility for financial help. The crucial point, in these situations, is that a male breadwinner is missing and no finite amount of social work, investigation, or coercion is going to change that fact. There are, therefore, millions of children, widows, old people, blind people, retarded people, and physically disabled people who cannot work and who have no one to feed them, clothe them, provide them with shelter. We can talk about getting welfare whores off their asses and into factories, we can pass laws requiring mothers of small children to undergo job training, and we can even believe that by trying to force husbandless mothers into jobs that we will solve the maid problem—but none of these issues is really relevant. Such persons should be provided with a simply-administered, steady, adequate source of income. (There may be other problems of a social service nature but such problems are separate, and easily separable, from the income problem.) The obvious solution is some form of income guarantee through one of the many means that have been proposed—such as a negative income tax. There is no need to complicate the problem with the exceptionalistic, means-testing, demoralizing practices that accompany the provision of welfare grants.

Problems of crime, policing, and law enforcement require both some redefinition of crime, and some reorganization of police practices. The first order of business is to clearly define white-collar crime as crime. The cheating, usurious slum merchant does harm to people. The price-fixing, union-busting, tax-evading corporation executive is a very costly person to the rest of us. The slum landlord causes not only physical misery, but actual disease and death. Such persons are, in the old phrase, enemies of the people; their activities should be given primary criminal definitions. If a man holds up a gas station and runs away with the day's receipts of $312, we do not send a government commissioner to bargain with him about how much of the $312 he might be willing to return, over how long a period of time, to the gas station owner. We send a cop to arrest him. Why should we bargain with the vice-president of a national corporation about the $312 million he stole from his customers? We should arrest him and charge him with grand larceny.

On the other hand, it seems almost masochistic to retain the criminal definition we apply, for example, to gambling and commercialized sex. All we are doing is guaranteeing a monopoly to organized crime, with all its associated evils of corruption of police and government officials. To define these activities as criminal is, first, to hand them over to the Mafia as

private preserves, and, second, to guarantee that organized crime will have a steady source of capital accumulation for their more injurious activities. Better to take these matters away from *Cosa Nostra* and put them into the solid, middle class businessmen's world, where they could be readily taxed, licensed, and regulated. The model is that of the traffic in liquor. During the days of Prohibition, the liquor business was in the hands of the gangsters—with all the attendant evils of gang wars, Al Capone, deaths and disease from impure liquor, and widespread corruption of public officials. Now we have respectable liquor store owners and large national corporations producing not only trustworthy booze and huge investments in advertising, but also great quantities of taxes to boot.

A final problem of redefinition involves offenses against public order—public intoxication, breach of the peace, loitering, vagrancy, disorderly conduct, etc.—which, along with traffic control, constitute more than one-half of current police workloads. These offenses are not crimes in the usual sense of the word; they may be irritating, or annoying or troublesome in general, but they are not really injurious to any one in particular. They should be bracketed together and treated as minor traffic violations are treated—offenses that violate the law, but that are neither harmful to others, nor contraventions of social goals or public policy. They can readily be removed from the realm of law-enforcement and assigned to a new category of order-main-tenance; this would require the creation and definition of a wholly new community service function, quite different from that of policing as we usually think of it.

Once we separate the functions of law-enforcement and order-main-tenance, the police problem and the "crime" problem are halfway solved. The police can then no longer confuse the two (in their own mind and the minds of the general public) by enforcing the main-tenance of the social order under the guise of arresting criminals who are no criminals at all—who may, at most, be offenders against public order. Order-maintaining activity—such as directing traffic, tagging illegally parked cars, keeping order in the streets, dealing with drunken citizens, intervening in minor personal disputes, and undertaking community service functions such as providing ambulances—do not have to be carried out by armed officers of social control and community power. In addition, standards for community order vary greatly from one neighborhood to another, and it would seem rea-sonable to have the process of maintaining order conform to these varying standards. I would propose that all of these functions now vested in municipal police, should be given over to community-based, community-controlled, order-main-taining public service organiza-tions. Partial models of such organizations are available in the functions that have been performed by air-raid wardens, meter-maids, part-time housewife traffic direc-

tors, and the improvised com-munity patrols that have operated with generally good results in a number of cities during civil dis-turbances.

Real crime, on the other hand, (including now, white-collar crime) should be dealt with by skilled, trained, well-paid professional police. They should spend all their time tracking down and arresting murderers, burglars, embezzlers, stock swindlers, bribers, usurers, adulterers of food and polluters of water, rent-gougers, racists, rapists, and dishonest public officials. Since it is abundantly evident that municipal police are, first, hope-lessly incompetent to perform such tasks, and, second, terribly subject to locally-inspired corruption, it is probable that law-enforcement should be organized on a regional, metropolitan, or even state-wide basis.

This would leave, as you may have noticed, no function whatsoever for minicipal police forces as we now know them. They could, con-sequently, be abandoned with no loss.

With policing and law enforce-ment thus limited in its scope to real crime, the problem of the poor and the black in the toils of justice would be reduced considerably. An ef-fective and well-financed public defender program and a systematic application to the poor of the prac-tice of "release on own recog-nizance" (often termed "R.O.R." or "no-bail" programs) would go a long way toward limiting fur-ther inequities.

11. ELIMINATING POVERTY

(Cont. from p. 213, Banfield, "Culture of the Lower Classes")

The lower-class household is usually female-based. The woman who heads it is likely to have a succession of mates who contribute intermittently to its support but take little or no part in rearing the children. In managing the children, the mother (or aunt, or grand-mother) is characteristically im-pulsive: once they have passed babyhood they are likely to be neglected or abused, and at best they never know what to expect next. A boy raised in a female-based household is likely at an early age to join a corner gang of other such boys and to learn from the gang the "tough" style of the lower-class man.

The stress on "masculinity," "action," risk-taking, conquest, fighting, and "smartness" makes lower-class life extraordinarily violent. However, much of the vio-lence is probably more an expres-sion of mental illness than of class culture. The incidence of mental illness is greater in the lower class than in any of the others. Moreover, the nature of lower-class culture is such that much behavior that in another class would be consid-ered bizarre seems routine. . . .

So long as the city contains a sizable lower class, nothing basic can be done about its most serious problems. Good jobs may be offered to all, but some will remain chronically unemployed. Slums may be demolished, but if the housing that replaces them is occupied by the lower class it will shortly be turned into new slums. Welfare payments may be doubled or tripled and a negative income tax insti-tuted, but some persons will con-tinue to live in squalor and misery. New schools may be built, new curricula devised, and the teacher-pupil ratio cut in half, but if the children who attend these schools come from lower-class homes, they will be turned into blackboard jungles, and those who graduate or drop out from them will, in most cases, be functionally illiterate. The streets may be filled with armies of policemen, but violent crime and civil disorder will decrease very little. If, however, the lower class were to disappear—if, say, its members were overnight to acquire the attitudes, motivations, and habits of the working class—the most serious and intractable pro-blems of the city would all disappear with it. . . .

Nothing except the elimination of lower-class culture would contri-bute as much to a general solution of the urban problem as would certain changes in public opinion—for example, greater awareness of the importance of class-cultural and other nonracial factors in the Ne-gro's situation and a more re-alistic sense of what levels of performance it is reasonable to expect from such institutions as schools and police forces and from the economy as a whole. However, it is very questionable to what extent, if at all, government can bring these changes about. It is a question also whether *if* it can bring them about it *ought* to—that is, whether the unintended and long-run effects of a strenuous exercise of its opinion-forming capacities would not be likely to change American society for the worse rather than for the better. . . .

There follows a list of measures that might well be regarded as feasible by one who accepts [my] analysis. . . . It will be seen that the list is rather short; that many of the items on it are not "constructive"— that is, they call for *not* doing something; and that far from being a comprehensive program for making the city into what one would like, it hardly begins to solve any of the problems that have been under discussion. Even if all the recommendations were carried out to the full, the urban situation would not be fundamentally improved. Feasible measures are few and unsatisfactory as compared to what it would be nice to have happen or what one would do if one were dictator. What is more to the present point, however, *hardly any of the feasible measures are acceptable.* The list is as follows:

1. Assure to all equal access to polling places, courts, and job, housing, and other markets.

2. Avoid rhetoric tending to raise expectations to unreasonable and unrealizable levels, to encourage the individual to think that "society" (e.g. "white racism"), not he, is responsible for his ills, and to

exaggerate both the seriousness of social problems and the possibility of finding solutions.

3. If it is feasible to do so, use fiscal policy to keep the general unemployment level below 3 percent. In any case, remove impediments to the employment of the unskilled, the unschooled, the young, Negroes, women, and others by (a) repealing the minimum-wage and occupational licensure laws and laws that enable labor unions to exercise monopolistic powers, (b) ceasing to overpay for low-skilled public employment, (c) ceasing to harass private employers who offer low wages and unattractive (but not unsafe) working conditions to workers whose alternative is unemployment, and (d) offer wage supplements in the form of "scholarships" to enable boys and girls who have received little schooling to get jobs with employers who offer valuable on-the-job training.

4. Revise elementary and secondary school curricula so as to cover in nine grades what is now covered in twelve. Reduce the school-leaving age to fourteen (grade 9), and encourage (or perhaps even require) boys and girls who are unable or unwilling to go to college to take a full-time job or else enter military service or a civilian youth corps. Guarantee loans for higher education to all who require them. Assure the availability of serious on-the-job training for all boys and girls who choose to go to work rather than to go to college.

5. Define poverty in terms of the nearly fixed standard of "hardship,"

rather than in terms of the elastic one of "relative deprivation," and bring all incomes above the poverty line. Distinguish categorically between those of the poor who are competent to manage their affairs and those of them who are not, the latter category consisting of the insane, the severely retarded, the senile, the lower class (inveterate "problem families"), and unprotected children. Make cash income transfers to the first category by means of a negative income tax, the rate structure of which gives the recipient a strong incentive to work. Whenever possible, assist the incompetent poor with goods and services rather than with cash; depending upon the degree of their incompetence, encourage (or require) them to reside in an institution or semi-institution (for example, a closely supervised public housing project).

6.   Give intensive birth-control guidance to the incompetent poor.

7.   Pay "problem families" to send infants and children to day nurseries and preschools, the programs of which are designed to bring the children into normal culture.

8.   Regulate insurance and police practices so as to give potential victims of crime greater incentive to take reasonable precautions to prevent it.

9.   Intensify police patrol in high-crime areas; permit the police to "stop and frisk" and to make misdemeanor arrests on probable cause; institute a system of "negative bail"—that is, an arrangement whereby a suspect who is

held in jail and is later found innocent is paid compensation for each day of confinement.

10.   Reduce drastically the time elapsing between arrest, trial, and imposition of punishment.

11.   Abridge to an appropriate degree the freedom of those who in the opinion of a court are extremely likely to commit violent crimes. Confine and treat drug addicts.

12.   Make it clear in advance that those who incite to riot will be severely punished.

13.   Prohibit "live" television coverage of riots and of incidents likely to provoke them.

There can be little doubt that with one or two possible exceptions these recommendations are unacceptable. A politician with a heterogeneous constituency would strenuously oppose almost all of them. In most matters, the actual course of policy is likely to be the very opposite of the one recommended, whichever party is in power. Government is more likely to promote unequal than equal access to job and housing markets either by failing to enforce laws prohibiting discrimination or by "enforcing" them in a way (for example, by "affirmative action") that is itself discriminatory. It is also more likely to raise expectations rather than to lower them: to emphasize "white racism"as *the* continuing cause of the Negro's handicaps rather than to de-emphasize it; to increase the minimum wage rather than to decrease or repeal it; to keep children who cannot or will not learn in school a longer rather than a shorter time; to define poverty in terms of relative deprivation rather than in terms of hardship; to deny the existence of class-cultural differences rather than to try to distinguish the competent from the incompetent poor on this basis; to reduce the potential victim's incentives to take precautions against crime rather than to increase them; to give the police less discretionary authority rather than more; to increase the time between arrest, trial, and punishment rather than to decrease it; and to enlarge the freedom of those who have shown themselves to be very likely to commit violent crimes rather than to restrict it. . . .

The American political style was formed largely in the upper classes and, within those classes, mainly by people of dissenting-Protestant and Jewish traditions. Accordingly, it is oriented toward the future and toward moral and material progress, for the individual and for the society as a whole. The American is confident that with a sufficient effort all difficulties can be overcome and all problems solved, and he feels a strong obligation to try to improve not only himself but everything else: his community, his society, the whole world. Ever since the days of Cotton Mather, whose *Bonifacius* was a how-to-do-it book on the doing of good, service has been the American motto. To be sure, practice has seldom entirely corresponded to principles. The principles, however, have always been influential and they have sometimes been decisive. They can

be summarized in two very simple rules: first, DON'T JUST SIT THERE. DO SOMETHING! and second, DO GOOD!

These two rules contribute to the perversity that characterizes the choice of measures for dealing with the urban "crisis. . . ." Believing that any problem can be solved if only we try hard enough, we do not hesitate to attempt what we do not have the least idea of how to do and what, in some instances, reason and experience both tell us cannot be done. Not recognizing any bounds to what is feasible, we are not reconciled to—indeed, we do not even perceive—the necessity, so frequently arising, of choosing the least objectionable among courses of action that are all very unsatisfactory. That some children simply cannot be taught much in school is one example of a fact that the American mind will not entertain. Our cultural ideal requires that we give every child a good education whether he wants it or not and whether he is capable of receiving it or not. If at first we don't succeed, we must try, try again. And if in the end we don't succeed, we must feel guilty for our failure. To lower the school-leaving age would be, in the terms of this secular religion, a shirking of the task for which we were chosen. . . .

Although it is easy to exaggerate the importance, either for good or ill, of the measures that government has adopted or might adopt, there does appear to be a danger to the good health of the society in the tendency of the public to define so many situations as "critical problems"—a definition that implies (1) that "solutions" exist or can be found and (2) that unless they are found and applied at once, disaster will befall. The import of what has been said in this book is that although there are many difficulties to be coped with, dilemmas to be faced, and afflictions to be endured, there are very few problems that can be solved; it is also that although much is seriously wrong with the city, no disaster impends unless it be one that results from public misconceptions that are in the nature of self-fulfilling prophecies.

Insofar as delusory and counterproductive public definitions of the situation arise from biases that lie deep within the culture (for example, from the impulse to DO SOMETHING! and to DO GOOD!), they are likely to persist in the face of all experience. To exhort the upper classes to display more of the quality that Trilling calls moral realism would be to offer a problem-begging "solution," since the very want of moral realism that constitutes the problem would prevent their recognizing the need of it.

The biases of the culture limit the range of possibilities, but they do not determine fully how the public will define the situation. This definition is in large part the result of a process of opinion formation that goes on within a relatively small world of officials, leaders of civic associations and other interest groups, journalists, and social scientists, especially economists; from this small world opinion is passed on to the public-at-large through the mass media, books, classroom instruction, campaign oratory, after-dinner speeches, and so on. Needless to say, a vast amount of misinformation, prejudice and illogic enters into the process of opinion formation.

POSTSCRIPT

ELIMINATING POVERTY:
AN UNWINNABLE WAR?

The book which, more than any other, alerted Americans to the persistence of poverty in our "affluent society" was Michael Harrington's *The Other America* (Macmillan, 1963). By the end of the 1960s a number of other books documenting the extent of poverty had appeared, among them Thomas Gladwin's *Poverty U.S.A.* (Little, Brown, 1967) and Nick Kotz's *Let Them Eat Promises* (Prentice-Hall, 1969). Meanwhile, President Johnson's "war on poverty" was generating a great deal of criticism. Daniel P. Moynihan, who is now a U.S. Senator from New York, wrote *Maximum Feasible Misunderstanding* (The Free Press, 1969) in the conviction that Johnson's poverty program played into the hands of radical activists and generated violence without relieving poverty.

It is often forgotten that Richard Nixon, who is usually thought of as a conservative President, offered Congress his own program for fighting poverty. Under the influence of Moynihan, who served as one of its early domestic advisers, the Nixon Administration proposed a "Family Assistance Program." FAP, as it came to be known, would have provided up to $2400 in cash grants annually, the sum to be adjusted downward in proportion to increases in the family's earnings. FAP passed the House of Representatives but was killed in the Senate by a crossfire of liberals, who thought $2400 was too little, and conservatives, who were appalled at the idea of any amount of guaranteed income. More recently, the Carter Administration has proposed to Congress a "welfare reform" plan which revives the principle of FAP and combines it with a program of government jobs for the poor and tax credits for the middle class. Its prospects for passage remain uncertain.

ISSUE 12
FREEDOM OF SPEECH—
FOR OBSCENITY?

"Congress shall make no law . . . abridging the freedom of speech, or of the press." The language is clear—or is it? The Supreme Court has often acknowledged that certain categories of speech or expression simply are not included within that constitutional protection, including lewd and obscene, libelous, or seditious speech, and "fighting" words which incite a breach of the peace.

Remarkably, the Supreme Court did not establish a constitutional rule for obscenity until 1957, although it has never since been entirely free of the issue. The 1957 decision (*Roth v. U.S.*) excluded obscenity from the constitutional protection accorded freedom of expression, as the Court had earlier suggested. Justice William J. Brennan, author of the *Roth* opinion, carefully distinguished obscenity from sex: "Obscene material is material which deals with sex in a manner appealing to prurient interests." As for "prurient interests," Brennan adopted a dictionary definition: "itching, longing; . . . lewd." For some people, the Bible or Shakespeare might cause itching or longing, so Brennan added that the "dominant theme of the material taken as a whole" must seem prurient to "the average person, applying contemporary community standards."

The Court was seriously divided in deciding *Roth*. Two Justices would not accept the argument that obscenity, or for that matter any other expression, should be excluded from First Amendment protection. Another Justice would have distinguished between the standards applied to the federal government and those applied to the states. (He would have given the states greater latitude to define obscenity according to their standards.) Still another Justice held that the crucial element was not the content of the allegedly obscene material but the way it was distributed and advertised, that is, its commercial exploitation.

Division on the Court became greater until on one decision day in 1966, seventeen different opinions were written in three obscenity cases. However, prosecution became more difficult; by 1966 the Supreme Court held that obscenity was not punishable unless it appealed to prurient interest *and* was "utterly without redeeming social value" *and* was "patently offensive."

By the end of the 1960s pornographic movies, sexually explicit magazines and topless bars had come up from the underground and become part of the contemporary landscape. If some Americans saw this as a healthy and inevitable change in mores, many others regarded it as a dangerous and ominous development, and they blamed the Supreme Court for creating a legal climate of "permissiveness."

Four new Nixon appointees reflected or responded to that criticism. In five obscenity cases decided in 1973, a new majority (the Nixon appointees plus Justice Byron White) made successful prosecution of obscenity easier, and therefore more likely. It is no longer necessary to demonstrate that the allegedly obscene material is "utterly without redeeming social value," only that it lacks "serious value." Furthermore, for the first time the Court made clear that the community standards to be applied were those of the local community. The increase in prosecutions since 1973 has been prompted not only by the change in judicial attitude but also by change in the postal law, allowing prosecution of obscene material in the place of delivery or receipt as well as the place of mailing. One consequence is that if a prosecution fails in one place, another can be attempted elsewhere. The pornographic film *Deep Throat* was tried and its producers and actors acquitted in Sioux Falls, Jacksonville, and Boston, with hung juries (no verdict) in Austin, Houston, and Beverly Hills, before conviction was secured in Memphis. The publishers of a weekly sex newspaper, *Screw,* were convicted in Wichita, Kansas where the publication was unavailable on the newsstands and fewer than twenty people in the state (including four postal inspectors!) had mail subscriptions. In 1977, Larry Flynt, publisher of *Hustler* magazine, with editorial offices in Columbus, Ohio, was convicted under Ohio law of pandering obscenity. All of these remain subject to further prosecution in other jurisdictions.

The issues are unlikely to be resolved by the Supreme Court or any other. "Does obscenity hurt?" is an empirical question, and psychologists, criminologists, and sociologists have long studied the question without reaching any consensus, and often without reaching any conclusion. The most that can be said is that the evidence isn't all in and, given the difficulties in conducting research in this area, it probably never will be. "Is obscenity immoral?," "Does it run counter to social values?," and "Is it offensive?" are all questions involving value judgments, and it is obvious that values differ. There are still other questions, questions of "pandering" (how the obscene material is advertised and marketed) and privacy (what are the rights of persons who would shun exposure of obscenity?).

In the following selections, Judge Jerome Frank offers a classic defense of the broadest latitude for free expression, including obscenity, while Harry Clor argues that liberty is not license and society's most fundamental values require that limits be set.

Harry M. Clor

OBSCENITY IS THE ABUSE OF FREE EXPRESSION

A new consideration has been introduced into the long-standing controversy over moral censorship and freedom of expression. Most people who write and debate about these matters have now come to agree that we are living through moral changes of such a magnitude as to warrant the designation "sexual revolution." There is, of course, little agreement about the value of this "revolution"—its potentialities for good or evil in our lives. Such ethical questions, questions about what is good for us and what is bad for us as human beings, are difficult to resolve with any certitude. Yet we cannot avoid grappling with the ethical issues if we are to arrive at reasoned judgments about the controversy over obscenity and about the sexual revolution which is now inextricably involved in that controversy.

The sexual revolution, or "the moral and sexual revolution," as it is sometimes called, may be said to have two distinguishing features—one in the realm of expression and the other in the realm of conduct. In recent years we have been witnessing a rapidly accelerating trend toward increasingly candid, or blatant, presentations of sexual and related subjects in literature and the arts, in public displays and advertising, and in public discourse generally. And, in the realm of conduct, we have been witnessing a similar trend toward sexual freedom, or promiscuity, among the young and in large sections of adult society as well.

Yet, in spite of this apparent moral and sexual revolution, the law continues to be concerned with the restraint of certain kinds of literature, motion pictures, and public performances as "obscene." The Supreme Court . . . has steadily and sharply confined the operation of obscenity laws. But the law may still act to prevent the commercial distribution of materials which, among other things, predominantly "appeal to prurient interests." It is an interesting question why legislative majorities (backed, according to most available evidence, by substantial popular majorities) continue to pass and support such laws. It is highly probable that the expanding market and multitudes of willing customers for erotic literature are provided, in part, from among the popular majorities that regularly indicate their support for censorship. The advocate of

Continued on p. 236

Excerpted from Harry Clor, "Obscenity and Freedom of Expression," in Harry M. Clor, ed., *Censorship and Freedom of Expression* (Rand McNally, 1971). Copyright © 1971 by the Public Affairs Conference Center, Kenyon College, Gambier, Ohio.

Jerome Frank

"AN INDIVIDUAL'S TASTE IS HIS OWN PRIVATE CONCERN"

Freedom to speak publicly and to publish has, as its inevitable and important correlative, the private rights to hear, to read, and to think and to feel about what one hears and reads. The First Amendment protects those private rights of hearers and readers. . . .

Some of those who in the twentieth century endorse legislation suppressing "obscene" literature have an attitude toward freedom of expression which does not match that of the framers of the First Amendment (adopted at the end of the eighteenth century) but does stem from an attitude toward writings dealing with sex which arose decades later, in the midnineteenth century, and is therefore labeled—doubtless too sweepingly—"Victorian." It was a dogma of "Victorian morality" that sexual misbehavior would be encouraged if one were to "acknowledge its existence or at any rate to present it vividly enough to form a lifelike image of it in the reader's mind"; this morality rested on a "faith that you could best conquer evil by shutting your eyes to its existence," and on a kind of word magic. The demands at that time for "decency" in published words did not comport with the actual sexual conduct of many of those who made those demands: "The Victorians, as a general rule, managed to conceal the 'coarser' side of their lives so thoroughly under a mask of respectability that we often fail to realize how 'coarse' it really was. . . ." Could we have recourse to the vast unwritten literature of bawdry we should be able to form a more veracious notion of life as it (then) really was. The respectables of those days often, "with unblushing license," held "high revels" in "night houses." Thanks to them, Mrs. Warren's profession flourished, but it was considered sinful to talk about it in books. Such a prudish and purely verbal moral code, at odds (more or less hypocritically) with the actual conduct of its adherents was (as we have seen) not the moral code of those who framed the First Amendment. One would suppose, then, that the courts should interpret and enforce that Amendment according to the views of those framers, not according to the later "Victorian" code. . . .

Continued on p. 242

Judge Jerome Frank, concurring opinion in *United States v. Roth*, 237 F. 2nd 796 (2nd. Cir., 1956).

12. FREEDOM OF SPEECH

(Clor, cont. from p. 234)

the sexual revolution and his frequent ally, the ideological libertarian, are inclined to explain this paradox as a result of sheer hypocrisy. Large sections of the American public are unwilling to acknowledge in public the sexual passions they indulge in private. But a somewhat different explanation is possible. As a private individual, the average American may be quite susceptible to the allure of prurient appeals. But in his capacity as a citizen and member of the public, and when called upon to render a judgment in that capacity, he still clings to the belief that there is something wrong with blatant appeals to prurient interest.

But what could be the matter with a prurient appeal? If "prurience" means, as courts have said, an arousal of "lust," and lust means sexual desire, what could possibly be wrong with that? We have it not only from the moral revolutionaries but also from the highest medical authorities that sexual desire is quite normal and healthy, and that it is the repression thereof which is unhealthy and productive of troubles. Why, then, should we disapprove of literature that stimulates a desire without which, as Judge Jerome Frank has seen fit to remind us, the human race would not survive? And should we not positively rejoice at the open and candid treatment of a subject so long shrouded in morbid secrecy?

Academic discussions of this issue frequently suffer from overabstraction: overabstraction in def-

erence, perhaps, to what remains of nonrevolutionary morality. The following are some more-or-less (but not wholly) concrete examples of the literature now prevalent as a result of the new candor and the new freedom of expression.

The "adult book shops" now flourishing in many of our larger cities feature what is called "spreader" pictorial magazines. These involve total nudity, very explicit portrayal of the female sexual organs (usually with the legs spread wide apart), and naked men and women posed together in provocative postures that stop just short of actual intercourse. Some of the magazines specialize in homosexual or lesbian portrayals. Often a large number of the "adult" shops are clustered in a central section of the city, with window displays advertising quite openly what is to be found inside.

One of the many New York "exploitation film" theaters just off Times Square recently featured a movie called *The Morbid Snatch.* Two men conceive and execute a plan to capture a young girl, imprison her, and compel her to submit to sexual acts of various sorts. The girl is drugged, confined in a basement, stripped naked, and subjected to sexual intercourse, first with one of the men, then with a lesbian, and then with both the man and the lesbian simultaneously. Periodically, the camera focuses very closely upon the sexual organs of all participants. Periodically also the girl (whose age is, perhaps by intention, difficult to determine; she could be as young as sixteen or as old as twenty-five) is represented as responding erotically to these acts. The sexual scenes, and preparation for them, constitute practically the sole content and surely the sole interest of this film. A companion film about twenty minutes long consists of nothing but close-up shots of a nude woman masturbating. The "coming attractions" promise films devoted to rape, violence, mass orgies, and the intercourse of women with apes.

Finally, consider the now standard theme of a whole *genre* of contemporary paperback novelettes—the systematic violation, humiliation, and domination of women. There are several variations on this theme. A recent novel, *The Orgiasts,* features the gradual introduction of a respectable woman to the practices of a "sex club," and her eventual complete subjection to the will and desires of its members. The plot is typical: by a combination of seduction and compulsion, the woman is induced to desire her own subjection. This is how it is done. Stage one: seduction. Stage two: she begs to be violated. Stage three: she is drawn irresistibly into deviant practices with multi-participation. Stage four: she has lost all will of her own and has become a tool at the disposal of the group. In conjunction with vivid description of the verbal side of this process, there is a detailed portrayal of its physical side—the woman's sexual organs and contortions while under the domination of passion.

Another variation on this theme involves heavy emphasis upon violence in connection with the sexual

act—the explicit interweaving of brutality and sensuality. In this kind of scenario, the woman is literally beaten into submission and is vividly portrayed as desiring and inviting this treatment. A recent novelette carries this principle to its utmost logical conclusion: the hero seduces women, tortures them, and then kills them.

Let us return to the original question. What is wrong with appealing to prurient interests? What, if anything, is the matter with the literature described above? If there is nothing the matter with it, then reasonable men are not entitled to be shocked by its relatively sudden liberation from social and moral restraints. Now, the moralist is inclined to answer our question with terms such as "smut," "filth," and "moral pollution," and many citizens are inclined to simply leave it at that. But revulsion and outrage do not constitute arguments. Common decency might suggest an obvious answer, but we can no longer take the claims of common decency for granted. This is a profoundly skeptical age in which, with regard to moral matters at least, little can be taken for granted. The rising generation of youth and many of their teachers do not accept the traditional ethical assumptions. Today's intellectual climate imposes a heavy burden of argument upon anyone who would defend any aspect of traditional morality.

Our question has two dimensions and can be broken down into two distinct inquiries. First, one must explore the nature of a "prurient appeal" and the intrinsic qualities of materials describable as prurient. And then, one must consider what social harms, if any, can result from the widespread circulation of such materials. If it can be reasonably concluded that legitimate community interests are endangered by obscenity, then there is a further question to be asked. What may organized society do to protect these interests?

The reader will note that I have presented my examples of obscene literature in a certain order and progressive sequence. They constitute a continuum of prurient appeals, beginning with those that arouse "lust" but do not portray violence, and concluding with those clearly recognizable as outright sadism. The intermediate forms portray sexual acts involving some degree of compulsion or constraint, but they do not portray torture or murder, and the infliction of physical pain does not constitute their explicit erotic appeal.

Now some of my readers may wish to argue as follows. There is nothing wrong with the "adult" pictorial magazines or with any other erotic material that simply appeals to normal sexual desire, but sadism is justly condemned. If moral judgment is to be rendered upon literature, it should be rendered at that point in our continuum where violence enters and is made sensually alluring. This argument relies on the distinction between erotic literature which portrays and, hence, stimulates normal sexuality and that which portrays and, hence, stimulates some perverted, distorted, or ugly form of sexuality.

This distinction has some merits but it is inadequate. It is inadequate for description and evaluation of our literary examples, and it is inadequate as a psychological analysis of what is going on between the reader or viewer and the prurient materials. Whatever is the perversion, distortion, or ugliness of outright sado-masochistic pornography, that perversion, distortion, or ugliness is also present in the "adult" pictorials, in a film or highly specific description of people copulating, however normally, and in the seduction scenes of *The Orgiasts*. The last literary items in our spectrum represent only the most extreme and flagrant form of an appeal that was present in all the items and which is present in all literature properly called "obscene."

We are on the way to understanding the nature of that appeal when we consider how the woman in the "spreader" pictorial is presented to the viewer. First of all, and most obviously, she is presented naked. What is normally concealed, and exposed only in private situations, is wholly exposed and placed conspicuously on public display. Secondly, she is presented as nothing more than an object for the gratification of the viewer's passions. She is not a woman but a plaything. All the indicators of human personality have been removed from the picture. What the observer sees is a person who has been stripped down to a mere body at his disposal. It can even be said that the body itself has been stripped down to a sexual organ; it is not the human body but an organ upon which the eye of the viewer is focused.

Essentially the same kind of voyeurism is solicited by the typical exploitation film and pornographic novel. The viewer of *The Morbid Snatch* is invited to enjoy the spectacle of a young woman reduced, as it were, to her parts and to a helpless object of manipulation. In *The Orgiasts* this appeal is made more explicit. The woman is represented as desiring her denigration to a passive tool, and the reader is thus made more consciously aware of what it is that he is invited to enjoy. By the time we arrive at that kind of pornography which specializes in cruel violence or brutishness, we should not be at all surprised. For there is a certain violence and brutishness in all the forms of obscenity examined here. Aspects of life believed to be intimately private are intrusively invaded, and the dignity of human personality has been violated.

In the most general terms, obscenity is that kind of representation which makes a gross public display of the private physical intimacies of life, and which degrades human beings by presenting them as mere objects of impersonal desire or violence. There are various forms of obscene portrayals, but they all have one thing in common—graphically and in detail they reduce human life to a subhuman or merely animal level.

In the usual pornographic novel, love is reduced to sex and sex is vividly reduced to the interaction of organs and parts of organs. The "characters" are not presented as persons: they are (or in the process of the plot they become) little more than sexual instruments, stimulating in a reader the desire for sexual instruments. This kind of literature is predominantly calculated to arouse depersonalized desire. This is what is really meant by "stimulating lust": the systematic arousal of passions that are radically detached from love, affection, personal concern, or from any of those social, moral, and aesthetic considerations that make human relations human. Persons then become *things* to be manipulated for the gratification of the manipulator. What is sometimes termed "the obscenity of violence" is only the logical conclusion of this way of viewing and representing human beings.

The foregoing description and judgment of obscenity has presupposed certain moral concepts. Expressions such as "the dignity of human personality" are in frequent use today, but we seldom explore with real care the meaning and implications of these concepts. More specifically, there is need for exploration of the relation between personal dignity and privacy, and between those feelings we call love or affection and privacy.

Imagine, hypothetically, a man who is required to perform every act of his life in public and in the nude. Would those observing his acts be able to respect him, and would he be able to form a concept of his own dignity? We may well speculate on why it is difficult to answer with a confident "yes." Our dignity, or sense of self-respect, appears to depend heavily upon there being some aspects of our lives that we do not share indiscriminately with others. A sense of self-respect requires that there be some things that are protected, shielded from the world at large, belonging to the individual alone or to his very special relationships. And it would seem that the body and some of its acts belong in this category, demanding a shield of privacy.

Our human dignity is often said to derive from the fact that we possess higher and rational faculties having primacy, or potential primacy, over the lower and merely animal appetites. It is the very essence of pornography that, in it, the lower appetites are rendered supreme. The more specifically human part of us is represented, to the extent that it is represented at all, as the slave of the passions. These passions are indeed powerful. In ordinary life we are assisted in controlling them by social conventions, such as clothing and various moral and aesthetic proprieties, including verbal proprieties. Without any of these conventions we would be constantly confronted with the animal side of our existence and reminded of its demands. The conventions, by partially concealing that side of our existence, serve to subordinate it; to put it in its proper place. Our hypothetical wholly-public man would be, like the characters in a pornographic novel, utterly without any of the protection which this concealment affords. . . .

Public concern about obscenity is sometimes justified on the grounds that salacious literature directly promotes "antisocial conduct." With regard to the direct effects of salacious literature upon the conduct of adults such evidence as we have is problematic and informed opinion is divided. While evidence does not preclude a reasoned judgment that exposure to obscenity is sometimes a factor in the causation of violent or indecent acts, the case for public concern about it cannot rest solidly on this consideration alone. The ultimate evils of unrestrained obscenity are more subtle and far-reaching. The ultimate evils include influences upon the cultural and moral environment of a people and, hence, upon mind and character. The fact that influences of this kind are always too subtle for exact measurement does not relieve us of either the responsibility or the opportunity for reasoning about them. . . .

The censorship of obscenity rests upon two presuppositions: (1) that its unrestrained circulation endangers values and qualities of character that are indispensable for responsible citizenship and decent social relations; (2) that in society's effort to preserve values and qualities that are important to it, there is a legitimate role for the law. . . .

Laws against obscenity constitute some of the community's rules of civility. They affirm that the society has a standard of decency and indecency—a public morality. The majority of us usually require some guidance from communal standards. And it would seem that no community of men can do without a public morality. By means of laws against the more extreme forms of obscenity, we are reminded, and we remind ourselves, that "We, the People" have an ethical order and moral limits. The individual is made aware that the community in which he lives regards some things as beyond the pale of civility. This educative function of obscenity laws is ultimately more significant than their coercive function. . . .

We might well consider whether, in the total absence of a public morality, it would be possible to protect children from obscenity. In an obscenity-saturated cultural environment, what good would it do to make laws forbidding the sale of prurient literature to children? . . .

Elsewhere I have suggested a legal formula for weighing and balancing the literary or intellectual qualities of a work against its prurient appeals. This "balancing" approach would have to include special provisions for protection of serious literature. It should be provided that in borderline cases the consideration of redeeming social importance shall always predominate. And it might be a further condition that works clearly acknowledged by the literary community as possessing *a high degree* of aesthetic worth are absolutely protected, regardless of their prurient effect on the average man. . . .

An ethic of self-expression need not result in unlimited sexual freedom and the wholesale dissolution of civility in self-indulgence. But when this result is avoided it is probably because the ethic of self-expression has been resisted and modified by a countervailing ethic. And the countervailing ethic cannot be expected to maintain itself without any attention from educational and other social institutions.

The most thoughtful proponents of the sexual revolution do not advocate or welcome unlimited sexual freedom. They seek a proper balance between individual spontaneity and restraint in the sexual relation, and they believe that this can be promoted by the new permissiveness. But a proper balance requires that there be guidelines and standards that sometimes take the form of rules, customs, and conventions. Guidelines and standards can also take the form of models of excellence— models of the better and the worse, the noble and the base, in sexual, moral, and aesthetic matters. But neither rules nor models of excellence can long survive in those places where nothing is taught and preached but liberation.

The total triumph of an ethic of self-expression would constitute a national catastrophe, endangering not just morality but freedom itself. The freedom to express ourselves is rendered meaningless when it becomes its own end and the only end. For, then, we lose the capacity to distinguish between a free exchange of ideas and an outburst of passion, between a genuine search for truth and an appeal to sensuality, between the art that ennobles and the pornography that debases. In such a climate of moral and aesthetic indifference, freedom of expression loses its justification.

And the consequences of its abuse may then become too great for the community to bear.

These larger ethical and cultural issues are beyond the reach of the law. They are questions of education in the broadest sense. We need a countervailing ethic.

(Cont. from p. 235, Frank, "An Individual's Taste")

The Statute, as Judicially Interpreted, Authorizes Punishment for Inducing Mere Thoughts, and Feelings, or Desires

For a time, American courts adopted the test of obscenity contrived in 1868 by L.J. Cockburn, in *Queen v. Hicklin*, L.R. 3 Q.B. 360: "I think the test of obscenity is this, whether the tendency of the matter charged as obscenity is to deprave and corrupt those whose minds are open to such immoral influences, and into whose hands a publication of this sort might fall." He added that the book there in question "would suggest . . . thoughts of a most impure and libidinous character."

The test in most federal courts has changed: They do not now speak of the thoughts of "Those whose minds are open to . . . immoral influences" but, instead, of the thoughts of average adult normal men and women, determining what these thoughts are, not by proof at the trial, but by the standard of "the average conscience of the time," the current "social sense of what is right."

Yet the courts still define obscenity in terms of the assumed average normal adult reader's sexual thoughts or desires or impulses, without reference to any relation between those "subjective" reactions and his subsequent conduct. The judicial opinions use such key phrases as this: "suggesting lewd thoughts and exciting sensual desires," "arouse the salacity of the reader," "allowing or implanting . . . obscene, lewd, or lascivious thoughts or desires," "arouse sexual desires." The judge's charge in the instant case reads accordingly: "It must tend to stir sexual impulses and lead to sexually impure thoughts." Thus the statute, as the courts construe it, appears to provide criminal punishment for inducing no more than thoughts, feelings, desires.

No Adequate Knowledge Is Available Concerning the Effects on the Conduct of Normal Adults of Reading or Seeing the "Obscene"

Suppose we assume, *arguendo,* that sexual thoughts or feelings, stirred by the "obscene," probably will often issue into overt conduct. Still it does not at all follow that that conduct will be antisocial. For no sane person can believe it socially harmful if sexual desires lead to normal, and not antisocial, sexual behavior since, without such behavior, the human race would soon disappear.

Doubtless, Congress could validly provide punishment for mailing any publications if there were some moderately substantial reliable data showing that reading or seeing those publications probably conduces to seriously harmful sexual conduct on the part of normal adult human beings. But we have no such data.

Suppose it argued that whatever excites sexual longings might *possibly* produce sexual misconduct. That cannot suffice: Notoriously, perfumes sometimes act as aphrodisiacs, yet no one will suggest that therefore Congress may constitutionally legislate punishment for mailing perfumes. It may be that among the stimuli to irregular sexual conduct, by normal men and women, may be almost anything— the odor of carnations or cheese, the sight of a cane or a candle or a shoe, the touch of silk or a gunnysack. For all anyone now knows, stimuli of that sort may be far more provocative of such misconduct than reading obscene books or seeing obscene pictures. Said John Milton, "Evil manners are as perfectly learnt, without books, a thousand other ways that cannot be stopped."

Effect of "Obscenity" on Adult Conduct

To date there exist, I think, no thoroughgoing studies by competent persons which justify the conclusion that normal adults' reading or seeing of the "obscene" probably induces antisocial conduct. Such competent studies as have been made do conclude that so complex and numerous are the causes of sexual vice that it is impossible to assert with any assurance that "obscenity" represents a ponderable causal factor in sexually deviant adult behavior. "Although the whole subject of obscenity censorship hinges upon the unproved assumption that "obscene" literature is a significant factor in causing sexual deviation from the community standard, no report can be found of a single effort at genuine research to test this assumption by singling out as a factor for study the effect of sex literature upon sexual behavior." What little competent research has been done points definitely in a direction precisely opposite to that assumption.

Alpert reports that, when, in the 1920s, 409 women college graduates were asked to state in writing what things stimulated them sexually, they answered thus: 218 said

243

men; 95 said books; 40 said drama; 29 said dancing; 18 said pictures; 9 said music. Of those who replied "that the source of their sex information came from books, not one specified a 'dirty' book as the source. Instead, the books listed were: The Bible, the dictionary, the encyclopedia, novels from Dickens to Henry James, circulars about venereal diseases, medical books, and Motley's *Rise of the Dutch Republic.*" Macaulay, replying to advocates of the suppression of obscene books, said: "We find it difficult to believe that in a world so full of temptations as this, any gentleman whose life would have been virtuous if he had not read Aristophanes or Juvenal, will be vicious by reading them." Echoing Macaulay, Jimmy Walker, former mayor of New York City, remarked that he had never heard of a woman seduced by a book. New Mexico has never had an obscenity statute; there is no evidence that, in that state, sexual misconduct is proportionately greater than elsewhere.

Effect on Conduct of Young People

. . . Judge Clark speaks of "the strongly held views of those with competence in the premises as to the very direct connection" of obscenity "with the development of juvenile delinquency." . . . One of the cited writings is a report, by Dr. [Marie] Jahoda and associates, entitled "The Impact of Literature: A Psychological Discussion of Some Assumptions in the Censorship Debate" (1954). I have read this report (which is a careful survey of all available studies and psychological theories). I think it expresses an attitude quite contrary to that indicated by Judge Clark. In order to avoid any possible bias in my interpretation of that report, I thought it well to ask Dr. Jahoda to write her own summary of it, which, with her permission, I shall quote. . .

Dr. Jahoda's summary reads as follows:

Persons who argue for increased censorship of printed matter often operate on the assumption that reading about sexual matters or about violence and brutality leads to antisocial actions, particularly to juvenile delinquency. An examination of the pertinent psychological literature has led to the following conclusions:

1. There exists no research evidence either to prove or to disprove this assumption definitively.

2. In the absence of scientific proof two lines of psychological approach to the examination of the assumption are possible: (a) a review of what is known on the causes of juvenile delinquency; and (b) a review of what is known about the effect of literature on the mind of the reader.

3. In the vast research literature on the causes of juvenile delinquency there is no evidence to justify the assumption that reading about sexual matters or about violence leads to delinquent acts. Experts on juvenile delinquency agree that it has no single cause. Most of them regard early childhood events, which precede

the reading age, as a necessary condition for later delinquency. At a later age, the nature of personal relations is assumed to have much greater power in determining a delinquent career than the vicarious experiences provided by reading matter. Juvenile delinquents as a group read less, and less easily, than nondelinquents. Individual instances are reported in which so-called "good" books allegedly influenced a delinquent in the manner in which "bad" books are assumed to influence him.

Where childhood experiences and subsequent events have combined to make delinquency psychologically likely, reading could have one of two effects: it could serve a trigger function releasing the criminal act or it could provide for a substitute outlet of aggression in fantasy, dispensing with the need for criminal action. There is no empirical evidence in either direction.

4. With regard to the impact of literature on the mind of the reader, it must be pointed out that there is a vast overlap in content between all media of mass communication. The daily press, television, radio, movies, books and comics all present their share of so-called "bad" material, some with great realism as reports of actual events, some in clearly fictionalized form. It is virtually impossible to isolate the impact of one of these media on a population exposed to all of them. Some evidence suggests that the particular communications which arrest the attention of an individual are in good part a matter of choice. As a rule, people do not expose themselves to everything that is offered, but only to what agrees with their inclinations.

Children, who have often not yet crystallized their preferences and have more unspecific curiosity than many adults, are therefore perhaps more open to accidental influences from literature. This may present a danger to youngsters who are insecure or maladjusted who find in reading (of "bad" books as well as of "good" books) an escape from reality which they do not dare to face. Needs which are not met in the real world are gratified in a fantasy world. It is likely, though not fully demonstrated, that excessive reading of comic books will intensify in children those qualities which drove them to the comic book world to begin with. an inability to face the world, apathy, a belief that the individual is hopelessly impotent and driven by uncontrollable forces and, hence, an acceptance of violence and brutality in the real world.

It should be noted that insofar as causal sequence is implied, insecurity and maladjustment in a child must precede this exposure to the written word in order to lead to these potential effects. Unfortunately, perhaps, the reading of Shakespeare's tragedies or of Anderson's and Grimm's fairy tales might do much the same. . . .

Maybe someday we will have enough reliable data to show that obscene books and pictures do tend to influence children's sexual conduct adversely. Then a federal statute could be enacted which would avoid constitutional defects by authorizing punishment for using the mails or interstate shipments in the sale of such books and pictures to children.

It is, however, not at all clear that children would be ignorant, in any considerable measure, of obscenity, if no obscene publications ever came into their hands. Youngsters get a vast deal of education in sexual smut from companions of their own age. A verbatim report of conversations among young teen-age boys (from average respectable homes) will disclose their amazing proficiency in obscene language, learned from other boys. Replying to the argument of the need for censorship to protect the young, Milton said: "Who shall regulate all the . . . conversation of our youth . . . appoint what shall be discussed . . . ?" Most judges who reject that view are long past their youth and have probably forgotten the conversational ways of that period of life: "I remember when I was a little boy," said Mr. Dooley, "but I don't remember how I was a little boy."

The Obscenity Statute and the Reputable Press

Let it be assumed, for the sake of the argument, that contemplation of published matter dealing with sex has a significant impact on children's conduct. On that assumption, we cannot overlook the fact that our most reputable newspapers and periodicals carry advertisements and photographs displaying women in what decidedly are sexually alluring postures, and at times emphasizing the importance

of "sex appeal." That women are there shown scantily clad increases "the mystery and allure of the bodies that are hidden," writes an eminent psychiatrist. "A leg covered by a silk stocking is much more attractive than a naked one: a bosom pushed into shape by a brassiere is more alluring than the pendant realities." Either, then, the statute must be sternly applied to prevent the mailing of many reputable newspapers and periodicals containing such ads and photographs, or else we must acknowledge that they have created a cultural atmosphere for children in which, at a maximum, only the most trifling additional effect can be imputed to children's perusal of the kind of matter mailed by the defendant. . . .

If the Obscenity Statute Is Valid, Why May Congress Not Validly Provide Punishment for Mailing Books Which Will Provoke Thoughts It Considers Undesirable About Religion or Politics?

If the statute is valid, then, considering the foregoing, it would seem that its validity must rest on this ground: Congress, by statute, may constitutionally provide punishment for the mailing of books evoking mere thoughts or feelings about sex, if Congress considers them socially dangerous, even in the absence of any satisfactory evidence that those thoughts or feelings will tend to bring about socially harmful deeds. If that be correct, it is hard to understand why, similarly, Congress may not constitutionally provide punishment for such distribution of books evoking mere thoughts or feelings about religion or politics which Congress considers socially dangerous, even in the absence of any satisfactory evidence that those thoughts or feelings will tend to bring about socially dangerous deeds.

The Judicial Exception of the "Classics"

As I have said, I have no doubt the jury could reasonably find, beyond a reasonable doubt, that many of the publications mailed by defendant were obscene within the current judicial definition of the term as explained by the trial judge in his charge to the jury. But so, too, are a multitude of recognized works of art found in public libraries. Compare, for instance, the books which are exhibits in this case with Montaigne's *Essay on Some Lines of Virgil* or with Chaucer. Or consider the many nude pictures which the defendant transmitted through the mails, and then turn to the reproductions in the articles on paintings and sculptures in the *Encyclopedia Britannica* (14th edition). Some of the latter are no less "obscene" than those which led to the defendant's conviction. Yet these Encyclopedia volumes are readily accessible to everyone,

young or old, and, without let or hindrance, are frequently mailed to all parts of the country. Catalogues of famous art museums, almost equally accessible and also often mailed, contain reproductions of paintings and sculpture, by great masters, no less "obscene."

To the argument that such books (and such reproductions of famous paintings and works of sculpture) fall within the statutory ban, the courts have answered that they are "classics,"—books of "literary distinction" or works which have "an accepted place in the arts," including, so this court has held, Ovid's *Art of Love* and Boccacio's *Decameron*. There is a "curious dilemma" involved in this answer that the statute condemns "only books which are dull and without merit," that in no event will the statute be applied to the "classics," that is, books "of literary distinction." The courts have not explained how they escape that dilemma, but instead seem to have gone to sleep (although rather uncomfortably) on its horns.

. . . No one can rationally justify the judge-made exception. The contention would scarcely pass as rational that the "classics" will be read or seen solely by an intellectual or artistic elite, for, even ignoring the snobbish, undemocratic nature of this contention, there is no evidence that that elite has a moral fortitude (an immunity from moral corruption) superior to that of the "masses." And if the exception, to make it rational, were taken as meaning that a contemporary book

247

is exempt if it equates in "literary distinction" with the "classics," the result would be amazing: Judges would have to serve as literary critics; jurisprudence would merge with aesthetics; authors and publishers would consult the legal digests for legal-artistic precedents; we would some day have a Legal Restatement of the Canons of Literary Taste. . . .

How Censorship Under the Statute Actually Operates

Prosecutors, as censors, actually exercise prior restraint. Fear of punishment serves as a powerful restraint on publication, and fear of punishment often means, practically, fear of prosecution. For most men dread indictment and prosecution; the publicity alone terrifies, and to defend a criminal action is expensive. If the definition of obscenity had a limited and fairly well-known scope, that fear might deter restricted sorts of publications only. But on account of the extremely vague judicial definition of the obscene, a person threatened with prosecution if he mails (or otherwise sends in interstate commerce) almost any book which deals in an unconventional, unorthodox manner with sex, may well apprehend that, should the threat be carried out, he will be punished. As a result, each prosecutor becomes a literary censor (dictator) with immense unbridled power, a virtually uncontrolled discretion. A statute would be invalid which gave the

Postmaster General the power, without reference to any standard, to close the mails to any publication he happened to dislike. Yet, a federal prosecutor, under the federal obscenity statute, approximates that position: Within wide limits, he can (on the advice of the Postmaster General or on no one's advice) exercise such a censorship by threat without a trial, without any judicial supervision, capriciously and arbitrarily. Having no special qualifications for that task, nevertheless, he can, in large measure, determine at his will what those within his district may not read on sexual subjects. In that way, the statute brings about an actual prior restraint of free speech and free press which strikingly flouts the First Amendment. . . .

The Dangerously Infectious Nature of Governmental Censorship of Books

Governmental control of ideas or personal preferences is alien to a democracy. And the yearning to use governmental censorship of any kind is infectious. It may spread insidiously. Commencing with suppression of books as obscene, it is not unlikely to develop into official lust for the power of thought-control in the areas of religion, politics and elsewhere. Milton observed that "licensing of books . . . necessarily pulls along with it so many other kinds of licensing." Mill noted that the "bounds of what may be called moral police" may easily extend "until it encroaches on the most unquestionably legitimate liberty of the individual." We should beware of a recrudescence of the undemocratic doctrine uttered in the seventeenth century by Berkeley, Governor of Virginia: "Thank God there are no free schools of preaching, for learning has brought disobedience into the world, and printing has divulged them. God keep us from both."

The People as Self- Guardians: Censorship by Public Opinion, Not by Government

Plato, who detested democracy, proposed to banish all poets; and his rulers were to serve as guardians of the people, telling lies for the people's good, vigorously suppressing writings these guardians thought dangerous. Governmental guardianship is repugnant to the basic tenet of our democracy: According to our ideals, our adult citizens are self-guardians, to act as their own fathers, and thus become self-dependent. When our governmental officials act towards our citizens on the thesis that "Papa knows best what's good for you," they enervate the spirit of the citizens: To treat grown men like infants is to make them infantile, dependent, immature. . . .

So, we come back, once more, to Jefferson's advice: The only completely democratic way to control publications which arouse mere thoughts or feelings is through non-governmental censorship by public opinion.

The Seeming Paradox of the First Amendment

Here we encounter an apparent paradox: The First Amendment, judicially enforced, curbs public opinion when translated into a statute which restricts freedom of expression (except that which will probably induce undesirable conduct). The paradox is unreal: The Amendment ensures that public opinion—the "common conscience of the time"—shall not commit suicide through legislation which chokes off today the free expression of minority views which may become the majority public opinion of tomorrow.

Private Persons or Groups May Validly Try to Influence Public Opinion

The First Amendment obviously has nothing to do with the way persons or groups, not a part of government, influence public opinion as to what constitutes "decency" or "obscenity." The Catholic Church, for example, has a constitutional right to persuade or instruct its adherents not to read designated books or kinds of books. . . .

In our industrial era when, perforce, economic pursuits must be, increasingly, governmentally

12. FREEDOM OF SPEECH

regulated, it is especially important that the realm of art—the non-economic realm—should remain free, unregimented, the domain of free enterprise, of unhampered competition at its maximum. An individual's taste is his own private concern. *De gustibus non disputandum* represents a valued democratic maxim. . . .

To vest a few fallible men—prosecutors, judges, jurors—with vast powers of literary or artistic censorship, to convert them into what Mill called a "moral police," is to make them despotic arbiters of literary products. If one day they ban mediocre books as obscene, another day they may do likewise to a work of genius. Originality, not too plentiful, should be cherished, not stifled. An author's imagination may be cramped if he must write with one

eye on prosecutors or juries; authors must cope with publishers who, fearful about the judgments of governmental censors, may refuse to accept the manuscripts of contemporary Shelleys or Mark Twains or Whitmans.

Some few men stubbornly fight for the right to write or publish or distribute books which the great majority at the time consider loathsome. If we jail those few, the community may appear to have suffered nothing. The appearance is deceptive. For the conviction and punishment of these few will terrify writers who are more sensitive, less eager for a fight. What, as a result, they do not write might have been major literary contributions. "Suppression," Spinoza said, "is paring down the state till it is too small to harbor men of talent."

POSTSCRIPT

FREEDOM OF SPEECH—FOR OBSCENITY?

Not all opponents of obscenity will concede, as Clor does, that the available evidence does not warrant a causal connection between obscenity and anti-social conduct. However, Clor's appeal is to society's right to preserve basic values, such as the privacy and dignity of human beings. What are basic "values" for Clor are matters of "taste" for Frank. Frank's most cherished value, which he believed was enshrined in the Constitution's First Amendment, is the right to advocate dissenting values.

Professor Clor has himself provided elsewhere the fullest philosophical analysis of the issue in the context of American practice. In *Obscenity and Public Morality* (University of Chicago, 1969), Clor developed at length a position similar to that expressed in this essay. From the perspective of a public prosecutor of pornography, Richard H. Kuh has written a non-technical defense of legal censorship in *Foolish Figleaves* (Macmillan, 1967). Charles Rembar, who was attorney for the defense in several leading obscenity cases, has written a lively defense of the right of obscenity in *The End of Obscenity* (Random House, 1968).

But there is no "end of obscenity" or of debate about it. Every age redefines it, and in the United States at the present time, we may suspect that every court defines it differently. The 1973 decisions are by no means the last word from the Supreme Court. Changing morals and changing issues, changing perceptions of the social consequences of obscenity and pornography, and (not least) changing membership of the Supreme Court will result in still more refinements of what legal standards are compatible with constitutional guarantees. Scholars will also contribute to clarification—and confusion—of the issue. The ten volumes of the presidential Commission on Obscenity and Pornography, published in 1970, have been followed by a number of technical studies on the relationship between obscenity and social behavior. Where evidence is likely to remain less than conclusive, advocates of opposed positions are likely to find confirmation of their biases.

ISSUE 13

THE MASS MEDIA: SHOULD GOVERNMENT GUARANTEE A "RIGHT OF ACCESS"?

The "mass media" of communication— newspapers, magazines, radio, and television—have been called the "fourth branch of government." The other three branches have the tangible powers to make laws, carry them out, and interpret them, but the mass media possess the fundamental democratic power to influence public opinion and thus to help shape the making, executing, and understanding of the laws.

This influence is not new, as evidenced in the amazing flood of books, pamphlets, broadsides, and newspapers which influenced colonial opinion in the American Revolution. This development was so important that John Adams felt it was decisive. He concluded: "The Revolution was effected before the war commenced. The Revolution was in the minds and hearts of the people." Thomas Jefferson stated that, were it left to him "to decide whether we should have a government without newspapers or newspapers without a government, I should not hesitate a moment to prefer the latter."

The new nation's indebtedness to free publication of opinion was acknowledged in the First Amendment to the Constitution, which proclaims: "Congress shall make no law . . . abridging the freedom of speech, or of the press. . . ." On its face the language is clear and unequivocal: government has no business interfering with the press. And if censorship—telling newspapers what they may *not* print—runs counter to the First Amendment, isn't the conflict even more obvious when the government presumes to tell newspapers what they *must* print?

Yet there are those who consider themselves ardent defenders of First Amendment freedom who at the same time defend the government's right to compel newspaper publication of items which the newspapers would not otherwise print. Indeed, the argument goes, there are times when compelling a newspaper to print something may be carrying out the spirit of the First Amendment. We cannot do justice to this seemingly paradoxical argument unless we understand how the press has changed in the nearly two centuries since the Constitution was written.

The changes have been enormous. A mass readership has replaced the literate elite of the eighteenth century. The telegraph, telephone, radio, and television have dramatically changed the ways in which news is presented and received. News reporting is very professional, in contrast to the crude partisanship of newspapers at the nation's beginnings. Of all the changes, the most noticeable—and disturbing—to those who wish to preserve the spirit of the First Amendment is the evidence that control of newspapers (and the other newer media) has become concentrated in fewer and fewer hands. Only fifty-eight cities and towns in the United States have competitive newspapers. Three national networks largely dominate television broadcasting. Elsewhere, in book and magazine publishing, similar if less dramatic concentrations exist.

The Supreme Court has said that the First Amendment rests upon "the principle that debate on issues should be uninhibited, robust, and wide-open." But what if uninhibited and robust debate is squelched not by the government but by the media? Imagine that a town's only newspaper prints a scorching criticism of a political candidate shortly before the election, and the aggrieved candidate requests space for reply. If the newspaper refuses, has it not replaced "uninhibited, robust, and wide-open" debate by controlled, unhealthy, and one-sided debate—that is to say, by no debate at all?

Such a case is not purely hypothetical. In Miami in 1972, Pat L. Tornillo Jr., a candidate for the Florida state legislature, asked the *Miami Herald* for space to respond to editorial attacks on him. When he was refused, he sued under a Florida "right of reply" statute, and won in the Florida courts. In *Miami Herald v. Tornillo* (1974), however, the U.S. Supreme Court reversed, upholding the newspaper. Even so, the Court's opinion was not unsympathetic to Tornillo's side of the argument. Chief Justice Warren Burger said that the purpose of the First Amendment was to keep government out of the editor's chair, but he agreed that the growing concentration of newspapers can lead to abuses of power by these conglomerates.

The "right of access" issue, then, is far from being settled, at least in the realm of public opinion. In the following selections, Professor Jerome Barron of George Washington University Law School, who argued Tornillo's case before the Supreme Court, presents the case for such a right, while reporter Thomas Powers discusses the dangers of giving government such powers over the press. Both were written before the *Tornillo* decision.

Jerome A. Barron

THE RIGHT OF ACCESS
TO THE MEDIA

Freedom of the press is one of the more attractive phrases in American life, law, and myth. What does it mean? Why is it an important value in our society? Minimally it promises that newspapers cannot be restrained or intimidated by government for what they allow to be printed in their pages. The First Amendment to the U.S. Constitution states: "Congress shall make no law abridging freedom of speech or of the press.". . .

Changes in our approach to freedom of the press are bitterly resisted. Now an access-oriented approach is attacked as a violation of the concept because, it is urged, the Constitution speaks only to government and not to private power groups. But the law of freedom of the press was extended from the national to the state governments in the past without constitutional amendment. The Supreme Court said the word "liberty" in the Fourteenth Amendment ("No state shall deprive any person of life, liberty, or property without due process of law") was a concept sufficiently broad to warrant the conclusion that it obligated the states to respect freedom of the press. I believe that the reference to freedom of the press in the First Amendment itself permits an interpretation today which will make the concept continuingly vital and meaningful. Such an interpretation would permit governmental action to provide for positive expression.

Our approach to freedom of the press has operated in the service of a romantic illusion: the illusion that the marketplace of ideas is freely accessible.

After the first World War, in a case involving a socialist who was prosecuted for distributing leaflets which were allegedly designed to "cripple or hinder the United States in the prosecution of the (first) World War," Justice Oliver Holmes wrote a memorable opinion:

> But when men have realized that time has upset many fighting faiths, they may come to believe even more than they believe the very foundations of their own conduct that the ultimate good desired is better reached by free trade in ideas—that the best test of truth is the power of the thought to get itself accepted in the competition of the market and that truth is the only ground upon which their wishes can safely be carried out.

Continued on p. 256

Thomas Powers

THE DANGERS OF "RIGHT TO REPLY" LAWS

Everyone in the United States is in favor of a free press, until you get down to particulars. Then qualifications abound. Justice Hugo Black was almost unique in saying that freedom of the press was absolute and anyone could print anything he liked, from libel to pornography, without exception. His fellow justices have generally argued that the First Amendment has its limits, without always being able to agree as to just what they are, and the general public feels that some things—but not always the same things—go too far. Fraudulent advertising, say, or advocating the violent overthrow of the republic. The CIA insists it may censor its agents' memoirs, John Mitchell tried to prevent the *New York Times* from printing the Pentagon Papers, and Herbert Marcuse thinks no one should have the right to advocate racism. When it comes to particulars the press does not want for adversaries.

For all the argument, however, it has generally been accepted in this country that a free press is the bedrock of political liberty. Without the right to say what they think, however intemperate, wrong-headed or wounding, the people would be powerless. The Supreme Court explicitly recognized this in 1964 when it unanimously ruled that public officials are not protected against public accusation, even when false, unless they can prove a "malicious" intent or "reckless disregard" of the facts.

"Debate on public issues should be uninhibited, robust and wide-open," the Court said, "and it may well include vehement, caustic and sometimes unpleasantly sharp attacks on government and public officials." In effect, the Court agreed with Harry Truman that public officials who can't take the heat should stay out of the kitchen.

No ruling is so firm that it is not subject to revision, however, and the present Supreme Court, a different body from the one which ruled so unequivocally ten years ago, is being asked to turn down the temperature. The case currently before the Court is *The Miami Herald Publishing Company v. Pat L. Tornillo* and the law at issue is an alluringly-named Florida statute which grants every candidate for public office a "right to reply," at equal length and in a space of equal prominence, to any newspaper attack on his personal character or public record. . . .

Continued on p. 262

Reprinted by permission of Commonweal Publishing Co., Inc. From Thomas Powers, "Right-to-Reply Laws," *Commonweal*, May 17, 1974.

13. THE MASS MEDIA

(Barron, cont. from p. 254)

A half a century later, Holmes' eloquent description of the free marketplace of ideas depicts an ideal, not a reality. There *are* enormous limitations on the "power of thought to get itself accepted in the competition of the market." In Holmes' concept of the marketplace of ideas the only limitation on the currency of ideas is an intellectual one. But there is no free trade in ideas. Ideas in a mass society are transmitted in the mass communications media of television, radio, and the press. Admission to them assures notoriety and public response. Denial assures obscurity and, apparently, frustration.

We assume that the only obstacles to debate and discussion are the penalties that the state may apply to unpopular debate and provocative discussion. Our law of freedom of expression, however, has done very little to insure opportunity for freedom of expression.

The traditional liberal position on ideas is essentially Darwinian. Ideas engage in a life of mortal combat and the fittest survive. In this struggle, the continuing menace has been seen to be government. That private power might so control the struggle of ideas as to predetermine the victor has not been considered. But, increasingly, private censorship serves to suppress ideas as thoroughly and as rigidly as the worst government censor. . . .

There is inequality in capacity to communicate ideas just as there is inequality in economic bargaining power. Indeed inequality of power to communicate is usually one aspect of inequality in general economic bargaining power. In the broadcast media, the VHF television outlets are almost completely in the hands of network affiliated stations, and possess the mass audience. The licenses of these stations are almost invariably renewed by the Federal Communications Commission at three-year intervals. The unregulated daily newspaper industry is equally unfriendly territory for new entrants and new voices. The cost of establishing a competitive daily newspaper is all but absolutely prohibitive. . . .

If a community has only a single daily newspaper, many issues and topics excluded from it will not be sufficiently newsworthy for mention in print media elsewhere. This element of public dependence on the single community daily makes the case for compulsory entry a strong one. Sometimes, a similar necessity may exist even in a magazine. A very recent decision has produced the first American legal recognition of access to a magazine. A group called the Radical Lawyers Caucus sought to place an ad in the *Texas Bar Journal* to publicize its meeting during the Texas bar convention in San Antonio. The proposed ad announced that a hotel suite had been rented and that the lawyers were planning to discuss national problems and pass out literature about them.

The *Bar Journal* refused the ad on the ground that state bar rules prohibited accepting political advertisements. As is not unusual in these cases, the Radical Lawyers Caucus had no difficulty in showing that the *Bar Journal's* definition of political was not so detached as it might have been. The *Bar Journal* editors had reprinted an editorial from the *Dallas Morning News* on the Chicago Seven, as well as a resolution by the state bar committee supporting the President's Vietnam policy and denouncing antiwar demonstrators. Counsel for the Bar said that permitting "political advertisements" would lead to ideological warfare and injure the State Bar's image of disinterestedness.

The federal court decided in favor of the Radical Lawyers Caucus. The *Bar Journal*, as a state agency, could not accept commercial advertising to the exclusion of editorial advertising. Furthermore, since it had printed editorials and resolutions from bar committees, the *Bar Journal* was hardly in a position to maintain its claim to be politically neutral. The court said that it was "unquestioned" that the *Bar Journal* refused the ad because of its content rather than from any general advertisement policies. Censorship on the basis of content is clearly a violation of the equal protection and free speech guarantees of the Constitution. . . .

The print media cannot continue to evade legal responsibilities. The idea of access cannot stop with the electronic media. The same wire services feed both broadcasters and newspapers. Often the same

corporations and families own a television outlet and the only daily newspaper in a community. . . .

Daily newspapers are not scarce like broadcasters because of inherent technical limitations, but because of economics. The number of American daily newspapers of general circulation has steadily dwindled. Today there are less than 1800 in this country. The cost of establishing a daily newspaper is of such heroic dimensions that few are foolish enough to try.

Historians of journalism record that in revolutionary eighteenth century America, many printers operated on an open-to-all-comers basis. Printers published little weeklies which reflected their own passionately felt views, but customarily allowed their rivals to hire out their facilities. Entry into the world of public and political debate is no longer so informal. The nineteenth and early twentieth centuries brought the rise of great mass circulation daily newspapers. But for fifty years, the steady pattern of the American press has been a decline in numbers. Famous journals of all political stripes have perished—the Republican New York *Herald Tribune,* the Democratic Boston *Post,* the radical *P.M.*

In 1909-10, 2202 daily newspapers were published, compared with 1761 in 1961. But the decline in numbers has by no means led to a decline in influence. It is sometimes said that the loss of alternatives to American newspaper readers is not necessarily a matter for alarm since the rise of the electronic media, radio and television, provide an alternative forum. The American Newspaper Publishers Association contends, for example, that there is competition in news and advertising between the print and the broadcast media. But the reality is that often the print media compete with broadcast media, not in ownership or in content, but only in technology.

In 1963, 153 of the 563 television stations were newspaper affiliated. In 26 communities the only newspaper has an interest in the only television station. Daily newspaper circulation is over 60,000,000 but the number of cities possessing dailies with competing ownership has decreased from 117 to 58.

Twenty-eight of the 69 newspapers published in the country's top 25 television markets have ownership interests in television stations in the community where they publish. Moreover, in the few communities where one of two daily newspapers operates a television station, the nontelevision affiliated newspaper is at a competitive disadvantage. That does not augur well for the survival of the non-affiliated competitor.

There is a temptation to seek vigorous enforcement of the anti-trust laws in order to inhibit and perhaps to break up concentration of ownership and control in the media. It must always be remembered, however, that our objective is a multiplicity of ideas rather than a multiplicity of forums. Obviously, when media outlets have a common ownership, the existence and the exercise of independent editorial opinion in each is suspect. The chain newspaper is not only a monopoly voice in a community; very often, it is not even a community voice. The International Typographical Union has described the chain newspapers as follows:

> The chain paper, with wire services, "canned" features and editorials, and a modicum of local news, can be managed like a chain store or hotel.

In 1962, 46.9 percent of the total daily circulation of American newspapers and 53.7 percent of the total circulation of Sunday newspapers was held by chains. The big twelve newspaper chains are Hearst, Chicago Tribune, Scripps-Howard, Newhouse, Knight, Cowles, Ridder, Cox, Gannett, Chandler (*Times-Mirror*), Ochs Estate (*New York Times*) and Triangle. The circulation of these twelve chains amounted to 20.4 million or 34.4 percent of the circulation of all daily newspapers. Sunday circulation of the Big Twelve totaled 21.8 million, or 45.2 percent of all Sunday circulation.

From all these figures, the International Typographical Union concluded that "the free and independent press guaranteed by the First Amendment stands to be forfeited to monopolists and absentee owners unless remedial measures are taken." It is difficult to understate the monopolistic character of the American press. As of 1962 the following states were without any competitive dailies: Alabama, Delaware, Georgia, Idaho, Kansas, Louisiana, Maine, Minnesota, Montana, Nebraska, New

Hampshire, New Mexico, North Carolina, North Dakota, Oklahoma, Rhode Island, South Carolina, Utah, Virginia, West Virginia, and Wyoming.

The possibility of new entrants into the daily newspaper business are probably more hypothetical than real. Concentration of ownership in the media generally, and a monopoly newspaper press specifically, are the reality now and in the foreseeable future. Take a single statistic: in 1968, out of more than 1500 cities with daily newspapers, only 45 had competitive newspapers. Diversity must be accomplished within the existing outlets. How can that diversity be obtained? Direct entry into the press is what is necessary. But such entry is difficult. The pressure for access therefore manifests itself in and outside the media. . . .

As the law presently stands, broadcasters face an obligation to provide an opportunity for reply and to some extent for debate, but they have no general duty to provide access to broadcasting. Newspapers are under no obligation to provide space for reply, debate, or access. Indeed in all but two American jurisdictions, publishers have no obligation to provide a right of reply even when they libel someone. The libel area highlights the contrast between the press situation and broadcasting. In 1964 the Supreme Court radically revised the law of libel. The theory was that the freer newspapers were to criticize and discuss public men and public issues, the more "robust and wide-open" debate would be.

In even a primitive understanding of debate, there must be an assumption that if a newspaper says X, then someone must have an opportunity to say anti-X. Yet that is not what happens now when a newspaper libels a public person. The newspaper may attack public officials and private persons with public reputations with less fear of being subject to a heavy judgment than ever before. If any provision for reply is given by the newspapers to the victims of their attacks, it is entirely voluntary. Is that debate?

The paradox is that the Supreme Court in 1969 required debate and reply in broadcasting and in 1964 entrenched the pre ailing lack of legal or social responsibility on the part of the press. The cases can be differentiated. In the broadcasting case, Congress by law had required fairness to include a right of reply to personal attacks. Therefore the Supreme Court had only to decide whether such an interpretation was consistent with freedom of the press. Their enormous contribution was that they did. In fact, they went further and indicated that legal mechanisms for dialogue implemented First Amendment values in a medium where access was limited economically and technologically. The newspaper libel case in 1964 between an Alabama public official and the *New York Times* did not present a direct question of the validity of right of access legislation. But neither was the Court presented with any statute which said that where public men are attacked by newspapers, the standard for recovery should be the heavy one of having to show that the particular libel was published in malice, i.e. with reckless disregard of the truth or falsity of what was said. Yet the Court carved out such a rule by interpreting the First Amendment as demanding the criticism of government and the encouragement of debate on public matters.

There is no objection to giving new perspectives to basic constitutional guarantees to give them continuing contemporary force and vitality, but the price of a new constitutional immunity ought to be some corresponding constitutional obligation. If libel law is to be softened to encourage newspapers to be more adventurous and daring on matters of public concern, then surely the same First Amendment which authorized the Court to change the law of libel should have been used to provide at least some new opportunities for participation in the press by the newspaper public. Where a public man as a result of the new rule has lost his right to a judgment for money damages against a newspaper, the newspaper should have to provide him with space for a right of reply. Such a rule is minimum decency.

On the access front, the Court in *New York Times v. Sullivan* missed a splendid opportunity to declare a constitutional duty to publish editorial advertisements. Just the announcement of such an obligation as a constitutional duty of publishers and a constitutional right of readers would have greatly enhanced the powers of communication of all groups in one-newspaper communities.

When the Supreme Court's broadcast access case and its newspaper libel case are put beside each other, is not the position of the press anomalous? Since there are far more broadcast outlets in the United States than daily newspapers, the argument is ludicrous that affirmative legal obligations must be imposed on broadcasting because it is a limited access medium. In the United States all the important media are limited access media.

There are now signs of change which suggest that the rights of the readership to the press which serves them will eventually be recognized. In June 1971 the Supreme Court, in a decision which extended the considerable immunity from libel which newspapers already enjoy to all situations where "the utterance involved concerns a matter of public or general interest," explicitly recognized for the first time the problem of access to the media. Furthermore, the Court's remarks unquestionably revealed sympathy for the proposition that as a First Amendment matter there is a right of access to the press.

The context was a case involving a broadcaster who was sued for libel and who was given the benefit of the rule that to collect for libel a public figure must prove "actual malice," i.e. reckless disregard for the truth or falsity of what was said.

The argument was pressed at the Supreme Court bar by Ramsey Clark that the rule of relative libel immunity for the media in defamation cases would leave private individuals helpless. Those individuals having no access to the media could be pitilessly defamed and the newspapers would be immune to any legal responsibility to the subject of their attacks. Media publicity might destroy someone and then there would be no recourse. At this point, the Court for the first time saw the connection between relieving newspapers from fear of libel suits and the need for access to the press.

If the states were concerned about securing redress for private individuals wounded by media publicity, said the Court, a remedy should be sought in arming them "with the ability to respond, rather than in stifling public discussion of matters of public concern." Debate, not damages, was the answer. In a footnote, Justice Brennan developed this idea. I quote it in full because it may well be a guide to the future of access to the press:

> One writer in arguing that the First Amendment itself should be read to guarantee a right of access to the media not limited to a right to respond to defamatory falsehoods, has suggested several ways the laws might encourage public discussion. Barron, Access to tl Press—A New First Amendment Right, 80 Harv. L. Rev. 1641, 1666-1678 (1967). It is important to recognize that the private individual often desires press

exposure either for himself, his ideas, or his causes. Constitutional adjudication must take into account the individual's interest in access to the press as well as the individual's interest in preserving his reputation, even though libel actions by their nature encourage a narrow view of the individual's interest since they focus only on situations where the individual has been harmed by undesired press attention. A constitutional rule that deters the press from covering the ideas or activities of the private individual thus conceives the individual's interests too narrowly.

A Supreme Court exhortation that judges should take into account the individual's interest in access to the press is encouraging for the future. If constitutional adjudication can provide for access to the press, then the Court must think that the state action problems which the lower federal courts and the newspaper industry have made so much of are not insurmountable. The Court's remarks about access to the press appear at least to imply that a right of access to the press can be fashioned by the courts as a matter of First Amendment interpretation.

Attention is at last being given to the idea that the First Amendment grants protection to others in the opinion-making process besides those who own the media of communication.

13. THE MASS MEDIA

(Cont. from p. 255, Powers, "The Dangers of 'Right to Reply' ")

The Florida law is misnamed because it does not really grant a candidate a "right" to reply; that is something which the Constitution already protects. Instead, it guarantees a forum for reply, something quite different. The notion is not a new one. Even A. J. Liebling, hardly an opponent of the First Amendment or a friend of official-dom, once wrote that "Freedom of the press is guaranteed only to those who own one." This position has been defended most vigorously by Jerome Barron, a Florida law professor representing Tornillo, who argues that the First Amendment is empty if it does not implement, rather than simply protect, an individual's right to print his views. The Florida court largely accepted Barron's view, citing the steady decline in newspapers and suggesting that the public ought to have a Constitutional right of access to the ones that remain.

This argument is not without merit. There is very little competition between newspapers on the local level and the potential for abuse is obvious. Indianapolis and Manchester, New Hampshire, are cases in point. If the attack on Tornillo had come from a local television station, the FCC's "fairness doctrine" clearly would grant him the right to reply on the attacking station. By extension, then, the argument goes, he ought to have a right to defend himself against the *Herald* in the *Herald*. Theoretically a city could have a dozen newspapers but in fact most Americans now live in one-newspaper towns, which means that an injured aspirant for public office must reply in the paper which attacks him, or he cannot reply at all. Telling him that he is free to start his own paper is like telling a traveler bound for Chicago that he may start his own railroad. It is a freedom without substance, a pious fraud.

The problem with "right to reply" statutes is not so much their ostensible purpose, which is high-minded and unexceptionable, as their effect, which would be to grant for the first time a degree of public control over the editorial content of newspapers. That degree might be small to begin with, but once conceded it would tend to grow. This, of course, would be denied vigorously in any Congressional debate over a "right to reply" statute, but the government also promised, when it finally got a wiretap law in 1968, that it would never dream of tapping or bugging anyone but gangsters and spies. That is the sort of promise which the fox gave to the gingerbread boy, when he offered to ferry him across the river.*

There are two important ways in which "right to reply" statutes would undermine the freedom they are alleged to enhance. The first is that they would tend to become

---

*The too-trusting gingerbread boy, it will be remembered, started out on the fox's back, and ended inside his stomach.

universally applicable. Why, after all, should a "right to reply," or guaranteed forum, be uniquely reserved for candidates for elective office, as stipulated in the Florida statute? Officials, union leaders and anti-war activists are just as vulnerable to newspaper "attack" and could fairly demand an equal right to reply. Clive Barnes can destroy a young playwright with a single review; why shouldn't playwrights have a right to reply in the only space which counts, the theater page of the *Times*? What about all the other people who can claim they have been injured by newspaper comment? The coaches of losing teams, for example, or lawyers defending unpopular Presidents? The list is endless: baby doctors accused of treason, nominees for the Supreme Court who are not comfirmed by the Senate, union leaders convicted of murder, Secretaries of Defense charged with war crimes, the builders of aircraft which fall out of the sky, press secretaries ridiculed for dismissing lies as "inoperative," Jesuits charged with anti-Semitism, generals who do not win wars, the mothers of assassins. Presumably they, too, are protected by the First Amendment. They are in no position to start newspapers. Why should they be denied the guaranteed forum for reply which Florida now grants to every candidate for a local school board? It is a short step, after all, from candidates to elected officials, and from elected to appointed officials, and thence to everyone else.

The rule of universal applicability also means that a "right to reply" to *newspaper* attack would quickly be extended to every other sort of periodical, from trade journals to diocesan newspapers, and ultimately even to books. The number of magazines is diminishing, too, and it would hardly be consistent with the First Amendment to grant the ones that remain a unique freedom to print criticism which was denied to newspapers, or to expose officials to attack from one quarter while protecting them from another. Magazines are more intimate than newspapers and the threat to free speech inherent in "right to reply" statutes is somehow clearer in their case. Would it enhance freedom of the press to require Catholic magazines to print the views of abortionists? Must the *New Leader* provide a forum for Stalinists? Should Lester Maddox have a right to space in *The Race Relations Reporter?* Must the *Audubon Magazine* offer its gorgeous pages to Western Senators who favor the poisoning of coyotes? Many small magazines of opinion are sustained only by conviction. They could hardly survive a situation in which half of every deficit dollar was a free gift to their bitterest opponents.

The second danger grows out of the first. Who is to decide what constitutes an "attack," its precise length and the prominence of its position in the paper? Would an attack on "Congress" for dragging its feet on impeachment be answerable by each and every Representative? Who would answer attacks on "the public" for its indifference to freedom of the press, or on "teachers" for their insensitivity to the richness of ghetto English, or on "the oil industry" or "the automotive industry"? If every citizen were not to be the sole judge of whether or not he had been attacked, at what length and how prominently, then some public institution would have to act as arbiter. Its power would be very great indeed. If there were no appeal of its decisions its power would be totalitarian, and if there were appeal there would be no end to them. Almost every story in every publication would be the potential focus of a legal struggle as bitter as a custody fight. The purpose of "right to reply" statutes might be to guarantee a forum for the voiceless, but their effect would be to establish a degree—and inevitably a growing degree—of public control over the press. It is not hard to see who would benefit. Would a "right to reply" board be less instinctively sympathetic to the President in its rulings than the Internal Revenue Service officials who praised him for the neatness of his tax returns? A man who would believe that, as the Duke of Wellington said in another context, would believe anything.

"Right to reply" advocates misunderstand—unless they understand only too well—the purpose of the First Amendment, which is to protect the freedom of citizens to publish their views, not to guarantee their fairness. The men who wrote the Constitution were hardly indifferent to such matters, but they concluded that fairness, like moderation and wisdom, could not be imposed upon political debate.

Any attempt to do so, they felt, would inevitably favor one faction over another, with the most likely beneficiary the faction in power. "Fairness" is not the object of political struggle, after all, but only a means, an intellectual style, a tone intended to persuade. Political partisans can and do resort to ridicule, invective and exhortation as well as to reason. It is hardly fair to say of Gerald Ford that he has played too much football without his helmet. Perhaps in strict fact he *always* wore his helmet. Nixon was not being fair in 1952 when he attacked the Democrats as the party of "Communism, corruption and Korea." Barry Goldwater was unfair in 1964 when he called Lyndon Johnson "the biggest faker in the United States" and Bobby Kennedy was unfair in 1968 when he said Johnson was "calling upon the darker impulses in the American spirit." Unfair attack is the common coin of politics. The lack of "fairness" may work for or against an advocate; that is a tactical question. But if his freedom to speak and publish is to have substance, the choice of words must be his alone.

The legal arguments in favor of "right to reply" statutes are so strained, and the consequences of their acceptance so clear, that it is hard to see how the Supreme Court could accept them. And yet . . . it might. There is a lot of hostility toward the press in this country, for the same reason there is a lot of hostility toward city hall, General Motors and the Internal Revenue Service, because they are huge, indifferent and inaccessible. Arrogance is the least congenial of human failings. Attacks on freedom of the press get as far as they do, which is farther all the time, because a lot of people would like to see the *Times* taken down a peg or two and either do not see or do not care that their own freedom would inevitably be compromised as well.

It is unfortunate that the press must be the chief defender of the press in these matters; it makes freedom of the press seem somehow self-serving. The *Times* may argue that it is defending the people's freedom in defending its own but this has a specious ring to it, like Charlie Wilson's assurance in the 1950s that what's good for General Motors is good for the country. Things were different in the 18th century when starting a newspaper was a week's work for a handful of men; citizens then were jealous of their right to publish unimpeded because it was a right they might reasonably expect to exercise. But

in the age of media giants like *Time-Life*, CBS, the *New York Times* and the *Washington Post,* when starting a newspaper is beyond all but centi-millionaires, it is easy to see freedom of the press as little more than an institutional prerogative. This ignores the importance of small papers and magazines, many of which have an infuence greater than their circulation, but it is an opinion widely held all the same.

The best cure for the ills of democracy, it is said, is more democracy, and the best cure for the failings of newspapers would be more newspapers. Let a hundred flowers bloom! But how are we to start more newspapers, when the necessary investment is in the tens of millions and the chances of financial success are problematic at best? That, as they say, is another subject altogether. In the meantime we must protect the independence of the newspapers that survive, even as we criticize their performance, because if they cannot publish without let or hindrance, who can?

POSTSCRIPT

THE MASS MEDIA:
SHOULD GOVERNMENT GUARANTEE A
"RIGHT OF ACCESS"?

An exact counterpart to the *Tornillo* case, except that it involved a radio station instead of a newspaper, was the case of *Red Lion Broadcasting Co. v. FCC*, decided by the Supreme Court in 1969. A right-wing radio station in the town of Red Lion, Pennsylvania, had broadcast an attack on Fred Cook, a liberal jounalist. Cook demanded air time to reply, and was refused. He appealed to the Federal Communications Commission, which then ordered the station to broadcast Cook's reply. The station appealed to the Supreme Court. But in that case, unlike *Tornillo*, the Court agreed that the government could enforce a right to reply. How, then, can we distinguish between *Tornillo* and *Red Lion*?

The usual distinction is that radio and TV, unlike newspapers, are "limited-access" media. The only difficulty with the "limited access" argument is that it can also be used to describe our nation's newspapers. If access to the air waves is limited by the laws of electronics, access to the print media is also limited— by the laws of economics! Thomas Powers admits that, in our age of media giants, "starting a newspaper is beyond all but centi-millionaires."

A number of books published in the 1970s have explored the problems of government censorship and media distortion. On the latter problem see Edward Jay Epstein, *News From Nowhere* (Random House, 1973), an important criticism of network news. For a lively account of newspaper reporting—and misreporting—during a presidential campaign, see Timothy Crouse, *The Boys on the Bus* (Random House, 1973). The other danger, of government interference with freedom of the press, is explored by Sanford Ungar in *The Papers and the Papers* (Dutton, 1972). Ungar's book is a study of the Nixon Administration's attempt to prevent the publication of the top-secret "Pentagon papers."

The goal of free speech, or at least its justification in a democracy, is not simply to let people sound off. It is to provide us with the widest variety of clashing viewpoints. Anything, therefore, which puts a damper on that grand debate ought to be suspect. In most cases, probably, the chief danger is government interference. But as we watch TV and read newspapers we should also be alert to those obstacles to the free trade of ideas which come from the media themselves. For, as the Supreme Court said in the *Red Lion* case, "it is the right of the viewers and listeners, not the right of the broadcaster, which is paramount."

ISSUE 14

DOES DETENTE
GIVE AWAY TOO MUCH?

Ever since British Prime Minister Chamberlain appeased Adolf Hitler in 1938 and consented to the dismemberment of Czechoslovakia in the hope of thus averting war (which came the following year, because Hitler's appetite for more territory was unappeased), a foreign policy of appeasement has had a bad name.

Appeasement was the charge hurled against those who sought to negotiate trade, disarmament, or peace with the Soviet Union in the so-called "Cold War" era of the 1950s and 1960s. The lesson we had bitterly learned, that "you can't do business with Hitler," applied with equal force to Stalin and other Communist rulers. Non-appeasement meant "standing up to the Soviets," "calling the Communist bluffs," preparedness for nuclear war which some critics of Communism thought was inevitable and others thought was most likely if we betrayed any weakness. At one time such policies were called "brinkmanship," standing at the edge of the awful precipice which if overstepped would plunge us into a holocaust.

One consequence of American toughness was gradual escalation of our involvement in the war between North and South Vietnam. If South Vietnam fell, the "domino theory" proclaimed, Laos, Cambodia, Thailand, and other Asian nations would fall behind it. If we failed to repel Communist aggression in that unknown-to-Americans corner of the world, Communist aggression would be encouraged elsewhere. To do less was appeasement. But as the containment of communism came at an increasing price in lives, material, and morale, an increasing number of Americans questioned the fundamental tenets of "cold war" anti-Communism.

In the meantime, the notion of a monolithic "Communist conspiracy" had lost much of its credibility. By the mid-1960s it was apparent that Russia was no longer the unchallenged leader of world Communism. On the contrary, fear of a Soviet-Chinese alliance against the West had been allayed by the deep rift that developed between the two great Communist powers. European Communist nations and parties displayed increasing independence. "Third World" countries grew in number and political influence, and neither the United States nor the Soviet Union could take their support for granted. Soviet non-intervention in Vietnam did not support the thesis of world conquest.

The most dramatic symbolic expression of a changed American attitude toward Communism came in President Nixon's unprecedented trips to visit the Russian and Chinese heads of state in Moscow and Peking. Whether the initial idea to undertake these trips was the President's or the Secretary of State's, it was Henry Kissinger, first a foreign policy adviser and then Secretary of State under Presidents Nixon and Ford, who fashioned the foreign policy of "detente," or relaxation of tension. At the heart of Kissinger's policy was the conviction that the United States and the Soviet Union could negotiate about such matters as nuclear arms limitations and foreign trade, with both sides benefiting from the exchanges. To its supporters, detente was a major step toward lasting peace; to its critics, it was simply a new form of appeasement.

So the foreign policy argument is joined again. There are many differing views that insist we must do more and even risk more in the quest for understanding, trust and the reduction of armaments, but no view has been so influential as that of Henry Kissinger, the architect of detente. The critics, represented here by James E. Dornan, Jr. and Peter C. Hughes, see detente as giving more than we get, inducing a false sense of security, encouraging repression within Russia and aggression outside it, and making widespread war more, not less, possible. The specific issues are likely to change but the fundamental choice—rapprochement or resistance, detente or deterrence—is likely to remain essentially the same for years to come.

Henry Kissinger

DEFENSE
OF DETENTE

This is an important anniversary. A year ago today, on October 8, [1972] came the break through in the Paris negotiations which led soon afterward to the end of American military involvement in Viet-Nam. It is stangely difficult now to recapture the emotion of that moment of hope and uncertainty when suddenly years of suffering and division were giving way to new possibilities for reconciliation.

We meet, too, at a time when renewed conflict in the Middle East reminds us that international stability is always precarious and never to be taken for granted. Pacem in Terris remains regrettably elusive. However well we contain this crisis, as we have contained others, we must still ask ourselves what we seek beyond the management of conflict.

The need for a dialogue about national purposes has never been more urgent, and no assembly is better suited for such a discussion than those gathered here tonight.

Dramatic changes in recent years have transformed America's position and role in the world:

—For most of the postwar period America enjoyed predominance in physical resources and political power. Now, like most other nations in history, we find that our most difficult task is how to apply limited means to the accomplishment of carefully defined ends. We can no longer overwhelm our problems; we must master them with imagination, understanding, and patience.

—For a generation our preoccupation was to prevent the cold war from degenerating into a hot war. Today, when the danger of global conflict has diminished, we face the more profound problem of defining what we mean by peace and determining the ultimate purpose of improved international relations.

—For two decades the solidarity of our alliances seemed as constant as the threats to our security. Now our allies have regained strength and self-confidence, and relations with adversaries have improved. All this has given rise to uncertainties over the sharing of burdens with friends and the impact of

Continued on p. 272

Henry Kissinger, "Moral Purposes and Policy Choices," *Department of State Bulletin*, October 29, 1973.

James E. Dornan, Jr., Peter C. Hughes

THE DANGER OF "DETENTE AT ANY PRICE"

The American Mission in World Politics

More than two hundred years ago, at the close of that period of American history which has been felicitously designated "the seedtime of the Republic," John Adams set down his thoughts on the historical significance of the American experience with republican government. "I always consider the settlement of America with reverence and wonder," he wrote, "as the opening of a grand scene and design in Providence for the illumination of the ignorant and the emancipation of the slavish part of mankind all over the earth." Adams was by no means alone in the view that the United States, as an almost-unique embodiment of social and civic virtue, was destined to make a major contribution to the political reformation of mankind. Such convictions have been prominent throughout the nation's history: statesmen with political outlooks as divergent as those of Hamilton and Wilson have beguiled themselves with the belief that the American system would become the political model for the entire world, and that American power might be the instrument for the establishment of representative government on the widest possible scale. The crusading spirit perhaps most fulsomely expressed in John Kennedy's inaugural address thus appears to have deep roots indeed in the nation's political character.

To such beliefs about the unique nature of the American polity can also be traced the origins of what George Kennan has called the "legalistic-moralistic" approach to foreign policy, in which American values and interests broadly interpreted become the primary standard for judging the behavior of other nations. As Kennan has emphasized, the United States has been particularly prone to judge international events from its own special perspective, and commonly has failed to consider adequately the legitimate views of other nations in the process. We have thus frequently been accused of exhibiting a narrow "absolutism" and a hypocritical moralism in our foreign relations.

These criticisms are not totally without foundation. . . . But so consistent and pervasive have been the assertions of higher purpose that most students of American diplomacy have concluded both that these claims have been more

Continued on p. 279

14. DETENTE

(Kissinger, cont. from p. 270)

reduced tensions on the cohesion of alliances.

—Thus, even as we have mastered the art of containing crises, our concern with the nature of a more permanent international order has grown. Questions once obscured by more insistent needs now demand our attention: What is true national interest? To what end stability? What is the relationship of peace to justice?

It is characteristic of periods of upheaval that to those who live through them they appear as a series of haphazard events. Symptoms obscure basic issues and historical trends. The urgent tends to dominate the important. Too often goals are presented as abstract utopias, safe havens from pressing events.

But a debate, to be fruitful, must define what can reasonably be asked of foreign policy and at what pace progress can be achieved. Otherwise it turns into competing catalogues of the desirable rather than informed comparisons of the possible. Dialogue degenerates into tactical skirmishing.

The current public discussion reflects some interesting and significant shifts in perspective:

—A foreign policy once considered excessively moralistic is now looked upon by some as excessively pragmatic.

—The government was criticized in 1969 for holding back East-West trade with certain countries until there was progress in their foreign policies. Now we are criticized for not holding back East-West trade until there are changes in those same countries' domestic policies.

—The administration's foreign policy, once decried as too cold war oriented, is now attacked as too insensitive to the profound moral antagonism between communism and freedom.

One consequence of this intellectual shift is a gap between conception and performance on some major issues of policy:

—The desirability of peace and detente is affirmed, but both the inducements to progress and the penalties to confrontation are restricted by legislation.

—Expressions of concern for human values in other countries are coupled with failure to support the very programs designed to help developing areas improve their economic and social conditions.

—The declared objective of maintaining a responsible American international role clashes with nationalistic pressures in trade and monetary negotiations and with calls for unilateral withdrawal from alliance obligations.

It is clear that we face genuine moral dilemmas and important policy choices. But it is also clear that we need to define the framework of our dialogue more perceptively and understandingly.

The Competing Elements of Foreign Policy

Foreign policy must begin with the understanding that it involves relationships between sovereign countries. Sovereignty has been defined as a will uncontrolled by others; that is what gives foreign policy its contingent and ever-in-complete character.

For disagreements among sovereign states can be settled only by negotiation or by power, by compromise or by imposition. Which of these methods prevails depends on the values, the strengths, and the domestic systems of the countries involved. A nation's values define what is just; its strength determines what is possible; its domestic structure decides what policies can in fact be implemented and sustained.

Thus foreign policy involves two partially conflicting endeavors: defining the interests, purposes, and values of a society and relating them to the interests, purposes, and values of others.

The policymaker therefore must strike a balance between what is desirable and what is possible. Progress will always be measured in partial steps and in the relative satisfaction of alternative goals. Tension is unavoidable between values, which are invariably cast in maximum terms, and efforts to promote them, which of necessity involve compromise. Foreign policy is explained domestically in terms of justice. But what is defined as justice at home becomes the subject of negotiation abroad. It is thus no accident that many nations, including our own, view the international arena as a forum in which virtue is thwarted by the clever practice of foreigners.

In a community of sovereign states, the quest for peace involves a paradox: The attempt to impose absolute justice by one side will be seen as absolute injustice by all others; the quest for total security for some turns into total insecurity for the remainder. Stability depends on the relative satisfaction and therefore also the relative dissatisfaction of the various states. The pursuit of peace must therefore begin with the pragmatic concept of coexistence—especially in a period of ideological conflict.

We must, of course, avoid becoming obsessed with stability. An excessively pragmatic policy will be empty of vision and humanity. It will lack not only direction but also roots and heart. General de Gaulle wrote in his memoirs that "France cannot be France without greatness." By the same token, America cannot be true to itself without moral purpose. This country has always had a sense of mission. Americans have always held the view that America stood for something above and beyond its material achievements. A purely pragmatic policy provides no criteria for other nations to assess our performance and no standards to which the American people can rally.

But when policy becomes excessively moralistic it may turn quixotic or dangerous. A presumed monopoly on truth obstructs negotiation and accommodation. Good results may be given up in the quest for ever-elusive ideal solutions. Policy may fall prey to ineffectual posturing or adventuristic crusades.

The prerequisite for a fruitful national debate is that the policy-makers and critics appreciate each other's perspectives and respect each other's purposes. The policymaker must understand that the critic is obliged to stress imperfections in order to challenge assumptions and to goad actions. But equally the critic should acknowledge the complexity and inherent ambiguity of the policymaker's choices. The policymaker must be concerned with the best that can be achieved, not just the best that can be imagined. He has to act in a fog of incomplete knowledge without the information that will be available later to the analyst. He knows—or should know—that he is responsible for the consequences of disaster as well as for the benefits of success. He may have to qualify some goals, not because they would be unesirable if reached but because the risks of failure outweigh potential gains. He must often settle for the gradual, much as he might prefer the immediate. He must compromise with others, and this means to some extent compromising with himself.

The outsider demonstrates his morality by the precision of his perceptions and the loftiness of his ideals. The policymaker expresses his morality by implementing a sequence of imperfections and partial solutions in pursuit of *his* ideals.

There must be understanding, as well, of the crucial importance of timing. Opportunities cannot be hoarded; once past, they are usually irretrievable. New relationships in a fluid transitional period—such as today—are delicate and vulnerable; they must be nurtured if they are to thrive. We cannot pull up young shoots periodically to see whether the roots are still there or whether there is some marginally better location for them.

We are now at such a time of tenuous beginnings. Western Europe and Japan have joined us in an effort to reinvigorate our relationships. The Soviet Union has begun to practice foreign policy, at least partially, as a relationship between states rather than as international civil war. The People's Republic of China has emerged from two decades of isolation. The developing countries are impatient for economic and social change. A new dimension of unprecedented challenges—in food, oceans, energy, environment—demands global cooperation.

We are at one of those rare moments where through a combination of fortuitous circumstances and design man seems in a position to shape his future. What we need is the confidence to discuss issues without bitter strife, the wisdom to define together the nature of our world, as well as the vision to chart together a more just future.

Detente
With the Soviet Union

Nothing demonstrates this need more urgently than our relationship with the Soviet Union.

This administration* has never

---

*Editor's note: Kissinger was speaking for the Nixon administration.

had any illusions about the Soviet system. We have always insisted that progress in technical fields, such as trade, had to follow—and reflect—progress toward more stable international relations. We have maintained a strong military balance and a flexible defense posture as a buttress to stability. We have insisted that disarmament had to be mutual. We have judged movement in our relations with the Soviet Union not by atmospherics but by how well concrete problems are resolved and by whether there is responsible international conduct.

Coexistence, to us, continues to have a very precise meaning:

—We will oppose the attempt by any country to achieve a position of predominance either globally or regionally.

—We will resist any attempt to exploit a policy of detente to weaken our alliances.

—We will react if relaxation of tensions is used as a cover to exacerbate conflicts in international trouble spots.

The Soviet Union cannot disregard these principles in any area of the world without imperiling its entire relationship with the United States.

On this basis we have succeeded in transforming U.S.-Soviet relations in many important ways. Our two countries have concluded a historic accord to limit strategic arms. We have substantially reduced the risk of direct U.S.-Soviet confrontation in crisis areas. The problem of Berlin has been resolved by negotiation. We and our allies have engaged the Soviet Union in negotiations on major issues of European security, including a reduction of military forces in central Europe. We have reached a series of bilateral agreements on cooperation—health, environment, space, science and technology, as well as trade. These accords are designed to create a vested interest in cooperation and restraint.

Until recently the goals of detente were not an issue. The necessity of shifting from confrontation toward negotiation seemed so overwhelming that goals beyond the settlement of international disputes were never raised. But now progress has been made—and already taken for granted. We are engaged in an intense debate on whether we should make changes in Soviet society a precondition for further progress or indeed for following through on commitments already made. The cutting edge of this problem is the congressional effort to condition most-favored-nation (MFN) trade status for other countries on changes in their domestic systems.

This is a genuine moral dilemma. There are genuine moral concerns on both sides of the argument. So let us not address this as a debate between those who are morally sensitive and those who are not, between those who care for justice and those who are oblivious to humane values. The attitude of the American people and government has been made emphatically clear on countless occasions in ways that have produced effective results.

275

The exit tax on emigration is not being collected, and we have received assurances that it will not be reapplied; hardship cases submitted to the Soviet Government are being given specific attention; the rate of Jewish emigration has been in the tens of thousands, where it was once a trickle. We will continue our vigorous efforts on these matters.

But the real debate goes far beyond this: Should we now tie demands which were never raised during negotiations to agreements that have already been concluded? Should we require as a formal condition internal changes that we heretofore sought to foster in an evolutionary manner?

Let us remember what the MFN question specifically involves. The very term "most favored nation" is misleading in its implication of preferential treatment. What we are talking about is whether to allow *normal* economic relations to develop—of the kind we now have with over 100 other countries and which the Soviet Union enjoyed until 1951. The issue is whether to abolish discriminatory trade restrictions that were imposed at the height of the cold war. Indeed, at that time the Soviet Government discouraged commerce because it feared the domestic impact of normal trading relations with the West on its society.

The demand that Moscow modify its domestic policy as a precondition for MFN or detente was never made while we were negotiating; now it is inserted after both sides have carefully shaped an overall mosaic. Thus it raises questions about our entire bilateral relationship.

Finally, the issue affects not only our relationship with the Soviet Union but also with many other countries whose internal structures we find incompatible with our own. Conditions imposed on one country could inhibit expanding relations with others, such as the People's Republic of China.

We shall never condone the suppression of fundamental liberties. We shall urge humane principles and use our influence to promote justice. But the issue comes down to the limits of such efforts. How hard can we press without provoking the Soviet leadership into returning to practices in its foreign policy that increase international tensions? Are we ready to face the crises and increased defense budgets that a return to cold war conditions would spawn? And will this encourage full emigration or enhance the well-being or nourish the hope for liberty of the peoples of Eastern Europe and the Soviet Union? Is it detente that has prompted repression—or is it detente that has generated the ferment and the demand for openness which we are now witnessing?

For half a century we have objected to Communist efforts to alter the domestic structures of other countries. For a generation of cold war we sought to ease the risks produced by competing ideologies. Are we now to come full circle and insist on domestic compatibility as a condition of progress?

These questions have no easy answers. The government may underestimate the margin of concessions available to us. But a fair debate must admit that they are genuine questions, the answers to which could affect the fate of all of us.

Our policy with respect to detente is clear: We shall resist aggressive foreign policies. Detente cannot survive irresponsibility in any area, including the Middle East. As for the internal policies of closed systems, the United States will never forget that the antagonism between freedom and its enemies is part of the reality of the modern age. We are not neutral in that struggle. As long as we remain powerful, we will use our influence to promote freedom, as we always have. But in the nuclear age we are obliged to recognize that the issue of war and peace also involves human lives and that the attainment of peace is a profound moral concern.

The World as It Is and the World We Seek

Addressing the United Nations General Assembly two weeks ago, I described our goal as a world where power blocs and balances are no longer relevant; where justice, not stability, can be our overriding preoccupation; where countries consider cooperation in the world interest to be in their national interest.

But we cannot move toward the world of the future without first maintaining peace in the world as it is. These very days we are vividly reminded that this requires vigilance and a continuing commitment.

So our journey must start from where we are now. This is a time of lessened tension, of greater equilibrium, of diffused power. But if the world is better than our earlier fears, it still falls far short of our hopes. To deal with the present does not mean that we are content with it.

The most striking feature of the contemporary period, the feature that gives complexity as well as hope, is the radical transformation in the nature of power. Throughout history power has generally been homogeneous. Military, economic, and political potential were closely related. To be powerful, a nation had to be strong in all categories. Today the vocabulary of strength is more complex. Military muscle does not guarantee political influence. Economic giants can be militarily weak, and military strength may not be able to obscure economic weakness. Countries can exert political influence even when they have neither military nor economic strength.

It is wrong to speak of only one balance of power, for there are several, which have to be related to each other. In the military sphere, there are two superpowers. In economic terms, there are at least five major groupings. Politically, many more centers of influence have emerged; some 80 new nations have come into being since the end of World War II, and regional groups are assuming ever-increasing importance.

Above all, whatever the measure of power, its political utility has changed. Throughout history increases in military power, however slight, could be turned into specific political advantage. With the overwhelming arsenals of the nuclear age, however, the pursuit of marginal advantage is both pointless and potentially suicidal. Once sufficiency is reached, additional increments of power do not translate into usable political strength, and attempts to achieve tactical gains can lead to cataclysm.

This environment both puts a premium on stability and makes it difficult to maintain. Today's striving for equilibrium should not be compared to the balance of power of previous periods. The very notion of "operating" a classical balance of power disintegrates when the change required to upset the balance is so large that it cannot be achieved by limited means.

More specifically, there is no parallel with the 19th century. Then the principal countries shared essentially similar concepts of legitimacy and accepted the basic structure of the existing international order. Small adjustments in strength were significant. The "balance" operated in a relatively confined geographic area. None of these factors obtain today.

Nor when we talk of equilibrium do we mean a simplistic mechanical model devoid of purpose. The constantly shifting alliances that maintained equilibrium in previous centuries are neither appropriate nor possible in our time. In an age of ideological schism the distinction between friends and adversaries is an objective reality. We share ideals as well as interests with our friends, and we know that the strength of our friendships is crucial to the lowering of tensions with our opponents.

When we refer to five or six or seven major centers of power, the point being made is not that others are excluded but that a few short years ago everyone agreed that there were only two. The diminishing tensions and the emergence of new centers of power have meant greater freedom of action and greater importance for all other nations.

In this setting, our immediate aim has been to build a stable network of relationships that offers hope of sparing mankind the scourges of war. An interdependent world community cannot tolerate either big-power confrontations or recurrent regional crises.

But peace must be more than the absence of conflict. We perceive stability as the bridge to the realization of human aspirations, not an end in itself. We have learned much about containing crises, but we have not removed their roots. We have begun to accommodate our differences, but we have not affirmed our commonality. We may have improved the mastery of equilibrium, but we have not yet attained justice.

In the encyclical for which this

conference is named, Pope John sketched a greater vision. He foresaw "that no political community is able to pursue its own interests and develop itself in isolation" for "there is a growing awareness of all human beings that they are members of a world community."

The opportunities of mankind now transcend nationalism and can only be dealt with by nations acting in concert:

—For the first time in generations mankind is in a position to shape a new and peaceful international order. But do we have the imagination and determination to carry forward this still-fragile task of creation?

—For the first time in history we may have the technical knowledge to satisfy man's basic needs. The imperatives of the modern world respect no national borders and must inevitably open all societies to the world around them. But do we have the political will to join together to accomplish this great end?

If this vision is to be realized, America's active involvement is inescapable. History will judge us by our deeds, not by our good intentions.

But it cannot be the work of any one country. And it cannot be the undertaking of any one administration or one branch of government or one party. To build truly is to chart a course that will be carried on by future leaders because it has the enduring support of the American people.

So let us search for a fresh consensus. Let us restore a spirit of understanding between the legislative and the executive, between the government and the press, between the people and their public servants. Let us learn once again to debate our methods and not our motives, to focus on our destiny and not on our divisions. Let us all contribute our different views and perspectives, but let us once again see ourselves as engaged in a common enterprise. If we are to shape a world community we must first restore community at home.

With Americans working together, America can work with others toward man's eternal goal of a Pacem in Terris—peace abroad, peace at home, and peace within ourselves.

(Cont. from p. 271, Dornan & Hughes,

"Danger of 'Detente . . .' ")

than mere rationalizations for other drives, and that they have had a significant impact upon the selection of ends and means in American foreign policy as well. To that extent, American diplomacy does exhibit a pattern different from that of other nations.

In recent years many critics have come to consider the belief that the

United States has a distinctive role to play in world politics to be deleterious to the development of a successful foreign policy. Even before the Vietnam War, there existed an ample literature urging a scaling down of American pretentions and a redefinition of the goals of American policy in more modest and prudent terms. As the nation's involvement in Vietnam deepened, that view became a consensus; and although even the academic critics of America's "crusading interventionism" by no means abandoned the view that the United States should play a large role in world politics, it became virtually *de rigueur* in the scholarly community to espouse the so-called "limitationist" viewpoint concerning the goals of American policy. . . .

Both President Nixon and his National – Security – Advisor-become-Secretary-of-State believed (even before 1969) that popular discontent with Vietnam had undermined the consensus concerning America's role in the world which had sustained United States foreign policy since the 1940's. Both Nixon and Kissinger, in fact, believed that virtually all of the forces and factors which had shaped world politics during the first two postwar decades had ceased to be operative.

The principal changes were said to be six in number. First, Japan and the nations of Western Europe, the latter gradually drawing closer together economically and politically, have recovered from the ravages of World War II, and are capable once again of assuming major roles in the world political system. Second, the new nations of Africa and Asia have substantially matured since the early post-independence period, and now appear able to resist external aggression and hold their own in relations with bigger powers. Third, the one-time communist monolith has been shattered, replaced by a loosely organized bloc whose members quarrel as often as they cooperate. Fourth, U.S. military preeminence has given way to a condition of strategic parity between the U.S.S.R. and the United States, reducing American freedom of maneuver in crisis situations but simultaneously creating new possibilities for detente based on a "stable balance of terror." Fifth, the old "isms"—the once-vibrant ideologies which for twenty years animated the foreign policies of the great powers—have lost their vitality, and more traditional national goals such as security and economic progress have become the primary concerns both of the United States and the Soviet Union. Finally, our own foreign policy is now inhibited by serious internal constraints, one of the several aftermaths of the Vietnam War. Our citizens' "psychological resources" have been exhausted, their "moral strength" has been undermined, and the nation's ability to play a major role in world politics is therefore considerably diminished.

Mr. Nixon's world view thus combined both pessimism and optimism. Although the power of the United States is in decline, especially relative to that of the Soviet Union, other changes which are occurring in the world are more favorable to American interests, especially if the latter are more restrictively defined than in the past. A substantially reduced role of America in maintaining world security, Mr. Nixon believed, was both desirable and possible; moreover, for the first time since the end of World War II, there existed an opportunity to create a "new structure of relations" with our traditional adversaries and thereby achieve a "durable peace" which will survive at least until the end of this century. Particularly if the economies of the U.S. and the U.S.S.R. could be bound together through a series of interlocking agreements, the Soviets would have a "vested interest" in continually-improving relations with the West. Somewhat later, as events in the Middle East and the massive post-SALT Soviet military build-up aroused doubts about the assumed Soviet desire for a constructive relationship with the United States, administration spokesmen began to stress the necessity of avoiding nuclear war as the primary rationale for the policy of detente.

Mr. Nixon's efforts to redirect American foreign policy, of course, were considerably reinforced by the views of Mr. Kissinger. At least since 1965 Kissinger has believed that the Soviet Union and Communist China are basically satisfied and status-quo powers, increasingly anxious for cooperative relation-

ships with the United States. His views on defense policy also strongly buttressed Mr. Nixon's new approach to American foreign policy. Since virtually the start of his academic career in the mid-fifties Kissinger has believed that the maintenance of a strategic balance between the two major powers is relatively easy when both sides possess invulnerable second-strike forces. He is also convinced that, beyond their deterrent effect, strategic nuclear weapons have very little operational significance for oreign policy. Precisely because of the awesome power of nuclear weapons, he has insisted, once a "stable" nuclear balance has been achieved no rational leader would be tempted either to launch an all-out war or to try to utilize strategic weapons to advance his nation's political interests. Hence, he has been relatively uninterested in the niceties of the nuclear balance and in the significance of numerical disparities in numbers of missiles deployed by the major powers. Finally, he has long argued that under conditions of nuclear stability thus defined the prospects for significant arms control agreements between the superpowers improve substantially. It was the combination of Mr. Kissinger's views on detente and on military strategy and Mr. Nixon's convictions concerning the possibilities of improved relations with the U.S.S.R. which constituted the driving force behind the Nixon Administration's national security policy.

The often-voiced charge that the

14. DETENTE

Nixon Administration never adequately defined or articulated its foreign policy objectives is thus without merit. Virtually from the outset the administration made the achievement of detente with the U.S.S.R. its primary goal. Vital foreign policy tasks such as repairing strained relations with our European and Asian allies and restructuring the international trade and monetary systems, to say nothing of developing a coherent long-term strategy for dealing with the developing continents, were all sacrificed—and continue to be sacrificed—to the pursuit of improved relations with the Soviet Union. The "shocks" administered to Japan in 1971 and the pronounced deterioration in relations within the NATO Alliance during the first two years of the second Nixon Administration testified clearly to the new pecking order for adversaries and allies within that Administration's policy. At the same time, under the tutelage of Messrs. Nixon and Kissinger the United States renounced, even as an ultimate objective of policy, any intention to effect a fundamental change in the nature of the Soviet regime; indeed, not only great-power status but also a right to "natural expansion" in the Middle East and elsewhere were conceded to the Soviets. Even the much-heralded "opening" to China appears in retrospect to have been primarily designed to goad the Soviets more rapidly down the road to detente.

The Administration's efforts to redefine America's global interests can be similarly understood. Many critics have suggested that the so-called Nixon Doctrine contained no clear standards defining the conditions under which the United States would use force to defend its interests abroad. Hence, they argued, it remained uncertain what policy the U.S. might follow if and when local defense forced proved inadequate in areas of American concern. Both Mr. Nixon and Mr. Kissinger, however, gave ample indication that they expected direct American involvement to be rarely necessary. The reason once again had to do with their views on the emergent relationship with the Soviet Union. If Soviet-American hostility is waning due to changes in Soviet ambitions, and if wise American diplomacy can be expected to lead to further improvements in relations between the two superpowers in the future, then America's fundamental security position is markedly improved. Not only is the danger of a military confrontation with the U.S.S.R. substantially diminished, but there is no longer any need to "contain Communism" through a complex array of treaties and alliances. As the Cold War passes, according to this view, American interests abroad shrink commensurately. Herein may lie the explanation for what was the Nixon Administration's apparent lack of concern over both the relative decline of American military power and the probable political consequences of that decline. In this respect the

SALT agreements are the perfect strategic expression of the Nixon Doctrine itself.

The Adequacy of the Kissinger Foreign Policy

The willingness of the Soviet Union to pursue policies of restraint, therefore, is a crucial element in the new grand design for American foreign policy. Unfortunately, thus far there have been few signs of any such willingness on the part of the U.S.S.R., and the argument that Soviet foreign policy objectives in their broadest definition have decisively changed is not a great deal more compelling now than when it was first raised not long after the revolution of 1917. . . .

Even the various SALT agreements, frequently cited by the Administration as the principle evidence to date of a favorable trend in Soviet-American relations, contain no Soviet concessions. Although the U.S.S.R. has agreed to halt further antiballistic missile (ABM) construction and consented to build no more ballistic missile launchers after specified totals have been reached, there were no signs that they were contemplating extensive ABM construction in any event and no hard evidence—despite Nixon Administration claims to the contrary—that they had previously intended to add to their arsenal large numbers of missile launchers beyond the total permitted by SALT . . . .

In fact, since SALT I was signed the Soviets have embarked upon a program of military development which is staggering in scope and intensity, and which will nullify any remaining American advantages within several years. . . .

It is thus uncertain in the extreme whether "nuclear parity" with the United States is or ever has been a Soviet objective. On the contrary, available evidence indicates that the U.S.S.R. is seeking superiority over the United States in every significant area of military power. The relevant question, of course, is *why*.

No one would suggest that a Soviet nuclear attack "out of the blue" is probable, either now or in the foreseeable future. What is far more likely is an effort by the U.S.S.R. to exploit its growing strategic advantage for political purposes. The historical record indicates that the Soviets aggressively attempted to exploit their military capability for political purposes even when they were substantially inferior to the United States in strategic striking power, especially during the Khrushchev era. Neither have they been reticent in calling attention, before a variety of audiences, to their existing margin of superiority in intercontinental ballistic missile launchers. Were the Soviets directly or tacitly to bring their strategic advantage to bear during an international crisis, the U.S.—or its allies—might readily be intimidated. Given existing strategic realities, any Western leader would hesitate to challenge a direct Soviet military threat when a vital interest of the U.S.S.R. was at stake, much less employ strategic weapons in the event of lower-level Soviet aggression. . . .

In any case, if the course of Soviet military development holds out little hope that detente has become a reality, neither is the political record very promising. While there is not space within the scope of this essay to analyze thoroughly the general course of international politics since SALT, even a capsule review of recent events is sufficient to indicate that the Soviets have no more sought to contribute to the "momentum of detente" within the political sphere than within the military arena.

There have been no serious concessions by the Soviets in any of the several ongoing negotiations with the Western powers on political and military issues. The talks on mutual force reductions in Europe are presently deadlocked, apparently awaiting the next American accommodations. The Conference on Security and Cooperation in Europe is also deadlocked, in this case over Western European insistence that the Soviets agree to permit more "human contacts" between their people and those of the West. As for other areas of potential political conflict between the two superpowers, the record speaks for itself. Not only were the Soviets intimately involved in the preparations for the Middle East War, but virtually to the day that the oil embargo was lifted they continued to urge the radical Arab states to maintain it in force. There is no evidence to indicate that they have supported Mr. Kissinger's

efforts to move the opposing parties towards a mutually satisfactory settlement since the embargo ended. Brezhnev himself has repeatedly stated during the period since SALT I that the ideological and political struggle between the two powers will go on. In fact, at a conference of Eastern European party leaders in mid-1973 he explained that the precise purpose of the Soviet policy of detente with the Western powers was to buy time for the Soviets to acquire total strategic superiority over the West; at that point, he said, the U.S.S.R. would set about to achieve the reorganization of world politics on its terms, which has always been the ultimate objective of Soviet foreign policy.

There is, in short, no evidence whatsoever that there exists at present a true detente between the U.S. and the U.S.S.R., even if we define detente, in a minimum way, to mean acceptance by both the U.S. and the U.S.S.R. of the pre-SALT military balance as a permanent condition of international life. Much less is there a true detente if that word is defined more broadly as a situation in which both superpowers agree to pursue foreign policies which are essentially status-quo in nature.

A belief in the existence of detente between the superpowers has encouraged false hopes and has stimulated wishful thinking in the West. In the resulting euphoria, thoughtful and objective analysis of the military and political threats we confront from the U.S.S.R. in today's world has been rendered extraordinarily difficult. Even a-mong those on the political Left whose enchantment with the U.S.S.R. has recently faded, there is little appreciation of the significance of the Russian military buildup; and in the highest councils of the present Administration the conviction that detente is a reality is deep-seated indeed. There are thus few obstacles in the path of the Soviet drive toward military and political preeminence.

Toward a More Viable Foreign Policy

As with most issues of public policy, perhaps it is best to return to *what is*, to certain observable facts about the behavior of nations and about the universe of international politics. As the French scholar Raymond Aron has recently reminded us, only "a small power restricts its ambitions to physical survival and the preservation of its legal independence and its institutions." A great power, on the other hand, "over and above physical security, moral survival, and the well-being of its inhabitants, acts to achieve an (often) ill-defined purpose, which I should call the maintenance or creation of a favorable international environment." Isolationism in the United States, he adds, has been largely discredited because five times in the twentieth century in moments of profound crisis the United States has found it necessary to undertake a major military intervention in Europe or Asia. The issue, he suggests, is not what the United States might prefer to do, but what it has done and will continue to do: "The real question is whether nonalignment and the refusal of 'entangling alliances' would not give rise some day to crises from which once again, however much it wished to abstain, the American Republic would be incapable of standing aside."

In arguing that, whatever its formal doctrine, the United States would find a policy of isolationism impossible to maintain in practice, Aron is not succumbing to the determinism of the power realists or the para-Marxists, who also assert—albeit for quite different reasons—that the United States is compelled to play a substantial role in world politics. Neither is he merely arguing, with Thucydides, that the interests of states tend to expand with their power. On the contrary, he is asserting that power is not the sole, and often not even the primary, determinant of human action, and therefore that the behavior of men and nations cannot be explained in terms of power alone:

Drawing a distinction between physical security and the creation of an environment favorable to the expansion of the national values, though valid analytically, is rather hazardous. No great power defines its national interest simply as its physical security. Diplomats think and act within a world already structured by animosities, principles, or sympathies which cannot be reduced to calculations of strength or considerations of balance.

285

14. DETENTE

If this argument is correct—and the historical experience of all great nations goes far toward confirming it—it suggests at least the beginnings of an answer to the questions raised earlier concerning the purpose of American policy. Self-interest and principle are inextricably intertwined as motives for the foreign policies of all nations, although of course the mix will differ in each individual case; moreover, it is when the demands of self-interest and the demands of principle reinforce one another that policy tends to be most consistent and effective.

In the present instance, both principle and self-interest point clearly to a firm United States policy stand toward the Soviet Union. At the level of principle, it is difficult to maintain that the Soviet regime is morally superior to the American. Whatever may be the thrust of the changes which have occurred in the U.S.S.R. since Stalin, the Soviet regime remains a tightly-controlled, one-party dictatorship. All political dissent in the Soviet Union is carefully circumscribed, and respect for basic human freedom and dignity is virtually nonexistent. The United States, by way of contrast—and, more broadly speaking, the civilization of the West in general—embodies principles of politics which are eminently defensible on ethical grounds, however imperfectly some of those principles may be realized in practice. Thus the Western nations have the right and the obligation to defend their values and principles and the political

systems based upon them, and indeed to extend their influence where it is possible and prudent to do so.

At the level of self-interest, it is clear that the threat to American interests abroad and even to our security and survival is increasing rather than diminishing. What is therefore required in response is a policy toward the U.S.S.R. based on a clear apprehension of current realities rather than on desires and dreams. In the words of Defense Secretary Schlesinger, "unless we are to plan only by intuition, we must continue to build our peace structure on the hard facts of the international environment rather than on gossamer hopes for the eminent perfectability of mankind." And whatever the professed fears of Mr. Kissinger regarding the danger of nuclear war, there *do* exist options for the United States other than holocaust or the supine acceptance of Soviet political and military supremacy.

To be sure, a realistic policy toward the U.S.S.R. cannot, under current circumstances, advocate a crusade to roll back the Iron Curtain or to bring down the Soviet regime by force. As Burke long ago taught us, prudence is the central virtue of politics, and in the nuclear age such a policy could result only in disaster. By the same token, the time has long since passed when we could attempt an international quarantine of the U.S.S.R., or even refuse to negotiate with the Soviets on the whole range of East-West issues. In any event there can be few objections raised against the concept of detente properly defined, or against a policy of detente properly pursued. What the United States requires is consistent firmness and realism in assessing Soviet intentions and policies and in devising responses to them.

Future arms control agreements, for example, must be based on true equivalence, and must not proceed from the Kissinger assumption that one-sided agreements are satisfactory solely because they contribute to the "momentum of detente." Trade agreements likewise must contain equal economic advantages for both powers, and under no circumstances should strategic materials or military-related technology be transferred to the U.S.S.R. Finally, even arms control and economic agreements limited by these principles must be offered to the U.S.S.R. at a price. That price must be a demonstrated moderation in Soviet behavior, at home and abroad—in Europe and in the Middle East as well as on such issues as submarine deployments in Cuba and the emigration of dissident minority groups from the Soviet Union. Pressure on the U.S.S.R. emanating from Senator Jackson and elsewhere on the latter issue has already led to some modification of Soviet policies. If the Soviets are seriously interested in obtaining access to American technology, a consistent U.S. hard line on the emigration issue—which will serve to demonstrate to others

our continuing moral commitment—might well lead to further changes in Soviet behavior. If not, nothing of consequence will have been lost, and an increased knowledge of Soviet intentions and flexibility will have been gained. . . .

It has obviously not been possible within the scope of this essay to specify in detail the kind of foreign policy which we believe necessary for the United States. Enough has been said, we hope, to indicate the nature of the approach. More than a decade ago, in one of his most illustrious books, a well-known professor of international relations wrote cogently of the relationship between power, principle, and world order:

> Whenever peace—conceived as the avoidance of war—has been the primary objective of a power or a group of powers, the international system has been at the mercy of the most ruthless member of the international community. Whenever the international order has acknowledged that certain principles could not be compromised even for the sake of peace, stability based on an equilibrium of forces was at least conceivable.

The professor was Henry A. Kissinger. The hour is now late. But there is still time for the United States to heed his warning, and to substitute for "detente at any price" the difficult decisions and sacrifices dictated by principled realism.

POSTSCRIPT

DOES DETENTE GIVE AWAY TOO MUCH?

Part of the difference between Henry Kissinger and his critics stems not from conflicting "principles" of foreign policy but from different perceptions of the facts. Is the U.S.S.R. really building a military force superior to ours? Are the Soviets really insincere in their professed desire to limit armaments? Are they really trying to put one over on us, and are they succeeding? These empirical issues can only be resolved by careful intelligence work. Yet the reader must have noted the larger issues lying behind them: To what extent should American foreign policy be an expression of American ideals? Does America have a unique mission in the world? How tough should we be in dealing with the Soviets, and what are the limits to toughness? These kinds of issues have been in the background of many foreign policy debates since the "Cold War" began in the 1940s, and they are likely to remain there through the end of the 1970s.

"Realism" or "pragmatism" in American foreign policy, of which the Kissinger statement is a recent example, was first argued in systematic form by Hans Morgenthau in a classic work, *Politics Among Nations* (Knopf, 1948). A cogent reply to Morgenthau's thesis came from Robert E. Osgood, in his *Ideals and Self Interest in America's Foreign Relations* (University of Chicago, 1953). By the end of the 1960s the belief in the viability, not to say exportability, of American ideals had reached a nadir, at least in the academic community. An expression of that pessimism can be found in Andrew Hacker's *The End of the American Era* (Atheneum, 1968). But perhaps that "end" has itself ended. A more recent book, Paul Eidelberg's *Beyond Detente* (Sugden, Sherwood, 1977) argues for a reassertion of American ideals in foreign policy.

It may well be that the period of "detente" is ending. The Soviets have expressed their deep resentment of President Carter's statements on "human rights," regarding them as an attempt to meddle in Soviet domestic affairs. Soviet hostility to Israel's position in the Middle East conflict and a hardening Soviet line toward Jews and dissidents in the U.S.S.R. have caused many American liberals to reconsider their initial support of detente. At the present time it seems unlikely that the "Cold War" will return with all its former intensity. But the experiences of the last twenty years should teach us that all sorts of unlikely things can happen in foreign policy.

ISSUE 15

CAN CONSERVATION
MEET OUR ENERGY NEEDS?

"With the exception of preventing war, this is the greatest challenge our country will face during our lifetimes." That is how President Carter characterized "the energy crisis." Most Americans have had a sense of crisis, in their experience one year of waiting in long lines at filling stations for rationed gasoline, in the next year being told to lower thermostats, and in the year after that seeing factories and schools shut down for want of fuel.

But is there really a crisis? Public opinion polls show a majority of Americans suspecting that the shortages are contrived by the oil companies in order to force up prices. Ironically, the oil company executives themselves argue that the crisis is in a sense artificial, but for them the culprit is not big business but big government. Instead of fixing prices for gas and oil, they contend, the government should let companies charge whatever the market will bear, thus providing them with the financial incentives to look for new supplies. In reply, critics of the oil companies point to the enormous profits already amassed by them and ask why these profits have not led to a more intensive search for new supplies.

And so the argument rages. Each side scores its points, but neither has contributed very much to a consensus on public policy. To get out of this well-traveled circle we need to see the crisis in larger perspective.

In the first place, we must see "the energy crisis" not only as a crisis of oil and gas, but of other essential commodities as well. The Western states are suffering for want of water, and in many areas of the country Americans are feeling the pinch of scarcity when it comes to clean air, open space, woodland, wildlife, and unpolluted waterways. Like it or not, an era has come to an end—one in which Americans could think that there was no end to nature's abundance—and its passing cannot be blamed entirely upon the oil companies. For Americans have consumed their resources at an alarming rate. A Ford Foundation study concluded that American per capita energy consumption is six times greater than the world average. We have deserted our railroads and streetcars and subways in favor of cars, trucks, and planes, which are far less economical in fuel consumption. Our cars have been giant gas-guzzlers, and we have torn up the countryside to install new suburbs which are almost entirely dependent upon them. Our homes have been poorly insulated, and practically every year some new gadget, often of dubious value, gets plugged into their circuits. Out in the countryside, animal manures from cattle feedlots wash downhill to pollute the rivers; manures are no longer used to fertilize the soil, having been replaced by artificial fertilizers made from natural gas. Our newer, hybrid crops require enormous doses of pesticides and herbicides, derived from fossil fuels. As a result, farming today uses more petroleum than any other single industry.

What are we to do about the depletion of America's energy resources? The creation of a federal department of energy implies a commitment to finding solutions, but what should they be? Broadly speaking, two basic philosophies have emerged.

The first puts its greatest emphasis upon conservation: a more controlled use of pesticides; a greater use of animal fertilizers; better home insulation; the reprocessing of garbage and sewage; smaller, more fuel-efficient cars; increased use of mass transit. Those who take this approach contend that, since America is running out of non-renewable resources, we must make sacrifices and move toward a more modest scale of living.

The second school of thought insists that the only real solution to the energy crisis is to find new sources of energy. In the long run, solar, wind, fusion, and geothermal energy may supply our needs, but for the present we must search for new supplies of fossil fuels. To the conservationist's claim that there is not much left to be found, the advocates of this school reply: we've heard that before! In the 1920s, they often remind us, the alarm went up that we were nearly out of petroleum—and then came the discoveries in Texas and Oklahoma. American brain-power, they add, is itself a source of energy, and given the right incentives it can search out and find new energy supplies. Conservation may be a good in itself, but it should not be seen as a solution to the present crisis, which is primarily a crisis of supply.

These two contrasting approaches are typified in the following selections. President Carter's messages to the American people and to Congress in April of 1977 urged an effort that in his words would be "the moral equivalent of war." Professor Eugene Bardach scathingly criticized the tenets of the President's program in an essay that was published a year before that program was announced.

Jimmy Carter

THE MORAL
EQUIVALENT OF WAR

Tonight I want to have an unpleasant talk with you about a problem unprecedented in our history. With the exception of preventing war, this is the greatest challenge our country will face during our lifetimes. The energy crisis has not yet overwhelmed us, but it will if we do not act quickly.

It is a problem we will not solve in the next few years, and it is likely to get progressively worse through the rest of this century.

We must not be selfish or timid if we hope to have a decent world for our children and grandchildren.

We simply must balance our demand for energy with our rapidly shrinking resources. By acting now we can control our future instead of letting the future control us. . . .

The oil and natural gas we rely on for 75 percent of our energy are running out. In spite of increased effort, domestic production has been dropping steadily at about 6 percent a year. Imports have doubled in the last five years. Our nation's independence of economic and political action is becoming increasingly constrained. Unless profound changes are made to lower oil consumption, we now believe that early in the 1980's the world will be demanding more oil than it can produce.

The world now uses about 60 million barrels of oil a day, and demand increases each year about 5 percent. This means that just to stay even we need the production of a new Texas every year, an Alaskan North Slope every nine months, or a new Saudi Arabia every three years. Obviously this cannot continue.

We must look back into history to understand our energy problem. Twice in the last several hundred years there has been a transition in the way people use energy.

The first was about 200 years ago, away from wood—which had provided about 90 percent of all fuel—to coal, which was more efficient. This change became the basis of the Industrial Revolution.

The second change took place in this century, with the growing use of oil and natural gas. They were more convenient and cheaper than coal, and the supply

Continued on p. 294

Jimmy Carter. Address to the American People on Proposed Energy Policy; delivered over television and radio from Washington, D.C., April 18, 1977 and Jimmy Carter, Address to Congress on Proposed Energy Policy; delivered April 20, 1977 before a Joint Session of Congress.

Eugene Bardach

"A SOLUTION IN SEARCH OF A PROBLEM"

I own a 1961 Buick with a 440-horsepower engine. With its anti-smog device and its large engine, in normal city driving it gets about six miles per gallon. It uses premium-grade gas, which presently sells for about 65 cents per gallon in my city. The fuel cost alone of my daily round trip to my office, which is about a mile and a half from my home, is therefore just over 30 cents. A pity, you might think, that I acquired this gas-guzzling monster in that dim past before the energy crisis struck. I must avow, however, that I bought this car in August 1975.

Despite appearances, my purchase was based on conscious calculation. I intended to use the car almost exclusively for trips back and forth to my office, a level of usage that would bring my annual fuel bill to around $120. I reasoned that no old car in my price range could cut more than $60 off this annual fuel bill and that this car, which was being sold by a long-established service-station owner in my neighborhood, would save in annual repair expenditures more than it would cost in higher outlays for fuel.

If I did what was right for myself, though, did I also do what was right for society? Since everyone who counts seems to agree that as a nation we must conserve energy, I am clearly out of step. But, say I, the appearances are again deceiving. Actually I am aiding the conservation effort: if I did not own this car, whoever owned it in my stead might drive 500 miles per month instead of a mere 100 miles. Although I did not particularly intend to help the energy-conservation effort when I bought the car, I am not unwilling to take credit when it can be had cheaply.

Well, perhaps not so very cheaply, since many people initially regard this line of reasoning as blatant sophistry and condemn me twice over for advancing it. Yet it is correct, at least as far as it goes. There are only two obvious alternatives for the disposition of this ancient Buick: either someone uses it or it goes to the junk heap. Sending it to the junk heap is absurd, however. Can one seriously justify scrapping all that good steel and glass, all those nicely harmonized gears and pistons and valves, in the name of conservation? If not, then someone must use the car, and I am probably the best such someone.

Continued on p. 303

15. CONSERVATION

(Carter, cont. from p. 292)

seemed to be almost without limit. They made possible the age of automobile and airplane travel. Nearly everyone who is alive today grew up during this age and we have never known anything different.

Because we are now running out of gas and oil, we must prepare quickly for a third change, to strict conservation and to the use of coal and permanent renewable energy sources, like solar power.

The world has not prepared for the future. During the 1950's, people used twice as much oil as during the 1940's. During the 1960's, we used twice as much as during the 1950's. And in each of those decades, more oil was consumed than in all of mankind's previous history.

World consumption of oil is still going up. If it were possible to keep it rising during the 1970's and 1980's by 5 percent a year as it has in the past, we could use up all the proven reserves of oil in the entire world by the end of the next decade.

I know that many of you have suspected that some supplies of oil and gas are being withheld. You may be right, but suspicions about the oil companies cannot change the fact that we are running out of petroleum.

All of us have heard about the large oil fields on Alaska's North Slope. In a few years when the North Slope is producing fully, its total output will be just about equal to two years' increase in our nation's energy demand.

Each new inventory of world oil reserves has been more disturbing than the last. World oil production can probably keep going up for another six or eight years. But some time in the 1980's it can't go up much more. Demand will overtake production. We have no choice about that.

But we do have a choice about how we will spend the next few years. Each American uses the energy equivalent of 60 barrels of oil per person each year. Ours is the most wasteful nation on earth. We waste more energy than we import. With about the same standard of living, we use twice as much energy per person as do other countries like Germany, Japan and Sweden.

One choice is to continue doing what we have been doing before. We can drift along for a few more years. Our consumption of oil would keep going up every year. Our cars would continue to be too large and inefficient. Three-quarters of them would continue to carry only one person—the driver—while our public transportation system continues to decline. We can delay insulating our houses, and they will continue to lose about 50 percent of their heat in waste.

We can continue using scarce oil and natural gas to generate electricity, and continue wasting two-thirds of their fuel value in the process.

If we do not act, then by 1985 we will be using 33 percent more energy than we do today.

We can't substantially increase our domestic production, so we would need to import twice as much oil as we do now. Supplies will be uncertain. The cost will keep going up. Six years ago, we paid $3.7 billion for imported oil. Last year we spent $36 billion—nearly 10 times as much—and this year we may spend $45 billion.

Unless we act, we will spend more than $550 billion for imported oil by 1985—more than $2,500 for every man, woman, and child in America. Along with that money we will continue losing American jobs and becoming increasingly vulnerable to supply interruptions.

Now we have a choice. But if we wait, we will live in fear of embargoes. We could endanger our freedom as a sovereign nation to act in foreign affairs. Within 10 years we would not be able to import enough oil—from any country, at any acceptable price.

If we wait, and do not act, then our factories will not be able to keep our people on the job with reduced supplies of fuel. Too few of our utilities will have switched to coal, our most abundant energy source.

We will not be ready to keep our transportation system running with smaller, more efficient cars and a better network of buses, trains and public transportation.

We will feel mounting pressure to plunder the environment. We will have a crash program to build more nuclear plants, strip-mine and burn more coal, and drill more offshore wells than we will need if we begin to conserve now. Inflation will soar, production will go down, people will lose their jobs. Intense competition will build up among nations and among the different regions within our own country.

If we fail to act soon, we will face an economic, social and political crisis that will threaten our free institutions.

But we still have another choice. We can begin to prepare right now. We can decide to act while there is time. . . .

Our national energy plan is based on 10 fundamental principles.

The first principle is that we can have an effective and comprehensive energy policy only if the Government takes responsibility for it and if the people understand the seriousness of the challenge and are willing to make sacrifices.

The second principle is that healthy economic growth must continue. Only by saving energy can we maintain our standard of living and keep our people at work. An effective conservation program will create hundreds of thousands of new jobs.

The third principle is that we must protect the environment. Our energy problems have the same cause as our environmental problems—wasteful use of resources. Conservation helps us solve both at once.

The fourth principle is that we must reduce our vulnerability to potentially devastating embargoes. We can protect ourselves from uncertain supplies by reducing our demand for oil, making the most of our abundant resources such as coal, and developing a strategic petroleum reserve.

15. CONSERVATION

The fifth principle is that we must be fair. Our solutions must ask equal sacrifices from every region, every class of people, every interest group. Industry will have to do its part to conserve, just as consumers will. The energy producers deserve fair treatment, but we will not let the oil companies profiteer.

The sixth principle, and the cornerstone of our policy, is to reduce demand through conservation. Our emphasis on conservation is a clear difference between this plan and others which merely encouraged crash production efforts. Conservation is the quickest, cheapest, most practical source of energy. Conservation is the only way we can buy a barrel of oil for a few dollars. It costs about $13 to waste it.

The seventh principle is that prices should generally reflect the true replacement costs of energy. We are only cheating ourselves if we make energy artificially cheap and use more than we can really afford.

The eighth principle is that government policies must be predictable and certain. Both consumers and producers need policies they can count on so they can plan ahead. This is one reason I am working with the Congress to create a new Department of Energy, to replace more than 50 different agencies that now have some control over energy.

The ninth principle is that we must conserve the fuels that are scarcest and make the most of those that are more plentiful. We can't continue to use oil and gas for 75 percent of our consumption when they make up only 7 percent of our domestic reserves. We need to shift to plentiful coal while taking care to protect the environment, and to apply stricter safety standards to nuclear energy.

The tenth principle is that we must start now to develop the new, unconventional sources of energy we will rely on in the next century.

These ten principles have guided the development of the policy I would describe to you and the Congress on Wednesday.

Our energy plan will also include a number of specific goals, to measure our progress toward a stable energy system.

These are the goals we set for 1985:

—Reduce the annual growth rate in our energy demand to less than 2 percent.

—Reduce gasoline consumption by 10 percent below its current level.

—Cut in half the portion of United States oil which is imported, from a potential level of 16 million barrels to 6 million barrels a day.

—Establish a strategic petroleum reserve of one billion barrels, more than six months' supply.

—Increase our coal production by about two thirds to more than 1 billion tons a year.

—Insulate 90 percent of American homes and all new buildings.

—Use solar energy in more than two and one-half million houses.

—We will monitor our progress toward these goals year by year. Our plan will call for stricter conservation measures if we fall behind.

I can't tell you that these measures will be easy, nor will they be popular. But I think most of you realize that a policy which does not ask for changes or sacrifices would not be an effective policy.

This plan is essential to protect our jobs, our environment, our standard of living, and our future.

Whether this plan truly makes a difference will be decided not here in Washington, but in every town and every factory, in every home and on every highway and every farm.

I believe this can be a positive challenge. There is something especially American in the kinds of changes we have to make. We have been proud, through our history, of being efficient people.

We have been proud of our ingenuity, our skill at answering questions. We need efficiency and ingenuity more than ever.

We have been proud of our leadership in the world. Now we have a chance again to give the world a positive example.

And we have been proud of our vision of the future. We have always wanted to give our children and grandchildren a world richer in possibilities than we've had. They are the ones we must provide for now. They are the ones who will suffer most if we don't act. . . .

From Address to Joint Session of the United States Congress, April 20, 1977:

Our first goal is conservation. It is the cheapest, most practical way to meet our energy needs and to reduce our growing dependence on foreign supplies of oil.

With proper planning, economic growth, enhanced job opportunities and a higher quality of life can result even while we eliminate the waste of energy.

The two areas where we waste most of our energy are transportation and our heating and cooling systems.

Transportation consumes 26 percent of our energy, and as much as half of that is waste. In Europe the average automobile weighs 2,700 pounds; in our country 4,100 pounds.

The Congress has already adopted fuel efficiency standards, which will require new cars to average 27.5 miles per gallon by 1985 instead of the 18 they average today.

To insure that this existing Congressional mandate is met, I am proposing a graduated excise tax on new gas guzzlers that do not meet Federal average mileage standards. The tax will start low and then rise each year until 1985. In 1978, a tax of $180 will be levied on a car getting 15 miles per gallon, and for an 11 mile-per-gallon car the tax will be $450. By 1985 on wasteful new cars with the same low mileage, the taxes will have risen to $1,600 and $2,500.

All of the money collected by this tax on wasteful automobiles will be returned to consumers, through rebates on cars that are more efficient than the mileage standard. We expect that both efficiency and total automobile production and sales will increase under this proposal. We will insure that American automobile workers and their families do not bear an unfair share of the burden. Of course, we will also work with our trading partners to see that they are treated fairly.

Now I want to discuss one of the most controversial and misunderstood parts of the energy proposal, a standby tax on gasoline. Gasoline consumption represents half of our total oil usage.

We simply must save gasoline, and I believe that the American people can meet this challenge. It is a matter of patriotism and commitment. Between now and 1980 we expect gasoline consumption to rise slightly above the present level. For the following five years, when we have more efficient automobiles, we need to reduce consumption each year to reach our targets for 1985.

I propose that we commit ourselves to these fair, reasonable and necessary goals and at the same time write into law a gasoline tax of an additional 5 cents per gallon that will automatically take effect every year that we fail to meet our annual targets.

As an added incentive, if we miss one year but are back on track the next, the additional tax would come off. If the American people respond to our challenge, we can meet these targets, and this gasoline tax will never be imposed. I know and you know it can be done.

As with other taxes, we must minimize the adverse effects of our economy—reward those who conserve and penalize those who waste. Therefore, any proceeds from the tax, if it is triggered, should be returned to the general public in an equitable manner.

I will also propose a variety of other measures to make our transportation system more efficient.

One of the side effects of conserving gasoline is that state governments collect less money through gasoline taxes. To reduce their hardships and to insure adequate highway maintenance, we should compensate states for this loss through the highway trust fund.

The second major area where we can reduce waste is in our home and buildings. Some buildings waste half the energy used for heating and cooling. From now on, we must make sure that new buildings are as efficient as possible, and that old buildings are equipped, or "retrofitted," with insulation and heating systems that dramatically reduce the use of fuel.

The Federal Government should set an example. I will issue an executive order establishing strict conservation goals for both new and old Federal building—a 45 percent increase in energy efficiency for new buildings and a 20 percent increase for existing buildings, by 1985.

We also need incentives to help those who own homes and businesses to conserve. Those who weatherize buildings would be eligible for a tax credit of 25 percent of the first $800 invested in conservation, and 15 percent of the next $1,400.

If homeowners prefer, they may take advantage of a weatherization service which all regulated utility companies will be required to offer. The customer would pay for the improvements through small, regular additions to monthly utility bills. In many cases, these additional charges would be almost entirely offset by lower energy consumption brought about by energy savings.

Other proposals for conservation in homes and buildings include:

—Direct Federal help for low-income residents.

—An additional 10 percent tax credit for business investments.

—Federal matching grants to non-profit schools and hospitals.

—And public works money for weatherizing state and local government buildings.

While improving the efficiency of our businesses and homes, we must also make electrical home appliances more efficient. I propose legislation that would, for the first time, impose stringent efficiency standards for household appliances by 1980.

We must also reform our utility rate structure. For many years we have rewarded waste by offering the cheapest rates to the largest users. It is difficult for individual states to make such reforms because of the competition for new industry. The only fair way is to adopt a set of principles to be applied nationwide. I am therefore proposing legislation which would require the following steps over the next two years:

—Phasing out promotional rates and other pricing systems that make natural gas and electricity artificially cheap for high-volume users and which do not accurately reflect costs.

—Offering users peak-load pricing techniques which set higher charges during the day when demand is great and lower charges when demand is small.

—And individual meters for each apartment in new buildings instead of one master meter.

Plans are already being discussed for the TVA system to act as a model for implementing such new programs to conserve energy.

One final step toward conservation is to encourage industries and utilities to expand "cogeneration" projects, which capture much of the steam that is now wasted in generating electricity. In Germany, 29 percent of total energy comes from cogeneration, but only 4 percent in the United States.

I propose a special 10 percent tax credit for investments in cogeneration.

Along with conservation, our second major strategy is production and rational pricing.

We can never increase our production of oil and natural gas by enough to meet our demand, but we must be sure that our pricing system is sensible, discourages waste and encourages exploration and new production.

One of the principles of our energy policy is that the price of energy should reflect its true replacement cost, as a means of bringing supply and demand into balance over the long run. Realistic pricing is especially important for our scarcest fuels, oil and natural gas.

15. CONSERVATION

However, proposals for immediate and total decontrol of domestic oil and natural gas prices would be disastrous for our economy and for working Americans, and would not solve long range problems of dwindling supplies.

The price of newly discovered oil will be allowed to rise over a three-year period, to the 1977 world market price, with allowances for inflation. The current return to producers for previously discovered oil would remain the same, except for adjustments because of inflation.

Because fairness is an essential strategy of our energy program, we do not want to give producers windfall profits, beyond the incentives they need for exploration and production. But we are misleading ourselves if we do not recognize the replacement costs of energy in our pricing system.

Therefore, I propose that we phase in a wellhead tax on existing supplies of domestic oil, equal to the difference between the present controlled price of oil and the world price, and return the money collected by this tax to the consumers and workers of America.

We should also end the artificial distortions in natural gas prices in different parts of the country which have caused people in the producing states to pay exorbitant prices, while creating shortages, unemployment and economic stagnation, particularly in the Northeast. We must not permit energy shortages to balkanize our nation.

I want to work with the Congress to give gas producers an adequate incentive for exploration, working carefully toward deregulation of newly discovered natural gas as market conditions permit.

I propose now that the price limit for all new gas sold anywhere in the country be set at the price of the equivalent energy value of domestic crude oil, beginning in 1978. This proposal will apply both to new gas and to expiring intrastate contracts. It would not affect existing contracts.

We must be sure that oil and natural gas are not wasted by industries and utilities that could use coal instead. Our third strategy will be conversion from scarce fuels to coal wherever possible.

Although coal now provides only 18 percent of our energy needs, it makes up 90 percent of our energy reserves. Its production and use create environmental difficulties, but we can cope with them through strict strip-mining and clean air standards.

To increase the use of coal by 400 million tons, or 65 percent, in industry and utilities by 1985, I propose a sliding-scale tax, starting in 1979, on large industrial users of oil and natural gas. Fertilizer manufacturers and crop dryers which must use gas would be exempt from the tax. Utilities would not be subject to these taxes until 1985, because it will take them longer to convert to coal.

I will also submit proposals for expanded research and development in coal. We need to find better ways to mine it safely and burn it cleanly, and to use it to produce other clean energy sources. We have spent billions on research and development of nuclear power, but very little on coal. Investments here can pay rich dividends.

Even with this conversion effort, we will still face a gap between the energy we need and the energy we can produce and import. Therefore, as a last resort we must continue to use increasing amounts of nuclear energy.

We now have 63 nuclear power plants, producing about 3 percent of our total energy, and about 70 more are licensed for construction. Domestic uranium supplies can support this number of plants for another 75 years.

Effective conservation efforts can minimize the shift toward nuclear power. There is no need to enter the plutonium age by licensing or building a fast-breeder reactor such as the proposed demonstration plant at Clinch River.

We must, however, increase our capacity to produce enriched uranium for light-water nuclear power plants, using the new centrifuge technology, which consumes only about 1-10th the energy of existing gaseous diffusion plants.

We must also reform the nuclear licensing procedures. New plants should not be located near earthquake fault zones or near population centers, safety standards should be strengthened and enforced, designs standardized as much as possible and more adequate storage for spent fuel assured.

However, even with the most thorough safeguards, it should not take ten years to license a plant. I propose that we establish reasonable, objective criteria for licensing, and that plants which are based on a standard design not require extensive individual design studies for licensing.

Our fourth strategy is to develop permanent and reliable new energy sources.

The most promising is solar energy, for which much of the technology is already available. Solar water heaters and space heaters are ready for commercialization. All they need is some incentive to initiate the growth of a large market.

Therefore, I am proposing a gradually decreasing tax credit, to run from now through 1985, for those who purchase approved solar-heating equipment. Initially, it would be 40 percent of the first $1,000 and 25 percent of the next $6,400 invested.

Increased production of geothermal energy can be insured by providing the same tax incentives as for gas and oil drilling operations.

Our guiding principle, as we developed this plan, was that above all it must be fair.

None of our people must make an unfair sacrifice.

None should reap an unfair benefit.

The desire for equity is reflected throughout our plan:

—In the wellhead tax, which encourages conservation but is returned to the public;

15. CONSERVATION

—In a dollar-for-dollar refund of the wellhead tax as it affects home heating oil;

—In reducing the unfairness of natural gas pricing;

—In ensuring that homes will have the oil and natural gas they need, while industry turns toward the more abundant coal that can also suit its needs;

—In basing utility prices on true cost, so every user pays a fair share;

—In the automobile tax and rebate system, which rewards those who save our energy and penalizes those who waste it.

I propose one other step to insure proper balance of our plan. We need more accurate information about our supplies of energy and about the companies that produce it.

If we are asking sacrifices of ourselves, we need facts we can count on. We need an independent information system that will give us reliable data about energy reserves and production, emergency capabilities and financial data from the energy producers.

I happen to believe in competition, and we don't have enough of it.

During this time of increasing scarcity, competition among energy producers and distributors must be guaranteed. I recommend that individual accounting be required from energy companies for production, refining, distribution and marketing, separately for domestic and foreign operations. Strict enforcement of the antitrust laws can be based on this data, and may prevent the need for divestiture.

Profiteering through tax shelters should be prevented, and independent drillers should have the same intangible tax credits as the major corporations.

The energy industry should not reap large unearned profits. Increasing prices on existing inventories of oil should not result in windfall gains but should be captured for the people of our country.

We must make it clear to everyone that our people, through their Government, will now be setting our energy policy.

The new Department of Energy should be established without delay. Continued fragmentation of Government authority and responsibility for our nation's energy program is dangerous and unnecessary.

Two nights ago, I said that this difficult effort would be the moral equivalent of war. If successful, this effort will protect our jobs, our environment, our national independence, our standard of living and our future. Our energy policy will be innovative, but fair and predictable. It will not be easy. It will demand the best of us, our vision, our dedication, our courage, and our sense of common purpose.

This is a carefully balanced program, depending for its fairness on all its major component parts. It will be a test of our basic political strength and ability.

(Cont. from p. 293, Bardach, "A Solution in Search of a Problem")

But perhaps the argument does not go far enough. At issue is not merely conservation but *energy* conservation. When pushed to this point, energy conservationists do one of two things. Either they relent and agree that saving the Buick is a lesser evil than scrapping it—even though not an absolute good—or they stand firm and admonish me to drive the car to Mexico, where I should turn it over to a poor rural family that will convert it into a housing unit.

So ardent, then, is the love of certain energy conservationists for BTU's (British Thermal Units) of gasoline and other combustible hydro-carbons. And so great is their distaste for a 1961 Buick. A Buick is only a car, but BTU's are a precious legacy which we must transmit intact to our descendants. A 1961 Buick is a vulgar sort of thing, but BTU's are energy. . . .

If energy conservation meant doing things which saved money as well as BTU's, and which imposed no added inconvenience in time or other intangibles, everyone would agree not only on the principle but on the details. Almost surely there are conservation practices which, if undertaken, would make us in at least some few respects better off and in no respects worse off. The most commonly mentioned measures which probably fit this description are better design of new buildings; retrofitted insulation in many old buildings; more efficient space-heating systems; energy-efficiency labeling of appliances; and restoring normal competitive forces in the transportation sector by phasing out government regulation. . . .

Other practices. . . deserve a more skeptical reception. All those pertaining to the industrial sector, for instance, raise the question: if they are so good why has industry not undertaken them already? If the answer is that the price of energy has historically been too low to make such practices worthwhile, then the past is clearly no guide to the future. Given the prospects of considerably higher energy prices in the future, businessmen should change their ways. If they do not change to more energy-efficient processes in every case, the explanation could lie either in the force of habit or in the fact that the practices alleged to save money as well as energy. . . are actually financially unattractive to the businessmen who must bear the costs and risks.

There is no need to be querulous, however. If we can get something for nothing we should find out where and how, and then just do it. The real problems arise when we are asked to exchange the costs of energy conservation for the benefits of energy conservation.

[Zero Energy Growth (ZEG)] would shift large numbers of people from automobiles to bicycles and mass transit. It would locate some 17 million people in "new communities" of large multi-family units, the major advantage of which would be reduced commuting distance to places of work. It would encourage vacations closer to home. These do not seem like entirely costless shifts in style of living or in consumption patterns.

A more serious question than what the costs might be, however, conerns the prospective benefits of reduced energy consumption. A careful look at the alleged benefits reveals that either they are illusory or else they can be achieved more effectively through other means. Reduced energy consumption might be a by-product of employing these other means, but in no case would it make sense to treat reduced energy consumption either as an end in itself or as the primary instrument of attaining other public purposes.

One alleged benefit of energy conservation is decreased vulnerability to "the oil weapon," that is, an embargo of Arab oil similar to the one we experienced in 1973-74. It is misleading, though, to see this primarily as an energy problem. It is a problem of unreliable supply sources for a critical commodity. In such cases the standard response is to hold unusually large reserves, i.e., a stockpile. Automobile manufacturers, for instance, stockpile steel when they expect a long steel-workers' strike. Coal-burning electric utilities stockpile coal when they anticipate a lengthy coal-miners' strike. We presently hold large stockpiles of certain materials, like aluminum, for military emergency. Thus, stockpiling is a standard protective strategy for any con-sumer faced with unreliable supply sources, whether the sources be domestic or foreign and no matter the physical nature of the commodity.

No one knows how much oil is presently held as a hedge against an embargo. Private parties have an incentive to conceal such information, since in the event of an embargo there will be strict price controls and a black market to which access will be simpler if government agencies are kept in the dark about the parties' pre-embargo holdings. We can be sure, though, that the present inventories in private hands are not large enough, since the prospect of price ceilings strongly discourages appropriate private hoarding behavior. The Federal Energy Administration, in *Project Independence Blueprint*, estimated that the 1973-74 embargo reduced GNP by $10-20 billion. The FEA further calculated that a one-million-barrel-per-day supply interruption lasting one year could cost the economy about $33 billion and that, given certain cost assumptions for creating and maintaining a stockpile, the nation would be well advised to store enough oil to offset this shortfall if the chances are any more than one-in-five of its occurring in the next ten years. The same basic conclusion is reached by Princeton economist Robert E. Kuenne and his colleagues from the Institute for Defense Analyses in a recent issue of *Policy Analysis*. They recommend a storage program of some 4.4 billion barrels, to be held mainly in salt domes in the Gulf of Mexico, which would permit a daily draw-down of 4 million barrels over a three-year period. The storage cost would be about 96 cents per barrel per year, or less than 10 per cent of the present OPEC price per barrel.

Of course, if one is willing to threaten, or actually use, force either to deter an embargo or to terminate it once it is in progress, a much smaller, and correspondingly less expensive, storage program would be optimal. Energy conservation is therefore like the threat of force: it can reduce the size, and therefore the expense, of the optimal stockpile, provided that it is directed specifically at insecure oil imports. Some form of tariff or import quota is the instrument with the required accuracy of aim, however, not energy conservation in general. Once imports are limited, energy conservation, in the sense of reduced consumption, will come about automatically, provided the federal government permits the price mechanism to work unimpeded.

There is no doubt that reduced imports, with or without higher prices will increase the pressure to develop domestic energy sources. There is also no doubt that such development will have adverse effects on the environment. Preventing or minimizing such effects is another primary objective of the energy-conservation movement.

Some preliminary questions that must be raised in this connection concern the magnitude of the effects and how strongly we wish to avert them. In general, the answers are that, in the realm of conventional fossil fuels, the likely effects will not be as large or as severe as many or most environmentalists seem to fear. Even a dozen large strip-mining operations would be virtually lost in the vast spaces of the Northern Great Plains; the stripped lands can almost always be restored to their original (flat) contours; and perhaps half of these lands (or more) can be successfully revegetated in a five- or ten-year period. Offshore oil and gas development along most of the East Coast will not affect recreational and aesthetic uses of the coastal zone, since the prospective drilling sites are almost all 50-100 miles from shore. The development will not be visible, and accidental oil spills will almost never reach shore. The environmental outlook for offshore oil and gas development in Alaska is generally less favorable, but only a careful site-by-site analysis will reveal where energy development would entail costs which outweigh the benefits.

More generally, in the area of fossil-fuels development the interesting decisions are almost always site-specific. This is as true for coal development in Wyoming and Montana or offshore oil on the East or West Coasts as it is for the Alaskan sites. It should be obvious that a generalized policy of promoting energy conservation gives absolutely no guidance on such matters. All it tells us is that, overall and in the long run, energy conservation will permit us to develop fewer such sites than we otherwise would, a virtual truism. As with reducing oil-import vulnerability, the sensible policy would be to focus on the desired level of environmental protection, and if possible on its location as well, and then to let conservation come about as a by-product through a rise in prices. By some perverse illogic, ZEG advocates seem to have made environmental protection into the by-product rather than the objective, and ZEG into the objective rather than the by-product.

The same argument applies with even greater force to policy decisions concerning the management of nuclear-fission technologies. Nuclear power is very worrisome indeed, much more so than conventional fossil fuels. What to do with spent, but still dangerous, nuclear fuels is the outstanding problem, though there are other unresolved questions as well. [ZEG advocates] are much more concerned about nuclear power than about any or all fossil-fuel developments, and rightly so. If this reading is correct, then one must wonder how ZEG addresses the problem. Technically, a ZEG world dominated by nuclear-fission energy sources is no less conceivable than a ZEG world with no fission reactors at all. Whether we want one or the other or something in between is too important a social decision to be left to the vagaries of a diffuse policy of energy conservation.

The third popular reason advanced on behalf of energy conservation is that we should protect the welfare of future generations. Fossil fuels are a finite, and hence depletable, resource, the argument runs, so we ought not to squander them on ourselves at the expense of our descendants. Energy conservation will curb our self-indulgence.

This argument is in one sense irrefutable: a BTU of coal, oil, or gas burned up today is burned up forever, and in its raw form it is absolutely unavailable to our descendants. However, we would probably injure rather than benefit our descendants by transmitting these BTU's in raw form rather than in the form of capital equipment, which is at least one other form that BTU's can take. All other things being equal, capital is better, since it embodies not only energy but materials and labor and technology. On the other hand, it is obvious that the majority of BTU's used in any time period are allocated to consumption rather than to capital formation. Is there reason to think that this allocation is inequitable, that it is tipped too much in favor of consumption at the expense of capital?

I suspect not, although this is frankly a question to which no one has a definite answer. The first point to note, though, is that at least since the beginnings of capitalism each generation has been, on the average, better off than its immediate predecessor, largely because it has inherited its predecessors' accumulated capital stock. If this process continues, regardless of the intergenerational distribution of fossil-fuel stocks, our descendants will owe us a debt rather than vice versa. If the process does not continue, on the other hand, the distribution of fossil-fuel stocks might have little to do with the fact. The idea of "capital stock" in this context is quite inclusive. It embraces knowledge, for example, and the capacity to transmit and increase knowledge. If the scholastic-aptitude-tests are any indication, each annual cohort of high-school graduates for the last twelve years has been less talented than its predecessor. In the final analysis, we may be sapping the welfare of future generations far more by our failing to replenish the talent pool than by our depleting the world pool of oil.

In any case, even if the depletion of the fossil-fuel stock is proceeding too rapidly, from the point of view of subsequent generations, energy conservation is not much of a solution. The solution is research and development. Ultimately, a technological breakthrough will be necessary, probably either in solar energy or in hydrogen-fusion technologies. If it does come, all the present talk of energy conservation will be seen as a historical curiosity. If it does not, energy prices will rise slowly to reflect fossil-fuel scarcities and the high cost of solar and other technologies. High prices will enforce a stern discipline on all users of energy and in that case too the present rhetoric about our "responsibility" to conserve energy will appear to have been irrelevant.

To sum up, then, energy conservation is a very blunt policy instrument when it comes to reducing our import vulnerability, protecting the environment, or transmitting an equitable stock of worldly wealth to succeeding generations. Although higher energy prices and reduced energy consumption may be a natural by-product of whatever we do to solve these problems, energy conservation is in no case the best strategy with which to approach them. Indeed, one ought to fear that the rhetoric of energy conservation might divert intellectual and political energy from real problems with real—and difficult—solutions. Most people find it easier and more entertaining to make up policies concerning the disposition of my 1961 Buick than to press for an adequate stockpile of crude oil in Gulf of Mexico salt domes or to argue for reasonable limitations on the growth of nuclear power.

If energy conservation cannot be justified on practical grounds, how explain its great popularity as a political rallying cry?

It is bold, it is comprehensive, it attacks many problems, and it seems to attack them root and branch. To brandish the sword of energy conservation is figuratively if not literally heroic. To ride a bicycle to work in the name of conservation is to place oneself in the tradition of Achilles, Hector, and Beowulf. Indeed, the energy conservationist reaches back to the heroic archetype, Prometheus—only in this case the aim is to take fire away from mankind rather than to bestow it. Hence the energy conservationist can burn with atavistic heroic ardor while at the same time moving comfortably within the anti-heroic tradition of modernism.

Like all heroes, the energy conservationist is doomed to become entangled in a web of troubles spun partly by himself. Once be-witched by the spell of a grand design, like energy conservation, it is almost impossible to back away and look forthrightly at the concrete problems for which it is alleged as a remedy. These too fall under the spell. A grand design, after all, requires a grand problem of which it can be worthy. Thus, in place of diverse problems with diverse names—oil-import vulnerability, environmental degradation, in-equitable wealth transfers to future generations—we get the single great woe, "the energy crisis." Once the talisman of energy conservation is in hand it creates and sustains the necessary demonology. If energy conservation is initially appealing because it is so bold, it retains its appeal because its very boldness dissolves the critical mind-set which might challenge its validity.

For those who disapprove of Western, and particularly Ameri-can, bourgeois materialism, energy conservation is the ultimate rhetorical weapon. "Consumption," Hannah Arendt warned in *The Human Condition*, "harbors the grave danger that eventually no object of the world will be safe from .... annihilation...." That warning came almost twenty years ago, and it may not have been clear then precisely what annihilation implied. Now it is clear: one day there will be an end to fossil fuels.

Being a natural resource, fossil fuels appear to give us something for nothing. Fossil fuels belong to the sun, not to man, and by using them we inevitably presume on the benevolence of powers not our own. The bourgeoisie has always done so, of course, and has always been despised for it by the aristocratic class and by intellectuals. First there was machinery. Then there was the economic dividend pro-vided by the division of labor. Next there was the capitalist miracle of compound interest. Yet the problem with attacking any or all of these wealth-increasing powers has been that defenders of the bourgeois order could argue that something for nothing was actually a good deal, and that even if the social cost were not literally zero, on balance and in the long run, it was fairly low. Now, however, the critics of the bourgeois order have an unassailable argu-ment: gains to man are won directly at the expense of nature. Con-temporary man's idle pleasures are made possible only by exploiting nature's eons-long frugality. The popular flavor of the argument is evident in the recent campaign literature of the energy conserva-tionists' favorite presidential can-didate, Congressman Morris Udall:

No longer can we continue our blatant waste of the world's limited supply of raw materials. Con-spicuous consumption must be eliminated from our lives, if we are to survive the long haul.
No longer can we as a nation afford the energy waste of gas-guzzling automobiles and meaningless mobility.
No longer can we overindulge ourselves with frivolous electrical appliances and gadgets cluttering up our kitchen counter-tops and our homes.

No longer can we rape the land and our environment to satisfy unlimited greed and desire for luxury.

Two years ago, if someone had asked how government might proceed to wage war on materialism and to alter the style of living of millions of Americans, I certainly would have been unable to propose a policy instrument. Suddenly, the instrument appears to be at hand. . . .

The psychological force of the energy conservationists' argument is remarkable. There is no getting around it, burning up the BTU's in a gallon of gasoline burns them up forever. They cannot be retrieved, reconstructed, recycled, or renovated. They are destroyed, and we are the agents of their destruction. Eloquent testimony about the deep reservoirs of guilt tapped by this fact is to be found in a letter by "a housewife and artist" published last winter in the New York *Times Magazine*. She rides a bicycle, keeps the heat down to 65 degrees, composts the family food scraps, saves newspapers, and has only two children. Still it is not enough:

> After all my efforts, I began to realize that to be alive now is to be guilty of shortening mankind's existence. I can't buy bread in a plastic bag, eat a hamburger, wear knit pants, or flush a toilet without being guilty of consuming some product that is either deadly to life's long-range continuance or in diminishing supply. So, I must cope with my individual guilt as a

modern consumer, or run naked into the woods and starve.

To assuage my guilt I have decided to conserve as much as physically possible, to use resources and technology efficiently, and to enrich life now by creating works of art. What more can I do?

Guilt is not the only psychological condition to which the doctrine of energy conservation speaks so compellingly. There are also infantile feelings of dependency. Energy is Mother Nature's milk for our industrial society. As consumers, we sense that it comes into our homes and automobiles virtually on demand. If it stops or slows down, we do not regard it as a problem of mere supply shortages or high prices—which could, after all, happen to any "ordinary" commodity—we see it as an ominous deprivation. We become petulant and demand of Father Government that he take the Mean Uncle oil companies in hand and stop them from interfering with Mother Nature's bounteous flow.

But one need not speculate about infantile needs to recognize that energy is a highly charged psychological symbol. An "integral part of the nation's life-support system," says *A Time To Choose*.* "Why should we mine coal in Montana, or drill for oil in Alaska, to keep the lights on in Tokyo?" is a favorite question of energy conservationists. The ultra-nationalism, and perhaps even racism, implied by such a question is normally not at all

---

*Final report by the Ford Foundation Energy Policy Project (Cambridge, Mass.: Ballinger Publishing Co., 1974). [Editors]

recognized, so powerful is the conception of coal and oil as some of the nation's vital signs. That the Japanese in exchange for our coal and oil will return to us radios and cameras and (very energy-efficient) automobiles seems like a contemptible answer.

Frugality and self-sufficiency are values defined by the exoteric doctrines of the energy-conservation movement. The movement has its esoteric side as well, however, with a special sort of fascination. It is a recurring disease of intellectuals to believe that there is a strong causal connection between social theory and social fact. The notion is that a great social transformation must be accompanied, if not always preceded, by a conceptual or theoretical breakthrough. Conversely, the conceptual breakthrough induces or speeds great social changes. The theoretical vanguard of the energy-conservation movement is presently at work developing what might be called the BTU theory of value. Eventually this theory will go the same way as the labor theory of value, but in the meantime it is capable of doing much mischief.

In its simplest form, the BTU theory of value holds that all human actions should be measured in terms of how much energy they require and that, for roughly equivalent actions, that action is to be preferred which requires less energy. Hence, mass transit is to be preferred to the private automobile, high-density residential development to low-density development,

and aluminum to steel in automobile construction.

The first problem with the theory is that roughly equivalent actions are not really equivalent. Mass transit, for instance, in many cases gives a lower quality of service than the private automobile. If the levels of service (convenience, reliability, comfort, etc.) were identical, then the mass-transit system would probably be prohibitively expensive. Herein lies the second, and more telling problem with the theory, namely, that energy is only one of many inputs into producing a good or service. To choose a production process on this basis alone is in effect to assume that, for each of the alternative processes being considered, all the other inputs are of exactly equal value.

Put this way, the theory is obviously untenable, but the scientific vanguard among the theoreticians has a solution: convert *all* inputs into BTU's and then choose the process with the lowest BTU consumption. This procedure is of course exceedingly complicated in practice. Although one can come up with BTU values for aluminum ingot, cement casing, and the like, it is a laborious task to estimate for any given process the relevant physical parameters of all the materials to which the appropriate BTU conversion factors are to be applied. The main difficulty is conceptual rather than practical, however, and the main conceptual difficulty is that some energy comes from the sun, which is free, while some energy comes from fossil fuels, which are not free. Energy which is free must either be excluded from the calculations or given some arbitrary value. It is no surprise that the theorists are in their greatest quandary about how to put a BTU value on human labor, which is ultimately nourished and sustained by crops and animals drawing on the sun's free energy. Even those who are willing to put some BTU value on labor are unable to differentiate between the BTU value of an unskilled worker and that of a brilliant engineer.

The most bizarre results of the BTU theory of value are evident when the theorists talk about energy-development policies. Do not develop an energy source, the argument runs, unless it will yield more energy than is consumed in developing it. This is the "net-energy-yield" test. It sounds plausible until one remembers that, given the second law of thermodynamics, every human action *except* developing energy resources represents a net energy loss for mankind. If the net-energy-yield test were to be applied more generally, we ought all to go immediately into rigor mortis, or at least assume the lotus position for hours on end. Why a social decision rule which gives preposterous results for any development decision outside the energy field, like building a ship or rehabilitating a slum or opening a copper mine, should make any more sense when it comes to digging coal or pumping oil is unfathomable.

Naturally, the BTU theory of value finds its most receptive audience among scientists. *Science* magazine recently published an article on the subject to which the editors gave the flattering subhead, "The energy unit measures environmental consequences, economic costs, material needs, and resource availability." The National Science Foundation Office of Energy Policy and the Energy Research and Development Administration (ERDA), both dominated by physical scientists, have taken steps to promote the BTU theory of value. It is easy to see why physical scientists should feel a significant emotional and intellectual affinity with a theory grounded in physical reality. In addition they are likely to welcome the BTU theory as a relief from the awful relativism with which conventional economics treats the matter of values. A final reason the theory is favored by physical scientists, and the one with the greatest explanatory power, I believe, is political. If the BTU theory of value is mishmash, it is at least scientifically esoteric mishmash. If we are ever so unfortunate as to have serious social decisions made using the BTU theory of value, it will almost surely be the physical scientists who dominate the political dialogue.

In sum, then, energy conservation is a popular political rallying cry not because of its intrinsic merit as an instrument of public policy but because it expresses the anti-bourgeois ideology of the dominant intellectual class and because it has a ring of rational self-sacrifice which

15. CONSERVATION

alleviates great psychological distress experienced by large segments of the public. As the BTU theory of value evolves into the movement's esoteric doctrine, the ability of ordinary people to pierce the veil of ideology and see that little or nothing lies behind it is likely to diminish even further.

Energy conservation is a solution in search of a problem. The problems it purports to solve are best addressed by other means. Our oil-import vulnerability should be dealt with by a combination of stockpiling, import quotas, and the threat of forceful intervention. Environmental degradation may be prevented by legal and administrative regulation and by appropriately scaled pollution taxes. Assuring energy for future generations requires a technological solution. The likelihood of finding such a solution will be determined by luck and skill, but the urgency with which it is sought will be powerfully determined by the actuality and the expectation of rising energy prices. By saving energy we can perhaps save our souls, but not much else.

It is very likely that reduced energy consumption will be a natural consequence of implementing most of the proposed solutions to these three problems. It is likely but not inevitable. If prices go up and we consume less than we otherwise would have, no great catastrophe will occur. The energy conservationists are right about that. On the other hand, we might be able to have our cake and eat it too. Everyone would be happy with that outcome except those energy conservationists who regard reduced consumption as an end in itself. At the present time, unfortunately, that description seems to fit a very large number of them.

POSTSCRIPT

CAN CONSERVATION
MEET OUR ENERGY NEEDS?

Obviously, Professor Bardach and President Carter would not totally disagree on how to deal with the "energy crisis." Both are prepared to endorse such energy-saving measures as better home insulation and more efficient heating systems; both want more research into solar power and other clean sources of power. Where they clearly differ is on the importance of conservation as a means of resolving the energy crisis. Bardach may well be right in his belief that new technological breakthroughs will turn the issue of energy conservation into "a historical curiosity." Still, it is hard not to sympathize with those who are appalled at America's waste of energy. The fact that Sweden, which uses much less energy than does America, enjoys at least as high a standard of living, shows that conservation does not have to cramp our "life style."

An interesting study of how societies adapt to changing supplies of resources is Richard G. Wilkinson's *Poverty and Progress* (Praeger, 1973). A more polemical work, but one which is solidly researched, is Walter A. Rosembaum's *The Politics of Environmental Concern* (Praeger, 1973). A reminder of how irrational our government can be in implementing energy policies is supplied by Theodore Lowi, *et al.,* in *Policide* (Macmillan, 1976), a case study of what happened when the Atomic Energy Commission decided to build an atomic accelerator in an Illinois town. Another book which is critical of our government's energy priorities is Wilson Clark's *Energy for Survival* (Doubleday, 1974). A good technical work is Hans Thirring, *Energy for Man* (Greenwood Press, 1968).

The energy program which President Carter outlined in this issue passed the House of Representatives in 1977, though with a number of modifications, including a deletion of the proposed gasoline tax. It was in the Senate, however, that the greatest damage occurred. The Senate deleted not only his provision for a gasoline tax, but also his proposed taxes on domestic crude oil and the industrial use of oil and gas, which together constituted the heart of his program. Moreover, the Senate voted to do exactly what Carter had said would be "disastrous for our economy and for working Americans": to remove all price controls from natural gas. At a press conference in October of 1977 the President reacted angrily, charging the oil and gas lobby with conspiring to commit "the biggest ripoff in history." Since the Senate and House versions of the energy bill still needed to be reconciled, Carter's hope was that the House version, which was acceptable to him, might prevail.

CONTRIBUTORS
TO THIS VOLUME

Editors

GEORGE MC KENNA was born in Chicago in 1937. He attended
high school in the city and received his bachelor's degree from the
University of Chicago in 1959, an M.A. from the University of
Massachusetts in 1962, and a Ph.D. from Fordham University in
1967. He has been teaching political science at City College of New
York since 1963. He edited, with his introduction and notes,
American Populism (Putnam, 1974), wrote a textbook, *American
Politics: Ideals and Realities* (McGraw-Hill, 1976), and has written
articles in the fields of American government and political theory.

STANLEY FEINGOLD was born in New York City in 1926.
He attended high school in the city and received his bachelor's
degree from City College of New York. He received his graduate
education at Columbia University and has been teaching political
science at City College since 1947. From 1970 to 1974 he was given
a special appointment as Visiting Professor of politics at the
University of Leeds, England. He writes and teaches in the fields of
American government and political theory.

Authors

ARLIN M. ADAMS has been a Judge of the U.S. Court of Appeals
(Third Circuit) since 1969. Judge Adams is also president of the
American Judicature Society.

EDWARD C. BANFIELD is professor of Urban Studies at
Harvard University and author of a number of articles and books on
urban problems, including *The Un-heavenly City Revisited,* from
which excerpts were taken for this book.

EUGENE BARDACH is a professor at the Graduate School of
Public Policy of the University of California at Berkeley and author
of *The Skill Factor in Politics.*

314

JEROME A. BARRON, a professor of law at George Washington University, argued the case for Florida's "right to reply" statute in *Miami Herald v. Tornillo*, decided by the Supreme Court in 1974.

DAVID BRODER, a columnist for the *Washington Post*, specializes in commentary on the American political process.

DAVID L. BAZELON has been Chief Judge of the U.S. Court of Appeals for the District of Columbia circuit since 1962.

JIMMY CARTER is the President of the United States.

HARRY M. CLOR is Professor of Political Science at Kenyon College and the author of *Obscenity and Public Morality*. Professor Clor has also edited *The Mass Media and Modern Democracy*.

The late MARTIN DIAMOND taught political science at several universities. In addition to periodical articles, Professor Diamond was co-author of *The Democratic Republic* and *Essays in Federalism*.

JAMES E. DORNAN, JR. is chairman of the department of politics at Catholic University and author of *Detente and the Impending Strategic Crisis*.

JOHN FISCHER is former editor of *Harper's*.

The late JEROME FRANK was a Judge of the U.S. Court of Appeals for the Second Circuit, and before that a federal commissioner. Judge Frank was the author of *Courts on Trial* and other books.

NATHAN GLAZER is professor of education and social structure at Harvard University, the co-author of *The Lonely Crowd* and *Beyond the Melting Pot*, and the author of numerous articles on contemporary social issues.

ARTHUR GOLDBERG was an Associate Justice of the United States Supreme Court before serving as the American representative to the United Nations. Mr. Goldberg is the author of several books and presently practices law in Washington, D.C.

WILLIAM T. GOSSETT practices law in Michigan. At the time he testified before the House Judiciary Committee on electoral reform, Mr. Gossett was President of the American Bar Association (1968-1969).

HERBERT HILL, formerly National Labor Director of the National Association for the Advancement of Colored People (NAACP), is currently a professor at the University of Wisconsin–Madison and author of *Black Labor and the American Legal System.*

PETER C. HUGHES is a Ph.D. candidate at Catholic University and an aide to Senator Harry Byrd of Virginia.

HENRY KISSINGER, former Secretary of State, now teaches international relations at Columbia University.

DONAL E. J. MACNAMARA is a criminologist and director of corrections programs at the John Jay College of Criminal Justice in New York. He is the author of *Corrections* and other books and articles.

The late sociologist C. WRIGHT MILLS was the author of numerous other works besides *The Power Elite,* including *White Collar* and *The Sociological Imagination.*

MICHAEL NOVAK is the Executive Director of EMPAC (Ethnic Millions Political Action Committee). Besides *Electing Our King,* from which the selection in this book is taken, he has written extensively on American culture and institutions.

GARY ORFIELD is a staff member of The Brookings Institution, engaged in basic research in governmental affairs. He is the author of *Congressional Power: Congress and Social Change,* from which the selection in this book was taken.

THOMAS POWERS received the Pulitzer Prize for national reporting in 1971. Among his recent books is *The War at Home,* a history of the anti-Vietnam war movement.

DAVID RIESMAN is a lawyer and sociologist who teaches at the University of Massachusetts. Besides *The Lonely Crowd,* Riesman has written a number of other books and essays on American society and culture.

WILLIAM RYAN is a professor of psychology at Boston College and a consultant in the fields of mental health, community planning, and social problems. Besides *Blaming the Victim*, from which the selection in this book is taken, his publications include *Distress in the City*.

H. R. SHAPIRO, author of *The Bureaucratic State*, writes on a variety of topics, from American education to our party system and legal framework.

THEODORE SORENSEN, former Special Assistant to President Kennedy, is the author of *Decision-Making in the White House* and *Watchmen in the Night*, which is excerpted in this book.

JAMES L. SUNDQUIST is a senior staff member of The Brookings Institution and the author of *Making Federalism Work* and *Politics and Policy*.

ERNEST VAN DEN HAAG lectures at New York University and the New School for Social Research. He is the author of *Political Violence and Civil Disobedience* and many other books and articles.

JAMES Q. WILSON is professor of government at Harvard University and the author of *The Amateur Democrat*, *Negro Politics*, and *Varieties of Police Behavior*.

ROBERT PAUL WOLFF is a professor of philosophy at the University of Massachusetts. Among his books are *In Defense of Anarchy* and *The Poverty of Liberalism*.

INDEX

Fossil fuels, 350, 308. *See also* Coal

Fourteenth Amendment, 141
and freedom of press, 254
and state's rights, 190

Frank, Jerome, 176, 233, 235, 236 242-250, 251

Free press, 255. *See also* First Amendment

Free speech, 232-233, 267

Friedman, Milton, 219

Fuel efficient standards, 297

Fulbright, J. William, 26, 119

Galbraith, John Kenneth, 26

Gallup poll
on political identification, 20
See also Polls

Gardner, Erle Stanley, 176

Gas, natural
modern use of, 292
price policy for, 300

Gasoline consumption, 298

Geneva Convention, 173

Geothermal energy, 301

Ghettos
crime rate in, 182, 183
See also crime rates

Gilmore, Gary, 168, 169

Gilpatric, Roswell, 26

Give-and-take theory
of government, 45
of pluralism, 57

Gladwin, Thomas, 231

Glazer, Nathan, 191, 193, 202-208

Goldberg, Arthur, 135, 136, 138-141

Goldwater, Barry, 264

Gossett, William T., 65, 66, 68-77

Government
balance theory of, 14-18
expansion of, 110
fourth branch of, 252 (*see also* Media; Press)
local, 28, 39
parliamentary system of, 130
popular, 23
referee function of, 59-60
state, 28

Graglia, Lino A., 209

Gravel, Michael, 72

Great Depression, and presidential power, 119

Green, Mark, 115

Grigby, Shaw, 173

Griggs v. Duke Power Co., 200

Groups

legitimacy of, 57
minority, 19, 25, 61, 156 (*see also* Affirmative action)
plurality of, 4, 6-10
pressure, 42, 43, 44, 46-55
types of, 56
veto, 6, 7, 8, 15
See also Interest groups; Political parties

Hacker, Andrew, 289

Haldeman, Robert, 106

Hamilton, Alexander, 20, 116, 271

Hand, Learned, 55

Harding, Warren, 52

Harlan, John Marshall, 140

Harriman, W. Averell, 26, 126

Harrington, Michael, 231

Hatfield, Mark, 72

Health care, and poverty, 221

Hereditary groups, 56

Hill, Herbert, 191, 192, 194-202

Hoffman, Paul, 26

Holmes, Oliver Wendell, 144, 254, 256

Homicide, criminal, 173
incidence of, 176-177
rate of, 185
See also Death penalty

Hook, Sidney, 194

Household appliances
efficiency standards for, 299
See also Conservation

Howe, Irving, 16

Hughes, Langston, 159

Hughes, Peter C., 269, 271, 279-287

Hunt, E. Howard, 106

Ideology, Mannheim's definitions, 45

Immigrant groups, discrimination against, 202

Impeachment
Congressional power of, 106
process of, 101

Independent voters, 20, 24

Inflation, 25, 295

Inouye, Daniel, 72

Institutions
power of, 11
trends in, 18

Interest groups
conflict among, 60
economic, 56
labor, 52, 57
politics of, 63

power of, 43
national v. sectional, 53
See also Pressure groups
Internationalism, 17
Isolationism, in U.S., 285

Jackson, Andrew, 2, 113
Jackson, Henry, 72, 287
Jaffe, Louis, 143
Jahoda, Marie, 244
James, Judson L., 41
Javits-Zablocki bill, 109
Jefferson, Thomas, 20, 113
Jencks, Christopher, 219
Job ratios, 198-199. *See also*
Affirmative action
John XXIII, 279
Johnson, Andrew, 51, 101
Johnson, Haynes, 27
Johnson, Lyndon, 26, 264
Johnson administration
and Vietnam War, 100
war on poverty of, 210
Journalists
focus of, 17
See also Press
Judges
discretionary power of, 155, 158
See also Courts
Judicial review
and civil liberty, 136, 138-141
limitation of, 134-135, 147
Juvenile delinquents, 157
effect of obscenity on, 244-245
See also Criminals

Kariel, Henry, 59
Kennan, George, 271
Kennedy, John, 26, 58, 110, 118, 271
Kennedy, Robert, 264
Kennedy v. Mendoza-Martinez, 136
Key, V. O., 31, 34, 75
King, Martin Luther, 121
Kirkpatrick, Evron M., 41
Kissinger, Henry, 26, 269, 270, 272-
279, 287, 289
Koestler, Arthur, 189
Kotz, Nick, 231
Krogh, Bud, 106
Kuenne, Robert E., 304
Kuh, Richard H., 251

Labor interests
and non-unionized workers, 57
and political parties, 52
Labor unions

and affirmative action, 194, 196-197
and electoral reform, 73
power of, 9
La Follette, Robert, 38
Laski, Harold, 170
Law, respect for, 144-145
Leadership
in American politics, 120-121
Federalist, 4
labor, 8
of president, 125
Lee, Richard Henry, 2
Leisure, and leadership, 4-5
Libel, Supreme Court on, 259-260
Liberalism, in Congress, 102
Liebling, A.J., 262
Life-fate, 12
Life sentence
deterrence of, 184
See also Death penalty
Lincoln, Abraham, 51, 76, 112, 113, 133
Lindsay, John, 35
Lippmann, Walter, 58
Literature, censorship of, 240-241
Lobby
nature of, 6
Local politics, character of, 8
Log rolling, 48
Lonely Crowd, The, 3
Longley, Lawrence D., 89
Lovell, Robert, 26
Lower classes, culture of, 213, 226-
230
Lowi, Theodore J., 63, 313

Macaulay, Thomas, 244
McCarthy, Eugene, 120, 121
McCloy, John, 26
McCord, James, 106
McGovern, George C., 72
McIntyre, Thomas, 72
McKinley, William, 6
Macmillan, Harold, 110
M'Naghten Rule, 175
MacNamara, Donal E. J., 169, 170, 172-
179, 189
McNamara, Robert, 26
Madison, James, 3, 20, 42-43, 67, 68, 77
Magnuson, Warren, 72
Maine, two-party collusion in, 35
Majority, rule of, 19
Mannheim, Karl, 45, 55-56
Mansfield, Mike, 72
Marchi, John, 35
Marcuse, Herbert, 255
Massachusetts
capital crimes in, 168, 169

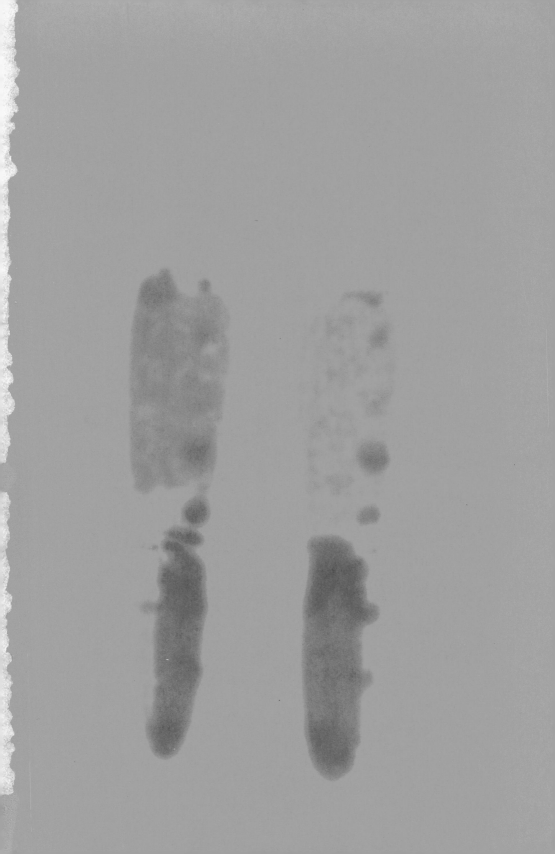